HUMAN RESOURCES FLEXIBILITIES IN THE PUBLIC SERVICES

International Perspectives

Also by David Farnham and Sylvia Horton

MANAGING THE NEW PUBLIC SERVICES
MANAGING PEOPLE IN THE PUBLIC SERVICES
NEW PUBLIC MANAGERS IN EUROPE
(*with John Barlow and Annie Hondeghem*)
PUBLIC MANAGEMENT IN BRITAIN

Human Resources Flexibilities in the Public Services

International Perspectives

Edited by

David Farnham

and

Sylvia Horton

First published 2000 by
MACMILLAN PRESS LTD
Houndmills, Basingstoke, Hampshire RG21 6XS
and London
Companies and representatives throughout the world

ISBN 0–333–73638–9

A catalogue record for this book is available from the British Library.

This book is printed on paper suitable for recycling and made from fully
managed and sustained forest sources.

10   9   8   7   6   5   4   3   2   1
09 08 07 06 05 04 03 02 01 00

Printed in Great Britain
by Antony Rowe Ltd., Chippenham, Wiltshire

This book is dedicated to the memory of

John Barlow

our colleague, friend and active member of the European Group of Public Administration

Contents

List of Figures and Tables

List of Contributors

Erik Beersen is a postgraduate student at the University of Twente, the Netherlands

June Burnham is Senior Lecturer in European Government and Politics, Middlesex University, England

Richard Cachares is a doctoral candidate in Public Administration, University of Illinois, Chicago, the United States

David Farnham is Professor of Employment Relations, Portsmouth Business School, University of Portsmouth, England

Annie Hondeghem is Senior Researcher at the Public Management Center, Catholic University of Leuven, and Professor in Public Administration at the Catholic University of Brussels, Belgium

Sylvia Horton is Principal Lecturer in Public Sector Studies, School of Social and Historical Studies, University of Portsmouth, England

Antoinette Kemper is a student assistant at the University of Twente, the Netherlands

Markku Kiviniemi is Research Manager in the Department of Political Science, University of Helsinki, Finland

Elke Löffler is an Administrator, OECD, Paris, France

Charles Montin is Directeur d'Administration, OTAN, Brussels, Belgium

Richard Murray is Chief Economist in Statskontoret, The Swedish Agency for Administrative Development, Stockholm, Sweden

Koen Nomden is a Researcher at the European Institute of Public Administration, Maastricht, the Netherlands

Salvador Parrado-Díez is Assistant Professor in Public Administration, Faculty of Humanities and Social Sciences, University Carlos III Madrid, Spain

Manfred Röber is Professor of Public Administration at the Fachhochschule für Verwaltung und Rechtspflege and Lecturer at the Free University of Berlin, Germany

F.F. Ridley is Emeritus Professor and Senior Fellow, the Liverpool Institute of Public Management, University of Liverpool, England

Renato Ruffini is Assistant Professor, Libero Istituto Universario Cattaneo, Castellanza, Italy

Trui Steen is a Research Assistant in the Public Management Center, Catholic University of Leuven, Belgium

James Thompson is Assistant Professor in Public Administration, University of Illinois, Chicago, the United States

Theo van der Krogt is Associate Professor of Organisational Sociology, Faculty of Public Administration and Public Policy, University of Twente, the Netherlands

Turo Virtanen is Professor of Administrative Science, Department of Political Science, University of Helsinki, Finland

Geoff White is Reader in Human Resources Management, the Business School, University of Greenwich, England

Preface

Over the past three years, members of the Personnel Policy Permanent Study Group of the European Group of Public Administration (EGPA), which is a section of the International Institute of Administrative Sciences, have been studying human resources flexibilities in their countries. This book is the result of that work. The research project, *Flexibility of Staffing and Personnel Systems in European Public Services*, was started at the EGPA annual conference in Budapest in 1996. Here a series of exploratory, national papers were presented and, after some productive debate and discussion, members of the Group agreed a common framework for further work. It was also decided to invite presentations of additional, thematic and comparative papers at the next EGPA Conference, to be held at Leuven in 1997. Those contributing to this current symposium presented final drafts of their papers at EGPA's Paris conference in 1998, where some final refinements of the research study were agreed. This was followed by submission of the following chapters by the contributors to this edited volume.

The changes taking place in public organisations throughout OECD countries, during the latter part of the twentieth century, have commanded intense national, international and professional interest. At first the focus was on the structural, financial and managerial changes taking place within public service organisations, which are incorporated in what was initially called the 'New Public Management'. The staffing implications of these changes only gradually became evident subsequently. One personnel management theme arising out of the New Public Management, the central focus of this book, is the extent to which public service organisations have adopted 'flexible' policies and practices regarding the selection, employment, rewarding, deployment and utilisation of the staff working in them. We describe these developments in this volume as 'human resources flexibilities'. This book seeks to address five broad issues about human resources flexibilities: what they are; what forms they take within public organisations; why they have emerged as a distinctive personnel strategy in the public sector; the factors facilitating or inhibiting them within particular countries and public services; and their consequences for governments, managers, public service staff and service users.

The book is divided into three parts. Part I introduces the concepts underpinning human resources flexibilities, the ways in which they can be classified and puts flexibilisation into a comparative perspective. It addresses three themes. First, the editors of this volume, Farnham and Horton, explore the flexibility debate. They consider the environmental contexts out of which demands for flexibilisation have emerged, and they distinguish between social push and economic pull factors. Tracing the origins and development of flexible working arrangements they demonstrate how current flexibilities incorporate the needs of public employers to overcome resistance to change, as well as to gain staff commitment to the organisations in which they work. They also provide a typology of current human resources flexibilities and conclude that employment flexibility is now a common phenomenon in the public services throughout Europe, and beyond, but unlike in the private sector, it is driven by largely political factors rather than strictly economic or technological ones (Chapter 1). Second, Ridley identifies some of the factors influencing flexibilities on a comparative basis and highlights the problems of making international comparisons. He goes on to examine the issues of employment status, career systems, selection and promotion and discusses the limits of flexibilisation (Chapter 2). Third, Virtanen, having provided his own conceptual framework for analysing human resources flexibilities, explores the relationship between flexibility, employee commitment and organisational performance, drawing on empirical data from surveys in Finland. His main conclusion is that there is no simple correlation between security of tenure and commitment and that commitment is only one factor in improving performance. However, both commitment and performance appear to decline significantly among those on fixed-term appointments in the later stages of their employment (Chapter 3).

Part II, the core of the book, consists of 10 national studies which examine the extent and scope of current human resources flexibilities in the public services. These studies provide in some detail the main developments in each country, thus enabling trends to be identified and comparisons to be made. Hondeghem and Steen start by examining recent innovations in ministries and public enterprises at federal level in Belgium, Flemish state level and local government in Flanders. A central conclusion for them is that human resources flexibilities support recent changes in the Belgium public sector, particularly devolution and decentralisation, and that flexibilities in staffing and personnel systems are conditional on decentralisation of decision-making. In the case of Belgium, contractual, pay, working hours and career flexibilities are the product of statutory regulations and collective bargaining (Chapter 4).

The extensive range of human resources flexibilities introduced into Finnish state administration by the Personnel Department of the Ministry of Finance are outlined and discussed by Kiviniemi and Virtanen. These have arisen out of other managerial reforms in the 1990s, such as decentralisation and the introduction of management-by-results systems. The State Civil Servants Act 1994 confirmed civil servant status as the primary type of employment in state administration but also aimed at converging conditions of service between civil servants and contractual state employees. Although symptoms of rigidity remain, a series of human resources flexibilities have been introduced including fixed-term appointments, contracting out, part-time work, overtime and 'part-time pensions'. The authors warn, however, that although efficiency gains are being achieved through human resources flexibilities, these may, in turn, strengthen an instrumental orientation to work by those affected by them (Chapter 5).

Burnham examines statutory and contractual flexibilities, part-time and flexible working hours and career and job mobility in France, coming to the conclusion that deep-rooted managerial and personnel reforms are difficult to achieve in French public administration. There are a number of reasons for this including absence of a free market ideology, weak political will by the governmental authorities and strong resistance by the trade unions. Further, members of the higher level *corps* are uninterested in major human resources reforms, largely because they are unlikely to get anything out of them and because they are too far removed from the everyday work experiences of their administrative and technical subordinates (Chapter 6).

Röber and Löffler show the limitations of human resources flexibilities in German public administration. The new thinking that has emerged in Germany is restricted largely to two areas: the introduction of elements of performance related pay to increase motivation of senior civil servants in state administration and the introduction, at local authority level, of some 'soft' forms of human resources management. The instruments used at local authority level include employee surveys, employee communication systems and 'performance agreements' between superiors and subordinates, with the purpose of improving employee motivation. As in France, and unlike in the United Kingdom, the political administrative system is difficult to change, partly because of lack of political will to do so. There are, however, some examples of part-time contracts, more family friendly policies and more vertical career mobility at local level, where these have been negotiated with the trade unions (Chapter 7).

The Italian administrative system was characterised in the late 1980s and early 1990s by rigidities in human resources management policies and practices, resulting in conflict between the administration and workers, complex recruitment procedures and public officials having little control over the managing of people. As a result of Ordinance 29/93, however, the Italian state is being transformed into a more customer-oriented, value for money administration. This is due largely to pressures to improve public finances in Italy, driven by the imperatives of economic and monetary union in the European Union, and growing citizen interest in better community services. Ruffini highlights the key changes in employment policy. These include basing public employment on civil law, giving responsibility for the managing of labour relations to individual organisations and introducing evaluation and performance practices into the administrative system. The human resources flexibilities that he identifies are pay flexibility, performance pay, career mobility, new pay scales and new types of employment contracts, though he suggests that while reform has started, change is likely to be slow and incrementalist (Chapter 8).

Parrado-Díez demonstrates that Spanish public administration has also undergone considerable change in the last two decades. This is associated with the transformation of a unitary, centralised state into a quasi-federal system, with a powerful regional level. Since the early 1990s, Spain has tried to reduce the size of its civil service to comply with government's aim of reducing public expenditure. While the numbers employed in central government have declined, those employed in regional authorities have increased as state functions have been reallocated. There has been an increase in those employed on temporary contracts in central administration in order to circumvent controls over staff numbers. Other devices being used include early retirement schemes, extended secondments to the private sector and increased use of short-term contracts or contracting out to obtain specialist staff. All politically appointed positions have become fixed-term, contractual posts and all top management appointments are on individual contracts. Rigidities continue, however, because civil servants retain security of tenure and cannot be dismissed. 'Employment plans' are being used to promote mobility, but with only partial success (Chapter 9).

In Sweden, human resources management is an integral part of a system of public management, which stresses performance criteria rather than regulatory rules, and where ministries determine policy and agencies execute them. Agencies are free to employ staff, dismiss them and set their own pay. Public employees are subject to general labour law that applies equally to the private and public sectors. The system of collective bargaining, the major means of determining the pay and conditions of public officials, has been reformed, with central negotiations leading to agreements providing only a 'floor' for local pay bargaining. There is no special recruitment, no security of tenure and no professional civil service *corps* and thus no institutional barriers to change. There is growing awareness, however, that central government needs to be regarded more as a unified concern. Some degree of re-centralisation, therefore, is likely to emerge to constrain the staffing and pay flexibilities which agencies currently have (Chapter 10).

Van der Krogt and his colleagues concentrate on human resources developments in central and local government in the Netherlands. In central government, most public employees have tenure but government and unions are investigating the possibility of increasing flexibility of working hours and opening hours, especially to meet the demands of seasonal workloads and public demands. The most common form of external flexibility in central government is hiring extra personnel through temporary employment agencies, whilst 'internal temporary employment pools' deal with changing workloads, especially for lower administrative functions. Since 1993, negotiations on terms and conditions of employment have taken place at national, sectoral and organisational levels. In local government, an important factor driving the search for more flexibility and mobility has been cost savings by the political authorities. Here part-time employment is normal, with local government employees having the right to work part-time, unless the interests of the organisation conflict with this. The unions have also negotiated a 36-hour week, with the aim of providing for more flexibility so that the 'released hours' can be allocated to the unemployed. In short, human resources flexibility and mobility are 'hot issues' in Dutch central and local government and it is public policy to increase both (Chapter 11).

In Europe, human resources flexibilities appear to have penetrated deepest in the UK's public services. Initially Horton compares the traditional bureaucratic model of personnel management with what is described as the 'new people management'. The first is associated with centralised, standardised, paternalist personnel policies and the other with more decentralised, flexible, business-oriented ones. She then examines numerical and working time flexibilities, contractual and distancing flexibilities, task and functional flexibilities and pay and personnel flexibilities in the civil service, National Health Service and local government. In general, there is clear evidence of all forms of flexibility across the public services although there are some significant variations between them. There is little evidence that the 'flexibility assault' is lessening under the New Labour administration, with its espoused concern for effective, efficient and quality public services (Chapter 12).

To provide an extra-European dimension to this volume, the editors invited Thompson and Cachares to examine developments in human resources flexibilities in the United States. Reporting on the National Performance Review (NPR), they note that particular emphasis is placed in it on the necessity of deregulating the processes of hiring, classifying, compensating, promoting and firing federal employees. According to their analysis, the NPR is based on the belief that bureaucratised rules and regulations impede the flexibility that is the requisite for 'good management'. The reforms recommended include: removing the extent to which line managers are subject to centrally-agreed rules, shifting the personnel role from one of policing policy to that of consultant and partner and granting individual agencies the authority to shape their own human resources policies. The NPR also wants increased attention to be given to quality of working life issues. In addition, there are proposals to create 'performance based organisations' modelled on Next Steps agencies in the UK. In Thompson and Cachares's view, deregulatory and decentralising trends are becoming pronounced in federal government and at state level, which could lead to a substantially different set of public services over the next few years (Chapter 13).

Part III is largely thematic and focuses on the comparative aspects of human resources flexibilities. White provides a comparative analysis of pay flexibilities in Europe, drawing in part on the material presented in the national studies. The themes he explores are the search for pay flexibility, trends in public sector pay, changes in the method and locus of pay determination, changes to grading systems and changes to pay progression systems. In his view, there are a variety of complex remuneration practices which do not readily suggest that a clear model is emerging. Large differences remain among countries, and sectors within countries. Different approaches to pay flexibilities appear to reflect different ideological objectives of the political authorities and different social value systems, with the UK, Finland and Sweden being strong on pay deregulation and the Latinate countries being more prone to continued centralised pay regulation (Chapter 14).

Nomden's analysis of flexible working patterns in European public administration concentrates on flexible working hours and flexibility of working life. In terms of flexible working hours, Nomden concludes that most European states allow public servants to work part-time, with some countries even providing financial incentives for workers to do so. In terms of flexibility of working life there is greater variation. Many public services offer early retirement, whilst others have more restrictive policies because of the costs involved. In other cases, those retiring early may take reduced pensions. But questions remain about how flexible these practices are in practice (Chapter 15).

In his analysis of flexibilities in international organisations, such as the UNESCO, UN, ILO, WHO and some 200 other supra-national bodies, Montin argues that the meaning and purpose of flexibility differ from its national equivalent and pressures for change have not been solely managerial. In spite of the diversity of their geographic membership, international organisations have a strict set of common rules concerning conditions of service, which are aimed at preventing competition amongst agencies hiring similar staff. The unity of these bodies is enhanced by frequent meetings between officials and mobility of staff, at senior levels, who have developed expertise in managing such organisations. This promotes mobility of ideas too. Montin goes on to discuss the specific traits of international organisations such as their autonomy, geographic distribution and co-ordination. Their style of management derives out of a framework of public law, which defines rights and duties of officials, widespread representation and consultation with staff and a developed system of arbitration. Such flexibilities that exist are limited to staffing flexibilities, where there are shortages of funds or political interventions, and some rather restricted pay flexibilities. Yet pay does not vary much because it tends to be agreed at co-ordinated level, irrespective of the importance or efficiency of specific agencies. The political drive for human resources management reforms and greater flexibility, in short, does not take the same form as in national systems, because they cannot be imposed from above (Chapter 16).

In the final chapter Horton and Farnham evaluate and review the nature, extent and impact of human resources flexibilities in the public services covered by this volume. Retracing the flexibility movement through three waves they clarify the macro contexts within which developments in human resources flexibilities have occurred. Drawing upon the chapters in the book and the work of the OECD they discuss the patterns of human resource flexibilities that can be observed. Whilst all countries practice contractual, working time, pay, working life and functional flexibilities the authors identify three groups. The first, displaying the most extensive range of human resources flexibilities, includes the UK, Finland, Sweden, the Netherlands and the US. A second group, including Belgium and France, practise most flexibilities but not as extensively or widely as the first. Finally the third group, comprising Germany, Italy and Spain appear to contain the most rigid systems with less flexibilities in each of the five categories. The authors examine the factors, which have influenced that pattern of development but emphasise a need for caution in drawing conclusions about the reasons for the similarities and differences. Pointing out that there is little evidence of any systematic evaluation of the effects of flexibilities on the major parties involved – governments, managers, public service workers and the users of public services, they identify some of the possible benefits and disadvantages for each stakeholder. In their concluding remarks Horton and Farnham draw attention to resistance to the flexibility phenomenon from those who defend the classic bureaucratic model of public service with its traditional public service ethos. Finally they highlight demands for a new public ethic to match the changing role of government and public management and for a new model organisation to balance the sometimes conflicting needs for flexibility and security.

The completion of this book would not have been possible without the involvement and co-operation of a number of people. First, the editors would like to thank EGPA for supporting this project and facilitating the participation of the contributors to the Personnel Policy Permanent Study Group over the past three years. We also wish to acknowledge the particular support given to us by our Co-Chair of this Group, Annie Hondeghem, throughout the duration of the project. Second, we would like to thank all the contributors for meeting the deadlines imposed by the editors, despite the multiple demands arising from their other professional commitments. Third, we thank Sarah Brown, Commissioning Editor at the publisher for her patience and support during the gestation, completion and publishing of this book. Fourth, the Study Group dedicates this book to the memory of one of its members, John Barlow, who, but for his untimely and premature death in 1997, would have been one of the contributors to this volume.

Finally, we have been highly interventionist editors in order to clarify the text, ensure consistency and contain the size of the book. We appreciate our colleagues' tolerance of this approach and hope that the resulting volume on human resources flexibilities is a readable, informative and reflective one in this important area of public management and employment relationships.

DAVID FARNHAM
SYLVIA HORTON

Part I
Introducing Flexibilities

1 The Flexibility Debate

David Farnham and Sylvia Horton

Flexibility in the recruitment, deployment and rewarding of human resources in organisations has been an issue of interest to governments, managers and academic observers since the 1960s. This chapter puts the concept of 'human resources flexibility' into context and provides some basic classifications of the flexibility phenomenon. It traces the origins and development of the flexibility debate, its perception by employers, employees and service users and the reasons for the introduction of human resources flexibilities into public services throughout Europe and the United States during the 1980s and 1990s. The word 'flexible' is defined in *The Oxford Guide to the English Language* (1984: 345) as 'able to bend easily', 'adaptable', and 'able to be changed'. The antonym of flexible is rigid meaning stiff, not bending, inflexible. Hegewisch (1999: 144) suggests that flexibility 'is more easily defined by what it is not – rigidity, stability, predictability – than by what it is'. The focus of this book is human resources flexibilities in the public services, what they are, how they are being dealt with and their impact on those involved with them. Flexibility is inferred as a condition where decisions about the employment of people, and how they are employed, can be easily changed or adapted to meet the needs of those demanding flexibility or the circumstances of the situation. Different actors in the public service – governments, employers and managers, staff or those using public services – are likely to perceive flexibility in different ways. Thus flexibility from the perspective of governments may be seen as the ability to choose freely levels of service provision, methods of delivery and costs and pricing of services, as well as containing public expenditure. Employers and managers, as suppliers of services, seek flexibility over the human resources they employ, including numerical control of staffing, the deployment of staff, their payment and utilisation because they are subject to financial constraints and need to control the labour process in their search for organisational efficiency. Those working in public-service organisations, in turn, see flexibility in terms of the control they want over their patterns of working, length of their working lives,

3

structure of their working day and content of the work they do. Finally, users of public services see flexibility in terms of access to services, their user-friendliness and quality of provision.

ORIGINS AND DEVELOPMENT OF THE FLEXIBILITY DEBATE

Concerns about flexible labour markets and flexibilities in employing people are not new phenomena or new policy issues and emerged with the development of industrial societies. In the nineteenth century and for much of the early twentieth century, the British labour market was a largely unregulated or flexible one from the perspectives of employers, workers and the state. Distinctions between 'wage' payments to manual workers – based on hourly rates of pay – and salaries to white-collar 'staff' – based on an annual, lump sum – became accepted practices in managing the employment relationship. These pay arrangements provided 'numerical' flexibility for employers who, in response to fluctuations in demand for their products, could hire additional workers or increase hours of work in times of market growth and lay-off workers or decrease hours of work in times of market contraction. Significantly, salaried staff or 'black-coated workers', who were literate, numerate and worked close to the centres of organisational power, normally received no extra payments from their employers for working in excess of their contractual hours but had higher status and more employment security. As the countries of mainland Europe and the western world industrialised, they developed similar arrangements in their private sectors. It was in response to deregulated labour markets that trade unions emerged in the mid and late nineteenth century. Their function was to enforce the 'common rules' of the trade through the device of the 'restriction of numbers' into the trade and the method of collective bargaining with employers, over terms and conditions of employment (Webbs, 1897). From the early twentieth century, collective bargaining was extended into the public sector too.

After the Second World War statutory regulation of employment relationships, including hours of work and minimum wages were introduced in a number of European countries. It was not until the 1970s, however, that legal regulation was introduced in Britain. Until then collective agreements, combined with state-created wages councils, which set minimum legally enforceable rates of pay for some groups of workers outside the collective bargaining system, covered over 70 per cent of the British labour force. In the 1970s the British system of voluntary joint regulation of terms and conditions of employment was supplemented by a series of legally enforceable job protection rights for workers, relating to redundancy payments, 'unfair dismissal' and anti-discrimination laws covering sex and race relations. Much of this legal interventionism was triggered by Britain's entry into the European Community, which was committed to harmonising basic employment standards in member states. In other European countries, a mixture of legal regulation and national and regional collective bargaining co-existed, although the degree of legal interventionism tended to be greater.

Arrangements for managing employment relationships in the public sector, however, ranged far more widely across Europe. In most countries there was a special legal status given to public officials and their payments and other terms and conditions of service were fixed by laws, which were periodically amended by governments-of-the-day. As the public sector expanded and employment increased, different employment statuses were created, some of which were not regulated by public law but by civil law, as in the private sector. In Germany, for example, three categories of 'public servant' were created: *Beamte* (public officials), *Angestellte* (public employees) and *Arbeiter* (workers). The legal status of *Beamte* is based on public law and they have a special service relationship with the state, involving strict duties, specific pay and conditions of work, including job security, and a career pathway. *Angestellte* and *Arbeiter*, in contrast, are employed under private sector law, even though their terms and conditions of employment are similar to those of *Beamte*. Another system, which emerged in Britain, was that of public-sector employment contracts. These were largely regulated by centralised, national collective agreements, which were incorporated into the individual contracts of employment of those working in the public sector. This system mirrored practice in the private sector, where individual, common-law employment contracts existed, which were also regulated, in many cases, by collective bargaining between employers and trade unions. In Britain, only the small senior civil service and armed services were outside that system. Their employment rules were not regulated by public law or statute but through the unique system of 'royal prerogative' (see chapter 12).

The contemporary flexibility debate began in Europe during the 1960s and has taken a number of different foci throughout the following 30 years. In the 1960s, 'flexibility of working life' was the subject of a series of OECD reports (Klein, 1965; Hallaire, 1968; OECD *et al.*, 1970; Seear, 1971). The circumstances within which this debate took place consisted of rising economic growth throughout OECD economies, increased levels of productivity, full employment and an expanding labour market. From 1960 to 1970, the GNP of the 20 OECD countries had increased by 55 per cent or 4.5 per cent per annum, while per capita income had risen by 40 per cent. There had also been a reduction in working hours, introduction of paid holidays and more leisure time. The concern was, with a growing working population, how jobs could be made available for all those wanting them. In order to make jobs available for young workers, one option was to provide opportunities for older workers to be eased out of the labour market. The rhetoric presented this in positive rather than negative terms, by focusing on quality of working life, the benefits of shorter working lives and freedom of choice for individuals. The hope was expressed that 'the increase in productivity will continue, that part of the parallel development in social welfare will find its expression in more time off work and that procedures will be worked out to enable workers to exercise a more deliberate choice as to the forms time off work may take'. By such means 'a fuller and more satisfying life, with more leisure, more choice of activities for free time, and fewer constraints in working life' would result (Evans, 1973: 11, 109).

The focus was on not only opportunities for earlier retirement but also 'new and more flexible forms for the allocation of working time over the day, the week, the year and the whole working life of the individual' (*ibid*: 11). Some studies placed more emphasis on 'social-pull' factors, that is the demand from workers, especially women, for new and more flexible forms of working time including part-time, job sharing and term-time working so that they could combine paid employment with child care and other family responsibilities. Questions about work over the whole active life of the individual were becoming subject to debate, experimentation, or definite reform in many countries. Preoccupation with this problem fitted into the general trend of the OECD's work at that time, which was increasingly concerned with stimulating policies designed to improve the quality of life as opposed to purely quantitative economic growth.

The flexibility debate in the late 1970s and early 1980s originated in quite different contexts and derived from different sources. The period of rapid economic growth experienced by OECD economies was slowing down and the structures of their economies were changing as a result of new technologies and increasingly deregulated world markets. The pressures were now 'economic push' factors and were again common throughout Western Europe and the US. Two major forms of flexibility in response to these economic-push factors were labour market flexibility and flexible employment practices, with one being of major concern to governments, the other to employers. The main elements acting on governments to initiate labour market flexibilities and on employers to initiate flexible working practices were:

- changing world markets and increased economic competition from both industrialised and newly industrialising countries, especially the 'tiger' economies in the Far East
- technological change, particularly the impact of information and communication technologies (ICTs) on data collection, communication and information exchange
- volatile product markets due to fast changing tastes, aggressive marketing and scientific and technological advances
- rising unemployment due to the effects of the above and the shift from industrial to post-industrial service economies.

First in the US and then in Britain and other English speaking countries, such as Canada, Australia and New Zealand, labour market flexibilities received growing attention by governments and academics throughout the 1980s. Labour market flexibility is based on the premises that labour market rigidities are a major cause of unemployment and loss of competitiveness, and that collective bargaining over pay and conditions, trade union organisation and legal employment rights for workers inhibit both job creation and spontaneous market adjustments to structural economic change. Within the UK, for example, the need for labour market flexibility became the overarching orthodoxy of successive Conservative governments between 1979 and 1997 which sought to promote a competitive, efficient and growing economy. Internationally, both the European Union (EU) and OECD identified improved labour market flexibility as the key to increased competitiveness and higher rates of economic growth (Employment Department, 1994; OECD, 1990).

Studies of the US and western European economies indicate that labour markets have become more flexible since the early 1980s, both in terms of employment flexibility and wages flexibility (Beatson,

1995; Katz, 1993; Vaughan-Whitehead, 1990). The main micro-economic indicators of employment flexibility are: increases in part-time employment; increases in working time; less constraints on employers engaging and dismissing workers; and greater functional flexibility within firms providing them with adaptability in allocating labour between different parts of the production process. Micro-economic indicators of wages flexibility, in turn, are demonstrated by decline in the coverage of collective bargaining and widening wage relativities, both regionally and sectorally (Brown, 1993; Elliot and White, 1993). In Japan and Germany, there is considerable flexibility in working time and labour mobility, whilst in the Nordic countries there is relatively little wages flexibility but high rates of mobility out of unemployment. In a number of EU countries, labour market flexibilities tend to be limited at the micro level, largely because of continuing labour market regulation, although some of that, as in the French introduction of the 35 hour week, is actually designed to increase employment possibilities (Horton, 1998). Beatson (1995) identifies a continuum with the US having the most highly deregulated labour market and the UK in an intermediate position amongst OECD countries with some features of its labour market resembling the US and others its more regulated EU partners. The most regulated labour markets are in Belgium, Germany and France.

The need for flexible working practices, and for firms to respond to changes in their market environments, stems from similar factors leading governments towards labour market flexibilities. These, to repeat, are: uncertainty and volatility in product markets; increased international competition; and accelerating technological change in the workplace. Discussion has focused around how far and in what ways organisations are reshaping their labour market and employment policies in the light of these econo-technological changes. An important debate about human resources flexibilities effectively started with the research of Atkinson (1985) and Atkinson and Meager (1986) in Britain. In his pioneering study, Atkinson (1985: 3) argued that under the influence of economic recession, uncertainty in the marketplace, technological change and reductions in working time, the length of the working week had been continually falling throughout the post-war period. British employers were beginning to introduce 'novel and unorthodox formations in their deployment of labour.' The emerging model was one of horizontal segmentation into a primary, 'core' workforce, conducting the organisation's key activities, surrounded by a cluster of secondary, 'peripheral' groups with a range of alternative contractual and working time arrangements. The core group, which had greater employment security, was required to be functionally flexible in the face of change, while peripheral groups provided numerical flexibility.

In their report for the National Economic Development Organisation (NEDO), Atkinson and Meager (1986: 2–11) modified the 'flexible firm' model to incorporate four main types of human resources flexibility: numerical, functional, distancing and pay.

- **Numerical flexibility** was defined as the ability of firms to adjust the number of workers, or the levels of hours worked, in line with changes in demand for them.
- **Functional flexibility** was defined as the ability of firms to reorganise the competencies associated with jobs, so that job-holders could deploy these competencies across a broader range of tasks. This could involve horizontal enlargement at the same skill level or vertical enlargement, upwards or downwards.
- **Distancing** was defined as the displacement of employment contracts by commercial contracts, as for example by sub-contracting. This type of flexibility was associated with the wish to concentrate corporate resources on competitive advantage or to find cheaper ways of undertaking non-core activities.
- **Pay flexibility** was defined as the ability of firms to adjust pay structures to encourage functional flexibility, match market rates for scarce skills and reward individual effort.

Atkinson and Meager raised a number of issues in their analyses of these flexibilities. These included: the rationale for flexibility; the permanency of the changes; whether there was mutual exclusivity of flexibilities; their impact on job segmentation; and whether there was common interest between employers and employees in the flexibility process. Their research, which sought to find answers to these questions, was based only on private organisations in selected industries, where they concluded employers were engaging in a 'flexibility offensive'.

Atkinson and Meager's research stimulated debate and gave rise to a number of critiques of their work and of the model of the flexible firm. In particular Pollert (1991) raised questions about the differentiation between core and non-core activities and whether all core activities were carried out by permanent full-time employees. Others questioned the empirical evidence and whether the model did describe what was happening within organisations. The British

Workplace Industrial Relations Survey (WIRS) of 1990 found that one-third of workplaces in their sample reported changes in working practices aimed at flexibility (Millward *et al.*, 1992), but other empirical evidence suggested that moves to increase the number of non-standard workers and improve flexibility of working practices owed little to a 'flexibility offensive'. Rather than a distinctive managerial strategy of flexibility, the findings reflected pragmatic and opportunistic responses by employers to high unemployment and weakened trade union influence. Other critics questioned how far functional flexibility was more than workers carrying out relatively minor additional tasks, ancillary to their main skills (Cross, 1988). WIRS 1990 found that changes in working practices amongst non-managerial staff were in fact limited to only eight per cent of establishments surveyed and that many of the reasons were the same as they had always been. These were for tasks requiring limited time for completion, the need to match staffing levels to product demand and providing cover for absent permanent workers. However, there was some evidence (McGregor and Sproull, 1992) that organisations were increasing the employment of non-standard workers for reasons more in line with the flexibility thesis, i.e. to reduce wage and non-wage costs. However, some research suggested that, from the employer's point of view, there were limits to using flexible working arrangements. One study of US-owned electronics plants in Ireland found that local managers were reluctant to use temporary workers because of: reduced commitment by temporary staff; problems in training them; conflicts between permanent and temporary workers; difficulties in terminating temporary staff once they had become integrated into the workforce; and being seen as operating different standards of treatment for these two groups of staff (Geary, 1992).

RECENT DRIVES FOR FLEXIBILITY

What was notable in this early 1980s debate on flexibility was the relative paucity of discussion about the application of the flexible firm model to public service organisations. In the initial findings of the 1998 Workplace Employee Relations Survey (WERS), however, there was more evidence of flexibility across the economy. It was reported, for example, that around 90 per cent of workplaces contracted out one or more of their internal services, such as building maintenance, cleaning, transportation of documents and security. This proportion was similar in both the private and public sectors, with workplaces in the private sector being more likely to contract out security and recruitment, 'whereas those in the public sector were more likely to contract out catering' (Cully and Woodland, 1999: 7).

In the latter part of the 1990s, there is evidence of a third wave in the flexibility debate. This again reflects the changing environment where new industries are dominating successful economies and where new skills are required of their labour forces. The premium now is on knowledge workers and the quality of human capital is seen as the key to economic success. Knowledge-based industries include high-tech manufacturing, such as computers and aerospace, and knowledge-based services such as finance, research and development, communications and training. The OECD economies are now major exporters of high-tech products, patents, trademarks and technical services and governments and employers are promoting the need for 'flexible workers'. Paye (1996: 4) argues that 'the development and diffusion of information technologies are central to the evolution of a knowledge-based economy. Increasingly knowledge can be transformed into information, codified and transmitted through computer and communications networks'. Costs of acquiring knowledge are lower, barriers to entry are demolished, natural monopolies are evaporating and new products and services are being created. Shorter product cycles, quick obsolescence of skills and intensified global competition are among the results. In this context, policies need to aim for two broad goals: increasing the capacity of workers and societies to adapt and minimising the social costs, especially for affected workers and communities. In the knowledge economy, the key resource is human capital and therefore the key investment must be in training and development. Life-long learning is identified as a vital part of people's lives.

The OECD is promoting the move towards flexible knowledge workers (OECD, 1996) and governments of member states of the EU and the US have policies designed to stimulate greater investment in human capital (Cervantes, 1996). Another dimension of this move to flexible key workers is a growing emphasis on direct participation in the workplace. The third wave in the flexibility debate encompasses calls for new forms of work organisations, partnerships and an alternative to the highly unregulated and low-wage American labour market model (European Foundation, 1997). The Employee Direct Participation in Organisational Change (EPOC) survey revealed growing interest in the 1990s in new forms of organising work, which would make European enterprises more competitive in global markets. The survey in 10 OECD countries found that 80 per cent of workplaces had some form of direct participation by employees. Respondents believed that direct participation had an impact on a range of key indicators of economic performance such as quality, output, costs, throughput times, absenteeism, sickness and in reducing staff numbers, including managers. 'The greater the responsibility given to staff, the better the results' (*ibid*: 204). Ingredients for success include education and training and employee involvement in introducing direct participation. There has been an increase in direct participation throughout Europe, but there is still a gap between Europe and Japan, where in Japan 90 per cent of manufacturing organisations and 80 per cent of services across both sectors practise group working.

The European Commission Green Paper, *Partnership for a New Organisation of Work* (European Commission, 1997), states that 'the policy challenges facing all organisations can be summarised in one question: how to reconcile security for workers with the flexibility that firms need' (Executive Summary). The Green Paper identifies a number of issues of concern to all with interests in organisational change including public authorities, the social partners (that is employers and trade unions across the spectrum of employment), educational institutions and bodies involved in social policy. These are:

- how to organise the necessary training and retraining so that the workforce can meet the increasing needs for skills and competencies
- how to adapt social legislation to take account of employment trends
- how to adapt wage systems along with organisational structures on which they are based
- how to adapt working-time arrangements in the light of the new situation
- how to take advantage of new employment trends regarding equal opportunities
- how to develop more flexible organisations in the public services
- how to provide adequate support for small organisations lacking resources and expertise to change.

Organisational change has been and continues to be a feature of both the private sector and public services throughout Europe and the US.

It is an aspect of flexibility, which has become increasingly important during the 1990s as governments have sought to create appropriate structures for delivering public services. There is also evidence that direct participation has increased, reflecting the need to overcome resistance to change as well as gain the commitment of staff to the goals and objectives of their organisations. Apart from the EPOC project, there is little comparative research on the management of the change process in the public sector.

There is another aspect of flexibility which has reappeared in the debate during the second half of the 1990s – namely reducing the working hours of those in employment to create working opportunities for the unemployed. Although the European Working Time Directive was introduced as a Health and Safety policy, it has been seen by governments as a way of providing scope for creating new jobs to absorb the hours 'released'. In France, for example, governments have imposed shorter working weeks and offered incentives to employers to create jobs. There has been a lot of opposition from both employers and employees for different reasons. Employers object to the removal of the option of overtime hours beyond 48 hours per week to deal with demand pressures, whilst employees have objected to loss of pay because of the restriction on the number of hours they can work. Loopholes in the Directive have greatly reduced the impact of the policy but the closing of those loopholes may begin to see some effect in the future. In most OECD countries, negotiated agreements on working hours in the public services are well within the limits set by the Directive, whilst essential services are excluded from its remit. Therefore its impact is likely to be limited in the public services *per se*. Contracted-out work may be affected, however, where private companies are not bound by contract compliance to offer standards of employment no worse than those in the contracting organisation.

TYPES OF HUMAN RESOURCES FLEXIBILITIES

A report prepared for the European Association of Personnel Management (EAPM), covering 32 organisations in 15 countries, claims that 'flexible working practices' are on the increase in all members of the EAPM, including public authorities. This section provides a framework for examining these, which goes beyond the basic model suggested by Atkinson and Meager. Using the EAPM study as a guide, six categories of flexibilities are identified: contractual flexibilities; flexibilities in working hours; pay flexibilities; flexibilities in the length of working life; task flexibilities; and flexibility in the location of work. These are merely heuristic devices, however, because, in practice, many organisations, including public services, use combinations of flexibilities to achieve their corporate goals, which are also linked with other organisational changes, such as decentralisation, contractorisation and human resources management (HRM).

Contractual flexibilities

These incorporate either non-permanent employment or sub-contracting arrangements and may be regarded as a form of 'distancing' as described in the research of Atkinson and Meager.

- *Non-permanent contracts.* These cover any form of employment other than permanent, unlimited contracts and include seasonal work contracts, temporary contracts, fixed-term contracts and short-term contracts.
- *Subcontracting.* This is the displacement of an employment contract by a commercial one as a means of getting a job done. Some subcontractors are self-employed but others can be full-time permanent employees in the contracting firm.

Flexibilities in working hours

These are nearest to the definition of numerical flexibility provided by Atkinson and Meagher and incorporate five sub-types of flexibilities.

- *Part-time working.* These are staff working less than the standard full-time norm within an organisation or sector, although the statutory definition of 'full-time' differs amongst countries.
- *Job sharing.* This is a form of part-time working where two or more employees share one job and where pay, holidays and other benefits are divided in proportion to the number of hours worked.
- *Flexitime.* These are arrangements where, within set limits, employees vary their starting and finishing times, provided they work the total number of hours agreed for the accounting period.
- *Annualised hours.* This is a form of working time by which employees are contracted to work a total number of hours per year, rather

than weekly. From the employer's viewpoint hours can be varied
on a daily, weekly or monthly basis.

- *Flexible daily hours.* This is a system whereby employees are paid
  only for the hours actually worked, arising from demands placed
  on the employer.
- *Overtime.* This is time worked by employees over and above
  normal contractual hours as defined by law or collective
  agreements.
- *Shiftworking.* This is where other workers doing the same jobs
  replace workers having completed a normal day's work. It covers
  a range of working practices such as double day shifts, staggered
  day shifts, night shifts, weekend shifts and continuous shifts.
- *Flexible weekly hours.* These cope with seasonal variations in
  demand for an employer's products or services.

Pay flexibilities

These are aimed at containing employment costs, linking pay and benefits more closely to individual and corporate performance, matching
market pay rates with workers who have scarce skills and providing
employers with more control over the pay-work bargain. The main
types of pay flexibilities are: decentralised pay bargaining; performance related pay; and profit related pay.

- *Decentralised pay bargaining.* This is where pay bargaining
  takes place at employer or establishment level as opposed to
  multi-employer or sectoral level. From the employer's viewpoint,
  decentralised bargaining has the claimed benefits of achieving flexible pay deals, dissociates union bargaining power and concentrates the bargaining power of the employer in slack labour
  markets.
- *Performance related pay (PRP).* This attempts to link an individual's pay with their performance and the extent to which
  they have met pre-agreed job targets with their manager. The
  claimed aims of PRP are: to help recruitment and retention;
  to facilitate changes in organisational culture; to weaken union
  power; to devolve personnel management functions to line
  managers; to reward and recognise 'good performance' by individual employees; to provide greater financial control and 'value
  for money' for the employer; and to encourage job and task
  flexibility.

- *Profit related pay.* This relatively new concept of reward management, currently encouraged by government policy in the USA and the UK, seeks to link increases in pay with the firm's profitability. It implies that paying flexible wages, in line with company profits, encourages firms to retain their employees in difficult times and reward them when times are good.

Flexibilities in length of working life

In addition to changing patterns of hours worked, there are also changes in patterns of working life.

- *Career breaks.* These are extended periods of unpaid leave from employment, with the intention of the worker returning to work with the same employer in the same or similar job. A modification of this is the secondment of staff with or without pay to other organisations to gain experience.
- *Early retirement schemes.* These allow employees to leave working life before normal retirement age. A variation of this is enabling people to reduce their working time in preparing for full retirement.

Task flexibilities

These are closest to the concept of functional flexibilities. Here job descriptions are drawn up to cover a range of tasks and to identify a range of competencies required to carry out the tasks. This enables individuals to cover a range of diverse activities and eliminates the traditional problems of job specificity and demarcation disputes. With the requirements of personnel flexibilities pressing on employers, traditional job boundaries are, according to the EAPM study, being firmly challenged.

Flexibility in location of work

This might also be seen as a type of distancing and largely takes the forms of teleworking, telecommunicating and working from home. It normally applies to traditional mobile workers (sales and maintenance staff), professionals, specialists such as managers, technical workers and office support workers.

DISCUSSION

The introduction of the wide-ranging types of flexibilities outlined above is associated with other managerial initiatives aimed at improving corporate performance, productivity and efficiency. As a result, some employers are using more sophisticated recruitment and selection systems (such as assessment centres and biodata), integrated staff appraisal systems, staff development programmes, culture change initiatives and more performance-focused reward systems. In English speaking countries, this approach to managing people has been identified with the emergence of a 'new' type of personnel management – 'human resources management' (HRM) (Storey, 1992; Beaumont, 1993; Beardwell and Holden, 1994; Hollingshead and Leat, 1995). HRM, with both its 'hard' and 'soft' sides, (Guest, 1987, 1990) is claimed to facilitate more efficient use of human resources, thus enabling organisations to meet their business objectives and helps in the recruiting, nurturing and developing of a flexible, trained workforce, comfortable with continuous change. Other related developments are total quality management systems (TQM), employee involvement initiatives, decentralisation and customer awareness programmes. These too are linked with creating, maintaining and managing a flexible workforce and meeting the corporate challenges arising from market competition and environmental turbulence. Whether these flexibilities and innovations actually achieve the objectives for which they are created is not definitively demonstrated. Nevertheless, they are powerful tools in the rhetoric of the 'new' management and in the managing of change.

Throughout the public services in all OECD countries the full range of flexibilities identified above are in evidence, although there are differences reflecting the varying types of political system and the varied contingencies of public organisations. These are illustrated in the country studies in this book. While focusing particularly on four categories of flexibility: contractual and distancing; numerical and working time; pay and personnel; and task and functional, no single template was imposed upon the contributors to this book. Each country is unique with its distinctive political institutions, legal framework, public service traditions and managerial structures and style. These are the variables which have fashioned the changes and trends, which are recorded, and the clue to why there are such differences and similarities.

Flexibility is now a common phenomenon in the public services and has been driven by political factors rather than by strictly economic ones, unlike in the private sector where flexibility is economically and technologically motivated. It is difficult to separate out the importance of economic-pull and social-push factors in either sector but the tradition of being a 'good employer' in the public services of some countries has also influenced responses to employee needs. Governments throughout Europe have been faced with the same environmental pressures from increased competition, globalisation, demographic change, rising public expectations of improved public services and competing ideologies about the role of the state in society. Each country had assumed an extensive welfare role post-1945 and, although levels of state expenditure and public sector employment varied, there was a common upward trend which was generally financed out of rising taxes and increased public borrowing. Faced with slowing or declining growth rates, and the need to increase the competitiveness of their economies, governments responded with policies of retrenchment, cuts in public spending and searches for greater efficiency in using government funds. Their actions were also influenced, either directly or indirectly, by the ideas of the New Right especially in the English speaking world, which was a political movement equipped with prescriptive policy recipes for dealing with the economic and political problems of the day (King, 1987; Massey, 1993; Farnham and Horton, 1993; Flynn and Strehl, 1996).

Responses to fiscal deficits and the influence of the New Right varied but there were sufficient similarities for academics to talk about 'megatrends' (Hood, 1991) and to identify the changes in and approaches to managing the public sector described as 'a new managerialism' (OECD, 1991; Pollitt, 1993; Farnham and Horton, 1996a; Zifcak, 1994). All governments have sought, to varying degrees, to reduce the size and scope of their public services and increase their productivity, efficiency and responsiveness. This was aimed at releasing resources for use in the so-called private wealth-creating sector, stabilising or reducing taxes, encouraging an enterprise culture and in some cases it resulted in the break up of state monopolies and the transfer of state enterprises and other activities to the private sector. In some countries, there has also been a concerted effort to reduce the power of civil servants, public-service professionals and trade unions, to resist change by installing managers to direct and control the use organisational resources. Markets or quasi-markets have been introduced to replace political decisions on allocation of resources and competition has become the mechanism for achieving greater efficiency, consumer choice, innovation and entrepreneurship in public organisations in countries like the UK and the US. The EU has also imposed external pressures on member states to contain or cut public expenditure in order to meet the criteria for entry into the single European currency and economic monetary union. Eleven countries met those criteria by January 1999, but only by reducing the share of public expenditure and public debt as a percentage of Gross National Product (GNP). The remaining four (Sweden, Denmark, Greece and the UK) are either aiming to meet the criteria for entry or have done so but are waiting to obtain the necessary political support to ensure ratification of entry (Sear, 1998).

Throughout western Europe and the US, the size of the public-sector workforce has tended to fall during the last 20 years, although the decline varies widely. Reductions have been obtained in various ways including privatisation, contracting out, and non-replacement of staff on retirement or exit and greater numerical flexibility. Public services have been exposed to a range of policies intended to simulate markets, encourage business approaches to management and introduce greater structural, functional and pay flexibilities within public organisations. These policies have included compulsory competitive tendering (CCT), market testing, contractorisation, agencification, financial reform, performance indicators or what is collectively described as 'new public management' (NPM). Forced to cope with declining resources in real terms, deliver cost reductions, meet rigorous efficiency and performance criteria and increasingly compete for business, top managers in public organisations have been confronted with situations not dissimilar to those facing senior managers in private-sector companies. It is not surprising, therefore, public managers are resorting to similar responses as their private-sector counterparts. Indeed, they have been positively encouraged by governments to look to successful private businesses for examples of 'best' management practice. There is now wide-spread acceptance by many political authorities that private-sector management practices are 'good' and 'efficient', while public-service ones are 'bad' and 'inefficient' and that traditional bureaucratic systems of public administration should move closer to the private management model (Farnham and Horton, 1996b). In these contexts, an important strategy for making public service organisations more efficient and more responsive to their clients' needs has been the introduction of a range of human resources flexibilities. It is these diverse patterns which constitute the central theme of the chapters in this book. In this way, further insights into these changes can be provided and similarities and differences across EU member states and the US can be highlighted.

References

ATKINSON, J. (1985). *Flexibility, Uncertainty and Manpower Management.* Sussex: Institute of Manpower Studies.

ATKINSON, J. and MEAGER, N. (1986). *Changing Patterns of Work: How companies achieve flexibility to achieve new needs.* London: NEDO.

BOYER, R. (ed.) (1989). *The Search for Labour Market Flexibility.* Oxford: Oxford University Press.

BEARDWELL, I. and HOLDEN, L. (1994). *Human Resources Management: A Contemporary Perspective.* London: Pitman.

BEATSON, M. (1995). *Labour Market Flexibility.* London: HMSO.

BEAUMONT, P. (1993). *Human Resource Management.* London: Sage.

BROWN, W. (1993). 'The contraction of collective bargaining in Britain'. *British Journal of Industrial Relations.* 31 (2).

CERVANTES, M. (1996). 'Helping industry help itself'. *The OECD Observer.* No 200, June/July.

CROSS, M. (1988). 'Changes in working practices in UK manufacturing, 1981–1988'. *Industrial Relations Review and Report.* No 415, pp 2–10.

CULLY, M. and WOODLAND, S. (1999). *The 1998 Workplace Employee Relations Survey.* London: Department of Trade and Industry.

ELLIOT, R. and WHITE, M. (1993). 'Recent developments in the industrial wage structure in the UK'. *Cambridge Journal of Economics.* Vol 17, pp 109–129.

EMPLOYMENT DEPARTMENT (1994). *Employment Department Group: Departmental Report.* London: HMSO.

EUROPEAN COMMISSION (1997). *Green Paper: Partnership for a New Organisation of Work.* European Commission: Brussels.

EUROPEAN FOUNDATION (1997). *New Forms of Work Organisation: Can Europe realise its potential?* Dublin: European Foundation for the Improvement of Living and Working Conditions.

EVANS, A. (1973). *Flexibility in Working Life.* Paris: OECD.

FARNHAM, D. and HORTON, S. (eds) (1993). *Managing the New Public Services* (1st edition). London: Macmillan.

FARNHAM, D. and HORTON, S. (eds) (1996a). 'Public Managers and Private Managers: Towards a Professional Synthesis', in Farnham, D. *et al.*, *New Public Managers in Europe: Public Servants in Transition.* London: Macmillan.

FARNHAM, D. and HORTON, S. (1996b). *Managing People in the Public Services.* London: Macmillan.

FLYNN, N. and STREHL, F. (1996). *Public Sector Management in Europe.* Hemel Hempstead: Prentice Hall.

GEARY, J. (1992). 'Employment flexibility and human resource management: the case of three American electronic plants'. *Work, Employment and Society*. Vol 6.

GUEST, D. (1987). 'Human resource management and industrial relations'. *Journal of Management Studies*. 24 (5), pp 503–21.

GUEST, D. (1990). 'Human resource management and the American dream'. *Journal of Management Studies*. 27 (4), pp 377–97.

HALLAIRE, J. (1968). *Part-time Employment*. Paris: OECD.

HEGEWISCH, A. (1999). 'Employment Flexibility', in Corby, S. and White, G., *Employee Relations in the Public Services*. London: Routledge.

HOGGETT, P. (1996). 'New modes of control in the public services'. *Public Administration*. 74 (1).

HOLLINGSHEAD, G. and LEAT, M. (1995). *Human Resource Management: An International and Comparative Perspective*. London: Pitman.

HOOD, C. (1991). 'A public management for all seasons'. *Public Administration*. 69 (2), pp 3–19.

HORTON, J.-L. (1998). 'The 35 hour week in France: potent remedy or lethal poison'. *Employee Relations Review*. December, No 7, pp 22–9.

HUTCHINSON, S. and BREWSTER, C. (1994). *Flexibility at Work in Europe: Strategies and Practice*. London: Institute of Personnel and Development.

KATZ, H. (1993). 'The decentralisation of collective bargaining: a literature review and comparative analysis.' *Industrial and Labor Relations Review*. 47 (1), pp 3–22.

KING, D. (1987). *The New Right: Politics, Markets and Citizenship*. Basingstoke: Macmillan.

KLEIN, V. (1965). *Women Workers: Working Hours and Services*. Paris: OECD.

KIRKPATRICK, I. and MARTINEZ LUCIO, M. (1996). 'Introduction: the contract state and the future of public management'. *Public Administration*. 74 (1).

MASSEY, A. (1993). *Managing the Public Sector: A Comparative Study of the United Kingdom and the United States*. Aldershot: Edward Elgar.

MCGREGOR, A. and SPROULL, A. (1992). 'Employers and the flexible workforce'. *Employment Gazette*. May.

MILLWARD, N., STEVENS, D., HAWES, W. and SMART, D. (1992). *Workplace Industrial Relations in Transition*. Aldershot: Dartmouth.

OECD et al. (1970). *Flexibility of Retirement Age*. Paris: OECD.

OECD (1990). *Labour Market Policies for the 1990s*. Paris: OECD.

OECD (1996). *Employment and Growth in the Knowledge-Based Economy*. Paris: OECD.

Oxford Guide to the English Language (1984). Oxford: Oxford University Press.

PAYE, J.C. (1996). 'Policies for a knowledge economy'. *The OECD Observer*. No 200 June/July.

POLLERT, A. (ed.) (1991). *Farewell to Flexibility?* Oxford: Blackwell.

POLLITT, C. (1993). *Managerialism and the Public Services*. Oxford: Blackwell.

SEAR, S. (1998). *Pocket Guide to the Euro*. Leigh-on-Sea: Glogold.

SEEAR, N. (1971). *Re-entry of Women to the Labour Market after an Interruption in Employment.* Paris: OECD.
STOREY, J. (1992). *Developments in the Managing of Human Resources.* Oxford: Blackwell.
VAUGHAN-WHITEHEAD, D. (1990). 'Wage bargaining in Europe: continuity and change'. *Social Europe.* Supplement 2/90. Luxembourg: Commission of the European Communities.
WEBB, S. and WEBB, B. (1897). *Industrial Democracy.* London: Longman, Green.
ZIFCAK, S. (1994). *New Managerialism.* Buckingham: Open University Press.

2 Public Service Flexibility in Comparative Perspective

F.F. Ridley

Flexibility in public services can mean a number of different things. And, within these different meanings, it can take different forms, involve different procedures and be considered from different comparative perspectives. To some extent, the meaning given to the term is affected by where one comes from. This may be the country or the interest, the perspective of academic or practitioner and, in the academic case, the discipline such as law, sociology, management or public administration in which the observer is trained. The individual's perspective is also influenced by the purpose of flexibility, what one hopes to improve through flexibility or to change, such as managerial efficiency, worker life-styles or user convenience.

What, then, is to be flexibilised? Human resources flexibility focuses on working practices, which range from use of staff, types of work they do, hours worked, types of employment contract they work under, the rewards they receive and length of their working lives. How these are determined and regulated varies. Some aspects of working practices may be determined by law or regulations, notably terms and conditions of service, hours of work and remuneration, whilst others are determined by collective bargaining between employer and employee representatives. A third method may be by employers unilaterally. In some countries conditions of service may be determined by specific laws which include civil service law, *statuts*, regulations and codes which have the force of laws. In other countries conditions may be determined by employment contracts. A complicating factor here is that 'contracts' may be another word for law and regulation. Further, flexibility ranges from the rules of employment to 'office practice'. These perspectives obviously overlap but what falls under 'legal rules' and what remains managerial discretion varies among countries. Some aspects of work, which can only be flexibilised in some countries through changes in the law or changing terms and conditions, can be changed in others through unilateral managerial decisions.

FACTORS INFLUENCING FLEXIBILITY

Flexibility of terms and conditions of public service employment can be found to some degree in all countries of Europe, though its nature, incidence and extent vary from country to country. The ease with which terms and conditions can be changed, the facility of reform, is affected by a number of factors. These include the constitutional framework, the nature of the political system, the legislative process, the traditions of employment relations, the administrative culture of the state system and, not least, its history. All the countries in this book, except the UK, have written constitutions. Their constitutions often set down rules, which govern the status, organisation, and procedures by which changes in the public service can be made. Furthermore, in federal systems, such as Germany, the constitution sets down procedures for decision making which complicate the process of change by involving both legislative chambers. In the UK, on the other hand, there is no special procedure to be followed or constitutional law to override parliamentary legislation on any matters relating to the public or civil service. The UK is also unique in having the historic royal prerogative powers of the Crown exercised by ministers, which gives them the power to change the structure of the civil service, its status, role and activities by executive decision without parliamentary involvement. The only exception is the civil service of Northern Ireland whose legal basis is found in the Government of Northern Ireland Act 1920. The British civil service (i.e. excluding Northern Ireland), which is subject to Crown prerogative, is regulated by ministers but in a system which now permits delegation of ministerial powers downwards. This provides considerable flexibility for executive agency heads to make changes to the structure, rewards and terms and conditions of civil servants subject to agreement with the civil service trade unions in some cases. The local government service in the UK requires no legislation to change its structure either, because it operates on the basis of contractual employment within the framework of ordinary employment law. Both UK cases are unusual in a European context. On the continent of Europe, public services are generally organised through law. The procedural dimensions of law reform are thus important. The legislative process and the politics of legislation differ. They either facilitate or hinder government projects, by reform from above, and shape the contents of reform measures from other sources, for example, the legislature itself. In many of the continental European countries, the multi-party system, frequency of coalition governments and legislative procedures impede executives from introducing change where conditions of service involve legislative rather than executive action, as in Belgium and Italy.

In the UK, reforms introduced into the public services since 1979 can in large part be attributed to strong reform-minded governments, with disciplined party majorities and executive powers to carry them through. Few politicians elsewhere in Europe have approached public service reform with that strength or made public service reform a central part of their political programme in the way that Margaret Thatcher, John Major and Tony Blair have done. Public service reform is on the agenda everywhere but nowhere else has it occupied as central a place in government policy as it does in the UK. No European parties or governments have shared the ideological drive of Thatcherism, Majorism or Blairism. Furthermore, parties of right and left in many of the countries of mainland Europe draw substantially on people with a public service background for their leadership, as in France and Germany. The other side of the power equation is the strength of public service unions to prevent change, shape it in their own interests and support the flexibilities which they are willing to accept. Public service unions appear strong in most western European countries, if in varying degrees, and are generally seen as 'social partners' in any discussion of reforms. In the UK, they too were near equal partners in pre-1979 negotiations about conditions of employment but their power was much tamed, although not extinguished, in the Thatcher years.

As important as other factors in understanding, explaining and constraining political and administrative change is history itself. Historically established ways of doing things are still embedded in the structures of governance and historically established ways of thinking about how things should be done are embedded in a country's political culture. New ideas about public service organisation, such as those of the New Public Management School, must compete with old ideas, reshape or replace them and that involves quite different situations from one country or group of countries to another. Public service cultures may be more or less open to modernisation and administrative sub-cultures to managerialisation, including human resources flexibilities.

PROBLEMS OF COMPARISON

One of the major problems in undertaking comparative national studies is that of language. The terms 'public service' and 'flexibility' are both ambiguous within a language and can have different meanings across languages. One risk in comparative studies is that one is not comparing like with like and it is clear from the country studies in this book that concepts and language do not travel easily across national borders. It is important therefore to look closely at definitions. Let us start with 'public service' to illustrate how problems of national differences arise. The term public service and associated terms like civil service are used differently from one country to another because they relate to different systems of public administration and to quite different political phenomena. First, the term 'public service' may refer to a group of people, such as state employees, a function or an institution, such as the health service. The public service may, in turn, refer to all those in public sector employment, including all public organisations and enterprises, or it may refer to only some personnel whose employment regulations are in some way specific and differentiated from other employees working in public organisations. For example, in some countries we can distinguish between personnel employed under administrative law and others employed under civil labour laws. In France, *la function publique* covers almost all public employees in central and local government, because both are subject to administrative law conditions. But in the UK, where there is no tradition of administrative law, there is a distinction between Crown-regulated appointments (civil service) and contractual employment (local government and the NHS). Germany with its administrative law tradition makes a distinction between three status groups of public officials, *Beamte*, *Angestellte* and *Arbeiter* but these statuses cut across the federal structure and all levels of government within the German state. There are also national distinctions between 'service' appointments and 'contractual' ones. These often relate to levels of work and distinguish public administration posts and clerical or industrial work, for example, with only the first being real 'officials' and therefore having a higher status. In many countries in this book employment contracts are being used as ways of over-coming restrictions on new appointments and both status position and terms and conditions of employment are the same as for career positions. Furthermore, in a cultural as well as a legal sense, large categories of staff may in some countries identify themselves with the public service, meaning service of the state/officialdom/special terms and conditions. In other countries, such people may not see themselves in the same light or be seen in the same light by the system as a whole. UK schoolteachers, for example, would not identify themselves as officials (or members of a translated *function publique*) and, though the government now determines salary levels, in other respects their conditions of employment are not public sector specific. The same applies to health service staff in the UK.

Because of the wide range of employment categories and legal statuses found across states, what are seen as flexibility reforms in some countries may simply mean bringing conditions of employment in those parts of the public sector where work differs little from the private sector closer to private sector conditions. Flexibility reforms in such cases are much less radical than flexibility in regard to officials engaged in tasks of public administration (the work of government) and are still seen as quite different from other workers with distinct conditions of employment. Also we need to be cautious about measuring the 'extent' of flexibility. If figures are produced to show how many people have had their conditions of employment changed, and these are used in cross-country comparisons with the hope of deducing trends, it is imperative that the comparisons are of like with like, such as administrative, clerical, industrial, educational or medical. We must remember that starting points for these groups, their legal status for example, may be different from one country to another. If we compare changes in 'status' groups (e.g. career appointed officials regulated by public service law, contractual staff employed under ordinary labour law), we must remember that these groups include a different mix of people from one country to another.

CONTRACTUALISATION

A major trend in public service management is often thought to be contractualisation of employment and, allowing for problems of differences in target groups noted above, there is certainly evidence of this. We return to a discussion of trends below but here it is worth staying for a little with definitional problems and issues of comparison they cause. The temptation is to contrast two situations: (1) career services where the position of staff is defined in detail by special codes, laws and regulations as in Germany, and (2) contractual employment, thought to be more flexible in a variety of ways, including the number and sort of staff that can be employed, methods of appointment and promotion and, of course, tenure. This view is an over-simplification at best and it can also seriously mislead. In continental Europe, contractual employment has often been used not to promote managerial efficiency, or make conditions of service more flexible, but to increase the size of personnel beyond what budget laws allow for established posts or beyond the numbers specified for particular categories or grades of officials in civil service laws. The motive quite often has been to circumvent limits on the growth of bureaucracy that parliaments tried to impose, as in Belgium. The fact that contractual employment could sometimes be presented as less permanent than for other staff sweetened the pill but, as noted below, the theory was not the practice. Another reason for using contractual employment has been to distinguish officials from lower status staff such as the distinction in Germany between *Beamten* and *Angestellten*.

Employment of both types, service and contractual, has been a common feature of many public services in Europe for a long time. However, employment of people on contracts may offer no more flexibility than statutory status, as they may have as much security of tenure and the same payment and conditions of employment as their higher status equivalents as in Germany and Belgium. Standardised terms are generally prescribed, with uniform systems of recruitment, uniform grades and uniform pay scales. Moreover, on appointment employees adhere to these terms, which makes their position little different from that of established officials accepting appointments. There is certainly no negotiated contract (see chapter 9 on Spain). True, disputes involving contract staff may be subject to different branches of law and a different set of courts, civil rather than administrative, but even that is not always the case, since contractual employment, as in France, may be in the framework of administrative or labour law. In the past, the situation of local government employees in the UK was not all that different from civil servants. Though based on individual contracts in law, these were written in relation to collective employer association and union agreements and linked to codes or 'books', known by colours, for different categories of staff, e.g. administrative, technical, manual. These defined recruitment and promotion procedures required qualifications, grades and pay scales, work time, sick leave, retirement and everything else. The point here is that contractual systems do not necessarily allow personnel managers greater freedom, whether in pay and conditions or indeed in work practice such as posting of staff.

Nor can one make firm statements that contractual employment gives less security of tenure and allows management to free itself of unsuitable staff, such as those who are incompetent or no longer required as work tasks change. In much of continental Europe, where security of tenure until retirement age is guaranteed for career officials, employees seem to have acquired similar rights and it is often hard to distinguish the two groups in this respect. In the UK, on the other hand, where the civil service never had security of tenure in law, as employment was at the will of the Crown, but had it in practice, this is no longer the case. The top 300 civil service posts in the Senior Civil Service (SCS) have recently been contractualised, are open to outsiders and are generally limited in time or at least subject to termination. Each member of the SCS has an individual contract, which is renewable. Renewal depends on performance and government need. Already two chief executives of departmental agencies have been dismissed (Polidano, 1997) and it is not uncommon for outsiders to be recruited to specific posts. But here too complexity of comparison occurs, because these are posts which are generally defined as 'political or 'discretionary' appointments in other countries of Europe. The size of the SCS in Britain is about the same as the number of political/discretionary appointments in Germany and the spoils posts available to an incoming president in the United States. In one sense, therefore, recent developments bring the UK closer to continental Europe but since appointments are managerial in the UK and remain political elsewhere, it is hard to see a meaningful flexibility trend here. On the other hand, a recent development in Germany, allowing for time-limited appointments to senior posts just below the 'political' level for efficiency reasons, reflect a potential trend as do other types of contractual employment notably for new, specialised types of work, for 'managerial' posts or for temporary needs. Contractualisation also refers to the process of outsourcing public service activities, so that delivery of services is carried out by private or voluntary organisations, whose employees are not civil servants or public officials. This form of privatisation, long practised in continental Europe in the field of social services, has been extended to all functions of government, including policing, criminal justice and defence.

In any discussion of flexibility through contractualisation, therefore, one needs to ask what sort of contract is involved. These may range from negotiated individualised contracts, non-negotiated (employer written) individualised contracts or non-negotiated standardised contracts (possibly prescribed in law or regulations). On a much larger scale, one may find standardised contracts for groups of people recruited to a service rather than appointed to a post. Even then, there can be major differences in the degree of flexibility allowed; especially if contracts of employment embody or refer to regulations as detailed as those for established staff. Finally, there are commercial contracts which may involve transfer of staff to the contractor or redundancy.

CAREER SYSTEMS

Career service systems also vary in the degree of flexibility they allow in career decisions, whether to management or staff. To some degree this reflects the extent of detail in the codes that regulate the service and the range of discretion they allow personnel management. This can be quite technical and easily overlooked (e.g. the width of pay bands in pay scales) and is a matter to which we return below in relation to flexibilisation of such codes. But it is important to remember in looking at trends that the starting point is not the same from country to country, as regulations can differ greatly in the detail of their prescriptions. Simplifications, even deletions, in one country, may not be much of a trend, if it merely brings that country closer to flexibilisation already found in the rules of other countries. Other limits on flexibility may be imposed by the structure of the civil service itself and to these we turn first.

Typical career systems involve two structures: a civil service grade system, 'rank in service', and a hierarchy of posts, 'rank in organisation'. If pay scales attach to rank in service rather than to posts, this creates serious problems if one wants to move to job evaluation and workload/responsibility related pay. This is sometimes met by the award of temporary, supplementary pay for holders of certain posts, which can easily lead to opaque salary structures with little real flexibility, as patterns are set. Even more of a problem for flexibility in deployment of staff is the internal structure within the civil service itself. Most civil services have horizontal classes and barriers to mobility between classes. Britain used to have over 1,300 classes based on generalist or specialist qualifications for entry but these were gradually abolished throughout the 1970s and 1980s. They were never a real barrier to promotion from bottom to top and about 40 per cent of civil servants obtained mobility across class boundaries. Such class structures persist elsewhere in Europe, generally linked to different levels of educational qualification at recruitment, with barriers to movement upward from one class to another. This may be a constraint on managers but it is an even more serious inflexibility for staff. Vertical divisions also prevent sideways movement from one branch of the service to another or indeed from one sort of post to another in the same ministry. The distinction between generalist administrative posts and specialist professional posts has also been largely removed in Britain, where appointments are increasingly based on the best person for the job. In contrast the French *corps* system based on exclusive claims on both horizontal and vertical positions remains largely in place despite some reforms (Rouban, 1998). From this perspective, flexibility involves dismantling barriers, in law or practice, allowing managers greater freedom in posting and above all opening career choices for staff. While this seems to be happening to some extent in most countries, the extent varies, reflecting above all the strength of established interests, civil service groups protecting their traditional patronage, as in France and Spain and to a lesser extent in Italy.

DEREGULATION, SELECTION AND PROMOTION

Human resources flexibilities may involve deregulation, changes in selection procedures and scope for exercising discretion over promotions. Deregulation can be achieved through transferring services or state activities and staff to another category of public sector institutions. In the UK under the Next Steps programme (Ibbs, 1998), executive activities of departments have been transferred to agencies headed by chief executives with responsibility for managing delivery of services to the public or other government departments. Other services may be transferred to semi-independent non-departmental agencies run by appointed boards or commercial services may be set up as public enterprises. Throughout Europe, similar practices are in evidence, although categories and titles vary from country to country. These options offer structural flexibility but personnel flexibilities may be and often are a by-product of wider managerial moves. Public service laws and regulations may also be made more flexible without such structural reorganisation. This can involve a variety of things such as:

- *recruitment* – by broadening qualification requirements or replacing examination scores by wider and more flexible personal assessments
- *promotion* – by less weight attached to service years
- *posting* – by opening posts to a wider range of staff
- *pay* – by introducing wider pay bands and allowing managers discretion where to place officials in their band differentiated pay scales for different groups within a service with non-automatic increments; elements of performance related pay)
- *grading* – through greater scope for job evaluation
- *tenure* – allowing for redundancy or early retirement.

Another aspect of flexibility may be a move from a uniform to a pluralist system for the civil service. In the federal state of Germany most civil servants are employed by the states (*Länder*), so the system is not *unified*, but it has a uniform set of rules covering personnel in federal, state and local institutions. In other federal systems, civil service, laws may be a provincial matter and greater diversity is thus possible because reforms may reflect different provincial views as in the US. In Britain, a major aspect of recent flexibilisation reforms has been the devolution of civil service management (e.g. recruitment, grades and pay) to departments and executive agencies. The managerial responsibility of chief executives includes decisions about number and type of staff within their block financial resources. Diversification of this sort is an aspect of flexibilisation but not a necessary one. Other countries are more strongly wedded to a principle of uniformity across services and across regions. Indeed, the German constitutional tradition requires the latter.

One could also consider flexibility in selection of staff. Everywhere there are rules to ensure 'fairness' at recruitment. Open competition and equality of opportunity, providing one is qualified to compete, are fairly universal general principles. However, in much of Europe, this still means competitive examination scores are the major determinant of entry. The British system, based upon extended interview systems, has always been much more flexible than the continental examination model which reflects a misplaced confidence in objective marking and an overvaluation of knowledge compared to personal competencies and skills. An element of flexibilisation might be allowing recruiting boards, even managers, greater freedom in selecting staff within frameworks that protect 'fairness'. A point can be made here about top appointments in the British civil service. Although 'open', i.e. advertised to outsiders and requiring only 'relevant' experience, the Civil Service Commission ensures that managerial flexibility in selection is not politicised. In other systems, however, it clearly is since sympathy with a political party may be as important as ability to do the job.

Similarly, one should look at the flexibility of promotion procedures, because these are often relevant to managerial decisions about deployment of staff. In career services, staff expect fairness in promotion since promotion is an essential part of the whole idea of a career service to which they have made a commitment. Seniority requirements have generally been flexibilised but elements still remain in many places. There may also be formalised procedures, such as independent promotion boards, to decide who is suitable for promotion, leaving the actual decision about filling a higher level post to management, a system that can frustrate both staff and mangers on occasion. Strangely, more attention is often paid to recruitment than promotion procedures yet it is the latter which determines who get to the top and direct public services.

DISCUSSION

What, after all this, do we then mean when we talk of flexibility in managing personnel in the public services? The debate about flexibility has largely focused on ways in which organisational structures, work processes and employment practices can enable managers to increase their own control over staff human resources in the workplace. There is of course another aspect, namely changes that enable staff to increase there own control over their working lives, through part-time work or better provisions for leave. Types of flexibility identified by the European Association of Personnel Managers (IPD, 1994) include working hours, location of work, length of working life, tasks and pay. Most of these seem to concern work procedures, which is not really the topic addressed here with its focus on public service law and regulation. The latter obviously cover pay systems, tenure and retirement. It is worth making the point, however, that work procedures may also relate to more formal aspects of civil service organisation, notably if much civil service work is seen as public administration, subject to administrative law, requiring specialised qualifications and a personnel of different legal status from employees in other sectors. In that case flexibility of personnel rules may be facilitated by changes in work procedures through which debureaucratisation of work precedes debureaucratisation of staff.

The point has already been made that one should probably distinguish between flexibility of civil service organisation in 'classical' administration, such as exercise of public authority, making official decisions, involvement in public policy and so on and other parts of the public sector such as commercial or educational activities. This is a distinction, incidentally, made by the European Court of Justice in regard to the posts member states may reserve for their own nationals and those that they must open to mobility of labour within the EU. Flexibility in the former, part of a managerialisation of public administration, involves a much more significant reform than in the latter. One might also distinguish between flexibility within the civil service proper, where it involves terms and conditions of employment on the one hand (i.e. laws and regulations) and management practices, on the other. Of course, management practices may be constrained by conditions of employment in the use of staff or in decisions about working hours. In any case, categorisations of this sort have their limits. Both those mentioned above, for example, relate to ideas about the 'right to manage', which is important in the context of New Public Management.

That personnel management in the public sector is changing everywhere, even if at different speeds and in different ways, is obvious and hardly surprising. More interesting, because more dramatic when it occurs, is how far such changes go in the narrower field of public administration. Is the incidence of reform in public sector employment more obvious in the industrial and commercial activities of the state or state education and health than in what might now be called the 'core activities' of government? For personnel managers that is probably not the key question. For students of public administration it is. The 'reinvention of government' went a long way in the US and the UK during the 1980s and 1990s and the tide looks unlikely to turn. Can one see similar trends in other countries of Europe? What follows makes no attempt to answer that question definitively but to make a number of general comments covering some aspects of the issues discussed above. This is a comparative volume, with excellent country reports. It is for its readers to make their own cross-country comparison, discover patterns and note differences. The concluding chapter also offers a synthesis of the evidence.

A starting point for this concluding discussion follows a question in the preceding paragraph. There does quite often seem to be a movement of organisations, previously run on administrative lines, to sectors where management is closer to private enterprise, commercial law and private sector labour laws. Privatisation is the extreme example. But such movement has also occurred within the public sector when government services have been turned into public enterprises such as state-owned companies or corporations run on industrial and commercial lines. A sort of halfway house situation is hiving-off delivery of services from ministries to executive agencies, as in Sweden, Finland and the UK. It is also found in some systems of local government, such as in the UK, where Direct Service Organisations are self-contained agencies within the local authority. Use of such public bodies now seems widespread and has probably brought some flexibility of employment with it, possibly as a by-product but in some cases one of the reasons for the change of organisational status. It also seems that the move to more flexible conditions of employment is part of a wider process of debureaucratisation, commercialisation and managerialisation. That said, one needs to look at the area of activity involved in different countries.

As regards contractualisation, there seems to be a widespread move to open top posts in public administration, as well as in industrial/commercial type agencies, though the employer-official relationship may remain that of a civil service appointee rather than a contractual one. This is established practice throughout continental Europe but the purpose in the past was political. Now one finds managerial arguments also. While tenure of such posts is discretionary, however, appointees from the civil service retain their right to civil service tenure and must be found other posts or pensioned if terminated in their political post in most European states, as in the mandate system in Belgium. A reform in some German *Länder* now allows for limited-term appointment to posts just below political level – a reform in German terms because the law gives civil servants the 'right' to their post, i.e. they cannot in theory be moved without their consent.

Of course that allows greater managerial flexibility as one can remove managers who prove inefficient but, in British eyes, where civil servants can be moved at any time, that is belated progress. How many countries have open competition for top posts with an end to the employment relationship at the end of the contract? Although there is little evidence of this type of post system, except in the US, there does seem to be a widespread desire to allow wider choice in the selection of efficient managers (officials with responsibilities of direction for those who do not like the new language) and to permit easier turnover, allowing removal of poor managers and providing an incentive to good performance. This trend, however, seems limited to the new public managers at higher levels, sometimes only at the highest, and affects the rank and file of ministry personnel much less (Farnham *et al.*, 1996).

Flexibility of conditions of employment giving management greater discretion at middle and lower levels could, as we have seen, involve recruitment, promotion, posting, pay, termination of employment and so on. The changes here are patchy and variable. The introduction of some elements of performance related pay or, with similar motives, making annual pay increments less automatic can often be observed. On the other hand, vertical and horizontal barriers that limit staff mobility seem as strong as ever in most cases. Contractualisation at this level also has its limits. Traditionally, it was used to get round legally set limits on civil service numbers or to distinguish real civil servants from a lesser breed of office staff but their position generally tended towards that of the tenured bureaucrats. Contractual employment is now used in some cases to employ temporary staff, where the time span for the work to be done is limited, or to employ specially qualified staff for new sorts of work that do not fit established personnel patterns. Here we see evidence of genuine managerial flexibility, although legal regulations over the length of such contracts and scope for renewal constrain managerial freedom.

Some trends relate to the economic or social policy of government. In the latter case, this sometimes responds to staff demands. An example of the last is reform to give staff greater freedom of lifestyle by allowing part-time work or flexi-time working hours. This can be put in the context of EU law on employment generally and may simply be a spillover into public administration of a wider trend in society. Job creation policy is another example, notably in France and the Netherlands, with provision for temporary jobs (really placements) at minimum wages to reduce unemployment and give young people work experience. The facilitation of early retirement, quite common, serves a number of purposes. It gives established staff another lifestyle choice, allows young people to be recruited or may be a way of reducing staff numbers and thus part of public expenditure policy. Neither schemes to allow public expenditure cuts nor schemes to make working life more flexible for staff, notably women, have much to do with new public management. They may, indeed, make personnel management less rather than more flexible. These are important trends, however, and reflect growing demands made on public service organisations.

Even more difficult than defining cross-country patterns of flexibility is assessing their effect. One can ask what is the effect in relation to different things. Does it reduce costs in public administration through greater efficiency in the use of human resources? Does it lead to more effective public administration and, if so, how? Is there better use of staff, better working methods and better motivation? Does it stimulate job satisfaction, such as freedom to manage or greater control over one's career? What are the most effective carrots (performance related pay) or sticks (reduced security)? Is it easier to introduce other reforms if conditions of employment are more flexible? Are staff less resistant to change, for example, or easier to fit into new institutional structures? Does it lead to cultural change in the public service, and if so how important is it compared to the impact of other reforms or, indeed, generational change in society? What is gained and what is lost as one moves from traditional bureaucracy to new public management? Once one starts thinking along these lines, the questions multiply and answers are likely to reflect personal views. There is much evidence in this volume, however, to stimulate readers and suggest some answers to them. Chapter 3 in particular raises the interesting issue of staff commitment in public service organisations.

References

FARNHAM, D., HORTON, S., BARLOW, J. and HONDEGHEM, A. (1996). *New Public Managers in Europe Public Servants in Transition*. London: Macmillan.

IBBS REPORT/CABINET OFFICE (1988). *Improving Management in Government: The Next Steps*. London: HMSO.

INSTITUTE OF PERSONNEL AND DEVELOPMENT (1994). *Flexibilities at Work in Europe*. London: IPD.

POLIDANO, C. (1997). *The Bureaucrat who Fell Under a Bus: Ministerial Responsibility, Executive Agencies and the Derek Lewis Affair*. Working Paper No. 1 Institute for Development Policy and Management: University of Manchester.

ROUBAN, L. (1998). *La Fin des Technocrats?* Paris: PRESES de Science Pol.

3 Flexibility, Commitment and Performance

Turo Virtanen

Flexibility of human resources management (HRM) is defined in this chapter as the managerial freedom to deploy staff within organisations to ensure the maximum efficiency and achievement of organisational goals. Staffs both individually and collectively are perceived as means or instruments of organisational productivity. Freedom of HRM, therefore, implies that the rules relating to the use of personnel can be formed and enforced by the organisation itself. This we define as *internal flexibility*. The internal environment of an organisation, such as its size, composition, culture and managerial style delimits or facilitates this freedom. But all organisations exist within an external environment and here flexible HRM is affected by the political, economic, social, technological and legal contexts which also impose important delimitations on management (Farnham, 1999). This we define as *external flexibility*. The more external flexibility there is the more there are opportunities for internal flexibility.

External environmental flexibility in recent years has been sought through choosing markets in preference to politics as the means of allocating resources and reflecting societal values. Lindblom (1977) argues that markets are preferable to politics (i.e. governmental allocation of resources) because they are:

- effective allocators of resources
- efficient co-ordinating mechanisms
- rational decision making processes
- enable choices to be made by individuals
- encourage resourcefulness and enterprise.

Markets are seen as turbulent, open-ended systems, which can grow and change with flexibility. This is, however, based on assumptions of free competition, open entry to markets and close regulation of markets to ensure control of their imperfections and their natural tendency towards monopoly (Seldon, 1990). For example, national collective bargaining is often considered to be a market imperfection because it hinders free competition in labour markets by creating a monopoly of labour supply. Also legal norms for working time and labour protection in general are seen as political interventions which impede the free working of the labour market and result in less than optimum allocation of labour resources.

Seldon identifies five main differences between politics (authority systems) and markets as:

- in markets people make decisions individually; in politics collectively
- in markets decisions are personalised; in politics they are submerged into the collective
- in markets individuals make decisions directly; in politics indirectly through delegates or representatives
- in markets people spend their own money; in politics politicians and governments spend their money for them
- in markets people are free to choose and can transfer their business; in politics they have no choice.

Politics, it is asserted, reacts too slowly, because it requires greater consensus than markets and in a democracy there are constraints upon governments which result in slow decision making, compromises, disjointed incrementalism and pragmatism (Lindblom, 1959). Also authority systems tend towards monopoly provision and highly bureaucratic and uniform systems of control. This leads to inflexibility.

As economies throughout the western world have moved towards markets since 1979, governments (politics) have sought to increase both labour market and organisational flexibility by deregulation policies. This has involved changes in the law regulating markets and, in particular, making it easier for private companies to enter markets, transferring public monopolies and other companies back to the market sector and amending or repealing legal restrictions on labour markets. However, there must be formal rules for markets to ensure that competition and fair play exist and these rules are defined by legislation. Consequently, the locus of authority for external flexibility lies both in markets and politics.

Table 3.1 displays the main forms of HRM flexibility organised by the dimension of flexibility and the main locus of the authority of flexibility. The distribution of different elements around the divisions of

Table 3.1   Main forms of HRM-related flexibilities

HRM Flexibility	**Internal Flexibility** *Locus of Authority Mainly Within Organisation*	**External Flexibility** Locus of Authority Mainly Outside Organisation	
		Demand and Supply in the Private Sector Markets	*Legislation, Power, Collective Bargaining Politics*
Working time	• part-time working • flexible daily hours • overtime • shiftworking • annual hours • fixed-term contract	• retirement by pension insurance • age structure of labour force • services to families with children	• early retirement schemes • sabbaticals • shortening sick leaves and maternity breaks • working time regulation • tightening unemployment benefits
Location	• geographical circulation, job transfer • virtual organisation: teleworking • office planning: front-office/back-office	• labour mobility • subcontracting • neighbourhood centres for teleworking	• movement allowances • tax policy on home-working • information technology policy
Task	• empowering management • job enlargement • job enrichment • allocation of health risks • multi-skilling • mixed-skilling • job retraining	• career mobility • subcontracting • competition in education markets • demonopolisation of professional know-how • availability of consults	• relaxation of job boundaries • deregulation of labour protection • deregulation of education: fragmentation of degrees • subventions of further education • retraining the unemployed
Pay	• openness to new incentives and continuous change • individual career planning • multiple contract types • performance-related pay • individual pay structures • individual coaching and mentoring	• head hunting • rental labour force • individual bargaining • salary competition	• political appointments • deregulation of minority and gender equality (affirmative action), child labour • deregulation of dismissals • recruitment and retirement age • employment legislation • deregulation of personnel's participation • local bargaining

internal and external flexibilities, as well as markets and politics, reflects the contemporary practice of HRM within western politico-economic systems. Some items can be put in more than one cell, because they are expressions of many dimensions of flexibility. The Table is intended to be indicative and a heuristic device for juxtaposing internal and external elements of flexibility and suggests that many forms of flexibility are related to essentially moral and political issues that are often overlooked or understated. The positive commitment to flexibility with its emphasis on enhanced freedom for both employers and employees understates the immoral consequences or outcomes, which can result from increased flexibility. Not every kind of flexibility is welcomed by those affected by it. For example legal deregulation of the labour market in the name of managerialism may give way to a loss of protection for workers and a real deterioration in their terms and conditions of employment.

The use of human resources in terms of time, place, task and pay are the major dimensions of HRM flexibility, both in the internal and external contexts, while the personal object of flexible HRM in both contexts is a worker, professional or manager. Beyond that there are wide national differences relating to recruitment from labour markets, types of employment and employment contracts, educational qualifications and payment systems, as the chapters in this book illustrate. The political context of HRM flexibility cannot be understated. Another important point is that flexibilisation does not treat all people equally and neither should it. Minorities, children and women may need inflexibility created by political pressure and legislation to protect them from the vagaries of the market and the in-built structural bias of market systems. What is equally important is that flexibility may affect behaviour in a variety of ways rather than uniformly. For example the motivation of public servants may change as they are treated more flexibly. If public servants are expected to be more flexible in terms of time, place, task and pay, will their values and goals related to public service remain untouched?

One of the central aims of new public menuyement (NPM) is to change the behaviour of public officials and we have been witnessing a gradual change of public service values and goals from an orientation to bureaucratic rules to one of productivity, economy, effectiveness and accountability to customers (Flynn and Strehl, 1996; Hughes, 1998; Farnham *et al.*, 1996). But increasing uncertainty related to many forms of flexibility appears to be affecting public servants' commitment to work and public service in general. The salaries of higher public servants have not been competitive in western countries for several decades, compared to salaries in the private sector. Part of the motivation of public servants, however, has been the security related to their careers, as well as morally and politically challenging work. When the flexibility mechanisms of new HRM make work resemble more the work done in the private sector without similar prospects in terms of salary improvement, commitment may weaken. Also where the quality of output cannot be easily measured, lack of commitment may endanger the quality of public service, at the same time as reducing the attractiveness of public service to the most able members of the society. Loss of commitment may also result in loss of performance, which is expected to increase with the application of HRM-related flexibility mechanisms.

There is very little empirical data on the impact of flexible HRM and in particular on the effect of new forms of flexibility on commitment of public servants. This is not a well-researched area prior to recent changes and so we do not know how committed public servants were in the past. The only indicators of satisfaction and positive orientation towards public service were competition for entry, retention rates and long service. Although we have not measured the commitment of public servants before flexible HRM, it is possible to analyse commitment with cross-sectional surveys comparing the responses of those public servants who are the objects of flexibility with those who are not. The purpose of this chapter is to describe how commitment to work and organisation is related to type of employment, and how they both are related to performance-awareness. Type of employment is defined here as (1) permanent jobs, (2) working on secondment (fixed-term job with permanent job in another organisation), (3) fixed-term jobs, and (4) part-time versus full-time job. The type of employment is chosen, because control is one of the basic instruments in making HRM more flexible. The assumption being made here is that commitment depends partly on tenure as an intervening variable and also on years of service in the agency. Both are included in the analysis.

The findings discussed in this chapter are based on a study of the Finnish public service carried out by the author in 1997 8 and two data sets: one collected by the University of Helsinki (Virtanen, 1997) and one collected by Statistics Finland. The first data set originates from research on the change of management systems and management practices of Finnish public agencies between 1995–8 with special emphasis on leadership culture. Management by results and leadership culture were studied in 17 public agencies, all financed by the state budget. Data was collected by questionnaires and surveys conducted on an annual basis with the first carried out in 1996. They cover all personnel in each agency (with minor exceptions). The response rate was 60 per cent in 1996 (N = 2,473), on which the results of this chapter are based. Because there is no random sampling but the selection of agencies is based on criteria that are theoretically relevant for the adoption of managerial instruments, the survey results do not represent the opinions of the entire state personnel. The data compiled by Statistics Finland, however, originates from research on the change of working conditions of the total work force in 1997 (N = 2,979). That data is based on random sampling and on-site interviews and the response rate was 79 per cent.[1]

EMPLOYEE COMMITMENT

The concept of HRM flexibility is closely related to the paradigm of New Public Management (NPM). The assumption is that increases in the flexibility of time, place, task and pay, together with performance measurement, adds to the standards of productivity, economy, effectiveness, quality, and accountability of public servants. HRM flexibility is considered to be, in part, a means of increasing efficiency, reducing costs, obtaining value for money, raising the quality of service and bringing about a stronger customer orientation. Key assumptions underlying this view are that individual employees are self-interested, seek job security, higher rewards and advancement opportunities. Any increase in uncertainty about continuous employment is likely to increase commitment to achievement of standards. Performance related rewards stimulate achievement of predetermined objectives and opportunities for advancement based on achievement stimulates that achievement.

Paradoxically, emphasis on motivation based on self-interest may open ways to intentions and behaviours that are in contradiction with many values of the public service ethos which is still supported throughout the public services. It is clear that the new entrepreneurial culture engendered by NPM can encourage unethical behaviour. Corruption related to public tendering and lobbying, responsiveness and accountability to 'best customers', connivance at legal norms, selective publicity, multiple commitments and fragmented loyalty are all examples of flexibility that can be considered to be in conflict with traditional public service norms. Of course, there are rules prohibiting overt behaviour of this type, and such behaviour was not unknown in traditional public services. But the increase in administrative/managerial discretion as to how goals are to be achieved, together with increasing differentiation of expert knowledge and work autonomy, as well as better access to information, has increased the importance of culture as a controlling factor in behaviour rather than formal norms. What are the incentives for public officials to conform to a public ethos in the 'culture of flexibilities'? Self-interest supports instrumental commitment to public service rather than a moral one. If moral commitment is publicly despised in the cynical atmosphere of disjointed 'post-modern ethics', it is easier to be morally flexible even by the standards of one's own conscience.

The data from this research do not include variables directly related to the public service ethos. This is compensated for by measuring the commitment to work and agency or organisation. Commitment is a concept that has been widely used to identify different aspects of personality and individual thoughts and behaviour in relations to community (Kanter, 1968). One theory of commitment (Becker, 1960) understands a commitment as a result of making a 'side-bet' or investment to certain types of behaviour by prior actions. Giving up behavioural consistency for short-term benefits leads to long-term costs that are bigger than anticipated long-term benefits. The literature on commitment reveals several foci of commitment: work commitment (Morrow, 1983); commitment to work group, supervisor, top management, union, and organisation (Becker, 1992); also commitment to profession, external funding agencies, and client (Reichers, 1985, 1986). Organisational commitment has been defined as 'the relative strength of an individual's identification with and involvement in an organisation' (Mowday *et al.*, 1982). In this view, commitment is characterised by strong belief in and acceptance of the organisation's goals and values, a willingness to exert considerable effort on behalf of the organisation, and a strong desire to maintain membership in the organisation (Mowday *et al.*, 1979).

Work commitment has been analysed and interpreted as the Protestant work ethic, career salience, job and work involvement as a central life interest, organisational commitment and union commitment (Morrow, 1983). Critics of the concept have argued that the component elements are insufficiently distinct to warrant separation and some are partially redundant (Morrow, 1983; Morrow and McElroy, 1986). In this study, work commitment is understood as a combination of job involvement and intrinsic motivation related to work (Virtanen, 1997). A seven-item measure was developed on the basis of additive scales used by Lawler III and Hall (1970). The measure of work commitment comprises variables that refer to the following work-related contents: career planning based on finding more interesting jobs, being a perfectionist about work, major satisfaction in life coming from success in job, the interesting things happening to oneself involving the job, doing work well gives a feeling of accomplishment, performing job well contributes to personal growth and development, doing job well increases feeling of self-esteem.

Within the academic literature **organisational commitment** is understood as a three-fold phenomenon comprising moral commitment, instrumental commitment and alienative commitment. It was partly adapted from the instruments developed by Mowday, Steers and Porter (1979) and Penley and Gould (1988), further developed by their pilot studies. In the work of Meyer and Allen (1997), **moral commitment** is described as a partial combination of affective and normative commitment, whilst **instrumental commitment** comes close to **continuance commitment**. The measure of moral commitment to an organisation refers to the following six variables:

- withholding telling negative stories about the agency to outsiders
- feeling upset when people say negative things about the agency
- willingness to put in a great deal of effort beyond that normally expected in order to help the agency be successful
- being proud to tell others about being part of the agency
- working in the agency really inspires the very best in the way of job performance
- leaving the agency results in feeling of guilt.

The measure of instrumental commitment to an organisation includes four variables

- career in the agency depends on possible pay rises
- the amount of work done for the agency depends on how much one is paid for it
- very small changes in the present circumstances would result in leaving the agency
- free-time is more important than the present job.

Finally, alienative commitment to organisation comprises the following five variables:

- feeling angry when thinking about work in the agency
- wanting to walk out of the agency and never coming back
- making a career in the agency would mean being overly compliant
- often feeling like wanting to 'get even' with the agency
- supporting the agency only to the extent it supports the respondent.

COMMITMENT AND TYPE OF EMPLOYMENT

Data collected on 17 public agencies indicate that *part-time* public servants are less committed to work than full-time public servants, and the former have stronger instrumental commitment to organisations than the latter.[2] Although the differences are small, this is what one would expect, because part-time workers are normally less exposed, than full-time workers, to the effects of organisational socialisation. On the other hand, part-time public servants working on fixed-term contracts are more committed to work than those working in permanent posts. The same applies to moral commitment, although the opposite is found in measures of instrumental and alienative commitment. This is contrary to what one would expect, because part-time employees with fixed-term contracts have probably fewer opportunities for organisational socialisation than others have. Amongst *full-time* public servants, those on fixed-term contracts are more committed to work than those on permanent unlimited contracts, while those working on secondment are the most committed to work. Alienative commitment is the lowest amongst the seconded and highest amongst permanent public servants. Instrumental commitment is lowest amongst seconded group, whilst in the case of moral commitment there is no clear difference. How can we explain the variation?

Secondment

Seconded public servants are generally in higher posts in the organisational hierarchy, they have better education and better salaries than the average official and they are also predominantly male in gender. This suggests that type of employment is probably not the only reason for their higher commitment figures – if even a reason at all. Seconded public servants may be originally more motivated to their work career than others. The variation shows, however, that perhaps the secondment procedure itself provides an outlet for commitment. Seconded employees are probably not 'social problem workers' with low work commitment, made to apply for temporary jobs elsewhere because their permanent employer would like to get rid of them. This could be a rival hypothesis. The variation is evidence about a form of HRM flexibility that can create an opportunity for commitment to increase or a career for those already favourably committed. The logic behind the possible increasing commitment is probably the following: an opportunity to choose a job one really likes with the background of a permanent job gives security and new challenges at the same time.

Voluntary secondment creates opportunities for the circulation of committed personnel and may even increase their work commitment while decreasing their instrumental and alienative commitment to organisation. The contribution given by seconded officials to their agency is partly shown by their number of overtime working hours during a busy month. It is clearly higher (27.4 hours) than for both permanent officials (15.1 hours) and fixed-term officials (13.9 hours). The same pattern is found in the percentage of overtime hours compensated in the form of free-time or additional pay. For seconded staff the percentage is 24.7, for permanent staff 30.4, and for fixed-term staff 37.0. The figures indicate that secondment can create *win-win situations*, where employees are well committed and their employers receive considerable contribution, partly as uncompensated overtime work unless higher basic salary is seen as compensation.

Fixed-term and permanent jobs

The higher commitment to work expressed by fixed-term public servants and their lower alienative commitment to the organisation, compared to permanent public servants, also needs explanation. The work may be more important to fixed-term employees, if they have to show their value as employees to justify their reappointment. Uncertainty would add to their motivation to work. At the same time their tenure is shorter than that of permanent public servants, which may not lead – yet – to 'getting fed up with all this'. The data show that alienative commitment to the organisation increases with the length of tenure among both fixed-term and permanent employees. However, with 78 per cent of fixed-term employees the tenure is less than two years, whilst only 10 per cent of permanent employees have worked for that time. This, together with lower alienation in the beginning of the service, makes the mean of alienation lower amongst fixed-term officials. Amongst permanent officials alienative commitment starts to weaken after 15 to 21 years of service and comes back to the same level as those with 3–6 years of service after more than 30 years. In the end, it is the *shorter tenure* of fixed-term employees that explains their lower alienation.

Work commitment of permanent public servants tends to decrease slowly by years of service, being at a lower level after 3–6 years than with fixed-term public servants with the same tenure. Fixed-term employees maintain the same level of work commitment as they started with up to 3–6 years of service. After 3–6 years, however, the work commitment of fixed-term employees decreases much more rapidly than that of permanent employees. The higher work commitment of fixed-term employees is partly explained by the on average shorter tenure. Also the pattern of change of commitment is different between these two groups. A year by year analysis indicates that for fixed-term public servants *the breaking point* is six years of service, while for permanent public servants there is no breaking point. After six years, work commitment goes clearly down having increased before that, instrumental commitment clearly goes up having decreased before that, and alienative commitment jumps up having increased before that. One has to remember, however, that we do not know the quality of the personnel working on fixed-term employment after six years of service. Because the data is cross-sectional, respondents in different stages of career are different people. It may be that favourably committed and qualified people have got permanent jobs after six years of service, while favourably or unfavourably committed but unqualified people remain on fixed-term posts still after six years.

Commitment is a dynamic phenomenon as it changes over time. But its dynamics are not easy to study. A panel data with repeated measure over a period of 20–30 years would reveal the pattern of change better than cross-sectional data. The study of our cross-sectional data suggests, however, that for permanent officials the pattern of change is different from that of fixed-term officials. Moral commitment to an organisation starts to strengthen after 15–21 years of service for permanent staff in the same agency, having slowly weakened before that. At the same point of tenure, both instrumental and alienative commitment also starts to weaken after having strengthened before that. Instrumental commitment is at its lowest level amongst those with less than one year's service while work commitment shows a continuing gradual decrease. It seems that the agency itself becomes more important than the work – in relative terms – after a considerable career in the agency. Part of these dependencies may be related to making a career within an agency rising from the lower to the higher levels of the organisation. Managers' moral commitment to the organisation is stronger, and their instrumental and alienative commitment weaker than are those of other superiors. The same applies to all those in higher positions. In this sense, commitment is clearly a *hierarchical* phenomenon. The same regularity holds for both permanent and fix-term public servants. Another reservation is that the structure and dynamics of commitment of different generational cohorts working in agencies may be different. The relevance of age has not been studied here but Meyer and Allen (1997: 44) state that the link between organisational tenure and affective commitment may really be because of employee age.

It seems that there is no crucial difference in commitment between permanent and fixed-term public servants in the first years of a career in the same agency. After six years, however, the commitment changes so clearly in a negative direction that one would need more arguments to insist that life-long fixed-time employment is a good instrument for HRM. To avoid the unfavourable development of commitment amongst fixed-term officials it is possible, at least in principle, to recruit openly for new staff to each post as it becomes vacant or is newly created. But if it is known in advance, that there is no hope for promotion and continuation, the commitment may be unfavourable from the start. There is no empirical data on this but the data of Statistics Finland show that threat of dismissal and unemployment is higher among fixed-term employees than among permanent employees. In state government, 14 per cent of permanent employees and 23 per cent of fixed-term employees see threat of dismissal in their job and 14 per cent of the group feel the threat of unemployment compared to 63 per cent of the latter group. The corresponding figures are eight versus 37 for dismissal and 10 versus 68 for unemployment in municipal government. In the private sector, the percentages are about the same: 12 versus 37 for dismissal and 12 versus 36 for unemployment. The small differences between sectors imply that uncertainty about continuity of employment is similar throughout the economy. All in all, one can conclude that even if there is greater uncertainty about job security among fixed-term than permanent employees, this does not mean that there is a crucial difference between the commitment of these two groups in the early stages of their careers.

Rivalry and commitment

There is another form of uncertainty that is more common among permanent than fixed-term employees. Especially in state government, the former group sees more often the threat of being transferred to another job (30 per cent) than the latter group (12 per cent). This implies that the commitment of permanent employees in state government is, to some extent, challenged by another kind of structure of uncertainty. This is partly expressed by the figures referring to rivalry in one's work-unit, originating also from the data of Statistics Finland. Permanent employees in state government perceive more rivalry for posts (83 per cent) than those in municipal government (61 per cent) or the private sector (66 per cent). Differences between the sectors are narrowest among fixed-term employees (58, 53, and 50 per cent respectively). The difference between permanent and fixed-term employees is greatest in state government (25 per cent) compared to municipal government (8), and private sector (16). Other comparisons of fixed-term employees further define the characteristics of state personnel. Employees of municipal government are most likely to find working on fixed-term contracts stressful and employees in the private sector the least stressful. Employees of state government see least difficulties in long-term orientation to work and are also least likely to feel themselves outsiders in their workgroup. Fixed-term employees of the municipal sector are least likely to criticise the faults they see but fixed-term employees in the state sector report most often that the uncertainty related to continuation of employment creates rivalry and conflicts. It seems that there is more rivalry in state government than other parts of the public sector but in the group on fixed-term contracts job insecurity is more general than in other sectors.

Uncertainty related to rivalry can be both favourable and unfavourable in terms of commitment. It is possible that permanent employment creates more opportunities and motivation and a positive orientation towards competition resulting in moral commitment to the organisation. It is also possible that rivalry is related to alienative commitment. The data reveal that, in all sectors, *permanent employees see more conflicts* between superiors and subordinates and between fellow-workers than fixed-term employees see. However, the data cannot directly reveal whether these conflicts produce favourable or unfavourable commitment. The data on 17 public agencies suggests, however, that rivalry is more likely to result in unfavourable rather than favourable commitment. It also confirms that rivalry is marginally stronger amongst permanent than fixed-term employees. Rivalry in superior-subordinate relations was measured by five variables. Its correlation to instrumental commitment was 0.39 and to alienative commitment 0.50 but correlation to work commitment was –0.10 and to moral commitment –0.19. The illegitimate power of the superior, another additive scale close to the idea of rivalry, was composed of five variables. Its correlation to instrumental commitment was 0.35 and to alienative commitment 0.55 but correlation to work commitment was –0.15 and to moral commitment –0.28. Also the illegitimate power of the superior was stronger among permanent than fixed-term employees, which further confirms the general trend.

The correlations are relatively high for instrumental and alienative commitment and they are practically the same for permanent and fixed-term employees. The variation suggests that rivalry and opposition to superiors may not represent favourable commitment that includes long-term commitment to the improvement of organisational practices. Rivalry and opposition are both stronger among permanent than fixed-term employees. Both increase by the tenure but for fixed-term employees the increase is stronger and the starting level is lower. This indicates that permanent employees are more critical right from the start of their tenure and that their commitment includes more questioning of the activities of superiors than the commitment of fixed-term employees. Criticism may be related to workloads, since the data of Statistics Finland indicates that the pace of working has tightened more amongst permanent than amongst fixed-term employees, in all sectors: state government (32 versus 8 per cent), municipal government (29 versus 12 per cent), and private sector (24 versus 13 per cent). Irrespective of sector, work tends to pile up more often among permanent than among fixed-term employees (64 versus 52 per cent), and the work is interrupted more often among the former than amongst the latter (57 versus 45 per cent). It seems that workload is experienced heaviest among permanent than among fixed-term employees. Again, this experience can be interpreted to represent either favourable or unfavourable commitment. Both moral and alienative commitments are compatible with the experience of 'a lot of work'. This is why it is important to analyse commitment and employment type in relation to performance.

COMMITMENT AND PERFORMANCE

A widespread belief is that at least some forms of commitment support performance (Meyer *et al.*, 1989). Having demonstrated that commitment varies according to type of employment, it is interesting to see if this is in any way related to performance. The data on 17 agencies does not include measures of objective performance but rather of 'performance-awareness'. Performance-awareness refers to respondents' claimed social behaviours and performance-orientation, like discussions with fellow-workers about productivity. These are interpreted as expressions of performance-awareness, not performance behaviours as such, because the researcher has no control for actual behaviours. The measure of performance-awareness comprised three additive scales: economy and productivity (eight variables), quality (four variables), and effectiveness (five variables). The opposite of performance-awareness was performance-ignorance (seven variables).

Most correlations between commitment and performance were weak (less than 0.30). Variation remained the same even if tenure was controlled for. The size of the correlation was in most cases practically the same for both permanent and fixed-term officials. This indicates that, with some exceptions, that neither type of employment nor tenure changes the weak connections between commitment and performance-awareness. However, the directions of correlations were systematic in all pairs. The correlations of work commitment and moral commitment to organisation were positive for all three forms of performance-awareness and negative to performance-ignorance. The highest correlations were between moral commitment and effectiveness-awareness (0.19 for fixed-term and 0.36 for permanent officials). The correlations of instrumental and alienative commitment to organisation were negative to all three forms of performance awareness and positive to performance ignorance. The highest correlations were between alienative commitment and performance- ignorance (0.53 for fixed-term and 0.47 for permanent employees) and between instrumental commitment and performance-ignorance (0.36 for fixed-term and 0.33 for permanent employees).

All this leads to the conclusion that performance-awareness is mostly independent of the work commitment and commitment to organisation but moral commitment and effectiveness-awareness support each other slightly among permanent employees. Performance-awareness is of course different from objective performance but they probably correlate positively. The results are not incompatible with other results, indicating that it is affective or value-based commitment to the organisation that supports performance, also measured by independently rated indicators, rather than continuance-based commitment emphasising costs and investments (Meyer *et al.*, 1989; Mayer and Schoorman, 1992; Meyer and Allen, 1997). The high correlations between performance-ignorance and instrumental and alienative commitment to organisation imply that the relative independence found here between commitment and performance-awareness may be partly caused by the characteristics of the measures themselves.

Analysis of linear dependencies is not able to reveal the possible non-linear variation of performance-awareness. It was shown above that tenure and commitment related non-linearly to each other, and commitment related to some degree to performance. Therefore, it is interesting to see how performance-awareness and performance-ignorance are related to tenure by employment type. The data show that awareness of economy and productivity and effectiveness are all strongest among permanent employees and weakest among fixed-term employees. Quality-awareness is strongest among those working on secondment and weakest among fixed-term officials. This implies that fixed-term employment and performance-awareness do not support each other as much as permanent employment and performance-awareness do. The result undermines the belief that uncertainty of employment adds to performance-orientation, a belief often connected to NPM. The data also show that performance-ignorance is strongest among permanent employees and weakest among fixed-term employees. In this sense, performance attitudes are a polarised phenomenon.

Analysis by tenure indicates that performance-awareness falls and performance-ignorance rises up after 3–6 years of service among fixed-term officials (awareness of economy and productivity increases till that point of time). Among permanent officials, performance-ignorance remains quite stable through the years of service, while performance-awareness starts to increase after seven to 14 years. Performance-awareness of permanent officials is higher in all stages of tenure than that of fixed-term officials. Also full-time employees have stronger performance-awareness than part-time employees, whether they are permanent or fixed-term. It is probable that the stronger experiences of heavy workload of permanent employees also bring with them higher performance-awareness. Evidence suggests that high performance-awareness, high workload experience, and permanent full-time jobs support each other. We have to remember, however, that this result is based on attitudes only.

Comparison of commitment by tenure and performance-awareness by tenure explains why there is a positive correlation between instrumental and alienative commitment and performance-ignorance but not between favourable forms of commitment and performance-awareness. Variation of performance-awareness by tenure is not linear, while that of work commitment and moral commitment is more so. Awareness of economy and productivity, and that of quality increases in the first and second years of service, decreases thereafter and starts to increase again after seven to 14 years, ending up with a slight decrease after 22–30 years. Effectiveness-awareness starts to fall immediately after employment starts and continues to do so till between seven to 14 years of service, after which it increases and then decreases, like the rest of performance-awareness. The curvilinearity probably refers both to cultural differences between cohorts that have entered public service at lower levels of the hierarchy and pursue a career via promotion through the ranks with more responsibilities for performance. It is symptomatic that effectiveness-awareness decreases steadily at the beginning of tenure. It may be due to disappointment among younger generations of public servants with their experience of public service and lack of congruence between expectations and experience. Performance-awareness decreases and performance-ignorance increases systematically when moving from higher to lower rank most clearly among fixed-term officials. Like commitment, performance attitudes seem to follow the hierarchy.

CONCLUSION

Commitment of public servants by type of employment tells something about the possible consequences of implementation of one form of flexible HRM. The consequences are connected to the motivation of public servants. Part-time jobs and fixed-term jobs are expressions of flexibility in relation to time. According to the data of this study, part-time public servants are less committed to work and have stronger instrumental commitment to agency than full-time public servants. Public servants working on secondment are the most favourably committed and their uncompensated contribution to the agency is also the highest. There is no crucial difference in commitment between permanent and fixed-term officials in the first five to six years of service, although experiences of uncertainty related to continuation of employment are stronger among the latter. With more years of fixed-term service, favourable commitment seems to become weaker. This may also be related to quality of the workforce who are not offered permanent jobs in the agency. The change of commitment of permanent officials follows a different pattern: favourable commitment increases after 15–21 years of service in the same agency after having decreased before that. This variation is also related to the cultural characteristics of different generational cohorts that have entered public service at different points of time but the data do not enable analysis of their effects.

Permanent employees see more rivalry in their agencies and oppose their superiors more often than fixed-term employees. This is especially true about rivalry in state government compared to municipal government and the private sector. Also among fixed-term employees, rivalry is seen more in state government but experiences of certainty are more general in this sector than in others. Rivalry and opposition to superiors both increase by tenure. However, experiences of rivalry and opposition seem to be more related to instrumental and alienative commitment than to work commitment and moral commitment. At the same time, workload is perceived as heavier among permanent public servants. It seems that this has to do with performance-awareness. It is stronger among permanent than fixed-term officials, in all stages of tenure. Performance-awareness is also stronger among full-time employees than part-time workers, whether they are permanent or fixed-term.

Performance-awareness seems to be mostly independent of favourable commitment but moral commitment and effectiveness-awareness support each other to some extent among permanent officials. Performance-ignorance coexists clearly with instrumental and alienative commitment to agency, in both types of employment. It seems that rivalry and opposition to superiors, heavy workload experiences and performance-awareness can coexist and increase by tenure but their connection to favourable commitment to agency is weak or non-existent. This supports the general outcome of previous research on commitment and performance. The connection is not unambiguous. Even at its best, commitment is only one factor improving performance or performance-awareness. However, the data imply that both favourable commitment and performance-awareness decrease among fixed-term public servants (not seconded) in their later stages of tenure. Further study of this dependence is necessary but must await a larger population of public servants that have long experience in fixed-time jobs without any permanent background office across national public services.

Notes

1. I want to thank researcher Hanna Sutela for being so helpful and processing the data of Statistics Finland according to my instructions.
2. All conclusions drawn from this data are statistically significant. Numerical data has been restricted in this text but can be obtained by contacting the author.

References

BECKER, H.S. (1960). 'Notes on the Concept of Commitment'. *American Journal of Sociology*. 66 (1), pp 32–40.
BECKER, T.E. (1992). 'Foci and Bases of Commitment: Are They Distinctions Worth Making?' *Academy of Management Journal*. 35 (1), pp 232–44.
FARNHAM, D. (1999). *Managing in a Business Context*. London: Institute of Personnel and Development.
FARNHAM, D., HORTON, S., BARLOW, J. and HONDEGHEM, A. (1996) *New Public Managers in Europe: Public Servants in Transition*, London: Macmillan.
FLYNN, N. and STREHL, F. (1996). *Public Sector Management in Europe*. Hemel Hempstead: Prentice Hall Europe.
HUGHES, O. (1998). *Public Management and Administration*. Basingstoke: Macmillan.
KANTER, R.M. (1968). 'Commitment and Social Organisation: A Study of Commitment Mechanisms in Utopian Communities'. *American Sociological Review*. 33, pp 499–517.
LAWLER, III, E.E. and HALL, D.T. (1970). 'Relationship of Job Characteristics to Job Involvement, Satisfaction, and Intrinsic Motivation'. *Journal of Applied Psychology*. 54, pp 305–12.
LINDBLOM, C. (1959). 'Incrementalism: The Science of Muddling Through'. *Public Administration Review*. 19, pp 78–88.
LINDBLOM, C. (1977). *Politics and Markets*. New York: Basic Books.

58   *Flexibility, Commitment and Performance*

MAYER, R.C. and SCHOORMAN, F.D. (1992). 'Predicting Participation and Production Outcomes Through a Two-Dimensional Model of Organizational Commitment'. *Academy of Management Journal.* 35 (3), pp 671–84.

MEYER, J. *et al.* (1989). 'Organizational Commitment and Job Performance: It's the Nature of Commitment that Counts'. *Journal of Applied Psychology.* 74, pp 152–6.

MEYER, J. and ALLEN, N.J. (1997). *Commitment in the Workplace. Theory, Research, and Application.* London: SAGE.

MORROW, P. (1983). 'Concept Redundancy in Organizational Research:The Case of Work Commitment'. *Academy of Management Review.* 8 (3), pp 486–500.

MORROW, P. and MCELROY, J. (1986). 'On Assessing Measures of Work Commitment'. *Journal of Occupational Behavior.* 7 (2), pp 139–45.

MOWDAY, R.T., STEERS, R.M. and PORTER, L.W. (1979). 'The Measurement of Organizational Commitment'. *Journal of Vocational Behavior.* 14, pp 224–47.

MOWDAY, R., PERTER, L. and STEERS, R. (1982). *Employee-Organization Linkages. The Psychology of Commitment, Absenteeism, and Turnover.* New York: Academic Press.

PENLEY, L. and GOULD, S. (1988). 'Etzioni's Model of Organizational Involvement: A Perspective for Understanding Commitment to Organizations'. *Journal of Organizational Behavior.* 9, pp 43–59.

REICHERS, A. (1985). 'A Review and Reconceptualization of Organizational Commitment'. *Academy of Management Review.* 10, pp 465–76.

REICHERS, A. (1986). 'Conflict and Organizational Commitment'. *Journal of Applied Psychology.* 71, pp 508–14.

SELDON, A. (1990). *Capitalism.* Oxford: Blackwell.

VIRTANEN, T. (1997). *Johtamiskulttuurin muutos ja tuloksellisuus. Valtionhallinnon uudistumisen seurantatutkimus 1995–98. Ensimmäinen väliraportti.* Helsinki: Valtiovarainministeriö, hallinnon kehittämisosasto.

Part II
Country Studies

4 The Belgian Public Services: Can Regulations go along with Flexible Personnel Arrangements?

Annie Hondeghem and Trui Steen

This chapter examines the extent to which flexible personnel arrangements can be found in Belgian public services. For this purpose a classification is used in which different forms of flexible working practices are identified: staffing flexibility, contractual flexibility, pay flexibility, functional flexibility, flexibility of working hours and working life, and career mobility. Also decentralisation is discussed, since it is seen as central to the concept of flexibility (Hondeghem, Farnham and Horton, 1996: 127). However, we take into account that flexibility cannot just be equated with the discretionary powers of employers relating to decisions on personnel matters. Different relevant actors, who have different perspectives on flexibility, are involved (Steen, 1997: 2). When looked at from the perspective of employees, flexibility relates to 'the capacity of employees to adjust the working situation as supple and adequate as possible to (changing) personal circumstances' (Trommel, 1987: 39).

In examining flexibility in different sectors of federal, state and local government in Belgium, this chapter is limited to ministries and autonomous public enterprises at federal level, Flemish state level and local government in Flanders. This means that little attention is given to personnel practices in the Walloon state and in Walloon and Brussels local government. In line with neo-institutionalist theory in political and organisational sciences, we describe the changes in the public sector as a process taking place within a framework fixed by institutional structures. This does not mean that institutional structures determine change, rather they restrict the space in which choices can be made. Institutional frameworks leave room for action and, moreover, are themselves produced and reproduced by action. The

Belgian situation can thus only be understood when taking into account the institutional context which is both triggering and hindering public sector reforms in general and personnel flexibility in particular. Before describing flexible working arrangements in the public sector in Belgium, the broader context of public sector reform is examined.

THE PUBLIC SECTOR IN BELGIUM

Between 1970 and 1993 four different state reforms converted Belgium from a unitary state into a federal state. Belgium consists of three communities – the Flemish, French and German community – and three regions – the Flemish, Walloon and Brussels region. The communities are based upon linguistic and cultural groups, while the regions are geographical areas. The regions and communities do not coincide, however, so the structure of the Belgian state is very complex. The distribution of public sector employment in Belgium, in 1998, is shown in Table 4.1.

As a major employer, the national civil service has served as a model for other sectors. Many practices observed at national level, therefore, also apply to other levels in the public sector. However, adjusting functions between levels of government meant a severe decrease in importance of the national civil service. Large numbers of civil servants were transferred from national level to 'state' level as a result of federalisation. After a series of reforms, national level has become more of a follower and the role as a triggering force has been taken over by 'state' public services. Without a legacy from the past and without serious budget problems, the new institutions at state level (e.g. the Flemish administration) have the opportunity to prove themselves. This opportunity was certainly seized on by the Flemish side and their positive experiences have inspired other administrative levels to modernise themselves.

Devolution and agencification have a long tradition in Belgium. Already by the end of the nineteenth century the so-called quangos came into being as autonomous institutions, linked with government but at a distance. The degree of autonomy of these institutions varies according to their status as *regies* (which are the least autonomous), public corporations, public financial institutions and autonomous public enterprises (APEs). This last category was created by law in 1991. APEs are found particularly in the transport and communica-

Table 4.1   Public sector employment in Belgium, 1998

	Number	%
Federal government	**195,683**	**23**
Ministries	59,286	7
Institutions		
Scientific	3,193	0
Regies and public corporations	21,050	2
Autonomous public enterprises	112,154	13
State government	**347,677**	**40**
Ministries	25,424	3
Institutions		
Scientific	245	0
Public corporations	49,879	6
Education	270,561	31
Community-commissions	1,568	0
Particular bodies	**75,603**	**9**
(courts, army, federal police)		
Local authorities*	**224,729**	**28**
Municipalities	124,856	14
Public welfare centres	80,291	9
Intercommunales	24,101	3
Provinces	15,481	2
Legislature	**2,742**	**0**
Total personnel strength	**866,434**	**100**

* numbers for local government employment
relate to 1994.
Source: Ministerie van Ambtenarenzaken, 1998.

tion sectors and include the Post, Belgacom (the former Telephone and Telegraph Company), the National Railways Company and National Company for Air Traffic. The formula of management contracts is used both at federal level, e.g. in the social security institutions, as well as at state level, where the Flemish government uses management contracts to steer institutions. These include the Flemish Transport Company, Flemish Institute for Technological Research, Flemish Employment Service (VDAB) and Flemish Radio and Television Company. Most of these autonomous institutions are active in sectors which are more exposed to competition than other sectors of government is active and they have therefore been subject to additional pressures for reform.

Local government – provinces, cities and municipalities, and local welfare agencies – occupies an important position in the public sector. Management reforms and innovations in personnel management in local government are however highly influenced by reforms in other parts of the public sector, especially state government. Finally a heterogeneous group of public organisations are put together under the title of 'particular bodies'. This group includes the army, courts and federal police force. Reform in these traditionally conservative organisations has recently been triggered by scandals and accusations of blundering by the federal police and the judiciary in the so called Dutroux affair.[1]

PRESSURES FOR REFORM AND TRENDS IN THE PUBLIC SECTOR

Since the national elections of 1991, the lack of legitimacy of the political-administrative system has become very clear. Traditional parties lost ground to extremist right wing and 'anti-political' parties. In recent years, several studies and public opinion polls indicate that the public's image of politics and government is not very positive. Public sector reforms have therefore aimed at increasing legitimacy by offering citizens more value for money. Second, an evolution towards an efficient, effective and economic administration is needed because of the enormous public debt at national level, whilst pressure is coming from the European Union to curb public expenditure. Third, the relationship between government and citizens is changing, since the citizen has evolved from a passive subject to a critical consumer. As a result, greater demands are being made on government. This requires a change towards client orientation, effectiveness and efficiency.

The reform process has, however, been slowed down by a number of factors. In the 1980s several constitutional changes had to take place before demands for a modern public sector could enter the political agenda. Government has been preoccupied with its own agenda of reform of the state and is paying the price for its slowness in attending to the political and social problems in society with its loss of legitimacy (Hondeghem, 1997: 39). The existence of two different political and administrative cultures in the Flemish and the Walloon communities is also hindering the reforms, not only at federal level but also at other levels, since organisational regulation has, up till now, remained a federal authority – e.g. the Royal Decree concerning the General Principles of the Public Servants Statute local government law. The administrative culture, which is very much juridically orientated, is itself a further constraint upon reforms in general. This juridical orientation builds on the French tradition of administrative law, in which central administrative values or ideas about 'good administration' (Hood, 1991: 10) are equality of rights, legal security and justice, rather than the three E's – efficiency, effectiveness and economy – with which new public management (NPM) is associated. In addition to factors triggering or hindering public sector reform in general, there are some forces which specifically counter trends towards more flexibility in the Belgian public services. Excessive regulation concerning the statute of the public servants is the most important factor impeding the evolution of public organisations towards modern public services.

Doeringer and Piore (1971: 1–2) describe the internal labour market (ILM) as 'an administrative unit, such as a manufacturing plant, within which the pricing and allocation of labour is governed by a set of administrative rules and procedures'. The authors point out that the utility of the concept does not solely depend upon the existence of administrative rules. It is important to take account of 'the rigidity of the rules which define the boundaries of internal markets and which govern pricing and allocation within them' (*ibid.*, 1971: 5). For Wise (1996: 100) the underlying notion is 'that organisations create closed systems for managing human resources'. Taking into account these characteristics, one can conclude that the Belgian public services are a typical example of an ILM : the allocation of positions is strictly regulated; rules on seniority, training, examination and merit determine mobility between positions; recruitment takes place in the lower grades, while vacancies in higher grades are filled through internal promotions; and the seniority criterion is not only a determining factor in the allocation of positions, but also equally important for remuneration of the public servant (Hondeghem, 1997: 11).

The question why public services and other organisations develop ILMs is mostly answered by referring to their functionality from a management perspective. The most important functions ILMs fulfil in both the private and the public sector correspond to the fact that ILMs [can] reduce turnover, develop company-specific skills, lower dependence on the external labour market, provide motivation, supply and select candidates for higher-in-house positions and increase the legitimacy of the authority structure (Sels, 1996: 6–7). In the Belgian context, the existence of an ILM and the rigidity in the ILM are due to clientelism and nepotism, which are fundamental characteristics of the Belgian political culture and to which the ILM offers strict rules that can lower the arbitrariness in the management of personnel (Hondeghem, 1997: 11).

Political appointments – appointments where the political affiliation of the candidate is a decisive factor – are old sores in Belgium (Hondeghem, 1990: 191). This situation stands in contrast with the principle of merit – appointments based on competence – which is a basic principle in the personnel statutes of Belgian public organisations. Recruitment is based on competitive examinations; promotions in turn are depoliticised by introducing criteria such as seniority, examinations, training and performance appraisal. Political appointments and other forms of clientelism and nepotism, therefore, can only be explained as deviations from the statute by the appointing body which misuses its discretionary powers. These practices have, in turn, resulted in fundamental mistrust of the political system by public servants. Because of the dysfunctions connected with these practices – demotivation of public servants, decreased efficiency and effectiveness – means are sought to increase objectivity of recruitment and promotion. These are found in regulations which restrict the discretionary power of appointing bodies and thus also limit flexibility of personnel management and hinder reform efforts (Hondeghem, 1990: 210–14).

Excessive regulations are also explained – and personnel management reform is further hindered – by the strong position of public sector unions. Public authorities are obliged to bargain before determining the working conditions of their public servants. They are however not legally bound by the outcome of these negotiations. The reason for this is found in the principle of statutory employment in the public sector. Statutory personnel are bound by a statute, which consists of a range of general, non-personalised regulations on the rights and duties of public servants. The statute is imposed unilaterally by government and can also be adjusted unilaterally in response to the changing requirements of the general interest (Van Praet, 1996: 35). Government is only morally and politically bound by the outcome of the bargaining. The role of unions is important, however, since public sector unionisation is relatively high in Belgium and public servants can use their union power to hold the government to its agreements (Janvier and Rigaux, 1987: 104; Vilrokx and Van Leemput, 1992: 379). Also the fact that unions are linked with the political parties of the government strengthens their position.

Despite counteracting forces, pressures for change have led to the gradual reform of the Belgian public sector. These reforms are found in different forms, as for example:

- introduction of new financial management systems in federal, state and local government
- gradual withdrawing by privatisation from some sectors including public financial institutions, transport and communication
- external devolution, including introduction of management contracts replacing the traditional hierarchical steering relations
- internal devolution as for example transformation of APEs into business-units responsible for their own results
- evolution towards a managerial model, where public managers with a broad responsibility are beginning to appear
- reforms concerning relations between the administration and citizens: e.g. elaboration of a citizen's charter to improve the 'client-orientation' of public services and enhance the legitimacy of the political-administrative system.

Also personnel management has been the object of a radical modernisation process in the direction of human resources management (HRM). Fundamental rights – security of tenure and careers – of the public servants are being questioned and demands for greater flexibility are being heard.

FLEXIBLE PERSONNEL MANAGEMENT IN THE BELGIAN PUBLIC SERVICES

Accumulation of regulations and rigidity of these rules have made it very difficult for public managers to conduct flexible HRM policies. Rules concerning remuneration and allocation of personnel were set down in detail in the so-called Camu statute established by Royal Decree in 1937 and have been little changed for half a century. Not until the 1990s were the rules reviewed to adjust the public service to the new structure of the State and face the new challenges of a modern administration. There is evidence of an evolution towards more flexibility, albeit the personnel statute remains the basic element in public sector employment relationships.

Staffing flexibility

In different sectors of the Belgian public services changes have occurred in staffing policy. At federal level a recruitment freeze, introduced for budgetary reasons, has not so much led to a reduction of staff, as to an upgrading of personnel. A similar trend is found in local government in Flanders where implementation of a new sectoral agreement has led to an upgrading of administrative personnel and a diminution of the number of manual workers and semi-skilled administrative workers. The example of local government, however, illustrates the inflexibility of staffing practices in the Belgian public sector. The statutory staffing of local government is depicted in personnel formations, which outline the number of posts in the different levels and grades for the statutory personnel. The relation between future services and the number and quality of personnel clearly indicates that personnel formations should not be static, but should rather be dynamic and adaptable. This is hindered, however, by the restricted flexibility of the procedure for adapting the personnel formation. Proposals have to meet with approval by city councils and Flemish Community. The administrative supervision procedures not only have an unfavourable effect on the time needed to adjust the personnel formation; they are also a serious limitation of local discretion since strict, but disputed directives are used to judge local decisions.

Contractual flexibility

The principle of statutory nomination is firmly anchored in Belgian administration and is strongly supported by the unions. Unions hold on to statutory employment as the standard because security of tenure is seen as granting an important advantage compared to the position of non-statutory personnel. According to the statute of public servants at national, state and local level, contractual personnel can only be engaged in exceptional situations. Nevertheless, actual practices diverge from the theory. In federal ministries 21 per cent of civil servants have contracts. In Flemish state ministries this is about 18 per cent. The proportion of contractual workers rises to 33 per cent in federal public institutions and 37 per cent in institutions at Flemish state level. In the provinces, less than two-thirds of personnel are employed under statute, whilst in the cities, municipalities and local welfare agencies the number of statutory personnel is less than half the total number of personnel (Ministerie van Ambtenarenzaken, 1998; Steen, 1997: 14). In public financial institutions statutory employment has already been exchanged for contractual employment. This was only achieved, however, when financial compensation was provided. At the VRT, the Flemish television station, only contractual personnel are to be engaged in the future. It is expected that the statutory nomination will be questioned shortly in all autonomous public enterprises (Hondeghem, 1997: 15).

The high number of non-statutory personnel can be explained partly by the rigidities of the statute. Contractual employment meets the concept of employers' flexibility far more closely than statutory employment. This is particularly the case for recruitment and dismissal (numerical flexibility). The number of contractual personnel raises problems for personnel management because of the deficient socio-legal position this group of personnel occupies, although they do the same work as statutory personnel (Steen, 1997: 15). By definition contractual workers have less security of tenure than statutory personnel. Other important disadvantages concern reduced possibilities of progression in the functional/financial career, differences in social security rights (pension) and exclusion from promotion. Contractual personnel either seek to regularise their situation by getting statutorily nominated or look for work in the private sector. Turnover of contractual personnel is therefore very high.

This intrinsic injustice in the organisation questions the tendency of holding on to statutory nomination. It seems more appropriate to evolve gradually towards convergence of labour relations in the public and private sectors. A number of benefits of statutory employment (for example social benefits) have been adopted by the private sector. Standardisation of the social statute for public servants and employees would also increase mobility between the public and private sectors. However, it will be some time before such reforms are adopted not least because of opposition from the unions (Hondeghem, 1997: 15).

WORKING HOURS AND WORKING LIFE

Public organisations in Belgium can implement different non-full-time employment systems for their personnel. The oldest regulations were introduced to grant employees the possibility of taking leave for personal reasons. This accords with the idea of employee flexibility, that is giving employees the opportunity to adapt their working time to family or other circumstances. Examples of such regulations are parental leave, long time absence due to personal circumstances, and leave in order to fulfil an apprenticeship or a probationary period in another public function. These regulations proved to have a *de facto* redistributive labour effect, although this was not originally intended. Since the 1980s government has started to refine and propagate a number of these measures and develop new measures to redistribute labour. Among the new regulations are provisions for reduced hours due to social or family reasons, absence for personal reasons, career interruption, part-time early retirement at the age of 55 and voluntary 'four day weeks' (Van Praet, 1996: 37–67).

Since most of these regulations are a response to the employees' demand for temporal flexibility, these measures can be classified as individual formulae, which respect the principle of voluntarism (Pollet and Sels, 1996: 77–8, 84). This leads to certain consequences. While the possibilities for voluntary part-time work are greater in the public sector than in the private sector, the actual percentage of non-voluntary part-time working employees is lower (Sels, 1992: 26–30). Although a number of these individual formulae are related to obligatory measures replacing personnel with unemployed persons, the labour redistributing effect of these measures is restricted. The basis of labour redistribution is determined by the workers' demand for temporal flexibility (Pollet and Sels, 1996: 78). The choice for individual and voluntary introduction of temporal flexibility also requires a certain amount of flexibility or adjustment on behalf of the organisation and investment in the training of temporary contractual personnel replacing other personnel.

Flexitime – differentiating starting and finishing times – is another widespread practice in government and an example of flexible practices meeting employees' demands. However, flexibility of working hours is implemented as a response to other drivers too, as for example the need to reduce rush hour pressures for public transport and road travel. Flexibility in time also fits in with efforts made by government to adjust the hours of service availability to the demands of clients. In Flemish state government the idea of 'service time' is being promoted. This means that during certain hours of the day, each service has to be available. Local government has a relatively long tradition of flexible opening hours. In other sectors, like federal government this tradition is non-existent and the move to extend opening hours is meeting more resistance.

PAY FLEXIBILITY

Changes in the structure of the pay system can be linked with a less hierarchical organisational structure in the public sector. Traditionally, public services are divided into 'levels', 'ranks', 'grades' and related 'salary scales'. An option taken in different governmental organisations has been to reduce the number of ranks, grades and pay scales. Division into levels is based on the nature of the work and on the existing system of education. Each level is subdivided into ranks which mirror the hierarchy within the system. Every rank consists of a number of grades, which are closely linked with the function of the public servant. The grade is the basis of the public servant's salary. Each grade has salary scales with incremental increases according to seniority. Salary scales are fixed after negotiations with the unions. This job classification system applies to the national civil service, public institutions and public service system of the regions. Consequently the job classification system in Belgium is rather centralised. A similar system is applied in local government, but without a subdivision of levels into ranks.

Recent reforms in the public sector have limited organisational discretion and flexibility in working out a pay system. This is illustrated by the implementation of the collective agreement for the local government sector, which dates from 1993 and determines the pay structure in local government in Flanders. Before the introduction of the agreement, cities and municipalities were largely free to determine the financial statute of their personnel. Each municipality had its own remuneration system, pay scales and diploma-bonuses. This local discretion was limited only by the fixed pay scales for top public servants, which were stipulated by the Minister of Internal Affairs. However, most cities and municipalities, with the exception of some medium-sized, regional and large cities, also followed reference scales for lower grades and levels (Van Hooland, 1992: 587–8, 591). In order to enhance uniformity, fixed salary scales for all local personnel were introduced and all non-legally regulated allowances were incorporated in these new salary scales.

Flattened organisational structures offer rather less career prospects than more hierarchical organisations. To compensate for reduced chances of promotion, due to the decrease in number of ranks and grades, the principle of a financial career has been developed. Every grade is now linked to a number of salary scales, so that a public servant can now pass through several salary scales even when remaining in the same grade. The system of 'financial careers' has been introduced at all levels of government: national, state and local government.

In the Flemish Community middle and top managers can receive a management premium from zero to 20 per cent on top of their normal salary. Also at national level the introduction of management premiums for top civil servants is planned, together with the introduction of the mandatory system. In the autonomous public enterprises management premiums exist for managers employed by mandate. Next to management premiums, the financial career is an instrument for rewarding 'good' performance. In Flemish state government the financial career depends on seniority and performance. In 1993 a system was introduced allowing civil servants to progress through their financial career in a faster or slower way, depending on their performance appraisal. The system of faster progress through the financial career has now been replaced by yearly premiums of 7.5 per cent of the salary, with a minimum of 750 Euro. In 1998, 365 out of more than 10,000 civil servants were given a premium, whilst the financial careers of 74 civil servants were slowed down.

In local government in Flanders progress through pay scales depends on seniority, training and also on performance appraisal. However, salary increases based on the financial career are limited. To get a real pay increase one has to develop a hierarchical career, where seniority, examinations and performance appraisal are major criteria. At federal level, due to budgetary reasons, progress in the financial career is limited by norms of 'social programmation'. This means that only a certain percentage of civil servants can pass to higher salary scales within their grade. Finally, in specific services, like merit-departments of the Flemish Employment Service, group premiums can be earned, related to the results of the group.

FUNCTIONAL OR TASK FLEXIBILITY

As in other countries, such as Germany and the UK, there is a close link between the grade and function of public servants. However, with increased specialisation, the number of grades increased markedly and this raised problems with respect to the mobility of public servants. Reform has drastically reduced the number of grades. This step back towards generalised grades has been compensated for by the introduction of job descriptions which can be adjusted according to the situation. No specific regulations are drawn up concerning functional flexibility, allowing public servants to change jobs during their career. The organisation of internal mobility belongs to the authority of the individual public organisation. However, political proposals demonstrate the intention to stimulate internal mobility within and between departments in federal and state government.

The new career system according to which public servants can get into a higher pay scale, while keeping the same grade, is called the 'functional career'. It is stated that introduction of the new personnel management and restriction of grades is leading to further enlargement of the tasks and responsibilities of public servants, which would mean a major step towards functional or task flexibility. However, since the essence of the system is that public servants get higher pay but keep the same job, the functional career could better be called an 'anti-functional career' or – as it was called above – a 'financial career' (Hondeghem, 1993: 626).

CAREER FLEXIBILITY

The public services in Belgium are traditionally characterised by entry at the bottom of the hierarchy and promotion from within. Division of the public services into levels is based on the education system: direct access to a level is only possible with the right educational qualifications. Promotion to a higher level is possible, however. Being an important feature of statutory employment, the career system is regulated in the personnel statute. Allocation of positions and mobility between these positions are strictly controlled. The requirements for progression in the hierarchical ladder are qualifications, seniority, training, exams, and/or performance appraisal. Determination of objective criteria, from which no deviations are allowed, supports the principle of the objectivity of recruitment and promotion. This principle in turn aims at lowering arbitrariness, clientelism and nepotism in personnel management issues. Regulation of the career and the fixed criteria for promotion, however, strongly restrict the possibility of having a flexible career policy. Therefore we can even speak of 'programmed careers' (Hondeghem, 1993: 616). This is the case especially in organisations where seniority is more important than other criteria, like performance appraisal.

In contrast with statutory personnel, contractual personnel are recruited for a specific post. However, since the new personnel policies place much emphasis on job definition and classification and on the financial career, an evolution towards a post system is taking place for statutory personnel as well. Also, top managers of public institutions – both quangos and autonomous public enterprises – are an important exception to the rule of recruitment taking place in the lower levels, while filling vacancies in higher grades through internal promotions. Top managers for autonomous public institutions can be recruited from outside the public service, albeit most directors are still recruited from within the organisation (Depré and Hondeghem, 1996: 87). Recent history shows, however, some examples of general managers being recruited with the help of head-hunters and coming from private companies, e.g. Kok, the former general manager of Belgacom and Degraeve, the general manager of the Flemish Radio and Television Company.

Although external recruitment is possible, most public servants spend their whole career in the same organisation and it is unlikely that this situation will drastically change in the near future. In local government, for example, the new sectoral agreement fosters mobility of personnel between the city or municipality and its local welfare agency, since local welfare centres have to implement the same personnel statute as the city or municipality. In practice, however, little or no use is made of this possibility. Also the high degree of uniformity of the administrative statute and pay system in the different cities and municipalities facilitates external mobility of personnel. The limited inclusion of required experience, or seniority achieved in other administrations or in the private sector can, however, have an opposite effect.

Next to external recruitment, the mandate system is also important in enhancing career flexibility in the public sector. The introduction of the mandate system enables the appointment of public servants to senior posts for a fixed period of five or six years and is designed to increase mobility at the top of the administration and enhance the innovative capacity of the organisation (Hondeghem, 1993: 616). The mandate system also makes top public servants more responsible and accountable. Mandated public servants have more autonomy concerning the means of their administration – personnel and finance – but are also held accountable for the results. At the beginning of the mandate, clear management objectives will be set down and at the end of the mandate, performance appraisal takes place. The mandate can then be renewed or incumbents are removed from office. External candidates are dismissed and internal candidates can return to their former function. At national level, the mandate system was agreed on for ministries and public institutions in 1994. Many practical difficulties and political obstacles have impeded this reform until now. Top managers in the autonomous public enterprises and in some public institutions are already employed by mandate. With the sectoral agreement of 1993 the mandate system is also possible in local government. Thus far the system has only been implemented in the city administration of Antwerp, which is the biggest local government in Flanders, having about 10,000 employees.

CONCLUSION

The discretionary powers of individual public organisations on personnel matters stand central to the concept of flexibility. Therefore, flexibility supports other changes in the public sector, such as devolution and decentralisation. Or, to put it even stronger, flexibility in staffing and personnel systems is conditional on decentralisation of decision making. (Hondeghem, Farnham and Horton, 1996: 127). It is exactly at this point that rigidity in personnel policies in the Belgian public sector appears. The personnel management practices being implemented in the public sector result from statutory regulations and collective bargaining. Except for some autonomous public enterprises, individual organisations are given little discretion to adjust personnel management decisions to local situations. Also within organisations there is still little evidence of devolution of responsibility for personnel management from central management to line departments. Yet this Belgian situation does not necessarily stand in contrast to practices in other countries. In the OECD report on public sector HRM reforms, it is stated that: 'despite stated commitments by most countries to human resource management reform, the pace of reform has often been slow with discretion and flexibility of line management hampered by detailed rules and regulations' (OECD, 1996: 10).

It is thus interesting to look at the flexible arrangements existing within the Belgian context. Table 4.2 summarises flexible personnel practices in the Belgian public sector.

A comparison across different organisations and types of flexible personnel arrangements shows that certain types of employment flexibility, such as contractual employment and flexible working time arrangements, are common throughout the Belgian public sector. In

Table 4.2 Flexible personnel practices in the Belgian public sector

	Federal ministries	State ministry (Flanders)	APEs and public institutions	Local government
Contractual flexibility	contractual employment: ±21%	contractual employment: ±18%	contractual employment: ±33–37%	contractual employment: ±33–50%
Pay flexibility	(management premiums) financial career	management premiums financial career	management premiums (group premiums)	financial career
Flexibility of working hours	different non-full-time employment systems (flexitime)	different non-full-time employment systems 'service time'	different non-full-time employment systems	different non-full-time employment systems flexitime
Career flexibility	(mandate system)	mandate system	mandate system	(mandate system)

recent years, experimentation has started with the mandate system – which uses fixed-term contracts for leadership positions – and with pay flexibility – as for example the management premiums. Both forms of flexibility are directed towards top and middle management, while for public servants at lower levels the system of a financial career has been introduced. The public sector is more rigid with regard to staffing and career policy. Also there is little evidence of functional flexibility.

In this chapter, flexible working practices have been classified into six categories. Other ways of classifying flexibilities of course exist, as for example division into quantitative and qualitative flexible arrangements. Quantitative or numerical flexibility relates to adjusting the number of workers or number of hours worked according to demand for work. Qualitative flexibility is connected with the qualitative aspects of working conditions and job content. It concerns employability of personnel, being able to fulfil different tasks. The most widespread types of flexibility, contractual employment and time flexibility, fall within the category of quantitative forms of flexibility. The Belgian public services seem to be slower than some other countries reviewed in this book in evolving towards more qualitative flexibilities such as task flexibility and outsourcing.

Forms of employment flexibility can be related to different drives towards flexibility. The demands of employees for opportunities to adjust the working situation to their personal lives, pressure from government to decrease unemployment rates, and the need of public organisations to reduce labour costs have all led to flexible arrangements of working time and working life. More recently there seems to be a change in the agenda driving flexibility as increased attention towards citizens as critical consumers has led to adjustments of working time to enable extension of hours of service. Other flexible practices, such as pay flexibility, can be related to the managerial imperative to increase efficiency in the public sector and improve the quality of the services or goods produced. This imperative not only encourages pay flexibility, but also other forms of personnel management flexibility and use of career policy to maximise the performance and motivations of public servants (Steen, 1997: 3).

Although certain flexibilities and inflexibilities are widespread throughout the public services, it would be wrong to consider the Belgian public sector as one uniform system. Increased autonomy of public institutions, at federal and state level, has led to variations in practices. In particular, in some APEs, new forms of flexible employment are being experimented with, such as the mandate system and performance related pay. Also the Flemish state government is demonstrating itself as being a young and dynamic institution. This also has a positive effect on local government, since state government has taken up the role as a model for other sectors within the public services. The public sector has, however, long been connected with the idea of 'good' employment practices, particularly in job security. Contractual employment has become widespread in the public sector and the deficient socio-legal position which the contractual employees are in questions the validity of holding on to the statutory nomination. It seems more appropriate to evolve gradually towards convergence of labour relations across sectors and employees.

Note

1. The Dutroux case, relating to a paedophile ring, led to the resignation of two ministers (Justice and Interior) in 1998 and to subsequent reforms of both the police and justice systems. Dutroux's case is still pending and he is expected to be brought to trial in 2000.

Abbreviations

APEs   autonomous public enterprises
HRM   human resources management

ILM   internal labour market
NPM   New Public Management
VDAB   Flemish Employment Service
VRT   the Flemish television station

References

DEPRÉ, R. and HONDEGHEM, A. (1996). 'Belgium', in Farnham, D., Horton, S., Barlow, J. and Hondeghem, A. (eds): *New Public Managers in Europe. Public Servants in Transition.* Basingstoke: Macmillan, pp 79–99.
DOERINGER, P.D. and PIORE, M.J. (1971). *Internal Labor Markets and Manpower Analysis.* Lexington: Heath Lexington Books.
HONDEGHEM, A. (1990). *De loopbaan van de ambtenaar. Tussen droom en werkelijkheid.* Leuven: VCOB.
HONDEGHEM, A. (1993). 'Het nieuwe personeelsstatuut: noodzakelijke en voldoende voorwaarde voor een goed personeelsbeleid?', in *De Gemeente*, 12, pp 613–18.
HONDEGHEM, A., FARNHAM, D. and HORTON, S. (1996). 'Working Report', in *New Trends in Public Administration and Public Law.* EGPA Yearbook. Annual Conference. Budapest, pp 127–30.
HONDEGHEM, A. (1997). 'The National Civil Service in Belgium', paper for the International Conference on Civil Service Systems in a Comparative Perspective. Bloomington, Indiana University.
HOOD, C. (1991). 'A Public Management for all Seasons?', in *Public Administration.* 69 (1), pp 3–19.
JANVIER, R. and RIGAUX, M. (1987). 'Individuele en collectieve arbeidsverhoudingen in de publieke en de particuliere sector. Een beknopte juridische vergelijking', in Gevers, P. (ed.): *Ambtenarenbeleid en arbeidsverhoudingen.* Brugge: die keure, pp 37–139.
MINISTERIE VAN AMBTENARENZAKEN (1998). *Overzicht van de personeelssterkte in de overheidssector. Toestand op 30/06/1997 en op 01/01/1998.* Brussels: Ministerie van Ambtenarenzaken.
OECD (1996). *Integrating People Management into Public Service Reform.* Paris: OECD.
POLLET, I. and SELS, L. (1996). 'Arbeidsherverdeling in organisaties: problemen en oplossingen', in Vanherck, R. (ed.): *Arbeidsherverdelende programma's: Instrumenten voor/tegen emancipatiebeleid?* Congresboek studiedag 8 juni. Antwerp: Provinciebestuur Antwerpen en Centrum voor Vrouwenstudies UIA, pp 77–110.
SELS, L. (1992). *Over-reguliere arbeid in over-gereguleerde organisaties?* Leuven: Steunpunt Werkgelegenheid Arbeid en Vorming.
SELS, L. (1996). *From Statute to Contract. Regulating the Employment Relationship in the Public Sector.* Leuven: Department of Applied Economics, Catholic University of Leuven.
STEEN, T. (1997). 'A New Personnel Management in Local Government in Flanders: Steps Towards More Flexible Arrangements?' Paper presented to the personnel Policy Study Group at the EGPA Conference. Leuven.

STEEN, T. (1998). 'Een nieuw en flexibel personeelsbeleid in de lokale besturen in Vlaanderen?' *Res Publica*. 40 (1), pp 79–97.
TROMMEL, W.A. (1987). *Flexibele arbeid: een werknemerstypologie*. 's Gravenhage: Wetenschappelijke Raad voor het Regeringsbeleid.
VAN HOOLAND, B. (1992). 'De wedden en lonen van onze ambtenaren: de lokale en provinciale sector'. *De Gemeente*. 12, pp 587–95.
VAN PRAET, B. (1996). 'Arbeidsherverdeling in de lokale sector', in Vanherck, R. (ed.): *Arbeidsherverdelende programma's: Instrumenten voor/tegen emancipatiebeleid?* Congresboek studiedag 8 juni. Antwerp, Provinciebestuur Antwerpen en Centrum voor Vrouwenstudies UIA, pp 33–76.
VEPSÄLÄINEN, K. (1994). *Henkilöstön Kehittäminen ankarassa muuto-spaineessa*. Helsinki: Painatuskeskus.
VILROKX, J. and VAN LEEMPUT, J. (1992). 'Belgium: A New Stability in Industrial Relations?', in Ferner, A. and Hyman, R. (eds): *Industrial Relations in the New Europe*. Oxford: Blackwell, pp 323–56.
WISE, L.R. (1996). 'Internal Labor Markets', in Bekke, H., Perry, J. and Toonen, Th. (eds): *Civil Service Systems in Comparative Perspective*. Bloomington and Ianapolis: Indiana University Press, pp 100–18.

5 Finland: the Development of a Performance Culture and its Impact on Human Resources Flexibilities

Markku Kiviniemi and Turo Virtanen

The chapter presents a general overview of flexible personnel management practices in the public sector of Finland. The traditional description of administration was based on functional sectors led by ministries but, for managerial and financial purposes, alternative functional classifications have been developed. Now there is a division into three main functional areas of the public sector which broadly reflect the major administrative policies of the 1990s (Hallintopolitkan suuntalinja, 1998). The three main areas are:

- *administration* including the functions of security and law and order
- *public services* to citizens and enterprises
- *market-oriented functions* including public enterprises and companies, as well as the productive and commercial tasks of the public sector.

According to Finnish administrative policy (*Laadukkaat palvelut*, 1998), the three functional areas of the public sector follow different principles in their activities. Administrative activities follow principles of democracy and good governance, legality and legal protection of citizens. Service activities follow principles of good service quality and citizen participation. Most public services are provided by the municipal sector. In 1996 the municipal sector consisted of 262 joint municipal boards and 453 municipalities. Joint municipal boards are associations of municipalities. Market-oriented activities follow mainly principles of competition in the marketplace. Administrative and service functions are carried out by state and municipal employers. Market-oriented functions are mostly provided by separate employers which in turn are public enterprises and companies. The civil service as an employment category is found only in administrative and service activities, not in market-oriented ones.

PERSONNEL IN THE PUBLIC SECTOR

The personnel policies of the state have long traditions which are closely connected with administrative and civil service legislation. The foundation of civil servants' position has traditionally been the independence of civil servants as a guarantee for objective, equal and just treatment of citizens and for the reliability and legality of the authorities. This tradition has implied an emphasis on the continuity and stability of careers, supported by traditional personnel policies. The 1990s brought changes in these policies.

The total number of state personnel in 1997 was 123,214 and the corresponding figure for the municipal sector was 418,000 (Ministry of Finance, 1998). The number of personnel has decreased markedly over the last decade: by 92,000 in state administration since 1988 and by 46,000 in municipal administration since 1990. The main reason for the decreases has been the transformation of several agencies into public enterprises and companies in which the personnel cease to be under the central personnel administration of the state or municipalities. The majority of the state's personnel (about 77 per cent) are civil servants, the rest are employed under employment contracts. In the municipal sector, 64 per cent of personnel are civil servants but the trend of the 1990s has been, contrary to that of the state, to increase the percentage of contracted employees. Joint municipal boards employ about 25 per cent of total personnel in the municipal sector, with the rest in the service of municipalities.

In 1997, the Finnish state sector employed about six per cent of the total national labour force and the municipal sector employed about 19 per cent – overall a quarter of the workforce. Within the state sector 25 per cent of personnel worked in education, 16 per cent in defence, 13 per cent in interior and nine per cent in finance. The rest were divided between the remaining eight sectors (Ministry of Finance, 1998). The largest state institutions by number of personnel are the country's 20 universities, national defence, police, road administration and tax administration. In comparison with 1985, personnel within traffic and communications has decreased dramatically because of reorganisations into public enterprises and companies. Only 20 per cent of state personnel work at the centre, the rest are spread throughout regional and local offices.

In the municipal sector, personnel broken down by functional area in 1997 were: health care 28 per cent, social services 27 per cent, education and culture 26 per cent, planning and public works six per cent, general administration three per cent and others nine per cent. Among state personnel 27 per cent had an academic degree in 1997 but for civil servants the percentage was 34 per cent. In the municipal sector only 15 per cent of personnel had an academic degree. Some 55 per cent of state personnel and 25 per cent of municipal personnel are male, whilst in the whole labour market the corresponding figure is 52.5 per cent.

REFORMS IN THE 1990s

Major reforms of the 1990s have been decentralisation and introduction of management by results. Decentralisation has affected both financial practices (budgeting) and personnel management. An essential change has been the increased autonomy of agencies and municipalities. The foundations for the reforms were laid in the 1980s. The work done by the Parliamentary Committee on Decentralisation (*Hallinnon hajauttaminen*, 1986) was an important step towards adopting a new line of thinking. Since 1987, a special Ministerial Committee on Public Management has been responsible for reform programmes. From 1991, government adopted a new procedure as a part of the annual budgeting cycle. Since then, preparation of the state budget has started by issuing a cabinet decision on the maximum level of total expenditures and a ceiling of expenditures for each ministry (frame-budgeting). Line ministries are expected to prepare their budget proposals so that their respective ceilings are not exceeded. The result has been a more disciplined budgetary process. In 1995, the present government made a politically-binding decision on total expenditures for the next four years when it first entered office. This multi-year approach to budgeting, combined with ceilings, has been assessed as a relatively efficient strategic instrument governing public expenditures.

At agency level, all government agencies implemented results-oriented management during the period 1990–95. Related to this approach is budgeting by results. A single appropriation is given by the state budget to each agency to cover its operational expenses and the agency can independently decide how to use it. Results targets for agencies are set out in contracts between ministries and agencies. Improving productivity, economy, quality and effectiveness are essential parts of the Finnish version of results-based management. Generally, the experiences of results-based management have been favourable. Although there are problems of implementation and accountability in contract-based management between different levels of state government, allocation of resources has improved, together with more cost-consciousness within agencies. Also increases in productivity have resulted but there are mixed effects of all the reforms, together with tightened state budgets. The introduction of net budgeting from 1993 has increased the financial powers of agencies but its real significance is limited to a few agencies which have substantial income other than from the state budget. Besides financial decentralisation, other tasks and functions have been delegated. This is related to administrative deregulation which has been going on since the late 1980s.

The trend towards decentralisation has also manifested itself in local government. The Local Government Act 1995 reinforced the self-governing status of municipalities. They have wide choice in arranging their organisation and responsibilities and collaboration between local authorities has been increasing. The state subsidy system to municipalities was reformed earlier, in 1993, to give wider possibilities for local authorities to use these subsidies. The former detailed costs-based system was changed into total subsidy sums based on indicators of population and local economy. The aim has been to encourage local authorities to operate in more economic and effective ways.

A salient trend of reforms has been the marketisation of public services. In the state sector, 24 different bodies have been reorganised into public enterprises or joint-stock companies since 1989. The biggest corporatised bodies have been the post and telecommunications and state railways, which now operate as state-owned companies. In a minor form, similar trends are observable in the municipal sector. Particularly in state administration, these reforms have resulted in a significant reduction of the number of personnel financed through state budgets.

Altogether, the administrative reforms imply significant changes in the public sector towards more flexibility in structures and functions. From 1987 onwards, the trends have been administrative decentralisation and deregulation. Budget reforms started the general trend to increase flexibility in resource management. In addition to financial management, increased flexibility covers personnel, materials and information management. These trends have been supported by the introduction of new information technologies. After the introduction of frame budgeting combined with budgeting by results and net budgeting, the focus has recently turned to personnel management.

STRUCTURAL AND SYSTEMIC REFORMS OF PERSONNEL POLICIES

The terms 'personnel administration' and 'personnel policy' came into Finnish discussions and organisational practices in the late 1960s (Palm and Voutilainen, 1970). They implied particularly an integration of decision-making within the area of personnel affairs and formulations of a new 'personnel perspective'. Before that time, the decisions related to personnel were characterised by diverse and separate practices (Lumijärvi, 1978; Kasvio, 1994). Personnel administration and policies were first formulated in the private sector and, in the early 1970s, these ideas entered the public sector. The central management of state personnel administration was organised as part of the Ministry of Finance. Another sign of institutionalisation was the beginning of central collective bargaining systems at the same time.

In the 1970s the development of personnel policies touched all different personnel functions (Keränen, 1979). The approach was characterised as 'holistic', which differed from earlier practices. Models of personnel planning were created, guidelines for recruitment were published and labour protection organisations were established. The State In-Service Training Centre was established in 1971 and personnel training plans were made in the agencies. Methods of personnel participation were developed under the concept of 'office democracy'. Research projects on working conditions were conducted. Also job descriptions and classifications were initiated. The principles and goals of personnel administration were formulated under the concept of personnel policy. In the 1970s, state agencies prepared their own documents on personnel policies. In 1979, government made a decision on the preparing of personnel policy programmes in state agencies, which set out the goals of state personnel policy, and was intended to be a framework for agencies. Programmes were prepared in the following years and had some impact on personnel practices. The programmes were not, however, binding and were criticised for their abstractness and too-general style.

In the 1980s, there was emphasis on management and new programmes of management training were introduced. Within the management-by-objectives tradition, emphasis was on the direction of functions and resources through objectives without much consideration of personnel issues. On the other hand, personnel management was based primarily on the tradition of personnel policy orientation, which emphasised the development of personnel competencies and motivations. The challenge for management training was to *integrate* these development traditions in practice. Case analyses of state agencies served to create broader managerial frameworks (Mikkonen, 1985). Development of personnel policies had a relatively strong tradition in state administration from the 1970s. The 1980s were a quiet period, with few new ideas, and although new conceptions of personnel policy had been elaborated in agencies, the centralised system of decision-making was a constraint and gave little room for manoeuvres in the agencies.

The progress of decentralisation, however, gradually created a base for new reforms of personnel policies. In 1991, government introduced a new policy, derived mainly from the proposals of the Personnel Committee of the State (*Henkilöstöpolitiikan uudistaminen*, 1990). Personnel policy was to become more flexible, competitive, active, decentralised and streamlined to meet the demands of the 1990s. Thus from 1990, reforms of personnel policies in state administration have been closely linked to goals of administrative reform. Essential structural reforms were introduced in the State Civil Servants Act 1994. This law confirmed civil service status as the primary form of employment in state administration but also aimed at converging conditions of service between civil servants and contracted employees. Only a few differences remain between civil servants and contracted employees. These concern procedures of appointment, official appointment and promotion criteria, the legal versus the contractual base of task definition, legal responsibilities and possibilities for employment continuation. Agencies have wide powers to both establish and abolish civil service and contracted posts within the limits of their budget. Fixing the size of the personnel establishment was removed from the state budget in 1996. This offers the possibility of hiring new personnel and funding out of the agency net incomes. A more traditional and still often-used way to hire personnel has been the use of general employment grants.

After 1988, the system of collective bargaining and collective agreements was reformed and partially decentralised in state administration. The goal has been to reinforce the system of agreements at agency level and so improve the possibilities for executing results-oriented pay policies in the agencies. At central level, general framework agreements for agencies are approved. Thus, to a certain degree, agencies can reform their pay systems and terms of employment for civil servants. By 1998, 50 different state agencies had utilised this possibility for 'specified contracts'. Also the possibility of individual agreements with civil servants was established. Working hours can be agreed at agency level within the limits set centrally.

Under the law, dismissal of personnel is possible on regulated grounds such as for 'economic and productive reasons'. This statement covers both civil servants and contracted employees. For civil servants, re-employment and retraining are the main alternatives before dismissal. For personnel adaptations, specific grants are available in the state budget. Each agency is obliged to try to work out a solution on these lines before making dismissals. The reforms of the 1990s have created bases for new, more decentralised personnel management practices. Generally, these reforms seek to abolish or relieve those problems which, in the 1970s and 1980s, were criticised as being over-centralised systems. Since the reforms, agencies have scope for determining their own personnel policies. They can recruit their main personnel from open labour markets which is typical of the Finnish public sector in general. They can promote staff mobility by using fixed-term appointments. In the 1990s, conditions of competence have been made more flexible by horizontally broadening their definitions.

Levels of personnel circulation and mobility, however, have remained low in the public sector in the 1990s. Within state administration only 2.3 per cent of personnel were mobile in 1996 including international mobility. Internal mobility of personnel within state administration was 2.6 per cent in 1997, which included all changes between the organisations of the state government. On the other hand, use of fixed-term service clearly increased. Fourteen per cent of personnel were doing fixed-term work within state administration in 1996 and eight per cent in the municipal sector (1995). The corresponding percentage for the total labour force was 16 per cent in 1997. Part-time employment has also increased in the 1990s: those doing part-time work in state administration were 7.3 per cent in 1996 and 9.1 per cent in 1997, compared with 2.7 per cent in 1990. In the municipal sector, the proportion of part-time workers was nine per cent in

1994. For the whole Finnish labour force, the figure was eight per cent in 1995.

Agencies can make agreements with the unions to introduce performance-related pay (PRP) systems. In the mid-1990s, PRP had been introduced in about 15 per cent of state agencies. Experiences of PRP systems have not been entirely positive, although several agencies have studied the possibilities of using them in the late 1990s. The general philosophy in reforming the pay system is to break monthly pay into three categories: pay for the requirements of the job, pay for personal qualifications, and pay for performance. Since 1995, all civil servants have had the right to negotiate individual agreements for a higher salary than that designated by the collective agreement. So far, this provision has been rarely used.

State agencies can independently decide on their personnel development and training policies. In the area of management training, strategic management has been organised at national level. These strategic training programmes attract participants from both the public and private sectors. Training related to European integration has increased markedly in state administration. The strategy for integrating training was laid down by the Ministry of Finance. At agency level, personnel development has been used as a tool for managing rapid and difficult change situations and for creating more flexibility in job content (Vepsäläinen, 1994). Personnel development and training have been decentralised areas of personnel management since the 1970s.

The Personnel Department of the Ministry of Finance is responsible for the state's general personnel policy. The Personnel Strategy of the State (Ministry of Finance, 1995) highlights fixed-term and part-time employment as means for human resources flexibilities. In addition, flexible job descriptions, flexible working hours, contracting out, telework, sabbatical leave and the provision of part-time pensions are highlighted for increasing personnel flexibility. In short, there have been significant increases in the means of flexibility within state administration in the 1990s. These have included:

- powers to establish and abolish posts, both civil service and con tractual ones
- size of an agency's personnel establishment is no longer controlled by the state budget
- partially decentralised collective bargaining and collective agreements

- possibilities for reforming pay systems and terms of employment
- local agreements on working hours
- dismissal of personnel on agreed grounds
- decentralised recruitment
- fixed-term recruitment
- part-time recruitment
- performance-related pay systems
- personnel development and training
- personnel circulation.

EXPERIENCES OF REFORM

The Department of Personnel of the Ministry of Finance has followed up implementation of the reforms. Two different studies have been addressed to state agencies, the first in 1996 (N = 113) and the second in 1997 (N = 125). The data from these studies reflect the experiences of the management of agencies. The Department of Political Science in the University of Helsinki also has collected data by interviewing agency managers in 1998. In the first survey (Ministry of Finance, 1997) managers were asked about the frequency of using different tools of flexibility. Only 18 different means were mentioned in the questionnaire and they do not cover all the potential means referred to above. The percentages of agencies using the different means are listed below in descending order. These percentages do not indicate the numbers of personnel but the numbers of agencies using the means:

- fixed-term employment 93%
- saving vacations for later years 90%
- employment by general employment grants 88%
- changing job content 79%
- contracting-out 78%
- part-time work 77%
- overtime work 72%
- timing of vacations 72%
- part-time pensions 57%.

These nine means of flexibility had been used in over half the agencies. Less frequent use was found for personnel circulation, early retirement and telework. Inclusion of part-time pensions and early retirement in the list is connected with increasing importance of policies for senior staff. The age structure of personnel is generally unbalanced with an over-representation of the age groups between 40–55. Some agencies have created their own programmes including specific 'senior flexibility'. Regarding flexibility of working hours, another survey (Ylöstalo and Rahikainen, 1998) shows that flexibility in times of arrival and leaving the workplace is much more general in state government than in municipal government, the private sector being somewhere in-between.

Agencies were asked also to assess the impact of these different means of flexibility on their productivity. The majority of agencies assessed the impacts to be positive for the following: development of job content, contracting-out and fixed-term employment. Over one third of the agencies assessed the impacts to be positive for employment by general employment grants, personnel circulation, timing of vacations and overtime work. Flexibility of working hours is also assessed as being positive but the negative impact is also apparent in terms of rising costs in the agencies. The positive impacts were assessed to be minor, if not totally absent, for early retirements, telework and part-time work. Generally, assessment of using flexibility was clearly positive. Similar assessments have been received from municipal and private employers. The impact is dependent not only on the specific flexibility but also the quality of preparing and planning its use in collaboration and in due time.

Agencies gave the general message that there are human resources flexibilities and that their use is now within the agencies' own responsibility. Even though there are enough potential means for flexible personnel management practices, the capacity to use them effectively is often limited. It takes time to determine the positive operational applications of flexibility developed at the system level. In the second survey (Pehkonen, 1997), a minority of agencies (40 per cent) agree with the proposition that changes in personnel management can be implemented without problems. In interviews with agency managers, reform of the pay system is a clear example of implementation difficulties. Managers accept pay reform to be positive, however, and they recognise their responsibility for undertaking its application in their agencies (Temmes *et al.*, 1998).

The empirical evidence suggests that structural and systemic reforms, as such, do not necessarily produce all the intended consequences at local level. There have been some shifts towards increased flexibility but simultaneously there are other factors restricting this. These include: tightened state budgets, a rigid labour market (with very low labour mobility) and the enduring effects of a traditional administrative culture. Macro-level economic conditions of the 1990s have constrained and hindered personnel policy reforms in agencies. Expenditure cuts are a major limiting factor in human resources policies. Low labour mobility, at around three per cent (the percentage of leaving personnel) in the state administration throughout the 1990s, is a further factor. There are of course differences between agencies but only 11 per cent of agencies assess that their personnel mobility is at a high level in terms of leaving personnel. Mobility is partly caused by changes in the formal organisation. Only six per cent reported that their internal personnel mobility was at a high level (Pehkonen, 1997). According to interviewed managers, low mobility constrains the possibilities for career development in the majority of agencies (Temmes *et al.*, 1998). In a survey (Pehkonen, 1997), 71 per cent of agencies said that they had enough autonomy in their personnel administration, whilst only 31 per cent claimed that their use of human resources was flexible in practice. Generally, personnel management flexibilities do not exist in the majority of agencies. Only 38 per cent had some flexibility programmes. Programmes for personnel circulation had been used only in 29 per cent of agencies. This situation is connected with the general scarcity of personnel management specialists.

Staff unions emphasise that personnel flexibility is not an end in itself but serves to improve the productivity and results of agencies. Unions also underline the importance of collaboration and co-operation between employers and employees. Unions are critical of the use of overtime, fixed-term employment and contracting-out. According to the unions, these three forms of flexibilities tend to decrease employment which is against an essential societal goal (Ministry of Finance, 1997).

Other surveys show staff reactions to HRM flexibilities. According to surveys of 17 state agencies (Virtanen, 1997, 1998), the threat of dismissal increased between 1995–96, although the increase stopped between 1996–97. Another survey (Ylöstalo and Rahikainen, 1998), based on random sampling, shows that dismissals and threat of layoffs have been decreasing in state government since 1993. This is probably related more to tighter budgets and gradual improvement of the state economy after 1995 than to HRM flexibilities as such. It is not surprising that satisfaction with the size and structure of pay has been decreasing, with staff considering that their opportunities to influence pay increments have diminished too. Willingness to accept fixed-term appointments has also decreased. Another survey (Ylöstalo and Rahikainen, 1998) shows, during 1995–97, that new, permanent appointments have been more common in the private sector than in the public sector, where permanent appointments were more rare in municipalities than in state government. In the sample of 17 agencies, willingness to accept personal salaries increased marginally between 1995–96 and remained the same between 1996–97. The results of replicated surveys in 1996 and 1997 show that leadership culture has become tougher: commitment to work and moral commitment to organisation have diminished, whilst instrumental and alienative commitment to organisation have increased.

It is difficult to estimate whether more flexible HRM policies have had any influence on these changes in leadership and workplace culture. These attitudinal changes may also be related to the increasing workload, which respondents report in both surveys. Two out of three respondents had done overtime during a busy month and about half of those doing overtime were compensated by additional pay or free time. The amount of overtime hours in a busy month was about 21 hours and only 29 per cent report full compensation for it. Overtime was especially done by those with a permanent position in another agency but worked temporarily in a fixed-term position ie on secondment. Compensation for their work was also lower. Flexibility of working time resulted in substantial amounts of uncompensated overtime work – the work that is normally not included in productivity calculations. Other studies show that overtime rose more in state government in 1997 than in municipal government, private-service industry or private-manufacturing industry (Ylöstalo and Rahikainen, 1998). Reduction in personnel was probably the reason for this, for only in state government was the decrease of personnel bigger than the increase. More often than in other sectors, overtime was not compensated at all in state government (*ibid.*).

The growing proportion of fixed-term appointments has not affected all public officials evenly. The results of the sample of 17 agencies showed that the higher the salary, the less officials there were on fixed-term appointments. In the lowest salary group the proportion was 28 per cent but in the highest salary group the proportion was five per cent. Although those who had a permanent job in another agency seemed to work overtime more often, they were at the same time more committed to their work (see Chapter 3). It seems that this group gained most from HRM flexibilities, at the same time as agencies benefited from their committed work behaviour. There were more managers and other superiors in this group than workers. They were also mostly men, while those appointed for fixed-terms without permanent positions in another agency were mostly women. The majority of part-time workers in this data were women, confirming the general trend found in other studies. Fixed-time and part-time flexibility was mostly gender-based flexibility, as was also found in the labour force as a whole (Sutela, 1998).

One of the tenets of the doctrine of new public management is that it empowers public managers. In the sample of 17 agencies, the influence of managers on the salary of staff has been slightly increasing. This probably reflects the general trend of decentralisation in state personnel policy. It seems that personnel do not generally oppose the increase of formal authority of their manager. The increase of one's own influence on pay that is paid in addition to the base salary appears to have a weak positive correlation with the increase of the superior's influence on the respondent's salary (0.34). If respondents were more satisfied with the size of their total salary, there was also more influence by the superior on their salary (0.32). This may reflect pay flexibility in that the superior has power to pay *more* than standard pay. Also satisfaction with the pay structure increased weakly in relation to the increase of a superior's influence on the salary (0.30). Perhaps the superior's influence made the structure more transparent and more related to individual work. One's own influence on pay rises was positively related to adequacy of performance measures (0.31). Probably these measures were developed together with the criteria of additional pay. The influence on these criteria was positively related to participation in decision-making on the required quality of work output (0.30).

It seems that satisfaction of personnel with forms of flexibility was also related to cultural issues. Willingness to change employer, even if the salary did not increase, was related positively to instrumental commitment to the organisation (0.35). It seems that labour mobility was related to instrumental rather than moral commitment. Satisfaction with the size of total salary and satisfaction with pay structure were negatively correlated with a tough leadership culture (−0.33 and −0.31 respectively). Although all correlations were relatively weak, the direction of dependence is important. Given this, it is understandable that, in the sample of agencies, the presence of PRP system did not mean that the moral commitment to the organisation or to work was lower than in the absence of that system. Probably more important is how the system is applied and the management style works. The social and cultural relations between management and staff determine the legitimacy of leadership which affects the reception of performance pay and other forms of HRM flexibilities. For example, in the Finnish National Road Administration (Finnra), the leadership culture is relatively soft, with a strong human relations orientation, while the opposite is true in the case of the National Board of Patent and Registration. Both have had a PRP system for several years. A short description of the experience of Finnra helps to illustrate the difficulties in implementing one form of flexible HRM.

Since the late 1980s, Finnra has experimented and employed a PRP system. The present system is based on collective pay for units, provided the total goal of a group of units (e.g. a district) is achieved. Experiences based on interviews and surveys of both managers and personnel describe the typical problems of performance pay also found in the literature (Laine, 1998; Kolu, 1991; Lawler, 1987). PRP is often considered so small in relation to total salary that the performance bonus is not regarded as an economic incentive. In Finnra, the maximum is six per cent at individual level. As a total sum the maximum is 3.5 per cent. It is difficult to set equally difficult goals for different units. Sometimes people do not understand the outcome, because they do not have a clear picture of the goals set for their unit, nor about the criteria for performance pay. The system is considered too complex but the wish to develop more precise measures to include all the different aspects of each function would lead to an even more complex system.

There is also a free-rider problem: performance bonus is paid to units, not to individuals. In spite of this, many seem to share the conviction that collective pay unites the interests of both the individual and the unit. Competition between individuals could end up with collective loss. At the same time, collective goals are considered too abstract and distant. A permanent problem is that even if pay is related to goals, the connection between actual performance and pay is weak. It is difficult to develop measures of performance pay for administrative functions and sometimes even the given goals are inappropriate for these tasks. There is a need to refine the system in order to differentiate between different groups and individuals within the unit. The system is not flexible enough. For example, independence of work in professional positions would support individual performance pay, while group pay would be more appropriate for more interdependent work. Leaders consider performance pay and the goal-setting related to it as useful instruments for management but subordinates complain they cannot take enough part in the goal-setting. In general, all share a positive attitude towards performance pay as it provides an opportunity to give feed-back and produces additional information useful in promotion and career planning.

EVALUATION AND CONCLUSION

Flexibilities in human resources management have increased in the context of administrative decentralisation and flexibilisation of resource management. In the Finnish case, decentralisation first led to budgetary reforms together with structural reorganisations. This provided the basis for flexibility in other areas of resource management which has been a gradual process over 10 years (1987–97). The process has consisted of several partial sub-reforms which had a relatively coherent continuity. This steadiness and persistence is seen as the strength of the Finnish reforms (Pollitt *et al.*, 1997). Flexibilisation of personnel management has progressed as a 'second wave' after financial and structural reforms. So far, the structural and systemic reforms have been principally accomplished and, therefore, new tools for flexible HRM are available. However, their adoption for regular use at agency level seems to be a long-term process. There is progress but it is uneven and the full impact of the reforms cannot yet be evaluated although some signals can be observed.

Assessments of agency managers imply that flexibility in personnel management has clearly improved at the systemic level although there are still symptoms of rigidity. These include the formal procedures in advertising open civil service posts, procedures for re-employment and impossibility of dismissal in cases of sickness. From the perspective of employers, flexibility in personnel management offers tools for adapting the quantity and quality of personnel and working hours to changing needs. Previously, control of the size of personnel has been the main method for flexibilisation, because the conditions of work have been inflexible. The structural and systemic reforms of the 1990s have been positive, because they have increased the tools available in managing of people.

Reformers of personnel management believe that the positive effects of flexibility include: lower personnel costs, rising productivity, better quality of service, possibilities for improving work motivation and lower staff absence. For personnel, increased flexibility may produce better possibilities for developing skills and improve work satisfaction. These positive effects present potential advantages of flexibility. To achieve these positive results, certain general principles are useful. In the Finnish experiences, they include:

- clear principles and policies on flexibility
- gradual implementation
- tailor-made applications in agencies
- commitment of managers
- consultation and co-operation with staff
- sufficient public information
- avoidance of discrimination
- systematic support and training
- voluntary basis
- continuous monitoring and evaluation (Ministry of Finance, 1997).

The conditions for effective use of human resources flexibilities require a lot of effort and, in practice, fulfilment of all conditions is rare. The managers interviewed gave a high priority to consultation and co-operation with personnel. The most positive solutions appeared to come from 'win-win situations'. According to empirical evidence, there have been many deficiencies in the practical implementation, often leading away from the ideal win-win situation. Quite often use of personnel flexibility results in increasing uncertainties in the working conditions. This usually leads employees to oppose or resist changes, which undermines positive possibilities for flexibilisation. However, there is evidence that a legitimate leadership culture supports, for example, pay flexibility. The prevailing administrative culture and its traditional 'leadership habits' often pose limits to open and positive communication between managers and personnel groups. Also lack of a longer time perspective often limits positive use of personnel flexibilities. Further, agencies may lack money for short-term flexibility costs even in cases when long-term effects should be economically positive.

It is important to recognise the context of human resources reforms in the evaluation of personnel management and its flexibilisation. There are at least three contextual factors affecting these reforms: the development of the public economy, changes in the labour market and administrative reforms. They probably all include both enabling and constraining elements for utilising flexible human resources practices. In the 1990s, the strict constraints on public spending and tight labour market have clearly constrained the real flexibilisation of personnel management. This was particularly true for the years 1991–94. After 1994, the labour market gradually become more mobile, although increased labour mobility has appeared mostly in the private sector. Strict economic policy still continues in the public sector. Administrative reform policies have been the main drivers of flexibilising human resources management and tightened budgets have provided a further impetus. With the shift towards decentralisation of resource management, together with more agency autonomy and responsibility, these policies have contributed several systemic reforms of HRM.

While responsibility for implementing flexible human resources policies in the late 1990s is clearly in the hands of agency managers, together with personnel specialists and staff, there are still important challenges left for the 'state employer', represented in Finland by the Ministry of Finance. The Department of Personnel identifies two major challenges: the increase of staff mobility and rectification of the age imbalance within state administration. These two challenges are macro-level structural problems which cannot be solved solely at agency level. National programmes are needed to make progress in these two areas. At agency level, the challenge of developing more flexible personnel management policies and practices is also a challenge for leadership. If structural uncertainty related to some flexible practices can be diminished by legitimate leadership, efficiency gains may be made. But if it cannot, efficiency improvement by flexibilisation may strengthen instrumental orientation to work and the organisation. This orientation may undermine the ideals of public service. Neither does it support long-term improvement of organisational practices. For this reason, it is important to adjust forms of flexibility to each type of job and groups of personnel separately.

References

Hallinnon hajauttaminen (1986). *Report of the Decentralisation Committee.* Helsinki: Government Printing Office.
Hallintopolitiikan suuntalinjat *Laadukkaat palvelut, hyvä hallinto ja vastuullinen kansalaisyhteiskunta. Government Decision-in-Principle* (1998). Helsinki: Edita.
Henkilöstöpolitiikan uudistaminen (1990). *Report of the Personnel Committee.* Helsinki: Government Printing Office.
KASVIO, A. (1994). *Uusi työn yhteiskunta.* Jyväskylä: Gaudeamus.
KERÄNEN, M. (1979). *Planering av statlig personalförvaltning.* Turku: Åbo Akademi.

Markku Kiviniemi and Turo Virtanen 97

KOLU, J. (1991). *Tulospalkkiojärjestelmä osana tulosjohtamista*. Henkilöstön kokemuksia tielaitoksen tulospalkkiojärjestelmästä. Helsinki: Finnra.

LAINE, J. (1998). *Tulospalkkiojärjestelmä ja työmotivaatio tiehallinnossa*. Yleisen valtio-opin pro gradu – tutkielma. University of Helsinki.

LAWLER, E. (1987). *The Designing of Effective Reward System. Handbook of Organizational Behavior*. Englewood Cliffs: Prentice-Hall.

LUMIJÄRVI, I. (1978). *Valtionhallinnon henkilöstöhallinnon hoidon kehityspiirteet ja nykytila*. Helsinki: Ministry of Finance.

MIKKONEN, R. (1985). *Viraston toiminnan analyysi toiminnan suunnittelua varten*. Helsinki: Valtion koulutuskeskus.

MINISTRY OF FINANCE (1995). *Valtion henkilöstöstrategia*. Helsinki.

MINISTRY OF FINANCE (1997). *Uudet henkilöstöstrategiset toimintatavat*. Helsinki.

MINISTRY OF FINANCE (1998). *Tietoja valtion henkilöstöstä 1970–1997*. Helsinki.

PALM, A. and VOUTILAINEN, E. (1970). *Henkilöstöhallinto*. Jyväskylä: Gummerus.

PEHKONEN, J. (1997). *Valtion henkilöstöhallinnon tila 1997*. Espoo: Suomen Gallup.

POLLITT, C. et al. (1997). *Trajectories and Options: An International Perspective on the Implementation of Finnish Public Management Reforms*. Helsinki: Ministry of Finance.

SUTELA, H. (1998). ?Muutoksia määräaikaisuudessa?, Hyvinvointikatsaus 2/1998: 24–7.

TEMMES, M. et al. (1998). *Henkilöstöpolitiikan uusi tuleminen*. Helsinki: Ministry of Finance.

VEPSÄLÄINEN, K. (1994). *Henkilöstön kehittäminen ankarassa muutospaineessa*. Helsinki: Government Printing Office.

VIRTANEN, T. (1997). *Johtamiskulttuurin muutos ja tuloksellisuus*. Valtionhallinnon uudistumisen seurantatutkimus 1995–98. First Report. Helsinki: Ministry of Finance.

VIRTANEN, T. (1998). *Johtamiskulttuurin muutos ja tuloksellisuus*. Valtionhallinnon uudistumisen seurantatutkimus 1995–98. Second Report. Helsinki: Ministry of Finance.

YLÖSTALO, P. and RAHIKAINEN, O. (1998). *Työolobarometri. Lokakuu 1997*. Työpoliittinen tutkimus 186. Helsinki: Ministry of Labour.

6 Human Resources Flexibilities in France

June Burnham

The French public sector is large by OECD standards; about a quarter of the French workforce is in public employment. The state provides a wider variety of utilities than in most west European countries, including electricity, gas, rail, post and telephone services, airlines, even a commercial bank. The French public service has a positive image, as witnessed in November 1995, when life in Paris and other cities was made difficult by public sector strikes and demonstrations, and yet support from the public remained strong. Despite their complaints about poor service from *guichets* (counters), parents want their children to become public servants, and only in part because of the stable career a mainly tenured service offers. The service has a feeling of self esteem, based on its undoubted contribution to France's economic development, territorial cohesion and even identity as a Republic at periods when political executives were weak. It has only recently begun to realise that it is not self-evidently a model for others in Europe and that it must fight to retain its special place in French society.

It is not just chance that the biggest moves towards more flexible structures, away from narrowly defined *corps* (occupational groups), and grades within *corps*, towards posts remunerated on the basis of responsibilities held or jobs done, can be seen in the public enterprises forced to adapt to an increasingly deregulated European Union. But it would be wrong to underestimate the internal demands for reform, especially by those responsible for managing delivery of services, whether in public enterprises, technical *grands corps*, ministries at field level (including the prefects) or local government. However, the public service background of many of today's political elite, typified by the President, Jacques Chirac, graduate of the Ecole Nationale d'Administration (ENA) and member of the *Cour des Comptes* (one of the top five *grands corps*), is as much a hindrance as a help to long lasting reform. Members of the higher corps have the capacity to resist or to promote change in the public service. But the *grands corps*, especially the administrative *grands corps*, are uninterested in managerial reform (Rouban, 1994: 12). It offers them no further reward and they are not in daily contact with practical issues of service delivery. ENA, which trains these officials, is particularly criticised because it offers 'its excellent students exceptionally good careers' with no incentive to invest their talents 'in the conception and management of innovation and change' (Nioche, 1995: 456). Reforms are generally stimulated by associations of more middle-ranking civil servants (*Services Publics*), groups of experts nominated on political grounds (Rouban, 1998: 33), and those nearest to the ground (Serieyx, 1994: xvii).

Unions too play a significant part in public personnel policies, since elected representatives of unions have had a statutory place since 1946 in discussions over pay and conditions of service. Though overall union membership is low at about 20 per cent (40 per cent in the education sector) (Chambron, 1993: 151) and fragmented between umbrella groups that reflect ideology or career status (Communist, Socialist, Catholic, middle management, education among others), any deal has to have the signature of a majority of unions. However, they are in competition with each other and undecided about their best strategies to retain members. On the one hand, unionists are seen by modernisers as holding back the type of 'public service' demanded by the public as shown by user surveys (*ibid.*: 151–2). On the other, the authority of the negotiators is contested by smaller unions at the grassroots defending the traditional statute (Rouban, 1998: 102). Unions resist breaches in the national system of career management, and block attempts at delegation and differentiation which are often the basis of flexibilisation, because their place at the statutory negotiating table is their main source of power (Chevallier, 1996: 200). Research on radical changes to employment conditions at France Télécom in the early 1990s showed that the relationship between unions and managers was not corporatist or even co-operative. Reforms took place because both sides agreed they did not want a solution to be imposed by the market (Reynaud and Reynaud, 1996: 111).

Luc Rouban (1998: 98) notes that modernisation of the French public services is not like that carried out elsewhere, for two main reasons. First, the free-market ideology held sway for only a short period in France. Second, reforms have been cut short by changes in political power, and each government's desire to do something dif-

Table 6.1   Staff in the French public sector in 1995

Public enterprises and bodies	1,830,000
Social security bodies	220,000
Central government staff	2,200,000
Local government staff	1,300,000
Hospitals	840,000
	6,390,000

Source: Ministère de la Fonction Publique
website, October 1998.

ferent from its predecessor, which French officials themselves describe as the 'stop-go' rhythm of reform. 'What is missing from reforms is duration' (Lebeschu, 1995: 452). 'In France one always comes up against the absence of political will over time' (Barouch and Chavas, 1993: 168).

STATUTORY AND CONTRACTUAL FLEXIBILITIES

The archetypal French public servant is a full-time tenured official (*fonctionnaire*) working for one of three 'public services': (1) the 'State public service' (*fonction publique de l'Etat*) of officials working in ministries and in some other administrative bodies; (2) the local government service (*fonction publique territoriale*) of officials working for elected local authorities and associated bodies; and (3) the hospital service (*fonction publique hospitalière*). Teaching personnel, including university lecturers, and most police officers are part of the State service; some school maintenance staff and other police officers belong to the local government service. Officials can move between the services, though few do so, because they share a basic 'general public service statute', revised in 1983 after decentralisation reforms. There are supplementary statutes for each service, amended from time to time.

Concentrating on the three public services might give a false impression of the French public sector, though some would argue that focusing on the core administration provides a better test of flexibility. Such an examination, however, would neglect flexibility gained from creating autonomous enterprises out of former ministries by alterations to the general statute, or flexibility provided by delivering services through such public bodies as the *Caisses d'allocations familiales* (CAF, supporting families), in which only the national director and finance officer are regulated by public law: their other staff are regulated by private employment law. In 1990 a new legal category (*exploitant public*) was invented for the Post Office and France Télécom, allowing serving *fonctionnaires* the right to remain *fonctionnaires* but outside the 'State public service'. They kept guarantees of tenure in exchange for accepting derogations from the standard *corps* structure, provided for in the 1984 statute of the 'State public service'. The nature of the bargain indicates flexibility within the statutes but also the reluctance of the public service to give up acquired positions, even under pressure of competition from French and other European operators.

In France any post that is not full-time, tenured and mapped-out is termed *emploi précaire* (precarious or insecure) which emphasises the negative aspects of flexibilisation, especially the risk of becoming unemployed. The positive aspects, however, for individuals, are a greater range of activities and responsibilities during a working life, working conditions which fit better with private life, the chance of being promoted more quickly and earning more if it is merited. For managers and employers it offers ways of using staff to best effect, according to their talents and availability and to respond to the ever-changing expectations of citizens and other parts of the public service.

In France tenure gives an official permanent entitlement to a post appropriate for his or her grade. Abolition of a post does not make the incumbent official redundant: the administration has to find a new post for the official at the same grade. The general public service statute restricts the use of non-tenured staff by making tenure a principle or norm. There were programmes giving tenure to serving non-tenured officials in 1950, 1964, 1975, 1983 and 1996, but these programmes never achieved their goals, because the practical needs of the service means new non-tenured staff are appointed, which in their turn lead to new plans to give tenure.

The public service statute allows some exceptions to full-time, tenured appointment, for example for discretionary appointments that allow political or individual preference. Ministers can nominate holders of about 450 director-level posts in ministries and in certain public bodies. Council leaders can nominate the holders of a range of posts, depending on the size of the council or services. In both cases, people appointed from the private sector are given a contract for an indefinite term (*contrat . . . durée indéterminée*) which can be brought

Table 6.2   Tenured and non-tenured staff in the
French public sector

Central government (in 1995)	
Tenured staff	1,629,000
Industrial staff	80,000
Non-tenured staff	200,000
	2,200,000
Local government (in 1994)	
Tenured staff	880,000
Non-tenured staff	330,000
Maternity home help	56,000
	1,266,000

Source: Ministère de la Fonction Publique
website, October 1998 (for central government)
and August 1998 (for local government).

to an end at any time. However, most such appointees are *fonction-naires*, who always have tenure. In central government their tempo-rary transfer (*détachement*), can be ended by the minister at any moment, and their *corps* finds them another post in their grade. This provision adds political flexibility to top appointments, profiting from the pool of reserve talent constituted by officials with a permanent place in a *corps*. In local government, displaced *fonctionnaires* are paid by the CNFPT (centre for the management of local government careers), whilst it finds them another post appropriate for their grade. This mechanism gave the leaders of autonomous councils real powers of appointment following the decentralisation laws of the early 1980s, while nevertheless assuring officials of a stable career or at least a con-tinued salary, since no council has the obligation to 'pick up' a dis-placed director.

More common exceptions to full-time tenure are fixed-term con-tracts and temporary posts, as well as part-time working (discussed later). Ministries and local government can engage staff on renewable three-year contracts, regulated by public law, if no existing *corps* has the capacity to fulfil the function, perhaps for innovative jobs. Local authorities are more likely to recruit non-tenured staff, as Table 6.2 makes clear. Over a quarter of their staff are non-tenured, whereas only 10 per cent of central government staff, nearly all teachers, are non-tenured.

Procedures for appointing temporary and contracted staff in local government are not so cumbersome as the competitive examination procedures for recruiting tenured staff but still provide only limited flexibility. A temporary official replacing a *fonctionnaire* who is sick or on training leave must have the same level of qualifications and abilities and is paid on the same range of the salary scale, though perhaps at its lower end. To recruit staff through three-year contracts, the council must make a formal decision on each case, specifying the terms of the job, its level of responsibility, the necessary qualifications, and show that no *corps* and grade can fill it. The salary scale must be fixed in accordance with these criteria, limiting cost-savings. In practice, human resources managers say, very few contracts can now be justified on the basis that no grade can fill the post, except for some specialised senior jobs (say, advising how to restore a historic area) which command high market salaries, and for some basic temporary or seasonal jobs paid at the national minimum wage. There is some argument between the experts interviewed on whether salary scales are mostly based on those of a tenured official and whether savings on 'bonuses' normally paid to *fonctionnaires* might outweigh the cost of employers' social security and health contributions (much higher than for fonctionnaires). In central government, the number of non-tenured staff has declined faster since the mid-1970s than the number of tenured staff (MFPRA, 1992: 184). Neither local nor central government are deliberately using contracts on any significant scale to replace tenured officials.

PART-TIME AND FLEXIBLE WORKING HOURS

As Table 6.3 indicates, local authorities are freer than ministries to use part-time working to provide extra staff at peak periods or to perform jobs that do not require a full week's work, an essential provision for thousands of small communes. They can create posts specially for *fonctionnaires* (*temps incomplet* or officials with part-time tenure). This facility does not exist in the 'State public service' but full-time tenured officials in all parts of the public service may be authorised to work part-time (*temps partiel*). From 1982 state officials could choose to work half-time as they near retirement and about one-third now take that option. These provisions were widened in 1994 to meet the needs of families and reduce unemployment. Part-time working can be demanded as a right for parents of children under three and

Table 6.3   Full-time and part-time staff in French
central and local government

Central government 1990 (excluding Post and Telephone)		
Full time	2,047,800	
Progressive retirement	14,400	
Other part-time	181,400	(9%)
	2,243,600	
Local government 1994		
Full-time	904,000	
Part-time	362,000	(29%)
	1,266,000	

Notes: December 1990 for central government;
January 1994 for local officials.
Source: Ministère de la Fonction Publique, 1992;
and August 1998 website.

in some other difficult family circumstances. Other staff can request a change to part-time working for up to three years, increased from one year pre-1994. Managers were invited to reorganise their offices to facilitate part-time working, and promised that gaps created would receive priority for allocation of replacement *fonctionnaires*. However, the Inspectorate-General of Administration 1998 report confirmed that the 'State public service was still backward in its recruitment of part-time permanent staff in comparison not only with the private sector but with local councils' (*Le Monde*, 30 January 1998). At present a head of service can refuse a request for part-time working on imprecise grounds ('the needs of the service') but a head of service who sees a use for part-time working has to wait for a full-time member of staff to make a request or depend on the central department allocating a suitable official. Mayors of rural communes also complain that their more flexible arrangements do not go far enough, since officials are not permitted to combine their public law work for the commune with private sector employment to provide a reasonable living.

However, some examples of the good use of part-time and short-term contracts to provide flexibility have been reported, notably in public sector organisations outside the 'three public services': in the CAFs, EDF (electricity) and Post Office (Lamarque, 1992; *Le Monde*,

12–13 January 1997; Mouret, 1994). Mouret's research on the Post Office showed that new part-time and short-term recruits were a-ccepted most easily by serving officials when used 'to deal with peak flows and provide holiday cover or where treated almost like a traditional apprenticeship, with a view to permanent employment, in a way that did not threaten existing employees' (*ibid.*: 151–2). The 1992 report of the French government's standing Committee of Inquiry into the Effectiveness of the Public Services showed that many types of administration were using working hours flexibly, for example decoupling staff working time from the times that services were open to the public. CAFs, whose staff are employed under private law, were particularly praised for introducing a variety of formulae such as annual hours. The report concluded that the obstacles to more flexibility in working hours were rarely 'social' (unions) or practical, but stemmed from 'a too rigid or traditionalist notion of the organisation of work in the public services' (Lamarque, 1992: 187). Six years later the annual report of the Inspectorate-General of Administration showed that introduction of flexitime had led to '*guichets*' being open to the public for fewer hours, because service heads found it too complicated to organise varying work schedules, and so limited opening times to core periods (*Le Monde*, 30 January 1998). Part-time working also creates particular problems in France because nearly half the part-timers want the same formula (80 per cent and not Wednesdays) since schools are often closed on Wednesday afternoon.

Even those in favour of part-time and short-term contracts stress the drawbacks (Rigaudiat, 1994: 124–6). The legal position is often unclear. Staff are sometimes recruited on dubious bases: temporary contracts for long term positions, training funds or 'pseudo research contracts'. A tribunal decision in 1996 that a canteen worker on a private law contract was an 'administrative official' embarrassingly added to official government statistics 20,000 people 'previously masked by being paid on various, varied budgets' (*Le Monde*, 14 October 1998). The Rigaudiat report said there needed to be a proper legal regime for non-tenured staff, either based on the general statute within public law or within private employment law. From an Anglo-Saxon viewpoint, there seems to be too much emphasis on looking for the ideal legal provisions, especially since half a million non-tenured officials already work in central and local government service as managers try to find ways to meet the demands of a modern service, demands from users, staff, senior managers and ministers. But it is likely that the debate over legal provisions hides a deeper debate over the uncertainties for the tenured public service that a policy of contracted employment would create. It is clear that the statute, like all 'written constitutions' slows down change, that is its role. However, as the Rigaudiat report emphasises, the statute is not a straitjacket: its provisions would allow 'dynamic job management' (1994: 134). It is rather the 'too rigid and traditionalist' notion of what constitutes 'public service' that needs to adapt, i.e. the administrative culture. The use of part-time and flexible working hours is still considered almost entirely from the point of view of public servants rather than of their clients.

CAREER AND JOB MOBILITY

The traditional rigidity of the French public service is expressed too in the annual finance law, which specifies the 'budgeted posts' (authorised posts) for each ministry, by division, by statute, by hierarchical category, between Paris and field services, and by status (tenured, contractual, auxiliary, temporary). This is suitable for a hierarchical, centralised system but not for the decentralising and managerial reforms promoted by governments since the 1980s. Cut-back formulae have been added since 1983, which direct divisions to freeze one in every two, three or four vacancies, or even all vacancies (1992). There are certain exemptions each year for priority categories (teachers in 1993), and the ministry of finance applies the rules 'with a certain flexibility' (Rigaudiat, 1994: 38). Yet it is difficult to see much room to manoeuvre at service level, especially as most ministries still allocate people to posts from the centre.

Mobility between posts

French officials are usually said to be fundamentally mobile because they are not recruited to a post, but possess a grade in a corps and can be transferred to any post corresponding to that grade and *corps* (Bodiguel, 1994: 77; Reynaud and Reynaud, 1996: 108). Separation of posts and grades provides a more flexible system than existed before 1946, when people could not be promoted to a higher grade unless a corresponding post was vacant and could not be appointed to a post of a higher grade unless they fulfilled the conditions for changing grade. In practice, officials can now refuse the first two appropriate postings; however, if they fail to accept the third they could be made redundant. The SNCF (railways) has relied chiefly on mobility to minimise staff reductions as it adjusts to European competition. It encourages requests for transfers to other areas or public organisations, gives training to enable an official to move to a vacant post in a higher grade, and requires junior managers to change their location and *métier* as a condition of promotion (Rigaudiat, 1994: 229–31).

There are some special mobility procedures, of which two add flexibility within the service: '*detachement*' and '*mise . . . disposition*'. This involves temporary transfer or secondment to another ministry, local authority, public enterprise or agency, which is new or expanding, or sees the usefulness of having an official with different experiences and contacts. For instance, in 1988 about 36,000 ministry officials were on *détachement* (about 1.5 per cent of State officials), including 17,000 in the French public sector, 16,000 abroad and 2,000 training for access to a different part of the public service (MFPRA, 1992: 288–9). *Détachement* is used to allow ministers to nominate *fonctionnaires* to about 400 posts in central administrations (deputy director and below). This provision is more about flexibility than politicisation, because it reduces the monopoly of certain *corps* over particular posts, and gives an element of reward and risk, since the minister can end the posting at any moment, when the official returns to a conventional post (Bodiguel, 1994: 72).

An OECD-PUMA survey (1997) of senior officials showed French officials move as frequently as UK civil servants and more frequently than those of other countries. However they move less frequently between ministries than officials in the Netherlands and UK, which is probably because of the influence of the *corps* over certain posts. Mobility is restricted by fragmentation of the public service into 1,700 *corps*; by complicated regulations that *corps* use to keep others out and a complex remuneration package difficult to reorganise. Other reasons include the consequences for families and especially the lack of information on vacancies. A real public jobs market does not exist in France (Bodiguel, 1994: 77–8). On the other hand, some senior officials say there is too much mobility, especially of senior managers, which leads to short-termism, to abandoning reform projects before they are well-rooted, and to destabilising managerial teams (Serieyx, 1994: xxii; DGAFP, 1993: 24). One prefect has spoken of setting himself six-month timescales to avoid disillusion (Lebeschu, 1995: 452–3). These observations are confirmed by the OECD-PUMA survey, where directors average four to five years in post and prefects only two years. But distinctions must be made (1) between geographic mobility and mobility of posts (the range of tasks people are prepared to do, either within the same office, or one after the other during their career); and (2) between different categories of officials.

Mobility between functions

Since the late 1980s, efforts have been made to reduce the barriers between *corps* and grades so that officials could perform a wider range of functions. The important 1990 pay-and-reform package (Durafour *accord*) included a protocol to reduce the number of *corps*. The only example found of a ministry undertaking a sustained project to combine *corps* was the Ministry of Agriculture (Barouch and Chavas, 1993: 128, 131). In other ministries change has been slow and the easiest groups, such as office support staff, were tackled first (DGAFP, 1993: 23; Quarr, 1997: 23). There were renewed government pleas in 1995 for fusion of *corps* within each ministry, and for common conditions of service across ministries to be developed to facilitate future mergers.

Some ministries, such as the Ministry of Education together with the Ministry of Youth and Sports, have changed from trying to fuse existing *corps* towards introducing broader groups based on professional skills, qualifications and competencies. The change of status of the Post Office and France Télécom in 1990 was accompanied by a radical restructuring of functions into 11 grades up career ladders based on 'professional domains', which give staff who opted to switch to the new system easier upward mobility and wider horizontal mobility between functions. The local government service in 1993 has drawn up lists of *métiers*, professional specialisms that include more than one *corps*, to aid mobility between different local authorities. In 1998, all five unions at ONERA, an aerospace research establishment, agreed to use 'classifying criteria' to sort officials into two occupational groups: engineer-research and management-administration, each with seven vertical levels according to the competencies required (*Le Monde*, 11 February 1998).

However, ONERA was forced to become functionally flexible to ease links with larger public research organisations such as the *Centre National de la Recherche Scientifique* (CNRS) after the fall of the Berlin wall made defence research vulnerable. The official Rigaudiat report (1994: 98–9) noted that a working group, organised by the Ministry of Public Service in 1990 (the Mariotte Group), had concluded that the traditional hierarchical classification, based on educational qualifications was outmoded. However, the group decided it would be inappropriate in central government to move to a system of 'classification criteria' like those being adopted in France Télécom and elsewhere, because of its potential expense, and the risk of creating a 'post-based' public service, a prospect which seemed unthinkable. Yet even pessimists think the Post and Télécom reforms might start a trend (Chevallier, 1996: 201).

PAY FLEXIBILITIES

Pay is determined at national level for the 'three public services': central government, local government and hospitals. Public enterprises conduct their own negotiations but still at national level. There is no current consideration of bargaining at local level over pay. However, in 1996 the then right-wing government suggested that other personnel issues could be dealt with at local level, which perhaps might lead eventually to decentralisation of pay bargaining. But the opposite, much stronger movement in the late 1980s and early 1990s to 'nationalise' and 'standardise' careers in the local authority service, in the name of equality and mobility, reflects more accurately the views of the French public services on flexibilisation of salary determination.

National pay determination

Levels of salaries are determined after a real process of collective bargaining between union representatives and employers, and then fixed by government decree. For the 'three public services' the employer is the minister for the public service; for state industries the relevant supervisory *'tutelle'* minister, for example the transport minister for the SNCF. Negotiations take place within parameters set by the prime minister and the political executive, heavily influenced by national budgetary requirements. But the government by no means gets what it wants, as shown by major strikes in November 1995, when up to two million people demonstrated against proposed changes to mechanisms for deciding public sector pensions, a reform that had, exceptionally, not been previously debated with the unions: the reform was dropped. On even minor changes on pay, staff-employer representative bodies have a statutory right to be consulted and changes must be submitted to parliament.

This system is flexible in being a genuine bargaining process across a broad range of personnel issues, including pay, in which representatives of public servants and government yield on some things to get other things they feel more important. There is flexibility in pay determination in that the bargainers find all sorts of ways to add bonuses, or adjust pay scales, to find what seems to them a fair balance. Indeed 'national' determination is a better term than 'central' determination because the outcome goes a long way to recognising grass-roots demands across the country. But there is inflexibility in that it is in the interests of the union leadership to keep pay determination at national level (Chevallier, 1996: 199) and the unions themselves are a significant cause of inflexibility in human resource management (Chambron, 1993: 151). There is inflexibility too in that national bargainers are deciding on fine detail. There is not much left for local managers of human resources to decide.

The remuneration structure for the 'three public services' is in principle simple and logical. There is a common pay scale of 'index points' (*grille indiciaire*), running from 100 to 800 which applies across the tenured service and to many non-tenured officials whose pay is linked to the scale. Annual pay negotiations determine the value in francs of the index point 100. Each grade in a *corps* has a minimum and maximum index point. Officials start at the lowest index point for their grade and, providing their performance is satisfactory, they move upwards through the scales. However, pay bargaining has spoilt the purity of the system. No one earns the theoretical minimum and many senior posts have salaries fixed beyond the scale, in francs. The difference between the lowest pay actually being paid to an official and the highest-paid is now about 1 : 6.5 (Bodiguel, 1994: 79). A far greater distortion to the scale is provided by the complex array of allowances and bonuses. In 1990 they were worth on average 20 per cent of total basic salary plus housing allowance, varying from nine per cent for unqualified manual workers to 52 per cent for very senior technical officials (Rigaudiat, 1994: 180–1), with an upwards trend since 1980 (Bodiguel, 1994: 80).

FLEXIBILITY IN PAY PROGRESSION

Pay progression is still dominated by incremental progression up the scales according to years of service, provided the appraisal mark (*note*) given by the line manager confirms 'that the manner in which the official works gives satisfaction' (MFPRA, 1992: 171). Some characterise notation as almost value-less (DGAFP, 1993: 23; Chambron, 1993: 167; Barouch and Chavas, 1993: 257) and it does seem at the mercy of formulae (a mark 10 per cent higher than average accelerates pay progress by one month but only for a maximum of half the officials in each *corps*; a mark 20 per cent higher accelerates it by two months for a maximum of a third of officials). Most allowances and bonuses are independent of performance or the particular demands of a post. But the 'new index bonus', which formed part of the Durafour reforms agreed in 1990, broke new ground in adding index points to the point on the salary scales reached by an official, in recognition for holding certain posts (manager, team leader, requiring specific technical competence). And there are tentative moves towards using bonuses and advances up the salary scales for working in more difficult conditions, such as in run-down urban areas. But individualisation of rewards remains rare.

The idea of performance incentives was in the minds of certain politicians and civil servants, notably in the 'modernising programme' led by the Rocard government after 1988. But it was easier to introduce collective rather than individual performance rewards, for instance office refurbishing or social welfare programmes. However, reports in the 1990s have shown that many senior officials think performance pay is a management tool they should have. The survey by Luc Rouban in the early 1990s found that two-thirds of senior officials considered that performance-related pay was essential for effective management. Younger people and technical *corps*, especially in the Post Office, France Télécom and the *Ponts et Chaussées*, were more willing personally to accept evaluation and its consequences for pay. But 21 per cent of the sample thought it went against their statute to be paid on performance (Rouban, 1994: 227). 'In the current state of things, it is contrary to the statute to be better paid' said one official (*ibid.*: 226).

France Télécom has been cited above as relatively revolutionary in its efforts to base officials' pay more on the post held – the functions performed and the competencies required – than on a grade within a *corps*. But part of the bargain made with the unions when this enterprise was created was that officials could keep their status as *fonctionnaire*. This exchange gave the stability and security offered by the statute which made other flexibilities more acceptable (Reynaud and Reynaud, 1996: 108). Though national pay arrangements are inflexible compared with more decentralised forms of bargaining that take place elsewhere, the pay negotiating process is used in France to promote other reforms in HRM. For example, the pivotal Durafour *accord* in 1990 (Ministére de la Fonction Publique: 1991) included a protocol to combine or close *corps* that would increase job mobility and versatility (though it has a long way to go), and to phase out the least qualified category of officials to achieve a better qualified though more costly workforce, more able to adjust to changing needs. Similar bargains in the Post Office and France Télécomhave facilitated a transition from a structure based on grades to one based on jobs and the relevant competencies.

CONCLUSION

The traditional argument is that tenure, with uniform conditions of work, guaranteed and sanctified by the state, is one side of the employment bargain and willingness to be mobile, to train, to be functionally flexible, is the other side. Certainly the France Télécom experience shows officials were more willing to shift to new, more flexible, but more risky structures because their jobs were not in question. But many examples given above show that the bargain favours the officials' side: they are more permanent than flexible. The Post Office and France Télécom, to succeed with their changes, had to guarantee officials that their new conditions of service would never be worse than their old ones. Almost all successful reforms have been the product of external forces: European competition for the 'network industries'; the budgetary effort to fulfil European currency conditions; family policy and unemployment policy have given civil servants the right to work part time. This feature of the French public service (but not only the French public service), not to feel within itself the need to move with the times, is seen as problematic. Many officials are convinced of the need for reform, especially in the technical *corps* and those closer to service delivery in local government and the field services. But it does not yet seem fully to be appreciated by the topmost officials or even by the 'street-level bureaucrats' of central ministries (see Bodiguel, 1996).

The groups who could drive change most easily are the top administrative *corps*, who are themselves flexible in the jobs they do – but who see nothing to gain from general reform. Even they are handicapped by changes in political direction, which have become more frequent since the mid-1980s. However, governments too need to reflect on the ends and the means of public service reform. As Luc Rouban says: 'If staff numbers are used primarily to manage macro-economic policy, modernisation of the public sector is bound to fail' (1998: 104). Such a short-sighted policy only confirms to the bulk of the public sector that 'flexibility' equals 'vulnerability': an attack on the public service rather than a means for it to adapt to an ever-evolving world.

Acknowledgement

The author would like to thank her friend and colleague Professor Jean-Luc Bodiguel of CRUARAP, Nantes University, for his thoughtful and constructive criticism of the draft chapter.

References

BAROUCH, G. and CHAVAS, H. (1993). *Ou va la Modernisation? Dix ans de modernisation de l'administration d'Etat en France.* Paris: L'Harmattan.
BODIGUEL, J.-L. (1994). *Les fonctions publiques dans l'Europe des douze.* Paris: LGDJ.
BODIGUEL, J.-L. (1996). 'Les fonctionnaires en proie au changement', in Gremion, C. and Fraisse, R. (eds), *Le Service public en recherche: Quelle modernisation?* Paris: La Documentation française.
CHAMBRON, N. (1993). 'Les Syndicats dans la modernisation de la fonction publique'. *Politiques et Management Public.* 11/1, pp 149–71.
CHEVALLIER, J. (1996). 'La reforme de l'Etat et la conception française du service public'. *Revue Française d'Administration Publique.* 77, pp 189–205.
DGAFP (1993). Direction Générale de l'Administration et de la Fonction Publique. *Documents d'étude sur la modernisation de l'administration.* Paris: La Documentation française.
LAMARQUE, D. (1992). 'L'apport de l'aménagement du temps de travail a 'l'amélioration de l'acceuil dans les services publics'. *Politiques et Management Public.* 10/2, pp 187–92.
LEBESCHU, J. (1995). Intervention in 'La Modernisation administrative en France: bilan et perspectives: débat'. *Revue Française d'Administration Publique.* 75, pp 449–58.
Le Monde, 12–13 February 1997. *Frédéric Lemaître.* 'EDF-GDF va proposer le passage – 32 heures – 40,000 agent'.
Le Monde, 30 January 1998. *Rafa % le Rivais.* 'Horaires variables: tout pour les agents, rien pour le public'.
Le Monde, 11 February 1998. (Anon.) 'D'peches: Classification'.
Le Monde, 14 October 1998. Rafa % le Rivais. 'Vingt mille employes de la fonction publique vont obtenir des CDI', p 36.

MFPRA (1992). Ministère de la Fonction Publique et des Reformes Administratives. *La Fonction publique de l'Etat 1992*. Paris: La Documentation française.

MINISTÉRE DE LA FONCTION PUBLIQUE (1991). *La Fonction Publique de L'Etat Rapport Annuel 1991* Paris: La Documentation français, pp 15–26.

MOURET, B. (1994). 'Flexibilité et changement à la Poste'. *Politiques et Management Public*. 12/3, pp 143–58.

NIOCHE, J.-P. (1995). Intervention in 'La Modernisation administrative en France: bilan et perspectives: débat'. *Revue Française d'Administration Publique*. 75, pp 449–58.

OECD-PUMA (1997). *Managing the Senior Public Service: A Survey of OECD Countries*. Paris: OECD.

QUARR, D. (1997). *La Fonction publique de l'Etat en 1993, 1994 et 1995*. Paris: INSEE.

REYNAUD, E. and REYNAUD, J.-D. (1996). 'March, du travail interne et organisation. La modernisation de France Télécom dans une perspective comparative', in Gremion, C. and Fraisse, R. (eds), *Le Service public en recherche: Quelle modernisation?* Paris: La Documentation française.

RIGAUDIAT, J. (1994). *Gérer l'emploi public*. Paris: La Documentation française.

ROUBAN, L. (1994). *Les Cadres superieurs de la fonction publique et la politique de modernisation administrative*. Paris: DGAFP and CGP.

ROUBAN, L. (1998). *La Fin des technocrates?* Paris: Presses de Sciences Po.

SERIEYX, H. (1994). *L'Etat dans tous ses projets*. Paris: La Documentation française.

7 Germany: the Limitations of Flexibility Reforms

Manfred Röber and Elke Löffler*

Given the fiscal deficits resulting from German re-unification in 1991, administrative reforms in Germany have been driven by the need to make savings. This implied downsizing on the one hand and an emphasis on the flexibilisation of resource management on the other hand. Personnel was mainly seen as a cost factor. However, the limits of a purely instrumental approach to administrative reforms soon become apparent as the hoped for efficiency gains did not materialise quickly enough. Administrative leaders of reform projects became more and more aware that they had failed to take politicians as well as personnel into consideration. According to a survey of the German Association of Cities in 1994, 70 per cent of staff in West German cities indicated that they were highly sceptical about administrative reforms. In a second survey in 1996, the number of public servants at local level, who were resistant to the changes had fallen to 50 per cent but in 1998 the figure increased again to 54 per cent. In East German cities staff members' scepticism towards administrative reform has been growing stradily, from 24 per cent in 1994–95, to 29 per cent in 1996 and 45 per cent in 1998 (Grömig and Thielen, 1996; Grömig and Gruner, 1998).

There is an increasing awareness in German public administration that personnel is also a key to productivity. It has to be reduced in size, but at the same time it is necessary to motivate staff better in order to unleash their hidden productivity potential. At present, this new thinking manifests itself in two major strands of personnel management reforms in the German public administration. The reform of the civil service law in 1997 has introduced elements of performance-related pay to increase the extrinsic motivation of senior civil servants in state administration. At local level, many municipalities are experimenting with 'soft' personnel management instruments such as employee surveys, employee dialogue, performance agreements between superiors and employees in order to improve the intrinsic motivation of public servants. Both forms of flexibility remain limited: in state administration, the introduction of some limited pay flexibility has occurred in the absence of modern human resource management (HRM), whereas at local level municipalities with modern HRM may not reward individual productivity and performance.

This chapter seeks to explain why the German public service is still relatively inflexible compared to the British civil service and comprehensive civil service reform is difficult to achieve. As the chapter shows, modernisation rather than structural transformation is the issue dominating the German public service at the present time.

A SINGLE CIVIL SERVICE AS A GUIDING PRINCIPLE

Germany's administrative system is to a large extent moulded by the country's constitutional principles. These are federalism which defines the *Länder* as members of the Federation yet retaining a sovereign state power of their own and local self-government which mainly operates on two levels, that of local authorities and counties (Wagener, 1990). Unlike in unitary states, central government only plays a moderate role in the direct administration and provision of public services. Most public services are administered by the 16 states (*Bundesländer*) and their 324 counties (*Landkreise*), 112 county boroughs (*kreisfreie Städte*) and nearly 15,000 local authorities (*Gemeinden*). The majority of local authorities are organised in local authorities' associations (*Gemeindeverbände*) in order to strengthen their administrative capacities. Moreover, public agencies as executing institutions and part of the indirect state administration (*Körperschaften, Anstalten* and *Stiftungen*) are responsible for special public duties for the whole area of the Federal Republic of Germany – like the Federal Labour Corporation (*Bundesanstalt für Angestellte*) or the Federal Insurance Corporation for Salaried Employees (*Bundesversicherungsanstalt für Angestellte*). These agencies which are governed by public law and at arm's length have a fairly high degree of autonomy which is more or less comparable to that of the British agencies established in the Next Steps Programme.

Due to the prevailing constitutional principles of federalism and local self-government, German public administration is considerably varied and complex. This framework has given rise to a whole variety of subnational peculiarities which diverge more or less in their administrative cultures. Nevertheless, the core elements of the German civil service are relatively uniform for public servants at all levels of government, with the term 'public servant' being used as a generic term to include civil servants (*Beamte*) as well as public employees (*Angestellte*) and public workers (*Arbeiter*). The reason is that the Federation has the right to determine the legal status of all public servants according to article 75, paragraph 1, Basic Law, as part of general legislation (*Rahmengesetzgebung des Bundes*) and to make decisions relating to pay and pensions for civil servants according to article 74a, paragraph 1, Basic Law, as part of concurrent legislation (*konkurrierende Gesetzgebung*). This means that unlike other federal states such as Canada and the United States, Germany has one single civil service. This lack of inter-governmental flexibility is justified with the need to avoid 'destructive competition' between vertical administrative levels as well as between states (*Länder*) or local authorities.

The prevailing philosophy of the civil service is enshrined in the German constitution especially by 'reserving to civil servants the right to act on behalf of the state' (article 33, paragraph 4, Basic Law) and by emphasising the traditional principles of the professional civil service (article 33, paragraph 5, Basic Law) (see Siedentopf, 1990: 237). Although there is no clearly defined enumeration of elements constituting the traditional principles of the professional civil service, some features are widely seen as characteristic such as lifetime occupation, an appropriate salary according to the maintenance principle (*Alimentationsprinzip*), loyalty, political neutrality and moderation, dedication to public service, no right to strike and subjection to special disciplinary regulations.

The traditional principles of the professional civil service only apply to civil servants (*Beamte*) and are not aimed at regulating the legal status of public employees (*Angestellte*) and public workers (*Arbeiter*). While the legal status of civil servants is based on public law with strict duties and sanctions, specific pay, health-care and pension systems, specific pre-entry-training and a cadre system with a career pathway, public employees and workers are subject to private sector law and public sector industrial relations. The dual employment structure of the public service is part of Germany's historical traditions. Due to these traditions, posts for civil servants have been established for law and order functions and must be reserved for them – according to article 33, paragraph 4, Basic Law. Even though the dual employment structure made sense in the last century, it has become less and less appropriate and relevant, since the boundaries between the two categories of service law have become increasingly blurred in practice. The vast majority of the 5.3 million people in the public sector in 1996 were either public employees (2.5 million) or public workers (0.8 million), with only 1.9 million being civil servants (Table 7.1).

The German career system is divided into four standard career structures which are the administrative class (*höherer Dienst*), executive class (*gehobener Dienst*), clerical class (*mittlerer Dienst*) and sub-clerical-class (*einfacher Dienst*). Each career structure consists of five grades, with a rising pay scale within the 'Salary Regulation A' (White and Löffler, 1998: 11; Röber, 1996: 173). The main characteristic of the 'Salary Regulation A' is that it provides increments every two years on the basis of a seniority allowance. In contrast to the salary system of 'Regulation A', top positions in the civil service – which are related to the leading grades in the administrative class – are remunerated according to a special 'Salary Regulation B' which does not contain any increments for seniority and income is irrespective of the officer's age or length of service. In the traditional German civil service system, a civil servant can only get appointed to the basic grade of one of the classes according to formal educational qualifications – like Abitur-examination (A-Level) and three or four years

Table 7.1   Distribution of public service personnel across administrative levels in Germany, 1996

Administrative Level	Civil Servants, Judges, Soldiers	Public Employees	Public Workers	Total
Federal Level	325,785	113,676	93,708	533,169
State Level (*Länder*)	1,244,382	998,751	186,751	2,429,884
Local Authorities	178,807	1,061,989	498,465	1,739,261
Railways	104,164	2,414	5,007	115,585
Indirect State Administration	49,181	360,101	53,282	462,564
Total	1,902,319	2,536,931	837,213	5,276,463

Source: Statistisches Bundesamt (1997), Statistisches Jahrbuch 1997, part 20.8.1: Beschäftigte nach Beschäftigungsbereichen am 30.6.1996, p 531.

studies at a *Fachhochschule* (University of Applied Sciences) for the executive class. Afterwards the civil servant can be promoted to the highest grade of the executive class, but not to a grade of the administrative class without further formal qualification (like a university degree or a similiar diploma as part of in-service training courses).

HUMAN RESOURCES MANAGEMENT REFORMS

In the last 10 years, the conventional system of personnel administration, which reflected the traditional bureaucratic model, has come under attack in many countries of the developed world (OECD, 1996). Even in less developed countries, the role of the traditional state and its public administration is more and more critically analysed (World Development Report, 1997). In the Federal Republic of Germany, the first serious attempt to modernise the traditional and fairly inflexible civil service was undertaken in the early 1970s when a 'Study Commission for the Reform of Public Service Law' (*Studienkommission für die Reform des öffentlichen Dienstrechts*) was established by the Federal government. It elaborated fairly ambitious and far-reaching proposals in order to change the traditional system of personnel administration. The most important shortcomings which were identified by the Commission were a lack of motivation amongst officers and poor performance, in terms of productivity. But due to strong reservations and resistance to any substantial change by public servants and their unions, only a small number of the Commission's recommendations were implemented. The 'Action Programme' of the Federal Government (*Aktionsprogramm zur Dienstrechtsreform*) of 1976 led only to minor changes in the pay system and in the vertical mobility of civil servants. Recent changes in personnel management seem to be more successful than previous attempts to modernise the old system of personnel administration largely because of changes in the environment. Financial constraints, shifts in public duties, demographic changes, changing values as well as an increasingly competitive environment are now creating a positive climate for change.

The German approach to administrative reform is very strongly focused on internal rationalisation in order to increase public sector productivity and achieve economic savings. Issues like local democracy (as, for example, in Scandinavian countries) or competitive pressure (as in the United Kingdom) have played a minor role in the German reform process until now. In addition to the introduction of new systems of cost accounting (in connection with the definition of outputs), and creation of less hierarchical organisational structures, personnel management has become an important element of administrative reform in Germany (Vaanholt, 1997).

The pace of reform at the three political and administrative levels in Germany is still, however, quite different. The local level – due to financial problems and direct contacts with citizens in public service provision – is far ahead in modernising organisational structures and decision-making processes compared with State and Federal levels. Nevertheless, some States have made progress in administrative reform (Bürsch, 1996) and even at federal level some changes have taken place during the last few years. At Federal level, examples are the Report of the Lean State Advisory Committee (1997) and the Civil Service Reform Law which was passed by Parliament (Deutscher Bundestag) in February 1997.

While the resolutions on HRM, in the Final Report of the Lean State Committee (1997: 102–7), refer to Federal level only and are not legally binding, the Civil Service Reform Law is of much greater importance for all parts of the German bureaucracy. According to the constitutional responsibilities of the Federation, this law sets the framework for personnel management in the German public service in general. The framework can be put into concrete terms by the States according to their special requirements in personnel management. Despite some criticism that many of the regulations fall behind what many scholars and critical practitioners consider necessary for introducing a modern HRM approach in the public sector (Oechsler and Vaanholt, 1997), one must accept that the Civil Service Reform Law is a first, small step in the direction of more flexibility in personnel management.

As mentioned before, German administrative modernisation has to be understood as a 'bottom-up process' (Klages and Löffler, 1995). Thus willingness to use new concepts of personnel management is greatest at local level. This is partly because the legal conditions at local level permit the introduction of more flexible methods of personnel management. As Table 7.1 shows, local authorities predominantly employ public employees and public workers, whereas civil servants are less prominent in local authorities than in state administration. Since regulations for public employees and public workers are based on private law and determined by public sector industrial relations, it is easier to experiment with new methods of personnel management for those groups than civil servants.

Another significant factor is that the Trade Union for Public Service, Transport and Traffic (*Gewerkschaft für öffentlichen Dienst, Transport und Verkehr*, ÖTV) has shown a positive attitude towards the introduction of modern HRM approaches in the German public sector (Mai, 1995: 325). In general, the ÖTV considers the modernisation of the public sector as the lesser evil, compared to privatisation of public services (see the official position of the ÖTV as adopted at the Annual Meeting of the ÖTV in 1996, reprinted in ÖTV, 1997: 131–7). Whereas the administrative modernisation politics of the ÖTV were rather passive and reactive until 1995–96, discussion about civil service reform with the Federal Government, as well as the increasing impact of the 'New Steering Model' on local government reforms (see Reichard, 1994 and 1997), made ÖTV take a more active role in the modernisation process in the German public sector. The second phase of the ÖTV-initiative 'Future of the Public Service' (*Zukunft des öffentlichen Dienstes*, ZöD) saw the development of a nationwide role and involvement of ÖTV in administrative reform

Table 7.2   Focus of modernisation activities of German cities, 1996
(in per cent)

Modernization field	Mod. is realized	Mod. is pursued	Mod. is planned (high priority)	Mod. is planned (low priority)	No mod. activities
Cost Accounting	2.4	47.1	37.1	6.7	6.7
Personnel developmment	6.7	37.8	37.1	6.2	12.4
Organizational development	6.7	46.2	28.6	6.7	11.9
Monitoring of contracted-out municipal services	7.1	17.1	23.3	19.0	33.3
Relationship between politics and administration	5.2	21.0	36.2	11.9	25.7

Source: Grömig and Thielen (1996), 'Städte auf dem Reformweg. Zum Stand der Verwaltungsmodernisierung', in: *Der Städtetag*, No 9, p 597 (modified by the authors).

projects, as the traditional approach to secure the influence of the trade union in administrative reforms from the centre reached its limits (Mai, 1997: 82f). This implies that ÖTV will continue to support reform experiments at local government level and, as well as co-ordinating and evaluating local government, will take a proactive role at regional level.

The fact that local authorities are especially affected by financial pressures has both positive and negative impacts on the relative importance of personnel management at German local government level. As the second survey of the German Association of Cities shows, most municipalities concentrate their present reform efforts on financial management issues and organisational development. However, more than one third of all modernising cities also have reform projects related to personnel management or consider it as a high priority of local government reforms.

The survey data in Table 7.3 also reveals that personnel management is still not seen as a reform objective in its own right. The large majority of cities has initiated public management reforms in order to increase the efficiency/effectiveness of local administration, improve citizen orientation and financial room for manouver but only a small proportion of the interviewed cities considered the motivation of their employees as a primary objective of reforms. The data also show that in 1994–95 only some 18 per cent of the cities thought that employee motivation was an important reform goal whereas in 1996 some 35 per cent and in 1998 31 per cent put staff motivation on the reform agenda. This confirms the hypothesis made at the beginning of the chapter that personnel is still predominately perceived as a cost

Table 7.3   Goals of modernisation activities of German cities, 1994–95, 1996 and 1998 (in per cent)

Year	Higher efficiency/ Effectiveness	Customer orientation	Cope with financial crisis	Increase the motivation of employees	Improve attractiveness for economic investors	Increase transparency of adminstrative acts
1994/95	92.6	58.9	49.1	18.3	–	28.6
1996	97.1	68.6	77.6	34.8	4.3	–
1998	96.0	77.0	74.0	31.0	13.0	–

Sources: Grömig and Gruner (1998), 'Reform in den Rathäusern. Neuste Umfrage des Deutschen Städtetages zum Thema Verwaltungsmodernisierung', *Der Städtetag*, No 8, p 582.

factor, not as a productivity factor, even though this view has been changing slowly.

Summing-up, reforms of personnel management have come on the reform agenda of German public administration again but unlike in Switzerland and Austria, abolition of the civil service status is not a political issue in Germany in spite of a permanent discussion on whether public employees (*Angestellte*) or civil servants (*Beamte*) are cheaper for the state. Nor have the Lean State Advisory Council or the Civil Service Law of 1997 dared to bring up the old issue of harmonising the dual structure of the public service in Germany. However, there is increasing awareness of the need to introduce more flexibility into a rigid public service in order to increase the performance of administrative personnel.

ELEMENTS OF FLEXIBILITY IN GERMAN PUBLIC ADMINISTRATION

The German civil service system has been relatively stable over a long time period. There have always been demands, by reform-oriented practitioners and scholars, to change the traditional system towards a uniform legal status for all public servants and reform the pay system. But due to the special politico-administrative system in Germany, including federalism, proportional representation, strong role of the state, constitutional guarantees for the status civil servants (Barlow and Röber, 1996), and due to the interests of the many beneficiaries and their representatives, unions as well as Members of Parliament, the traditional system of the German civil service has been relatively resistant to any major changes. Since abolition or modernisation of the special regulations for German civil servants require a constitutional amendment, and since civil servants are over-represented in Parliament, far-reaching changes have been impossible in the past and are unlikely to happen in the foreseeable future. This means that the system is likely to undergo only incremental changes and developments in certain elements and features. The Civil Service Reform Law can be seen as a small piece of evidence of such changes.

Employment contracts

The system of employment contracts is still rather inflexible. In general there is a distinction between three status groups: civil servants (*Beamte*), public employees (*Angestellte*) and public workers (*Arbeiter*). Due to historical traditions and according to article 3, paragraph 4, of the Basic Law, as stated above, civil servants should be responsible for those duties with regard to law and order functions. Employment conditions for civil servants are based on public law, which means that there are no employment contracts in the strict sense of employer-employee-relations:

> In public law, someone is a civil servant who holds a position of public service and loyalty to which he or she has been appointed by some proper document of appointment. A salaried employee, however, is a person who works in a job where he or she has to make contributions to the salaried employees pension-fund or whose job descriptions can be found listed in the employees salary scale or is covered by some other contractual agreement for salaried employees (Siedentopf, 1990: 241).

The contractual status of public workers who are mainly responsible for manual functions is similiar to the status of public employees. In practice, the categories of service law for civil servants, public employees and workers 'have become increasingly similiar and when allocating personnel one has ceased to make the fine distinction between sovereign and non-sovereign responsibilities' (Siedentopf, 1990: 237).

An important point in the Civil Service Reform Law – as far as employment contracts are concerned – is that civil servants will get the opportunity to work part-time (up to 50 per cent of their regular working hours) without any preconditions. In the past, they were not allowed to do this according to traditional principles of a professional civil service (*hergebrachte Grundsätze des Berufsbeamtentums*), especially the full dedication to public service. The exception was for family related reasons like bringing up children or looking after relatives who need special care. Someone who wanted to work part-time was signalling that he/she was not willing to dedicate themselves to public service completely. The new regulation for part-time work provides scope for greater flexibility in the form of flexible working hours, job sharing, 'working hours budgets over one year' (*Arbeitszeitkonten*) and sabbaticals. An important side-effect of the new regulation, however, is that some employers only appoint new civil servants as part-time civil servants in order to save money and/or to give more young people the opportunity to join the civil service. Similiar developments can be observed in contracts for public employees and workers. These actions by public employers meet with heavy disapproval by staff councils for civil servants (*Personalräte*), who criticise these regulations as non-acceptable compulsory part-time systems.

As far as we can see, these new regulations can hardly be regarded as far-reaching changes in the whole civil service system. Compared to many other countries, German public servants still have a considerable degree of job security. Even in those States or local authorities which have started their administrative reform projects under severe financial pressure, there was a broad consensus that nobody would lose their jobs as a result of the reforms. The ÖTV has adopted a policy to protect its members against the negative effects of administrative reforms by concluding so-called 'co-operation agreements' with the administrative chief executive and other involved parties in local government. A similiar kind of protective agreement may also be concluded between the staff council and local administration within the framework of the staff representation law of the States (*Landespersonalvertretungsgesetz*, LPVG).

By June 1997 there were 73 such agreements in existence. As Table 7.4 shows, there are fewer 'protection agreements' in East German municipalities. This may be explained by the fact that employee representatives in East Germany have been preoccupied with other personnel problems, so that there is little time to negotiate specific kinds of 'protection agreements'. This situation shows that the implications of 'New Public Management'-oriented reforms in the field of personnel management will be relatively moderate in terms of contractual flexibility but also in terms of numerical flexibility.

Table 7.4   Number of employee protection agreements in East and West German municipalities, 1997

	District-free cities	Cities and municipalities belonging to districts	Total
West German municipalities	30	30	60
East German municipalities	3	9	12
Total	33	39	73

Source: Müghe, 1997: 9.

Numerical flexibility

Although the effects of a 'New Public Management'-oriented reform approach on the system of German public management and on the attitudes of most public servants are not as strong as, for example, in many Anglo-Saxon countries, there are some real effects, especially on the size of the workforce. Employment statistics show that the number of staff members has been reduced considerably at all levels as shown in Table 7.5 Both at federal and local levels there has been considerable downsizing.

Some politicians give the impression that the most important area of redesigning public personnel management is further reduction of number of posts, because they consider the public administration, in particular the civil service, as heavily overstaffed (Kanther, 1995: 263). But international comparisons of the size of the public sector indicate that Germany takes a medium position within the OECD member countries (see Table 7.6).

But aggregate national employment statistics do not indicate the distribution of public servants over different functional areas and authorities. Some authorities are very short of qualified staff members, whereas others are overstaffed. Therefore, personnel policy must take into consideration a fair and legitimate distribution of different work loads in different parts of the public sector. Numerical flexibility for a single authority is made easier by new regulations which provide better opportunities for delegation (*Abordnung*) and transfer (*Versetzung*) of staff members. In the traditional system, it was nearly impossible to delegate or transfer someone against their will – even where duties of the respective authority had changed or had disap-

Table 7.5   Employment in the German public sector (excluding Federal Railways and Indirect Public service; Part time + full time)

	1991	1992	1993	1994	1995	1996	1997
Federal Government	652,000	625,000	602,900	577,600	546,300	533,169	526,431
Länder	2,522,000	2,452,000	2,462,000	2,481,000	2,478,000	2,429,884	2,401,665
Communities	1,990,000	1,986,000	1,874,000	1,792,000	1,715,000	1,739,261	1,683,521
Total	5,164,000	5,063,000	4,938,900	4,850,600	4,739,300	4,702,314	4,611,617

Source: PUMA (1991–95), data for years 1996, 1997 from Statistisches Bundesamt are provisional.

Table 7.6 Number of employees in the public
sector in OECD member countries, 1997

	as a % of total employment	as a % of total population
Australia	14.7	6.8
Austria	22.6	9.6
Belgium	18.6	6.8
Canada	19.9	9.3
Czech Republic	5.7	2.8
Denmark	30.3	15.3
Finland	23.1	9.7
France	24.7	9.5
Germany	15.3	6.4
Greece	12.5	4.7
Hungary	7.2	2.5
Iceland	18.5	8.9
Ireland	16.2	6.2
Italy	17.6	6.1
Japan	8.3	4.3
Korea	11.4	5.3
Luxembourg	–	–
Mexico	16.6	3.0
Netherlands	11.4	4.7
New Zealand	14.2	6.6
Norway	30.6	15.4
Poland	18.1	7.1
Portugal	18.9	8.2
Spain	15.1	4.9
Sweden	31.5	13.9
Switzerland	13.8	7.4
Turkey	7.3	2.5
United Kingdom	13.5	6.2
United States	15.2	7.4

Source: Analytical Databank, OECD.

peared completely. Under the new regulations, it is much easier to
transfer a civil servant to a different public employer for up to five
years, without the consent of the respective person.

The policy of downsizing without dismissing staff members has
already had the effect that very few new staff members have
been appointed and the workforce is ageing dramatically. Because
of the ageing workforce, innovation and flexibility are negatively

affected. Under these circumstances, it is difficult to motivate public servants for public management reforms. Many staff are suspicious that the introduction of new concepts of personnel management is a tricky strategy for downsizing in the disguise of administrative reforms.

As numerical flexibility, in terms of managing the total number of public sector employees, is relatively low in Germany, for the reasons set out above, all reform efforts concentrate on increasing numerical flexibility through financial means. In other words, 'global budgets of personnel costs' (*Personalkostenbudgetierung*) have become a key feature of local government reforms. The basic concept of personnel budgets is to plan the quantity of employment for the medium-term, which is not an easy task. The next step is to calculate a cost estimation on the basis of the personnel plan. The estimated budget costs for personnel then have to be distributed among different departments or administrative units. The latter have to manage their personnel costs within the limits of their personnel budget and report to the central unit to what degree they have achieved their performance targets on the basis of their given personnel budget (Zech, 1996). This new budgeting technique for personnel costs is used by many German cities.

Pay Flexibility

The traditional pay system for civil servants, as stated above, consists of a number of grades in each of the four classes of the career structure. Each grade is related to a fixed basic salary plus increments every two years on the basis of a seniority allowance (Röber, 1996). Other increments to the basic salary have only been provided for certain types of functions irrespective of individual results and performances. Similar regulations have been applied to public employees and workers. On the whole, there is very little flexibility. The reasons for this are quite obvious. 'As far as public employees and workers are concerned, collective bargaining between the Minister of the Interior, as the representative of state-employers, and the trade unions fixes national pay levels. Until today, German trade unions – in the private as well as in the public sector – still stick to country-wide pay agreements so that there is no flexiblity for agency-specific pay contracts' (Löffler, 1997: 79). Normally these agreements have been adopted for civil servants by Parliament because decisions on pay increases are agreed by Parliament and regulated by statute. This procedure is widely accepted in German society because people are not willing to accept large wage differences. Given this background, it is difficult to introduce new pay schemes which provide better opportunities for achievement-oriented salaries. But due to severe motivation problems in the public sector – according to some surveys up to 50 per cent of the total workforce do not identify themselves any longer with their duties ('inner dismissal' – *innere Kündigung*) – it was therefore necessary to open the traditional system for at least moderate changes towards incentives for staff members with 'exceptional performances' (*besondere Leistungen*). One approach to motivate staff members is – besides intrinsic work-related factors – to increase pay flexibility in order to strengthen the achievement principle and introduce adequate pay schemes.

The new Civil Service Reform Law opens up the opportunity for the Federation itself and for States (*Länder*) to introduce financial incentives 'for those staff members whose performance is higher than others'. It provides some elements which might be able to supersede traditional civil service regulations which are not conducive to the achievement principle. One element is that the system of increments every two years has been rearranged and no longer depends on seniority but on individual performance. The individual performance then 'determines how fast civil servants reach the next age step'. In addition to this, extra seniority pay is based on a regressive principle. This means that in the first professional phase, seniority pay is possible every two years; in the next phase, every three years; and in the last phase every four years. This implies that final salary is reached at a later age than before. This reform element clearly mirrors the aims of the Civil Service Reform Law, which is to increase public sector productivity but also reduce personnel costs. The cost neutrality performance-based promotion implies that faster promotion of some top performing civil servants has to be compensated by slower promotion of other civil servants (Oechsler, 1997).

Another element is that the Federation and the States are allowed to introduce single bonuses for exceptional results (*Leistungsprämien als Einmalzahlungen*) and extra pay for a limited period of one year (*Leistungszulagen*). In order to prevent decisions in accordance with the principle of 'giving everyone a slice of the cake' and excessive payments, bonuses and extra pay are restricted to 10 per cent of civil servants and extra pay must not exceed seven per cent of the initial or starting salary of the respective grade. Interestingly, the Federation as well as most of the States are still hesitating to introduce performance-related pay (PRP), either as bonus or as extra pay. They seem to be very uncertain about the validity of their appraisal systems. That is not very surprising because in practice these systems tend to lead to an inflation of the performance marks awarded. This means that personnel evaluation has very little significance for the promotion of staff and is certainly not very appropriate for PRP (White and Löffler, 1998). And public employers obviously seem to be afraid of poisoning the working atmosphere, because the overall majority of the work force will not – due to the tight regulation in the Civil Service Reform Law – benefit from extra money resources at all. The small survey we have been conducting at state level gives a very clear picture that the vast majority of the state governments are not yet ready to introduce even a relatively moderate system of PRP.

Although reservations against PRP in the German public sector can be regarded as an indicator of the attempt by some old fashioned bureaucrats to evade inevitable administrative modernisation, one must also see that there is still a heated debate among scholars of personnel management about the effects of incentive programmes. Some argue that extrinsic rewards like PRP only succeed in securing temporary compliance. 'When it comes to producing lasting change in attitudes and behaviour . . . rewards, like punishments, are strikingly ineffective' (Kohn, 1993: 55). By and large, the importance of PRP might be overestimated. Large-scale employee surveys have shown that in German public sector organisations 'intrinsic work-related factors such as "interesting", "meaningful", "makes fun", "offers change", "one can work independently", "can develop ideas", "responsibility", "challenging", "sense of achievement" are considered to be more important factors than performance-oriented and fair pay' (Löffler, 1997: 82, with reference to Klages, 1997).

CAREER MOBILITY

Mobility of staff – both horizontal and vertical – is rather limited in public administration in Germany. Many public servants have never worked outside the public sector; and even in the public sector itself horizontal mobility is relatively low. The repercussions in terms of selective perception or 'tunnel vision' and their negative effects on problem solving and innovative behaviour have been widely discussed. For that reason some states have introduced into their civil service laws regulations about job rotation as a requirement for getting a higher post and grade in the hierarchy – especially for posts in the administrative class (*höherer Dienst*). Limited mobility in the public sector can be regarded as indicative of a lack of any substantial personnel development strategies. In fact, in German public administration many have never heard of the term 'personnel development'. There is, however, some indication of change. Many municipalities such as the County Administration of Soest give high priority to personnel development in their administrative reform (Janning, 1994: 87f) and, even at the federal level, the Lean State Commission recognises the need for better personnel development in Federal ministries.

One of the biggest problems in the traditional system has been the difficulty of getting rid of poor performing top administrators and few civil servants have been downgraded for poor performance in practice. The Civil Service Reform Law provides two options for dealing with that problem. The first is to give somebody a leading position on probation for normally two years; after meeting all requirements associated with the higher position during these two years the civil servant will be permanently appointed. The second option is to establish temporary executive duties (*Führungsfunktion auf Zeit*) for civil servants who hold leading posts under the special 'Salary Regulation B', like heads of departments (*Abteilungsleiter*) and most of the heads of sections (*Referatsleiter*) in Ministries, and civil servants in grade A 16 who are heads of an authority (*Behördenleiter*). The Civil Service Reform law lays down that temporary executive duties are limited to two periods of office of no more than 10 years in total. After the second period the chief executive must be permanently appointed in the case of good performance or removed from office. Temporary executive duties are regarded as a good opportunity to correct inappropriate decisions and cancel the appointment of persons who are obviously not able to meet the requirements for top managers in the public sector. But there is also a lot of scepticism and criticism that these regulations will open the way to increased party politicisation of the higher ranks of the German civil service.

CONCLUSION

Despite several attempts to increase flexibility in personnel management practices, the German system is still relatively rigid compared to other countries, especially those which have made progress in implementing new public management-oriented reforms. Contractual, numerical, pay, and career flexibility are still relatively low in German public administration. In spite of continuing budgetary pressures, the prospects of fundamental changes in the German public service are rather limited. In contrast to the United Kingdom, and due to constitutional characteristics, the political-administrative system in Germany is difficult to change and there has been little political will to do so. However, there have been a number of 'soft' personnel management reforms in the German public sector that do not fall into the traditional flexibility framework. Innovative personnel management in German public administration, especially at local level, focuses on themes such as goal agreements between employee-supervisor, evaluation of superiors, employee surveys and training of superiors in leadership. All these approaches aim at increasing the flexibility of employees by shifting from a control-based command system to a more trust-based co-operative working style. In summary, human resources flexibility is limited in Germany and public managers are denied many of the options open to managers in other political/administrative systems. However, some developments, negotiated and agreed with the powerful trade unions, have increased flexibility for employers by allowing part-time contracts, more family-friendly policies and more vertical career mobility. The most significant feature of the change in Germany has been introduction of a new administrative culture where the focus is primarily on intrinsic rather than extrinsic motivation and rewards and which seeks to achieve increased performance and productivity through behavioural rather than structural change.

Abbreviations

PRP   performance-related pay systems
NPM   New Public Management
ÖTV   Trade Union for Public Service, Transport and Traffic
HRM   Human Resource Management

* The views expressed in this paper are those of the author, and do not necessarily represent those of the OECD, nor those of its Public Management Service.

References

BARLOW, J. and RÖBER, M. (1996). 'Steering not rowing. Co-ordination and control in the management of public services in Britain and Germany', in *The International Journal of Public Sector Management*, Vol 9, pp 73–89.

BÜRSCH, M. (1996). *Die Modernisierung der deutschen Landesverwaltungen: Zum Stand der Verwaltungsreform in den 16 Ländern*. Bonn: Friedrich-Ebert-Stiftung.

GRÖMIG, E. and THIELEN, H. (1996). 'Städte auf dem Reformweg. Zum Stand der Verwaltungsmodernisierung', in *Der Städtetag*, No 9, pp 596–600.

GRÖMIG, E. and GRUNER, K. (1998). 'Reform in den Rathäusern. Neueste Umfrage des Deutschen Städtetages zum Thema Verwaltungsmodernisierung', in *Der Städtetag*, No 8, pp 581–7.

JANNING, H. (1994). 'Personal- und Organisationsentwicklung in der Kreisverwaltung Soest', in Hill, H. and Klages, H. (eds), *Lernen von Spitzenverwaltungen. Eine Dokumentation des 2. Speyerer Qualitätswettbewerbs*, Berlin: Raabe Verlag, pp 85–97.

KANTHER, M. (1995). 'Rede des Bundesministers des Innern', in Banner, G., Biedenkopf, K. Eichhorn, P, Hagedorn, W. and Kanther, W. (eds), *Reformmodell Verwaltung*, Bonn: Bad Kissingen, DBB-Verlag.

KOHN, A. (1993). 'Why Incentive Plans Cannot Work', in *Harvard Busines Review*, September–October, pp 54–63.

KLAGES, H. (1997). 'Motivierung von Mitarbeitern durch Anreize? Ein Beitrag zum Thema "Human Resource Management in der öffentlichen Verwaltung"', in Lüder, K. (ed.), *Staat und Verwaltung. Fünfzig Jahre Hochschule für Verwaltungswissenschaften*, Berlin: Speyer, Duncker & Humblot, pp 455–76.

KLAGES, H. and LÖFFLER, E. (1995). 'Administrative Modernization in Germany – a Big Qualitative Jump in Small Steps', in *International Review of Administrative Sciences*, Vol 61, No 3 (September), pp 373–83.

LEAN STATE ADVISORY COMMITTEE (1997). Final Report. Bonn: Federal Ministry of the Interior.

LÖFFLER, E. (1997). 'Flexibilities in the German Civil Service', in *Public Policy and Administration*, Vol 12, No 4 (winter), pp 73–86.

MAI, H. (1995). 'Die Mitarbeiter im öffentliche Dienst als Träger der Verwaltungsreform', in *Verwaltung & Management. Zeitschrift für allgemeine Verwaltung*, Vol 1, No 6, pp 324–6.

MAI, H. (1997). *Dienstleistungen gestalten: Für einen aktiven Wirtschafts- und Sozialstaat*, Stuttgart: ÖTV-courier Verlag.

MÜGHE, G. (1997). *Vereinbarungen zur kommunalen Verwaltungsreform – Auswertung*, Stuttgart: . . .

OECD (1996). *Integrating People Management into Public Service Reform*, Paris: OECD.

OECD (1997). *Analytical Data Bank*. Paris: OECD.

OECHSLER, W.A. (1997). 'Reform des öffentlichen Dienstreichts – Aufbruch zu leistungsorientiertem Personalmanagement?', in *Die innovative Verwaltung*, Vol 2, No 3, pp 30–32.

OECHSLER, W.A. and VAANHOLT, S. (1997). 'Dienstrechtsreform – klein, aber auch nicht fein! Eine Stellungnahme aus personalwirtschaftlicher Sicht', in *Die Betriebswirtschaft*, Vol 57, pp 529–40.

ÖTV (1997). *Das Neue Steuerungsmodell der Kommunalen Gemeinschaftsstelle. Position der Gewerkschaft ÖTV*. Stuttgart: OTV.

REICHARD, C. (1994). *Umdenken im Rathaus. Neue Steuerungsmodelle in der deutschen Kommunalverwaltung*. Berlin: Sigma.

REICHARD, C. (1997). 'Neues Steuerungsmodell: Local Reform in Germany', in Kickert, W. (ed.), *Public Management and Administrative Reform in Western Europe*, Cheltenham: Edward Elgar, pp 59–79.

'RETHINKING REWARDS. WHAT ROLE – IF ANY – SHOULD INCENTIVES PLAY IN THE WORKPLACE?' (1993). *Harvard Busines Review*, November-December, pp 37–49.

RÖBER, M. (1996). Country Study 'Germany', in Farnham, D., Horton, S., Barlow, J. and Hondeghem, A. (eds), *New Public Managers in Europe. Public Servants in Transition*, London: Macmillan, pp 169–93.

SIEDENTOPF, H. (1990). 'The Public Service', in König, K., von Oertzen, H.J. and Wagener, F. (eds), *Public Administration in the Federal Republic of Germany*, Baden-Baden: Nomos, pp 235–46.

VAANHOLT, S. (1997). 'Human Resource Management in der öffentlichen Verwaltung'. Wiesbaden: Deutscher Universitätsverlag.

WAGENER, F. (1990). 'The External Structure of Administration in the Federal Republic of Germany', in König, K., von Oertzen, H.J. and Wagener, F. (eds), *Public Administration in the Federal Republic of Germany*. Baden-Baden: Nomos, pp 49–64.

WHITE, G. and LÖFFLER, E. (1998). 'Pay Flexibility in the German and British Civil Services', in *Employee Relations Review*, Vol 1, No 4 (March), pp 10–16.

WORLD DEVELOPMENT REPORT (1997). 'The State in a Changing World'. Oxford University Press.

ZECH, R. (1996). 'Planung, Steuerung und Kontrolle der Personalbudgets', in *Die innovative Verwaltung*, Vol 2, No 4, pp 16–19.

8 Employment Flexibilities and the New People Management in Italy

Renato Ruffini

Italy's public administration and the way in which it functions are greatly influenced by the history of the country, which saw the formation of the unitary State only in the second half of the nineteenth century. Unification took place in a very differentiated and fragmented social and cultural environment especially between the North and the South of the country. The building of the unitary state required homogeneity in the administrative system, which was pursued with the reforms of the 'Crispi period' (named after Francesco Crispi, a Minister of the Interior and later Prime Minister), between 1890 and 1910. These reforms introduced a classical bureaucratic model of public administration founded on principles of political neutrality, hierarchy and administrative acts according to pre-defined rules and undertaken by a qualified class of officials. This model of administration was centred on formality and regulated in detail by norms of positive law. Although it served the purpose of building an *identity* of the State, it was later exploited during the fascist period of the 1930s and 1940s to build a strong, *centralised* state. This process of centralising reform was imposed on regional traditions and cultures which have always been radically different. Although Italy is formally a unitary administrative system there are still strong regional and local differences in its functioning, with the result that there are great variations in performance levels throughout the country. Today, Italian public administration is still generally characterised by a classic bureaucratic model of personnel management (Farnham and Horton, 1997) and the effort to change towards a new people management is very difficult at both macro and micro levels of government.

At macro level it is not easy to move towards more flexibility because of difficulties in changing the legal framework (laws, regulations, codes, 'status' and contracts). Patterns of change in the public sector have therefore tended to be characterised by a general 'rules and regulations' approach. Innovations are aimed at finding a new balance in the system by redefining existing law, regulations and guidelines. Whilst institutional reforms emphasise the need to pursue economic viability and therefore require flexibility within each public organisation, responsibility does not always lie directly within the institution but with external bodies, i.e. higher-level decision making authorities or control authorities. This is particularly the case regarding public employment where matters relating to personnel are 'directed and controlled' by bodies external to the management of administrative organisations. Within this framework, improvements in the functioning of public administration should be automatic, as rules that constrain opportunistic behaviour become more defined and are externally set. However, history shows how a rigid legislative framework with too many rules can create a complexity of decision-making processes and implementation procedures which lead in turn to a proliferation of degenerating phenomena and actually reduces government's capacity to control the system as a whole.

At micro level in Italy, there are also outdated management and obsolete cultural models prevailing in individual public organisations which constrain the introduction of more flexible personnel systems. These models are too focused on administrative tasks and formal operating patterns rather than people management, which has remained underdeveloped.

In order to understand the causes and consequences of such rigidity in Italian public employment, it is important to note that historically the law excludes negotiation between the State and its employees and requires that each public authority determines its own relationship with staff. In other words all questions regarding personnel and organisation must by law be decided by the relevant political authority. The second point is that public employees are highly unionised and terms and conditions of employment are jointly negotiated between public authorities and trade unions. In the first decade of the twentieth century public employees sought basic principles of public employment comparable with those in the private sector, based on contractualisation. Contractual employment, however, was not formally started until 1983 with law No. 83, when to all intents and purposes the industrial relations process was 'privatised' (D'Orta and Talamo, 1996). According to this law, the contract was negotiated at central level (between government and trade unions) and collectively agreed decisions became law. The act declared that the aim was to increase flexibility in public employment. However the results were exactly the opposite, an increase in rigidity, because collective bargaining created more centralisation of policy and standardisation of practices in people management.

There was little delegation of policy discretion to operational managers involved with people management as all the policies, especially those relating to pay, grading, recruitment and staffing, were established centrally. As regard management style, there was also a preference for decision making by consensus between managers and staff and management and union. This situation created an extremely rigid human resources management (HRM) policy in Italy and this rigidity has been and still is generally considered the first cause of inefficiency of public administration.

CHANGE IN HUMAN RESOURCES MANAGEMENT

The practice of people management in the early 1990s was characterised by rigidities in both HRM policy and practice. This created an urgent need for change because of:

- high levels of conflict between workers and the administration, especially regarding job description and classification, the pay scale and recruitment procedures (both internal and external recruitment), which often led to court cases
- long and complex recruitment procedures (minimum one year) which left managers with no influence on the selection of personnel
- staff numbers were controlled by an external commission or public body and there was very low mobility, both internally and externally
- pay levels were negotiated at central level through collective bargaining. There were eight or nine pay levels that were also career grades. Career mobility was possible only through formal recruitment procedures and there was no pay progression or promotion system between grades
- there was a system of performance-related pay (PRP) but the value of this pay was generally limited and the public organisation did not develop a system of performance evaluation. Therefore this kind of reward had very little effect

- organisation descriptions at macro level (organisation structure) and at micro level (job design) were decided by law or by political administrators and not by staff managers.

It was evident in this situation that public managers had little influence or control over human resources in the workplace. As a consequence Italian public managers are unskilled in people management policies and practices and consequently cannot manage flexibility.

In 1993, during a period of great political and financial difficulties for the Italian State, the government, led by Prime Minister Amato, introduced an important reform of public employment with the ordinance No. 29/93. Initially the new provisions were oriented towards relieving the problems related to the cost and efficiency of public employment. In 1997 and 1998, the new government under Prime Minister Prodi strengthened the law by further increasing the decentralisation of decision-making in public administration. The ordinance No. 29/93 represents a major change in Italian public employment. This change, following the general trend of public reforms throughout developed countries, aims to transform an overloaded and unresponsive bureaucratic state into a lean, enabling, customer-oriented and 'value for money' administration. In particular, the declared aims of the ordinance are to introduce market forces and labour competitiveness into public administration to make it more like the private sector. This stems from the citizen's growing interest in community services and expectations of improved performance. At the same time, government considers the ordinance as part of the policy to improve public finance, required by European monetary union, bringing public sector labour costs in line with those of the private sector and with those of corresponding public services in the rest of Europe.

The key points of ordinance 29/93 relating to HRM are as follows:

- 'privatisation' of the regulatory framework. This means that public employment regulation is to be closer to the private sector. In particular, public employment is now based on civil law. With the reform, the collective agreement for public employment plays an enhanced role, whilst only some fundamental elements such as recruitment remain regulated by administrative law. Only certain public officials, in particular diplomatic corps, magistrates and armed forces, remain under administrative law

- employment relations, including individual contracts, are now defined within the boundaries of collective bargaining. Consequently disputes are settled by an ordinary judge instead of an administrative judge. This innovation is highly significant, as the administrative courts tended to favour the public approach to public employment, whereas labour agreements tend to merge such an approach with the principles of private employment
- full responsibility for the administration and management of labour relations rests with individual organisations. In particular law No. 29/93 specifies that every public organisation has the same powers as private employers
- a distinction is made between political administrators responsible for the definition of policies and related objectives, and monitoring the results, and managers responsible for managing technical, financial and human resources
- the start of an evaluation process and performance management practice in public administration
- introduction of flexibility practices in people management. In particular, these practices include pay flexibility with PRP, career mobility, new pay scales, procedures and rules for staff, new types of employment contracts such as part-time, flexible hours, on-call arrangements, home-working and term-time working and downsizing
- introduction of new rules and actors in labour relations. In particular a new agency for labour-union relations has been established, responsible for representing the administration (State, local authorities and other public bodies) in the collective bargaining process at central level. There are now two levels of negotiation: national and local. The former, however, remains the more important even if the process of decentralisation gives more power to local agreements which can use specific financial resources, not controlled by the Treasury.

The reform No. 29/93 has substantially modified HRM in line with a new public management orientation. As yet, however, the rules have not been fully accepted and put in place. In order to develop a real capacity to carry out new and more effective people management practice, it is necessary first to develop the abilities of managers and change the management ethos within public administration. Reforms began to be visible in 1997 with the implementation of the first collective agreement, but it is evident that the process of change has only just begun.

EMPLOYMENT CONTRACTS AND NUMERICAL FLEXIBILITY

Figure 8.1 shows the structure of public employment in Italy, by sector – central ministries, health, school/education, local authorities, universities, autonomous administrations and public agencies. Public employees are divided into five categories:

- statutory workers, a very small category with the exception of university professors
- non-statutory workers, managers and staff, representing between 55 and 85 per cent of all public employees
- part-time workers, not a significant number ranging from 0.2 to 1.5 per cent across public organisations
- other workers including those working flexible hours, on call arrangements, home-working, term-time working and other kinds

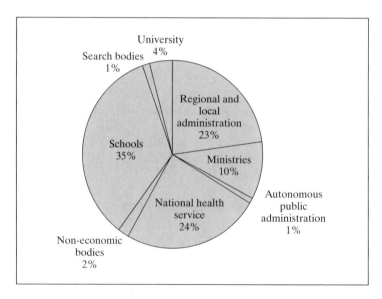

Figure 8.1 Breakdown of employment in general government in Italy, 1995
Source: Analytical Database. Rome: OECD.

of employment which do not have clear definitions used in the workplace. This group is growing but at the present time there is very little data on them

Occupational trends

Occupational trends are presented in Table 8.1 which show a small reduction of staff in both 1995 and 1996. This fall has been greatest in contractual employment and was caused principally by non-replacement of staff. In the same years, there was growth of part-time and temporary workers especially fixed- term contracts. Part-time work increased by 47 per cent in 1995 and 25 per cent in 1996, whilst other workers with different kinds of temporary contracts increased by 25 per cent in 1996. It is necessary to underline that percentage increases are high, because total numbers are small. If we consider the contribution of different kinds of contracts, we can say that the reduction of unlimited contracts was replaced by temporary and part-time contracts. The data also show a change in employment practices towards more flexible staffing policy but there is no evidence at present in Italian public administration of any real and strong downsizing policy. The only policy at present is a policy of non-replacement and, in general, the phenomenon of flexibility is extremely limited. However, there is a growing number of women in the workforce, especially in part-time work, and a falling proportion of men.

Table 8.1   Occupational trends in Italy, 1995–96

	1995		1996	
	Annual variation %	*Contribution to total growth %*	*Annual variation %*	*% Contribution to total growth*
Officials	1.3	(0.02)	−0.9	(−0.01)
Permanent contracts	−0.6	(−0.6)	−1.9	(−1.8)
Part-time	47.9	(0.2)	25.9	(0.2)
Temporary contracts	−3.1	(−0.2)	24.6	(1.3)
Total	−0.6	(−0.6)	−0.3	(−0.3)

Source: Dell'Aringa, 1998.

This general dynamic of occupational trends is different in different branches of Italian public administration. In particular downsizing is significant in the civil service and public agencies where it started in 1995 and was imposed by law. In Italy, the State budget is presented within the so called Law on the Finances of the State: This is generally discussed and voted by parliament every autumn. This yearly law and its attachments is the most important economic policy document in Italy. It includes information and gives guidelines on regulation, pricing, privatisation, taxation, public employment and other relevant economic matters for the specific year. In the national health service (−1.2%) and university sector (−1.9%), there has been a decrease in staff in recent years. In local government, in contrast, there has been a small increase and there is no evidence of downsizing.

Part-time employment

In 1995 and 1996 the number of part-time workers in the public sector was low. Although there was an increase of 30 per cent during that time, there was still under one part-time worker out of every 100 public workers in these two years. Only in local authorities, health services and universities did part-timers represent more than one per cent of the workforce. Part-time employment is rare in Italy generally, with part-time workers making up only two per cent of employees in the private sector.

Table 8.2   Part-time workers in the Italian public sector, 1995–96

	Per 100 workers		Female/male (%)	
	1995	*1996*	*1995*	*1996*
School	0.3	0.3	1.6	1.6
University	1.3	1.8	3.8	4.6
Local authority	1.2	1.5	5.1	5.8
Public agency	0.5	0.8	7.7	7.2
Health care	0.8	1.0	17.0	17.6
Civil service	0.2	0.6	6.5	4.8

Source: Dell'Aringa, 1998.

Fixed-term and temporary contracts

Temporary workers represented no more than seven per cent of the total workforce in Italian public employment in December 1996. This type of worker has risen from one in every 18 workers to one in every 14 since 1993. Education has more than 50 per cent of all temporary workers, 74 per cent of whom are women. The rest of temporary workers are in local authorities and health care, where 60 per cent are women. Temporary contracts have also developed amongst senior managers in recent years, in particular in local government. This kind of contract is being used not only for increased flexibility but also to shift power in the public sector from managers to politicians.

Organisational innovation

At micro level, public organisations are under a lot of pressure from central government to resort to more employment flexibility, because Italian public employment is considered to be inefficient, expensive and inflexible. In general public organisations try to respond to the rigidity of work with classical instruments, such as:

- organisational redesign to break down functional barriers
- job redesign
- increased functional flexibility with training to develop multi-skilled workers in non-professional areas and to facilitate role enlargement within professional groups. In recent years internal training is more focused on transferable management skills and less on professional qualifications. Unfortunately, despite commitments by governments, unions and managers, training expenditure is still well under one per cent in all the branches of public employment
- contracting out and outsourcing
- restructuring of the working week.

Local government and health services are two branches of government where most change is taking place and they are generally considered the most flexible. In general, however, there is little evidence of flexibility in Italian public services. Organisational innovation only began in the late 1990s and at the moment is not widespread. In general there is an implementation gap between the rhetoric and reality. One area where change is visible is in decentralisation of responsibility for recruitment. This delegation, again strongest in local authorities, enables organisations to determine their own staffing numbers, recruitment procedures and assessment, thus removing control by external commissions. It is also possible to privatise recruitment and regulate labour relations with individual private contracts for up to five per cent of top mangers, in each public organisation.

Pay flexibility and career mobility

Starting in 1994–95, collective bargaining has changed traditional pay structures and in some cases, especially for managers in local authorities and the civil service, doctors in the health service and primary school teachers, the change has been radical. At the macro level there are more then 100 pay items in three pay components: fixed wage (or basic wage), semi-fixed wage (or monthly variable component) and variable wage (or mid-year or year end bonus). Table 8.3 shows the pay structure of the public sector, using this classification. The figures illustrates that the fixed salary is 89 per cent for staff and 59 per cent for managers. This difference is due to the new pay system for managers in all branches of public administration called '*retribuzione di posizione*'. This is based on a job-evaluation system used to allocate managers in a grading structure decided autonomously by each public organisation. This payment is semi-fixed because it is linked to the job pro-tempore occupied by a manager appointed by the authorities of the organisation. This kind of payment has increased pay flexibility especially in large local authorities. The most common job evaluation system used is one specific to the public sector but some organisations

Table 8.3   Components of pay in the Italian public sector, 1996

	Fixed (basic wage) %	Semi fixed %	Variable %	Total retribution
Managers	59.6	24	16.4	100
Staff	89.1	3.3	7.6	100
Total	85.6	5.8	8.6	100

Source: Dell'Aringa, 1998.

have used private sector consultants. A similar pay system was introduced in 1998–99 for executive workers.

Regarding variable pay the figures in Tables 8.4 and 8.5 show that it represents less the 10 per cent on average of total pay in all public sectors, with a range between 4.5 to over 20 per cent. Discretionary salary includes over-time work which makes up more than half of total variable pay. PRP, merit pay based on individual performance evaluation (i.e. based on behaviour of the person) and group productivity compensation are present in most public organisations, especially for top managers, and in local authorities. Generally, their effectiveness is considered very low. The main problems are first, lack of discrimination in performance rating; second, relatively low levels of funding, which means that bonuses are of little value or are limited by quota,

Table 8.4   Components of managers' pay in the Italian public sector, 1996

	Total contribution				Variable component				
	Basic wage Fixed (%)	*Semi-fixed (%)*	*Variable (%)*	*Total (%)*	*Over time (%)*	*Allowance (%)*	*Merit Pay (%)*	*Other (%)*	*Total (%)*
School	–	–	–	–	–	–	–	–	–
University	73.1	1.6	25.3	100	72.3	19.8	7.9	–	100
Local authority	73.3	25.7	1	100	2.0	92.7	5.3	0.01	100
Public agency	61.2	15.4	23.4	100	27.8	51	21.2	0.003	100
Health care	56.5	25.7	17.8	100	12.8	5.2	67.5	14.5	100
Civil service	74.8	1.5	23.7	100	52.1	7.7	40.3	–	100

Source: Dell'Aringa, 1998.

Table 8.5   Components of staff pay in the Italian public sector, 1996

	Total contribution				Variable component				
	Basic wage Fixed (%)	*Semi-fixed (%)*	*Variable (%)*	*Total (%)*	*Over time (%)*	*Allowance (%)*	*Merit Pay (%)*	*Other (%)*	*Total (%)*
School	83.8	10.8	5.4	100	49.5	3.7	46.9	–	100
University	84.3	11.2	4.5	100	55.2	21.4	19.6	3.7	100
Local auth.	89.5	1.3	9.2	100	37	10.7	45.8	6.5	100
Public agency	73.9	2.4	23.7	100	13.3	37	49.6	0.09	100
Health care	80.7	5.4	13.9	100	15.7	6.2	36.1	41.9	100
Civil service	83.8	10.8	5.4	100	49.5	3.7	46.9	–	100

Source: Daell'Aringa, 1998.

with resulting staff dissatisfaction; third, a narrowing of the range and reduction in the size of awards.

In 1998, collective bargaining agreements in local authorities, health, public agencies, and the civil service radically reformed their grading structures. Until 1997, grading structures in all public administrations were uniform and rigid, based on eight or nine grades/levels that had 'narrow-bands' because there was only one pay level for each grade. This system had long been criticised as a barrier to organisational flexibility and a cause of low vertical mobility of workers from one grade to another and low horizontal mobility. Vertical mobility is difficult to achieve because movement between grades is considered as new recruitment and involves bureaucratic procedures based on administrative law. This means that internal promotion cannot be managed internally. The outcome is that it is almost impossible for qualified civil servants to be promoted to a higher grade. There are also barriers to horizontal mobility due to high task and defined job specifications. For example, in the civil service and health service there are a lot of occupational groups and criteria developed to classify positions which are defined by law. Similarly in local authorities job specification is determined by a special authority and is highly specific.

The new pay and grading system has the declared objective of improving organisational flexibility and is based principally on competencies. The grading system is very similar in all branches of the public sector and consists of four grades A, B, C and D. Each is a 'broad banded' pay scale, in which grades are linked to ranges on the scale. Each band has four to six steps defined by collective bargaining. Each pay step has a fixed amount but progression through the band is wholly dependent on performance, based on appraisal against predetermined objectives. Progression through the grades represents a career progression, e.g. from sub-clerical grade A or B to clerical grade C and on from C to executive grade D. Progression through the grades depends on the recruitment policy of individual organisations, which decide on external or internal selection and, in turn, depends on the internal competencies of the staff in relation to organisational needs.

Another area of change in Italian public employment since 1997 under government ordinance No. 396/97, has been in the field of collective bargaining, where local agreements are now more important. Especially in local authorities and health services, union policy has been to develop decentralised bargaining. The trend in both law and practice is towards greater autonomy for single organisations to negotiate salary increases within the limit of their own budget. In general, decentralised bargaining is focusing on the managing of additional compensation but lack of innovatory tools is restricting change.

According to OECD (1993) there are four main forms of pay flexibility: (a) the decentralisation of the pay determination process; (b) variation in pay systems between different organisations and/or groups of employees; (c) variation in pay rates in different categories or sub-sectors; and (d) individual or group-based variations in pay for a given job or position on the basis of factors such as skill, responsibilities or performance. In Italian public employment all four kinds of flexible pay forms are present. In particular forms (b) and (c) are developed and managed through collective bargaining and forms (a) and (d) are beginning to develop within single organisations. However, despite the rhetoric of reforms and some progress, the extent of flexibility in the pay system is very limited and Italian public organisations are still considered the 'kingdom of rigidity'.

EVALUATION

Since 1993, radical changes have occurred in the Italian public sector, especially in public employment. Greater human resource flexibility has been the objective of laws and ordinances by government. In Italy, as in the rest of Europe, decentralisation of responsibility for HRM from central government to departments or other public organisations and devolution of responsibility for HRM within public organisations to line managers are the stated governmental objectives. A policy to assimilate private and public employment rules has been developed. Despite general trends, however, it is difficult to claim that public organisations are flexible organisations, able to adapt themselves to changing circumstances, and using new patterns in people management in place of traditional bureaucratic models.

Given that policies for increasing flexibility in public employment are well known (OECD, 1996) and are being introduced in many European states, why has it been so difficult to achieve it in the Italian case? What factors are obstructing change in Italy? According to

Rebora (1998) the change process is characterised by different elements or variables including:

* *motivation to change*, involving all the forces stimulating change and determining the possibility of organisational evolution
* *organisational inactivity* or indolence involving those forces which steer an organisation towards stability
* *actors of change* or the people able to promote innovation within their organisations
* *change process and lever* involving all actions and interactions between people who develop innovation and specific instruments and procedures used by actors to hold the reins of change
* *patterns of organisational evolution* which are the result of the change process.

Using this model it is clear in Italy that change towards more flexible human resources policies and practices in accordance with the 'new people management' has encountered problems at each stage. Positive motivation to change has been politically driven and stemmed from both the scarcity of resources and the 'citizen's voice'. In contrast, negative forces impeding change have stemmed from a system of administration based on laws and ordinances, the culture of public sector workers and scarcity of competition within the public sector. Since 1990, there has been a proliferation of regulations each producing further regulations which have led to a regulation jungle making it very difficult to operate. The complexity of the decision-making process, due to over-regulation by laws and ordinances, also leads to strong contradictions in Italian public administration. The legislative tools, based on the traditional bureaucratic model of public administration, especially if overused, inhibit the development of new cultural models compatible with more performance-oriented practices. They create confusion and impede the implementing of reforms. The second problem is the culture of Italian public employees among whom seniority, stability, security and professional identity are still strong values. More and more senior managers pay attention to cost and flexibility but not to staff levels, as there is a commitment to the *status quo*. Managers prefer managing consensus instead of change.

As regards organisational inactivity, there are two kinds of problem: one concerning the behaviour of people, the other concerning organisational capabilities. At the first level, there is lack of managerial skill within public organisations that is hindering development of the flexible organisation model in HRM. As regards' organisational capabilities, public administration is overloaded with new procedures and new models of management and there are not enough resources of time, expertise, skills or finance to manage change.

For the agents and actors in the change process, there are two kinds of problem. The first is finding strong leadership in the organisation that can manage the change process. Generally politicians, managers and unions do not have a strong interest in increasing flexibility. Politicians are interested in decentralisation but not in devolution as they do not want to lose their power. Furthermore they do not want trouble with public officials and their unions. Managers are not used to having power in people management and do not know how to use it. Unions do not like too much flexibility, as they want to maintain centralisation to ensure standardisation and uniformity within employment relations. A second problem and brake on reform is the influence of external actors (the Treasury and administrative court) which are interested in maintaining central control of local public units. This creates a contradiction within the organisation which in managing this external control creates rigidity instead of flexibility.

To conclude it can be said that Italian public administration is clearly looking for flexibility. A reform process has now started and there is evidence of the beginnings of more pay, numerical and functional flexibility. However, many factors are impeding change and causing delays and inactivity. Change is likely to be a slow, although a certain process.

References

AIROLDI, G. (1995). *Ownership and governance: the case of Italian enterprises and public administration.* Milan: Egea.
DELL'ARINGA, C. (ed.) (1997). *Rapporto ARAN sulle retribuzioni 1996.* Milan: Franco Angeli.
DELL'ARINGA, C. (ed.) (1998). *Rapporto ARAN sulle retribuzioni 1997.* Milan: Franco Angeli.
D'ORTA, C. and TALAMO, V. (1996). 'Italy', in Farnham, D., Horton, S., Barlow, J. and Hondeghem, A., *New Public Managers in Europe. Public Servants in Transition,* Basingstoke: Macmillan, pp 215–39.
FARNHAM, D. and HORTON, S. (1997). *Employment Flexibility and the New People Management in the Public Services: the Case of the UK,* paper presented at the Annual Conference of EGPA, Leuven.
No. 83/1983. *General Law of Public Employment.*
OECD (1993). *Pay flexibility in the public sector.* Paris: OECD.

OECD (1996). *Integrating People Management into Public Service Reform.* Paris: OECD.

Ordinance 29/93. *Rationalisation of Public Bodies, Organisation and Reform of Public Employment.*

Ordinance 83/83 *General Law of Public Employment.*

Ordinance 396/97. *Modification of Ordinance 29/93.*

REBORA, G. (1998). *Organizzazione aziendale.* Rome: Carocci editore.

9 Introducing Rationality in Human Resources Management in Spanish Central Administration

Salvador Parrado-Díez

Spanish public administration has experienced a considerable change in the last two decades as a consequence of the political territorial decentralisation process (Parrado-Díez, 1996). Functions along with human and budgetary resources have been transferred from central to regional authorities with central administration left mostly with staff in charge of planning activities. Devolution of powers, however, has not been matched with the distribution of personnel. Some central organisations are overstaffed whilst the few agencies that deliver services directly to citizens are understaffed. Central units for human resources management (HRM) have devised several strategies both to comply with the general economic need to cut public expenditure through damping down growth in staffing and to centralise the system to introduce more rationality into personnel management. Public organisations and line managers have reacted against this centralisation process which is designed to bring more flexibility in HRM at the end of the day.

FACTORS INFLUENCING HUMAN RESOURCES FLEXIBILITIES

Reasons for adopting forms of flexibility in HRM are manifold (Maguire, 1993; Richards, 1995; Gustafsson, 1995). Four arguments explain why public organisations seek personnel flexibilities. First, by reducing the size of public organisations and staff costs, governments are aiming to dampen down public expenditure and, in particular, public-sector deficits (Richards, 1995; Maguire, 1993). Further, a flexible workforce is cheaper and more amenable to economies. Second, modernisation programmes contain reforms of personnel management methods and systems. Human resources are recognised as the engines propelling innovation. Successful introduction of new technology and management systems is dependent on staff commitment. Therefore personnel systems have to be adapted and based on a culture compatible with the aims and objectives of new systems (Klages, 1997). Further, if the state enters a territorial restructuring process, new allocation of resources and functions demand more flexibility of personnel to adapt to the new situation. Third, public employers have difficulties in competing with private employers in the recruitment and retention of highly qualified workers (Maguire, 1993; Gustafsson, 1995). Flexible and more attractive contracts bargained on an individual basis are designed to get and keep well-qualified staff. Fourth, a more controversial argument is that macroeconomic pressures require salary flexibility in both the public and private sectors (Maguire, 1993). An OECD report shows, however, that the link between macroeconomic policy and public sector pay is not easy to demonstrate and not all countries use public sector pay policy as a macroeconomic instrument (OECD, 1995).

These explanations of the shift to flexibility of human resources in public services may sometimes be contradictory. Measures to downsize the number of public servants, which aims to reduce the public deficit, could be contradicted by more flexibility of top management contracts (fixed-term contracts) or more freedom of pay determination leading to an increase in public spending. As Raadschelders and Rutgers (1996) show in their comparative study of the evolution of civil services, multiple and often conflicting objectives coexist in most systems. Some elements relate to governance; some link to personnel management and efficiency; and others concern financial or political accountability.

According to Richards (1995), the path to more flexible organisations varies for public and private agencies. In private enterprises, there is not a radical change from a rigid structure to a more flexible one but a continuing strategy of adaptation. Public organisations, however, have to break with the past in order to become flexible. Flexibility for public organisations entails transformation from a bureaucratic system, ruled by the need to achieve equity, coherence and procedural rectitude, into a managerial system focused on efficiency, effectiveness and value for money. Even though a more efficient and effective organisation is an avowed goal of governments, the essence of the state, promoting equal treatment of citizens and equal development of all communities within its boundaries, cannot be neglected. Laegreid (1995) demonstrates that both sets of ideas are paradoxical. Coexistence of both principles constitutes the paradox of the state's position on public human resources. On the one hand, the state is expected to ensure equality of rights and employment security whilst, on the other hand, it is expected to promote productivity and cost-effectiveness of public sector activities.

Human resources flexibilities in the Spanish public sector have been mostly driven by economic factors rather than by political ones, as in the United Kingdom (Farnham and Horton, 1997). Therefore, there has been a stronger attempt at reducing the size of the public sector by controlling numbers of public employees and by freezing salaries and only a limited attempt at reducing the scope of the public sector by privatisation. There has been almost no effort to encourage an enterprise culture. Besides the economic factors, the search for more flexibility of human resources has been encouraged by the emerging situation brought about by the territorial restructuring of the Spanish state. Redistribution of functions among levels of government – planning and co-ordination are mostly at national level and service delivery mostly at regional and local level – is demanding a more flexible use of personnel. Due to the devolution process and the importance of the role shift of central government public servants, this chapter focuses mainly on the central level.

In this chapter some categories of flexibility (numerical flexibility, length of working life, contractual flexibilities and pay flexibility) that Farnham and Horton (1997) have used from the European Association of Personnel Management are dealt with in order to examine the Spanish case. Before dealing with flexibility in detail, some introductory explanations of the effects of territorial devolution of power on central units for HRM are explored.

THE INFLUENCE OF REGIONALISATION ON HRM AT CENTRAL LEVEL

Reduction in the size of the public sector has taken place at the same time that state functions are being transferred to the regional level of government. The transformation of the unitary centralist, Napoleonic Spanish state into a 'quasi-federal' system with a powerful regional level, during the last two decades, has involved an ongoing redistribution of public servants amongst levels of government. Shortly, regional authorities will rank first as public employers, while national government will rank second in terms of numbers employed. Furthermore, national civil servants are changing their roles as the activities of planning and co-ordination remain at central level and, with few exceptions, delivery of services is being accomplished at regional and local levels.

As a consequence of this, HRM at national level is operating under four main tensions. First, the public sector must face the dilemma of doing more with less. If privatisation is not a feasible option, the only strategy is cutting the numbers of personnel employed. The need for flexibility of human resources is a direct consequence of the policy of reducing public employment. It may well be that the number of public servants should be reduced because there are too many and they are inefficient. However, most government reports deal rather with economic reasons for reducing numbers and not with issues of efficiency and effectiveness. Second, civil servants that have not been transferred from central level to regional authorities were mostly engaged in service delivery functions which have been devolved. The new planning and co-ordinating role of central organisations compels civil servants to adapt themselves to a new situation. Third, citizens are continuously demanding better services. In national government, this pressure is only felt in a few direct services that have remained with the centre (such as national police force, post office, tax collection, passports, driving licences, pension delivery, and so on). In these services, the number of staff is not enough to cope with citizen demand. There is therefore a mismatch of overstaffed co-ordinating and planning units and understaffed delivery organisations. Finally, differences of workload and salaries among civil servants delivering services and civil servants working as planners also brings another tension in the system. It appears that service delivery is more stressful than planning behind closed doors and this has led to increased demands for posts in decision-making and planning departments by those delivering services.

In order to resolve these tensions, two main strategies have dominated at central level. On the one hand, central government is trying to centralise the management of human resources by taking it away from the control of *corps* and ministry political appointees (Parrado-Díez, 1996). On the other hand, some organisations have tried to get a more independent status through autonomisation and through escaping from public law. Both strategies have influenced flexibility. The former trend confers rigidity on the system, with the promise of more flexibility for the future; the latter aims directly at more flexibility. Thus the centralisation process of HRM is a response to the need to reduce staff at any cost and is aimed at introducing some rationality into the system, before any serious attempt of granting more autonomy to line and personnel managers can be pursued.

FLEXIBILITY OF NUMBERS: A PRIMARY GOVERNMENTAL GOAL

Since the early 1990s, Spain has tried to downsize its civil service in order to comply with government's commitment to reducing public expenditure. Contraction started later in Spain than in other OECD countries for two reasons (Orgaz-Regúlez, n.d.). First, there was no growth in the welfare state until the transition to democracy in the late 1970s. Public expenditure increased from 23 per cent of GNP in 1970 to 40 per cent in 1990, which brought Spain up to the level at which France, Germany, the UK and US had been (37 per cent) throughout the period. Second, creation of autonomous regions brought about a major growth of staff in the new political-administrative bodies.

The overall size of the Spanish public sector has increased only slightly in the period 1990–97, from 1,388,553 to 1,525,522 public servants (police forces, military personnel and health staff are not included). The growth between 1993 and 1997 has been around 8,000 employees in absolute numbers. More relevant than the growth of personnel has been the internal redistribution of public sector employees among central, regional and local levels, as can be seen in Figure 9.1. While numbers of staff working in central government have declined, numbers of personnel in regional authorities have increased with the newly transferred services. A report from the International Monetary Fund (IMF 1996, cited in MAP, 1998) established that there is duplication of services in Spanish public administration and it recommended a reduction in the number of employees at central level, where there is now a limit of a 25 per cent replacement level. Growth of personnel numbers at local level is related to expansion of local activity, even though municipalities have not participated in the territorial distribution of power that took place.

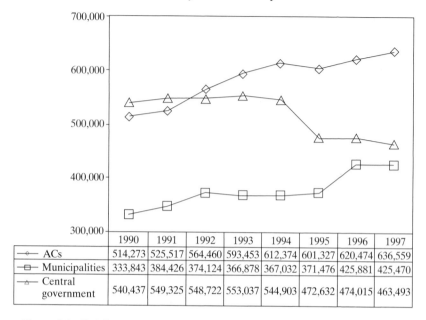

	1990	1991	1992	1993	1994	1995	1996	1997
—◇— ACs	514,273	525,517	564,460	593,453	612,374	601,327	620,474	636,559
—▱— Municipalities	333,843	384,426	374,124	366,878	367,032	371,476	425,881	425,470
—△— Central government	540,437	549,325	548,722	553,037	544,903	472,632	474,015	463,493

Figure 9.1   Public sector employment in Spain, 1990–97
Source: MAP (1998a).

Temporary jobs as a reaction to reductions in recruitment

There are three major ways of recruiting personnel. First, a civil service commission and/or the Treasury may monopolise recruitment. This is a very rigid selection mechanism but one in which uniform criteria are imposed in particular cases. In this instance, reactions to new demands for human resources are not promptly attended to. Second, a combination of central, departmental and other organisational units such as *corps* and autonomous agencies are responsible for recruitment. Where organisational units are converted into cost-centres, and line managers are responsible for goals, budgets and personnel, it follows that the same line managers should perform the recruitment function, adapted to their needs. Third, efficient and productive managers can be selected by specialised recruiting firms or head-hunters, as is the case in the UK (Richards, 1995) and Sweden (Gustafsson, 1995).

Central Spanish administration, since 1984, fits into the second pattern. Recruitment of new staff in central government has been partly centralised, so that MAP (Ministry for Public Administration) and MET (Ministry of Economy and Treasury) can control the size and costs of personnel through the Public Employment Offer (PEO). Part of recruitment was, however, decentralised. It was no longer mandatory for a great number of agencies to apply for approval of vacancies in the annual PEO. Apart from the dysfunctionalities that this measure has brought about, there has been inconsistency in controlling public expenditure. Some of the bodies that did not have to submit to PEO have enjoyed an increase in autonomy during the 1990s. The autonomy involved evasion from public law and is reflected in personnel management practices, whereby managers have freedom to hire staff and determine wages. For instance, between 1988 and 1992, around 30 bodies have experienced a change in their juridical status (Ariño and López de Castro, 1994).

PEO is meant to be an instrument with planning effects that should comply with the limit of the 25 per cent replacement figure. This goal, however, has not been fully achieved. While PEO has been absolutely restrictive (see the evolution of civil servant and labour force recruitment in Figure 9.2), the overall number of contracts has not diminished to the same extent because of growth of temporary contracts.

As can be seen in Figure 9.2, the number of civil servant entrants and number of labour contracts diminished from over 13,000 (adding both) in 1992 to under 300 in 1996. Before 1992, use of temporary employment was insignificant (MAP, 1998). Figure 9.2 shows that temporary contracts increased from 2,629 in 1992 to nearly 10,000 in 1994 and over 7,000 in 1996. Thus the avowed restrictive policy to cut down public expenditure, where most state functions are performed by other levels of government, failed. Contracts under temporary conditions constitute a flexible reaction from agencies to overcome central restrictive policies.

According to MAP (1998), temporary contracts are used for jobs of a 'permanent' nature in agencies where shortages of personnel are considerable, for example the Post Office, National Institute of Employment, Police forces, Treasury and Institute of Social Services. Temporary jobs have created a problem, as they have become structural to the system. As mandatory regulations compel that the public service should be staffed by civil servants, there has been the need to convert those on temporary labour contracts into permanent civil servants. Therefore, genuine temporary contracts, such as the needs

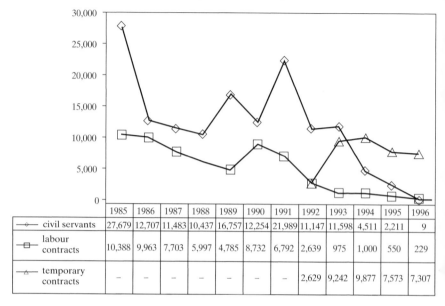

	1985	1986	1987	1988	1989	1990	1991	1992	1993	1994	1995	1996
—◇— civil servants	27,679	12,707	11,483	10,437	16,757	12,254	21,989	11,147	11,598	4,511	2,211	9
—□— labour contracts	10,388	9,963	7,703	5,997	4,785	8,732	6,792	2,639	975	1,000	550	229
—△— temporary contracts	–	–	–	–	–	–	–	2,629	9,242	9,877	7,573	7,307

Figure 9.2　Contracts by type in Spain, 1985–96
Source: MAP (1998a).

of Post Office during Christmas or elections, campaigns preventing
fire, income tax campaigns of the Tax Agency, extra-curriculum activities from the Ministry of Education and Culture, health services at
holiday times and others of a similar nature, have not remained time-
limited contracts. In this situation, reactions from the central authorities have been: first, the forbidding of temporary contracts and,
second, since 1996 (*Ley 13/1996*), PEO has been extended to all public
organisations of central government. Nowadays, even autonomous
agencies are subject to central control (MAP and MET) for new
contracts.

**Early retirement and career-break extensions as
means to downsizing**

Two further issues have influenced recruitment: early retirement and
career breaks. Government has used the early retirement scheme,
allowing employees to leave working life before normal retirement

age of 65, to cut numbers. More than 2,000 civil servants have accepted early retirement since 1994, although those in group B (three years at university) are the most represented of all groups (more than 40 per cent in each year of early pensioners) in early retirement (MAP, 1998a). There is no clear explanation for this pattern. There has been another piece of legislation that goes in the opposite direction to the above policy. While civil servants had to retire at 65, since 1997 legislation allows them to stay in service until the age of 70. It was first applied to university professors and magistrates. The members of other *corps* of top civil servants asked to have the same regulation. Top civil servants are more willing to remain in office – group A (five years at university or 69 per cent of those in retirement) and group B (three years at university or 40 per cent) than the rest (MAP, 1998a). There are clear advantages for the individual. However, from the organisational perspective if civil servants over 65 remain in office, this diminishes recruitment and old civil servants may pose obstacles to modernisation of the services.

In Spain, public managers have been allowed to spend several years in the private sector. Until 1996, there was restrictive legislation on career breaks and after 15 years in the private sector civil servants had to return to public administration or they lost the status of public servants. Some civil servants had to re-enter administration against their will and their entry caused uneasiness in the organisation, as they could choose where they wanted to work, independently of the number of staff in that particular organisation. Although there are no data to illustrate this problem, it was a concern of MAP for some years before a solution was found. Legislation in 1996 abolished the maximum period of time that civil servants may now remain in the private sector (*Ley 13/1996 de Medidas Fiscales, Administrativas y del Orden Social*).

New contracts according to groups

Reduction of recruitment according to different types of contracts has been uneven. In the recruitment function, as well as in other activities of the civil service, a distinction must be made between, labour contracts, 'street-level' and top civil servants. The change in the state's role from provider of services to enabler through privatisation, rightsizing and autonomisation has reduced the top civil service to a core of highly qualified generalists. Demand for specialists is increasingly covered either by contracting-out activities to the corporate sector or by employing individuals on specific contracts under labour legislation, as in the cases of computer experts, engineers, accountants, legal advisors and marketing personnel. Use of labour contracts may be misleading from the point of view of flexibility. Labour contracts for staff at lower levels are collectively bargained on a global and not an individual basis. Therefore, they are rather rigid. However, in relative terms, labour contracts are more flexible than civil servant status as the former are based on individual posts and the latter on careers or a constellation of posts in the administrative ladder. Furthermore, the recruiting process is much easier for the former.

As stated above many temporary contracts are converted into permanent ones. This is because the Constitutional Tribunal compels the public service to be staffed by civil servants. Hence many contracts must be converted into civil service status. This has posed some problems for the system, as the process of granting civil service status to contract staff has been criticised on the grounds that their public competition examinations were felt to be easier than those for permanent civil servants. It has become an unfair competition for those trying to enter public administration from the outside.

Cuts in recruitment of civil servants have been selective in terms of groups and according to level of education for entry. The recruiting policy of central government benefits mostly civil servants in group A (degree – five years at university level) who are in charge of planning activities. Civil servants in group B (three years at university), with implementation tasks, are no longer necessary, as delivery of services is performed elsewhere. Complete restriction on entry to groups C (advanced level) and D (education up to 16) is because they are overstaffed. The functions of group E (education up to 14 years of age), such as cleaning, concierge and the like, are being submitted to private contracts. This group is therefore likely to disappear.

Finally, since the early 1990s, politically appointed positions have become 'contract posts' with similar conditions to those in the private sector. These 'shielded contracts' (*contratos blindados*) include a huge indemnification in the case of dismissal and were banned by the last Socialist government. Private managers, however, can still be contracted to manage public corporations and autonomous agencies, under so-called 'Top Management Contracts' (TMCs – *contratos de alta dirección*) but with more moderate indemnification according to labour law, limited by government in an agreement of 1993 (Martínez-Moreno, 1994). TMCs have acquired increasing importance, especially in autonomous or 'quasi-autonomous' public bodies. Thus, in 1993, there were around 700 or 800 TMCs in different areas such as Spanish Television and Broadcasting, the Spanish Agency for International Co-operation, Post Office, Spanish Railways, hospitals and other public bodies (Jiménez-Asensio, 1996). In spite of few TMCs in public corporations and the contracting-out of some services at lower echelons of the administrative hierarchy, it cannot be claimed that recruiting techniques have become more flexible in the Spanish system in general. Recruitment of public servants is still largely based upon rigid principles for the great bulk of civil servants and those on labour contracts.

CAREER MOBILITY: FROM CENTRALISED FLEXIBLE PLANNING TO PIECEMEAL CENTRALISATION

Vertical promotion in the hierarchy, and horizontal mobility between the private and public sectors and amongst different organisations, are the means to increase flexibility from both the individual and organisational perspective. Opportunity for compulsory and voluntary mobility between and among different administrative levels, ministries and public corporations affects the degree of freedom that personnel managers possess to move human resources around and this depends on the degree of centralisation of the system. Compulsory mobility normally fits into the organisational perspective, while voluntary mobility may have professional and personal advantages. Both collective and individual compulsory transfers require political bargaining with trade unions in Spain. As stated above the distribution of human resources is geographically and functionally uneven in Spanish central administration (MAP, 1998). There are ministries and provinces with surpluses of personnel. For example, in the Ministry of Agriculture and in the province of Madrid, civil servants were not transferred to Autonomous Communities (ACs) and they are overstaffed, whilst in other ministries and agencies that deliver services such as the Traffic Agency and police forces, there are considerable shortages of personnel. The workload in such agencies is greater than in other public organisations, with co-ordinating functions and jobs less advantageous for public workers in terms of pay. These circumstances have had an enormous influence on the voluntary mobility and promotion of civil servants. Whenever a civil servant acquires enough experience in an intensive but relatively underpaid job in an agency, with high pressure from citizens for delivering services, he/she will end up applying for a job in an organisation with planning responsibilities, less workload and better pay.

There have been attempts to promote voluntary and compulsory mobility within the Spanish public service, away from relatively overstaffed units to those lacking staff, through employment plans (*Planes de Empleo*) introduced by Act of Parliament in 1993. As the public workforce cannot be dismissed either collectively or individually, in the case of redundant staff an Employment Plan, designed by any agency, could serve the purpose of moving resources to agencies where there is a shortage of personnel (Palomar-Olmeda, 1995). The success of this planning measure has been rather limited, however, since it was perceived in the media and by public employees as a means of making large numbers of public employees redundant. The agreement with trade unions recognises the limits of compulsory mobility and negotiation as the only acceptable mechanism for change. Nevertheless, distrust in employment plans remains. Only five employment plans were approved in 1995 and 1996 at the National Institute for Employment, the Post Office, Agency for Research on Energy and Environmental Issues, Ministry of Defence and Tax Agency – Information and Technology Services, under the Socialist government, and none under the Conservative government since 1996. All have been short-term and not medium or long-term negotiations. Although implementation of such plans has been assessed as positive, there are negative aspects that should be taken into account:

- none of the plans involved mobility of human resources or voluntary retirement provisions
- employment plans have been sectoral and not global and have not taken into account the new more regulatory and less executive tasks of central administration
- the plans have not introduced an overall strategy but only piecemeal measures
- plans have been designed by those agencies needing personnel and not by those with staff surpluses, so redistribution of resources has not taken place
- development of the plans has brought about unwanted salary increases (MAP, 1998).

Thus employment planning has not been enforced as intended but pressure on cutting public expenditure has continued. MAP has therefore devised other measures in an incremental, step-by-step process, bargaining with trade unions and trying to balance other agencies and organisational reactions.

Regarding the heterogeneous distribution of staff in geographical and functional terms, MAP has introduced mechanisms encouraging voluntary transfer of personnel from overstaffed ministries, with considerable reduction of functions due to devolution of services, to understaffed agencies at central level. In many instances, there are economic incentives to encourage geographical mobility. Top political appointees of ministries are very reluctant to get rid of their resources, however, as they consider human resources as the source of their power. So compulsory mobility has not yet been attempted. This would have to be agreed with trade unions and political appointees but negotiations are difficult on this question. To add to the difficulties new job offers in overstaffed agencies are not permitted.

Negotiations with trade unions are of crucial relevance in the whole procedure but fragmentation of the unions poses a problem for MAP officials. There are around 50 collective agreements between trade unions and the public authorities. This is a barrier to achieving a homogeneous policy and agreed objectives (MAP, 1998) and the process takes too long to cope with high pressure on the system to reduce public expenditure. The existence of so many different agreements between trade unions and the authorities is very dysfunctional, as all proposals require general agreements between trade union headquarters and top officials in ministries. This strategy is intended to produce homogenisation and unification of labour relations. More centralisation in labour relations is being sought in order to introduce more rationality in the system.

CENTRALISED PAY DETERMINATION

Some of the key characteristics of the rigid salary systems in both public and private organisations in Spain are: (1) negotiations are undertaken at national level and local conditions are not considered; (2) remuneration is largely administrative and its determination is centralised, without reference to performance or productivity; and (3) salary levels, grades and payment increase with seniority (Murlis, 1993). The introduction of more flexible rewards systems derive from three stimuli: to get better performance and productivity, prevent managers leaving for better paid positions elsewhere and attract managers from external organisations (OECD, 1993). The public sector's position in the salary market is not competitive, since it offers worse pay and conditions than in private enterprises for managers with the same type of rank and functions (Gutiérrez-Reñón and Labrado-Fernández, 1988). Adoption of TMCs, with highly improved salaries and fringe benefits, has served to attract some private managers into public corporations. Salary, however, is not necessarily the most relevant factor in motivating staff in public agencies. Other features of public tenure may be more attractive to private managers but the least they ask for is not to be worse off in public office.

The Spanish system of pay fits into a traditional pattern of organising rewards in public administration, according to the OECD criteria (1993). Pay is related to performance only through promotion to a higher-paid grade. Since 1984 (*Ley 30/1984*), there has been an attempt to link payment with performance (*complemento de productividad*) but, with few exceptions, performance related pay (PRP) does not really work in most Spanish public organisations as intended. This is because staff receive salary complements, without assessments of their productivity. In fact, PRP is normally attached to objectives. Management by Objectives (MbO) and Planning, Programming and Budgeting Systems (PPBS), already adopted by most Spanish administrations, should function as a basis for any allocation of PRP. The contribution of PPBS to better use of resources (Herrero and Querol, 1984) and use of objectives to guide appropriations in public organisations have, however, only been nominal in most instances. Autonomous agencies and public corporations are more adapted to manage by objectives and, for that reason, PRP has been more effectively implemented in some autonomous bodies. The National Institute for Social Security is a good example, where there is collective bargaining of objectives and PRP by both central divisions and provincial units. If there is achievement of objectives (partially or fully), PRP is paid to all staff in the provincial unit.

Performance-related payment is not the only device for determining degrees of flexibility in reward systems. There are other factors influencing rewards, which have not been identified in this chapter. These include the structure of public administration, public sector unions and collective agreements. Lack of adjustment of public wages to local labour market conditions, comparability with the private sector or the estimated rate of inflation are all indicators of rigidity in a reward system. All these features are encountered in the Spanish public sector, especially since there has been a movement towards more institutionalised pay arrangements and growth in trade union organisation in Spain. Nevertheless, the involvement of trade unions is not over-important, as pay determination is subject to unilateralist governmental patterns, which makes pay determination systems less flexible (see chapter 14).

CONCLUSION

There has been considerable political decentralisation in the Spanish public sector, through the creation of autonomous regional authorities since the early 1980s. Many former centralised state activities have been transferred to regional level. There has also been a slight reduction in the size of the public service in Spain over the last six years in order to contain public expenditure. This has been paralleled by a redistribution of employees between national and regional levels of government, as a consequence of territorial devolution of power. Until 1984, the system was controlled by *corps* and there was not enough power at the centre to rationalise or control the system. This lack of rationality has also been present in the recent transfer process. Planning and co-ordinating activities remain at central level with service delivery decentralised to the regions. This has resulted in a maldistribution of personnel. Distribution is uneven in two respects: (1) some provincial delegations have surplus of personnel, whilst others have deficits; (2) central organisations with planning duties are overstaffed and the few remaining central agencies that deliver services to the citizens are understaffed.

To date, central ministries in charge of human resources (the Ministry for Public Administration and Ministry of Economy and Treasury) have increased their power to control human resources including overall staff numbers, pay determination and inter-departmental mobility. Only some agencies have partially and temporarily evaded central control such as the Tax Agency, Post Office and National Airports. Increased centralisation has been enforced to avoid anarchy and to achieve real cuts in public sector expenditure. An overall strategy to encourage agencies with surplus staff to design schemes to deploy unnecessary personnel to other central organisations, through employment plans, has proved largely unsuccessful. This overarching strategy has been substituted with piecemeal measures that also aim at introducing rationality in the system. These include: non-replacement, controlling all applications for new posts, allowing early retirement, not compelling civil servants enjoying a career break to return to service and trying to avoid temporary contracts of a structural nature. There have also been attempts to redeploy human resources. A step-by-step strategy, being negotiated with trade unions, is bringing about some geographical and functional shift of staff between provinces and ministries. The process is slow and uneven but piecemeal intervention seems to offer certain promise of success.

Paradoxically, as there are efforts to increase the flexibility of the system, it is becoming more inflexible as the centre aims at greater control and room of manoeuvre for agencies is being restricted. Temporary contracts for jobs are more difficult to get and conversion of existing labour contracts into civil service status makes them as inflexible as other civil service contracts. It may well be that after this process of rationalisation, the political centre will devolve greater authority on HRM issues to personnel managers in different public organisations. But there is still a long and uncertain way to go in this respect.

Acknowledgement

I would like to thank Miguel Ordozgoiti, Deputy General Director of Planning and Recruitment of Human Resources, and Antonio Ramiro, General Inspector for Services, in the Ministry of Public Administration and other unnamed officials for their help in producing this chapter.

Abbreviations

ACs   Autonomous Communities
HRM   Human Resources Management
IMF   International Monetary Funds
MAP   Ministry for Public Administration
MbO   Management by Objectives
MET   Ministry of Economy and Treasury
PEO   Public Employment Offer
PPBS   Planning, Programming and Budgeting Systems
PRP   Performance-Related Payment
TMC   Top Management Contracts

References

ARIÑO, G. and LÓPEZ DE CASTRO, L. (1994). *Privatizar el Estado? Un retroceso en el camino de la Historia o la antítesis del Estado de Derecho*. Madrid: Fundscion BBV, Cuodernos de Ecamcia.
FARNHAM, D. and HORTON, S. (1997). 'Human Resources Flexibilities in the United Kingdom's Public Services', in *Review of Public Personnel Administration*, Summer, pp 18–33.
GARRIDO, F. (1994). 'Origen y evolución de las entidades instrumentales de las Administraciones públicas', in Pérez, A. (ed), *Administración Instrumental: Libro homenaje a Manuel Francisco Clavero Arévalo*, Madrid: Civitas, pp 27–45.
GUSTAFSSON, L. (1995). 'Promover la flexibilidad mediante políticas salariales: la experiencia de la administración nacional sueca', in OECD, *Flexibilidad en la gestión de personal en la Administración Pública*, Madrid: INAP, pp 37–54.
GUTIÉRREZ-REÑÓN, A. and LABRADO-FERNÁNDEZ, M. (1988). *La experiencia de la evaluación de puestos de trabajo en la Administración Pública*. Madrid: Ministerio para las Administraciones Públicas (MAP).
HERRERO, S. and QUEROL, V. (1984). *Técnicas presupuestarias en la Administración Pública*. Madrid: INAP.
INAP (1997). *Contribución al análisis de la Administración General del Estado: ideas para un plan estratégico*. (Mimeo.)
KLAGES, H. (1997). *Verwaltungsmodernisierung: 'Harte' und 'Weiche' Aspekte*. Speyerer Forschungsberichte, 172. Forschungsinstitut für öffentliche Verwaltung, Speyer.
JIMÉNEZ-ASENSIO, R. (1996). *Altos Cargos y Directivos públicos*. Oñati: Instituto Vasco de Administración Pública.
LAEGREID, P. (1995). 'Cambios de la política de personal en el sector público noruego', in OECD, *Flexibilidad en la gestión de personal en la Administración Pública*, Madrid: INAP, pp 55–66.
MAGUIRE, M. (1993). 'Flexibilité des rémunérations dans le secteur public – Vue d'ensemble', in OECD, *Flexibilité des rémunérations dans le secteur public*, OECD: Paris, pp 9–20.
MAP (1998). *Planificación de Recursos Humanos en la Administración General del Estado*. MAP (Secretaría de Estado para la Administración Pública). (Mimeo.)
MAP (1998a). *Informe sobre los Recursos Humanos en la Administración General del Estado*. (Mimeo.)
MARTÍNEZ-MORENO, C. (1994). 'La indemnización por cese de los altos cargos en el sector público estatal', in *Actualidad Laboral*, No. 17.
MURLIS, H. (1993). 'Stratégie de rémunération', in OECD, *Flexibilité des rémunérations dans le secteur public*, OECD: Paris, pp 203–34.
OECD (1993). *Pay Flexibility in the Public Sector*. Public Management Studies (PUMA). Paris: OECD.
OECD (1995). *Trends in Public Sector Pay in OECD Countries*. Paris: OECD.
ORGAZ-REGÚLEZ, M.J. (n.d.). 'La planificación de recursos humanos en las Administraciones Públicas. La Oferta de Empleo Público'. (Mimeo.)

PALOMAR-OLMEDA, A. (1995). 'Planes de empleo y reforma administrativa', in *Gestión y análisis de políticas públicas*, 2, pp 17–25.

PARRADO-DIEZ, S. (1996) 'Spain', in Farnham, D. *et al. New Public Managers in Europe. Public Servants in Transition.* London: Macmillan.

RAADSCHELDERS, J. and RUTGERS, M. (1996). 'The Evolution of Civil Service Systems', in Perry, J., Hans A., Bekke, G. and Toonen, T (eds), *Civil Service Systems in Comparative Perspective*, Bloomington: Indiana University Press.

RICHARDS, S. (1995). 'La flexibilidad en la gestión de personal: algunas comparaciones entre el sector público y el sector privado', in OECD, *Flexibilidad en la gestión de personal en la Administración Pública*, Madrid: INAP, pp 13–36.

10 Human Resources Management in Swedish Central Government

Richard Murray

Human resources management (HRM) is now an integral element of the new style of public management in Sweden, which stresses performance rather than regulation. The traditional system of government administration, which bore many of the characteristics of a classical bureaucracy until the mid-1960s, has been transformed into a more flexible post-bureaucratic structure. This chapter is confined to an examination of HRM in Sweden's central government and excludes both local government and the public utilities, such as telecommunications, postal services, air-traffic control and railways, which have long been run in a more businesslike manner. What holds for central government administration, however, also applies to other areas of the public sector, although trends there have either sped ahead or lagged behind those found at the centre. Public utilities have tended to lead the way, and must therefore be credited with inspiring developments in the rest of central government. Instead of relating how HRM has evolved in Sweden, this chapter describes the present state of the art. In particular it examines the ways in which HRM policies relate to other aspects of new public management (NPM) and describes the issues central to the current debates about HRM and flexibilities.

THE SWEDISH PUBLIC SECTOR

Sweden is famous for its very large public sector. In 1996, public spending made up 65 per cent of GDP, compared to the average of 50 per cent in OECD countries in Europe. The Swedish figure is, however, exaggerated in relation to those for other countries. This is because transfers are taxable, and because it excludes the interest income earned by central government from the huge public pension funds. Nevertheless, it is true to say, by international standards, that the public sector in Sweden constitutes an unusually large segment of the economy as a whole. Public consumption, i.e. the costs of providing health care, defence, police, education, etc, makes up 26 per cent of Sweden's GDP, whereas in most OECD countries the share is below 20 per cent. Employment in local and central government and in state-owned enterprises approaches 40 per cent of the labour force. The distribution of employment is shown in the Figure 10.1 below. Tax-financed central government accounts for five per cent of employment in the economy as a whole. When national state-owned enterprises and public utilities are included central government accounts for close to 12 per cent of employment. This is no negligible share but it is still dwarfed by local government, which accounts for 27 per cent of employment. The subject of this chapter is HRM for the five per cent working in the core of central government.

Central government in Sweden has a distinctive structure. It currently comprises 10 ministries, plus the Prime Minister's Office. These

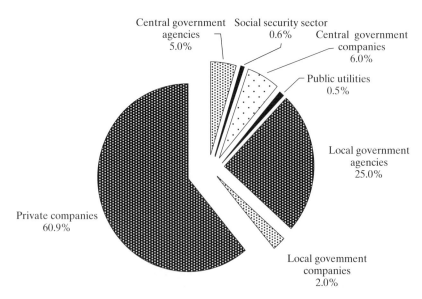

Figure 10.1   Employment in various sectors of the Swedish economy, 1996
Source: Statistics Sweden (1998).

ministries have almost exclusively policy-framing duties. All implementation of policies is carried out in more or less autonomous
agencies. The one major exception is the Ministry for Foreign Affairs,
which includes Swedish embassies abroad. The ministries employ
some 2,500 people, including embassies the number rises to 4,100. Of
this group, in 1994, only 650 employees were charged with responsibility for policy, the remainder having clerical duties (Parliamentary
Auditors, Report 1994–95: 25). Since Sweden's accession to the
European Union in 1993, the number responsible for policy has risen
slightly.

The majority of government employees, currently totalling some
130,000, work in agencies. Each agency is subordinate to a particular
ministry, in the sense that the ministry supervises the agency and
submits to Parliament proposals for legislation and the agency's
appropriations. The ministry drafts directives for the agency upon
which the government – the ministers collectively forming the Cabinet
– decides. Referring to separate ministries is somewhat misleading,
since no minister can decide single-handed on any matter of importance. Each minister presides over a ministry, but this means only
preparing decisions for the Cabinet. All ministerial decisions must be
taken collectively and the Cabinet includes all ministers, currently
numbering 20. Each minister is assisted by an average of around 35
policy advisors.

Terminological distinctions between the various levels of central
government are necessary. When the 'public sector' is divided into
'central government' and 'local government', 'central government'
refers to all government organisations that are not local, including the
Cabinet, ministries, agencies and public utilities. Agencies, of course,
have local branches and field administrations such as employment
offices or courts. Local government, in turn, has two tiers, the municipal and the regional, both run by democratically elected bodies.

HRM POLICY IN 1998

Central government agencies are free to hire and fire staff and set pay
rates at their own discretion. They are subject to general labour legislation that applies to private enterprise and government alike. A
special law for government employees merely adds a limited number
of specific rules for the public sector. These rules concern, for example,
the right to go on temporary leave to take other jobs and disciplinary

action against employees. Agencies bargain collectively through a special government agency – the Swedish Agency for Government Employers (*Arbetsgivarverket*, AgV) – that is completely controlled ('owned') by the other agencies. Its form is that of an economic association: agencies pay membership dues; the board is, although formally appointed by the Cabinet, elected by the other agencies' director-generals; and the director-general is appointed by AgV's own board. In all the other agencies, the agency head is a Cabinet appointee, and funds and directives are received from the Cabinet pursuant to parliamentary decisions.

AgV is a unique creation. It represents and fulfils the objective that the Cabinet should have nothing to do with pay negotiations and that this responsibility should be left squarely with agencies. The present arrangement is the outcome of painful past experience. In 1965 the task of pay negotiations was transferred from the Ministry of Finance to a newly created agency – the forerunner of AgV – but, despite its intentions to stay out of pay negotiations, the Ministry nevertheless became involved and all agreements were submitted to the Cabinet for final approval. The reason for this is obvious: pay increases are very costly. During the 1970s, adoption of incomes policies was a worldwide trend. In Sweden it prompted the Cabinet to intervene more vigorously in the pay-bargaining process. From 1979 to 1985, the Under-Secretary of State for public administration served as the board chairman of the pay-negotiating agency. In 1985, the Prime Minister took part in pay bargaining with the civil servants' union, then on strike. However, not even with this high-level political involvement was it possible to prevent paying increases beyond what was deemed macro-economically sound. A renewed effort was therefore made to free the Cabinet from responsibility for pay negotiations. But it took until 1994, when AgV was created, to find the formula.

AgV bargains with the public sector unions. There are three unions for employees in central government – for graduates, wage earners and a mixture of graduates and other white-collar employees respectively. Almost all employees belong to trade unions, and this puts the unions in a strong position. Most major labour disputes since 1965 have taken place in the public sector. Whether this is due to the high unionisation rate or to the comparative immaturity of the negotiating parties is debatable.

The trend towards the present system of HRM in central government began in 1965. In that year, central-government employees gained the right to strike. This applied to all categories of employees, even the military and police and on occasions they have used this right. The employers, now represented by AgV, can retaliate with lockouts. The only restriction on dispute action is that the action may be adjudged socially harmful for specific positions: a committee composed of employer and employee representatives may declare that a particular action such as strike, lockout or other industrial action, is socially harmful and put a stop to it. Over the years, very few incidents have been singled out in this way.

Despite negotiating rights and freedom to take action in industrial disputes, the traditional system of government pay, rigidly bound up with positions and grades, remained unaltered until 1977. Uniform changes in pay were decided upon in central negotiations and little scope for individual adjustments was provided. During the 1970s, a policy of reducing pay differentials was pursued and the result was a pay gap between the public and private sectors. This gap meant that public-sector employees were favoured in the low pay ranges and disadvantaged in the high. A 'double imbalance' was thus created.

The first players to react against this pay policy were employers representing public utilities. In the early 1980s, deregulation and competition began to be introduced in this sector, boosting the pressure to become more efficient. This in turn called for a more flexible pay system and more flexible HRM as a whole. In Sweden, unlike many other European countries, the economy in the 1980s was characterised by labour scarcity, which from time to time caused problems in recruiting specialist staff, such as data-processing experts, lawyers and economists, to central government. This, too, necessitated a more flexible pay policy. In 1978, the first step in the direction of a more flexible pay system was taken. One per cent of payroll expense was allocated for local negotiations and, in the ensuing years the rigid structure of grades was progressively dissolved. In 1985, the Cabinet submitted to Parliament a bill whereby the only goal of HRM policy for the future was to be the agencies' specific requirements for performing the functions assigned to them.

Today, central pay negotiations lead to agreements that provide a framework or rather a 'floor' for local pay negotiations. Local pay negotiations take place between the agency head, assisted by the staff division of the agency, and agency employees, i.e. their union representatives at the agency. Starting in 1978, exemptions from a centrally negotiated general pay rise were accepted to a limited degree. A specified sum was allocated for each agency to use for increments to pay strategic staff who were greatly in demand. The central agreement still, however, specified general pay rises for all staff grades.

Increasingly, the sums set aside for local negotiations grew. In 1990 the old grade system was abolished and pay rates began to be set individually, at each agency's discretion. In 1996, for the first time, no specification whatsoever was attached to the agreed sum of pay increases for each agency. Individual pay increases were entirely decided in local negotiations. The agreed sum then constituted a 'floor' for the negotiations that the unions were eager to exploit; and the agency was able to accept pay increases that, in aggregate, exceeded this floor.

This way of organising labour relations is modelled on the private business sector. Private enterprise has banded into industry-wide employer associations that are, in turn, organised in a single employers' federation. Labour is similarly organised in unions, divided along roughly similar lines. Trade unions form three main federations, and collective agreements are reached at industry level. The federations have long played a dominant role co-ordinating industry-wide agreements but in the early 1980s employers began abandoning this procedure, in favour of entirely separate collective negotiations for each industry. Central agreements are then followed by local agreements.

What distinguishes AgV from its private counterpart is that, basically, it confines itself to pay negotiations and general working conditions and does not act as a general lobbyist for its members *vis-à-vis* the Cabinet and Parliament. In central government, AgV is the only employers' association and does all the negotiating. There has always been some sort of co-ordination between employer organisations in central and local government.

GOVERNMENT EMPLOYEES

There is no such thing as a civil service in Sweden. Nor has Sweden ever had a civil service training college or anything similar. No special examination or test has ever been required for recruitment to central government. Government employees do not constitute a separate entity, distinct from ministries and agencies. A 'civil' or public servant is employed by a specific agency or by a ministry, not by central government as such, and an agency employee has a job only for as long as there is work to be done at the agency. When an agency is closed down, its employees lose their jobs. Promotion within one agency does not guarantee an equivalent position in another one.

The relationship between public service employees and the executive, whether it be a monarch or a democratically elected government represented by a cabinet, is crucial to the position of government employees. Back in 1611, King Gustavus Adolphus II created a central government in Sweden in which its employees had guaranteed tenure unless they committed some kind of criminal act and were sentenced in court. The reason, at that time, was to create a stable government during the ruler's absence on long war campaigns in foreign countries. In 1634 this rule was incorporated into the constitution and was retained until 1965. The arguments for the rule varied over time but, in general, it has been considered important for public-service employees to be independent of government and capable of acting with integrity. Today, this status applies only to judges. All other central-government employees may lose their jobs on other grounds than criminality but only according to clearly established rules e.g. dismissal due to shortage of work or misbehaviour on the employee's part. Most appointments are normally for an indefinite period although agency heads serve for six-year terms, which may be extended for three years at a time. However, during that time they may be relocated to other tasks.

The question therefore arises of how the administration's integrity is preserved under these new conditions. The answer is the agencies' autonomous standing. This has been seen as the most important safeguard of administrative integrity over the past century. It is rooted in the constitution, and has been guarded by the opposition, regardless of party affiliation, with meticulous care. Every year, a parliamentary debate is held on the ministers' and Cabinet's violations, if any, of the prohibition against interfering with the 'due process of administration'.

So with this strong agency position, how is it possible to delegate responsibility for pay without loss of control? What will stop agency heads from giving away taxpayers' money to their employees? As mentioned previously, there is no ceiling on pay rises in specific agencies, and pay rates are set individually for all employees. Here again, the model adopted is that of the private enterprise, where each company must decide how much it can afford to pay and still make a profit. For this model to function properly in the public sector, agency heads must act as true employers. Considerable efforts have been devoted to training agency heads to take on this responsibility, since the old system of centrally negotiated pay increases for each and every grade of government employees began to be dismantled in 1985.

Training may be necessary, but is not sufficient. If agency heads are to act as true employers, this has to be backed up by incentives. A prerequisite for the functioning of this model has therefore been reform of the appointments and the appropriation systems. The terms of service of agency heads have been shortened and they may now be removed from office and assigned to other duties by the Cabinet if they fail to perform. Since the introduction of this system, a small number of agency heads has been removed. Many served for decades in the past but regular review of the appointment makes that less likely today.

Reform of the appropriation system followed several years of intense political efforts, in the 1980s, to limit pay increases in the Swedish economy as a whole. The public sector was thought – erroneously, it was learnt later – to have been acting irresponsibly, paving the way for large pay increases in the economy as a whole. Paradoxically, the Ministry of Finance and the Ministry of Public Administration at that time exercised full power in pay negotiations. Repeatedly, however, negotiators came up with agreements deviating from the Cabinet's economic policy. This was the decade of active incomes policies in many countries. In some, such as The Netherlands, Denmark and Ireland, these policies appear to have been successful, but not in Sweden, where wage increases continued to be very high. Trade unions were well aware of the mechanisms of appropriation which were calculated by means of a formula that included agreed pay rises. Even if the appropriations had already been decided upon, agencies were compensated for pay agreements reached in the meantime. Unions therefore had no incentive to curb demands for higher pay. Neither had agency heads.

The system was, therefore, reformed in such a way that appropriations were calculated on pay rises in the export sector of private enterprise. Since Sweden is highly dependent on exports, it was considered crucial to adopt pay rises in the exporting sector of the economy as the benchmark. Pay motivated increases in appropriations are calculated upon the previous year's increase of salaried workers' pay in manufacturing. In addition, a reduction is built in, by targets for efficiency savings. Appropriations are nowadays adjusted only once a year in connection with the budget bill. Thus agencies are now given a cash limit on their expenditure that must be taken into account, both when pay rates are negotiated centrally and the 'floor' is set and when negotiated locally on an individual basis.

One flaw in the model, which has not been remedied to date, is that agencies can reduce their staff numbers and pay more to those remaining. To cover that eventuality, agencies could be made to sign contracts for specified outputs. Otherwise, they are free to reduce both output and staff in order to increase pay. Since 1985, efforts have been made to set up a system for monitoring agencies and their performance. Agencies are now obliged to report annually on their financial position and performance generally, in terms of output, quality, outcome. For the past couple of years they have been obliged to report interim, in a simplified way, on the first half of the year. But the quality and comprehensiveness of these reports still leaves a great deal to be desired.

Another flaw in the model is that agencies may have too short a planning horizon and consequently under-invest. Information technology (IT) is an increasingly important tool for enhancing the efficiency of services and the agencies' work requires continuous knowledge inputs. Their staff must be trained to keep up with developments. Until the early 1980s, ministries controlled the agencies' inputs in great detail. Staffing was specified for each level along with the appropriation, and the Cabinet appointed almost all staff. Under this system ministries were able, in principle, to ensure the requisite skills. Under the old system, too, an agency's organisation was prescribed by the Cabinet, which afforded scope for control of resources devoted to information, data processing, staff training and such functions that were deemed important to the agency's long-term functioning. Investments were controlled by special appropriations and monitored by specialist agencies, one for premises and one for IT.

All these features have now been eliminated. Agencies decide for themselves on the staffing needs to carry out their assignments and also on the most suitable organisation. In the transition from the old to the new system of public management, back in 1967 and 1970, two agencies were created to promote good HRM and adequate staff training at agency level. In 1992 the agency in charge of staff policy and training (the Swedish Institute for Public Administration, an amalgamation of the above-mentioned two agencies) was closed. Nowadays, agencies are left to themselves to handle this and may rely on services rendered by private consultants. The agency in charge of government premises was transformed into a limited company, and the agencies were given the right to rent premises from any property owner. There is no longer a requirement that IT investments be procured by a single, specialist agency.

Under these circumstances, what incentives can induce agencies to plan ahead? There are two powerful incentives in operation: one that has always existed and the other is the creation of NPM. Unionisation is high among government employees of all kinds. Almost every employee belongs to a union. And unions are keenly interested in the careers of their members, and therefore seek to promote training. For IT and other investments, agencies are entitled to borrow money up to specified limits. Amortisation and interest must be paid out of the annual appropriation. If the investment is profitable, i.e. if it lowers the costs of the agency's operations, it creates scope for pay increases. The incentive to save on costs has been underpinned by an appropriation technique that enables agencies to save unused funds for the years ahead, as well as, within limits, borrowing from future years. This incentive has proved to be quite a powerful one: after three years, agencies had saved and accumulated a sum total equivalent to 20 per cent of their annual appropriations.

THE LOGIC OF HRM AND NPM

New public management, introduced in 1985, had a long pre-history dating back to earlier efforts to introduce programme budgeting in the 1970s. Some advances had been made in the fields of accounting, performance measurement and global budgeting but most intended reforms remained to be made. Within nine years, with the formation of AgV marking the end of this reform period, they had been more or less completed. The reforms started in 1985 without a blueprint but set off a dynamic course of events with an outcome that is now known as NPM. In 1985, the reforms were not known as the 'new public management'. Instead the focus was on enhancing democratic and political control of administration and increasing its efficiency. This focus stemmed from the politicians' sense of having lost control. Expenditure was soaring and political goals were, again and again, not achieved. To achieve better control, a strategic choice was made. This strategic choice was to introduce performance management and control the administration through performance requirements and measurements of results, rather than through detailed regulation of inputs. This meant giving agencies greater responsibility for achieving their goals and for doing so in an efficient way. But it also meant that the Cabinet and its ministries assumed much more responsibility for formulating clear, relevant, challenging and realistic goals for the agencies.

Each agency head was made the focal point of accountability to the Cabinet. Accordingly, collective responsibility of agency boards was superseded by that of the agency head. For compatibility with this accountability, agency heads had to be given a free hand in reaching the agencies' goals. This meant they had to be given authority to organise their agencies in the most efficient way. Connected with organisation, and equally important, is the capacity to choose the right staff, hence the need to devolve the right to hire and fire to the agency head. Accompanying the right to hire and fire is responsibility for pay and this in turn entails accountability for costs. In addition the agency head had to be able to choose the optimal mix of resources and to be given responsibility for spending on premises, IT, staff, travel, bonuses, etc out of global appropriations. Within a short time of agency heads being made accountable, all the reforms at which programme budgeting had aimed for decades were realised.

Out of this situation and the specific circumstances of the time, the Cabinet derived a set of aims for HRM in the mid-1980s. Each of these is described and evaluated below. In evaluating the experience of HRM devolution it is important to keep in mind the specific prevailing circumstances. First, there was reduction of staff in central government, which fell by 20 per cent between 1980 and 1997. This was the result of incorporations of government services and also shifts of activity to central government, or from it to other levels of government. Second, there were the large number of reorganisations which meant that roughly 30 per cent of central-government employees experienced closure of their agency between 1990 and 1996. Third, organisational policies have been aimed at focusing the tasks of agencies, clarifying their roles and generally downsizing them.

One of the key objectives of HRM was to boost mobility of the workforce, both within central government and between central government, local government and private enterprise. However, experience has been to the contrary. Staff turnover, both in ministries and agencies, decreased sharply between 1986–87 and 1993–94 (see Table 10.1). Cutbacks heavily affected the number of staff and agencies had very little scope for taking on new staff members. No statistics are available on inter-sectoral mobility but there appears to be very little movement between business and the government sector. Specifically,

Table 10.1   Turnover of staff in Swedish ministries
and agencies, 1986 and 1994

Ministries	1986	1994
Managers	10.5	8.3
Other staff	16.8	9.6
Assistants	16.2	6.0
Agencies	*1986–87*	*1993–94*
Managers	10.2	4.7
Staff	9.9	5.2

Source: *Statlig personalpolitik (Central
Government Staff Policy)*, Parliamentary Auditor's
Report 1994–95.12.

HRM was aimed at increasing the mobility of agency heads and this
has been achieved to some extent. In 1994 the average agency head
had served only 4.5 years and almost 40 per cent had served no more
than 2.5 years (Parliamentary Auditors Report, 1995: 42).

A second objective of HRM was to professionalise managers. Here
some progress has been made. In the 1980s a special unit, within the
then Ministry of Public Administration, was created for selecting and
training managers. This unit was subsequently transferred to the
Ministry of Finance where training of new agency heads has been
intensified. Few new recruits to agency heads have had any previous
management experience. A very high proportion is recruited from the
committees that set up the new agency organisations, which very
often, recruit from the ministries (*ibid.*, p 42). It is difficult to establish professional criteria in the appointment of agency heads, since
such appointments are deemed to be of the utmost political significance. The opposition, of whatever party, constantly complains about
'political appointments'. There is no spoils system in Sweden and the
tradition, up to the early 1970s, was that 'civil service' careers extended
to agency-head level or even beyond, if they became under-secretaries
of state. However, with growing ambitions to control the administration, all political parties have accepted an increase in the number of
positions in the ministries that change with the cabinet, mainly under-
secretaries of state, who are ministers' spokesmen and political advisors. All cabinets have tended to make former political appointees, or
politicians, agency heads.

In the face of difficulties, under cutback policies, in acquiring staff with the requisite skills by recruitment, a heavy emphasis has been laid on staff training. The apprehension that agencies would be too short-sighted, hire less qualified people and forget about staff training has already been mentioned. This apprehension seems to have been unwarranted. In fact, central government has by far the most highly educated workforce of all sectors of the economy (see Table 10.2).

Fifty-seven per cent of staff in central government has completed post-upper-secondary (higher) education. In business and industry, the corresponding figure is 21 per cent. Figures for central government exclude public utilities like the railways, postal services, telecommunications, etc, but include universities and colleges which partly explains the significant difference. In areas like defence, police, business services, prisons, and the labour market, the share of staff with higher education varies between 47 and 59 per cent whilst in the cultural sector the proportion is 69 per cent, and nine per cent have PhDs. Although the concern has been that the public sector is unable to attract enough qualified employees, the problem seems rather to be the reverse: that it attracts far too high a share of the highly educated, leaving an insufficient number available for private enterprise. There has been a clear trend in educational level in central government with the proportion with higher education rising from 48 to 57 per cent since 1990. In the business sector, the rise has been from 17 to 21 per cent. At this stage, it is quite natural to ask how a marked rise in the

Table 10.2   Educational levels in various sectors of the Swedish public sector labour market in 1997 (per cent)

	Secondary school	High school	College	University graduate and post-graduate	Total
Central government	9	34	22	35	100
Municipalities	15	46	20	19	100
County councils	6	41	31	22	100
Business	27	52	12	9	100

Source: *Staten i omvandling 1988* (*The Swedish Central Government in Transition, 1998*), Swedish Agency for Administrative Development, 1998:15, p 122.

educational level has come about in the face of decreased turnover caused by downsizing. Difficulties in recruitment should have caused stagnation in staff skills, apart from the improvement brought about by staff training. But staff training cannot confer academic degrees, so it appears that the small scope for recruitment has been used with extreme strategic skill in enhancing the educational and skills level of the workforce. Moreover, agencies' downsizing has been selective: it is the less qualified they have let go.

Central-government employees receive nine or 10 days training a year, against five or six days in the business sector (*ibid.*, p 125). Since the 1980s there has been a major increase in training. Fear that devolution to the agencies would reduce training has been unfounded. Another apprehension that lack of HRM skills at agency level might cause working conditions to deteriorate is more difficult to evaluate. In various interviews, surveys and reports, the picture that emerges is that agencies have had a hard time coping with the increased stress caused by frequent reorganisations and staff cutbacks but not that it is due to ineffective HRM.

There have also been some interesting developments in pay levels and pay dispersion in the relationship between pay developments and decreased staff turnover. As stated above AgV, created in 1994, has been monitoring pay increases since then, in the various sectors of the economy. Pay has risen a good deal less in central government than in manufacturing (the benchmark) and slightly less than in the economy as a whole since 1995 (Table 10.3) The fear that agency heads would be unable to act in the interests of central government as employers seems to be unwarranted. In the longer term, employees in central government and private enterprise have been compared.

Table 10.3 Pay trends in the Swedish economy, central government and other economic sectors, 1995–97 (annual increase, per cent)

Manufacturing	5.5
Other private business	4.5
Central government	4.0
Local government	4.0
The Swedish economy as whole	4.5

Source: SOU, 1997a: 77.

Pay rises are calculated for similar groups of individuals on the basis of pay levels. In the above tables, pay increases are gross of all changes in pay levels and workforce composition. Research concludes that the central government sector never, in the period 1960–95, led pay trends. Rather, it lagged a year or two behind the private sector (AgV, March 1997). The lags may have been such that, in specific periods, pay rises in central government exceeded those in the private sector. Table 10.4 supports this conclusion. It could also be interpreted in such a way that central government led wage developments 1985–90. The correct interpretation, however, seems to be that wage developments in the central government lagged behind the private sector and yearly variations were larger until the early 1990s when wage developments in central government started to run parallel to the private sector. This harmonious development seems to be the result of all the reforms taken together.

One difficult question to answer, however, in this connection is whether central government should have aimed at an even lower rate of increase in relation to other economic sectors, since the overall policy has been one of downsizing. Keeping pay low would have induced more employees to leave the central government sector. Two facts, however, have to be borne in mind. The first is that downsizing has far exceeded that envisaged in any cabinet policy. Agencies have downsized and therefore been able to maintain pay levels for remaining staff. Moreover, downsizing has been greater than the reduction in work carried out. Agencies have replaced in-house staff by consultancy services and outsourcing. This is reflected in the trend of total costs. Costs (in fixed prices) have increased by nine per cent while staff have fallen by 18.5 per cent between 1980 and 1997. The wage share

Table 10.4   Pay rises for employees in Swedish central government and private enterprise for salaried staff (per cent)

Period	Central government	Private business
1985–90	48.9	46.4
1990–93	12.9	16.0
1993–96	15.4	15.4

Source: SOU, 1997a: 78.

of total costs has fallen from 59 per cent to 49 per cent with consultants, outsourcing and computers filling its place.

The second fact is that specific staff categories have been in short supply, especially in the fields of IT, the environment and tax auditing, and demanded pay increases. On many occasions in the 1980s, agencies were short of particular types of staff and experienced big problems in finding recruitment solutions. This has not occurred in the 1990s, owing to a more flexible pay-negotiation system. Whether the dispersion of pay has increased is hard to ascertain. Pay increases have varied strikingly among agencies (SOU, 1997a: 74), contradicting the supposed risk of agencies, being members of the same pay-bargaining organisation, keeping a jealously close watch on one another. Larger pay awards have been made in public utilities, such as roads, air-traffic control and railways. The judicial agencies and defence, too, have had above-average pay rises, while pay rates in environmental agencies have been the most sluggish. There is some evidence that more qualified staff have received higher pay increases than the less qualified. In one system of classification of positions the lowest group – out of five – has received rises of 12–13 per cent, whereas the highest group has obtained increases of between 15 per cent (for men) and 20 per cent (for women). Pay dispersion, measured as the difference between the highest and lowest quartiles divided by median pay, has increased somewhat, albeit surprisingly little.

Another apprehension that has proved to be groundless concerns equality between the sexes. Would decentralisation and increased freedom at local level be to the disadvantage of women? The answer seems to be no. During the 1990s, women have secured more equal

Table 10.5   Average pay rise in Swedish agencies
with more than 50 employees, 1993–96

Wage increase	Number of agencies
Less than 12 per cent	24
12–13.9 per cent	49
14–15.9 per cent	46
16–17.9 per cent	21
18–19.9 per cent	5
More than 20 per cent	4

Source: SOU 1997a: 76.

Table 10.6   Pay dispersion and female relative pay in Sweden, 1990–96
(per cent)

Year	1990	1991	1992	1993	1995	1996
Wage dispersion	30.5	30.1	30.6	31.8	31.2	31.4
Overall female relative pay	84.1	84.3	84.6	84.9	85.1	85.8

Source: *Studier av lönebildning på det statliga området* (*Studies of Pay Formation in the Central Government Sector*), Swedish Agency for Government Employers (AgV), March 1997:10, and Schager and Andersson: 28.

status, more women have been promoted to managerial positions and, as mentioned above, their pay increases have exceeded those of senior male employees (SOU, 1997a: 75).

The ageing of the labour force has long been considered a problem. In 1963 the average age of central government employees was equal to that of private employees: 38 years. By 1997 the average central government employee was 44 years old, while the private employee was 40 (Parliamentary Auditors, Report, 1994–95, 12: 12). The government sector as a whole expanded during the 1960s and 1970s, absorbing the generation born in the 1940s. This generation now fills most government positions and leaves very little room for recruitment. Starting in 2005, this generation will be retiring and, over the next 10 years, a very high proportion of government employees will vacate their positions. Recruitment needs will then be staggering and the difficulties in overcoming the loss of continuity very grave. Agencies do not appear to have addressed this problem (Swedish Agency for Administrative Development Report, 1998b: 108).

Finally, what happened to output and efficiency? Have pay increases and general working conditions been salvaged at the cost of diminished staff and output? There are many factors causing productivity change, but the overall verdict is in favour, rather than against, HRM devolution. An upward productivity trend began even before the new system of public management was launched in the late 1970s. This corresponded with the first series of cutback efforts in central government. That trend has persisted and has not been reversed by HRM devolution. Rather, the continued upward trend has been a condition set for the new system of public management and decentrali-

Table 10.7   Productivity trends in Swedish central government, 1960 to 1997, excluding defence (annual change, per cent)

Year	1960–65	1965–70	1970–75	1975–80	1980–85	1985–90	1990–97
Productivity	−1.3	−2.2	−3.0	1.9	1.2	0.1	0.8

Source: *Produktivitetsutvecklingen i statsförvaltningen 1990–97* (*Productivity Trends in Central Government Administration, 1990–97*), Swedish Agency for Administrative Development 1998:23.

sation of all means of production to agencies and their heads. The view that the cutbacks of the 1990s could never have been achieved without this devolution is frequently voiced (SOU, 1997a).

CRITIQUE AND DISCUSSION

The evaluation undertaken by the government commission of inquiry on the delegation of employer responsibility in central government (SOU, 1997a) concluded that delegation had worked well. Central government is not in the vanguard of pay increases although these have been used to recruit staff with requisite skills and reward good work. The commission emphasised the need to induce agency heads and their personnel staff divisions to behave more like private-sector employers and rejected any reversion to more centralised HRM. However, it recognised the need for the ministries, especially the Ministry of Finance, to be informed about HRM and pay policies at local level, and therefore suggested a stronger monitoring scheme. This scheme has been created and has operated since 1998. It requires agencies to report annually to the Ministry of Finance on their staff situation, according to a standard classification and on pay increases for the various categories of employees such as managers, core staff and support staff.

This monitoring enables the Ministry to keep an eye on developments, so that pay increases do not get out of hand. At the same time, it challenges the role and position of AgV, the agencies' pay-negotiating organisation. A tension between the Ministry of Finance and AgV was evident when the monitoring scheme was introduced. The monitoring scheme is an interesting indication of the need for a strategic view of HRM, despite the praise of decentralisation. The strategic needs are to secure staff with requisite skills in the long run; to recruit and train agency heads adequately; to achieve good working conditions throughout central government; to realise equality between the sexes; and, finally, to prevent individual agencies from engaging in a pay spiral, thereby causing central government to start leading pay trends in the economy.

The Parliamentary Auditors' conclusion three years earlier (*Statlig personalpolitik* [*Central Government Staff Policy*], Parliamentary Auditors, Report 1994–95.12) had been less favourable. They closed their report with the recommendation that the cabinet should develop and adopt a plan for HRM, and require agencies to comply with that plan. This divergence in conclusions and recommendations may be due either to the progress made since then or to a different set of values, with the Parliamentary Auditors favouring more uniformity throughout central government than the commission. The Commission on Administrative Policy (SOU, 1997b) also dealt with HRM, but its approach was somewhat different. It was concerned particularly about the 'fragmentation' of central government into several distinct and contradictory cultures: first, the authoritative handling of citizens' rights and duties; second, service-mindedness; and, third, pure business. Another factor contributing to fragmentation, in the Commission's view, was emphasis on individual organisational performance. For central government – the state – to be coherent, common values and attitudes are needed. The commission felt that elimination of purely business activities would facilitate the return to a traditional civil service. The Commission regarded HRM in the context of the power relationship between politics and administration. Compared with earlier commissions of inquiry and official reports on this matter, it leaned towards a stronger position for the administration. The way to achieve this, in the Commission's view, is to strengthen the position of the individual civil servant. The Commission could have argued for a return to lifelong employment and irremovable civil servants but, instead, recommended that ethical standards be raised in the corps. To support high ethical standards, the Commission suggested enlarged scope for punishing civil servants for misconduct.

The Commission was also concerned about the power relationship between the head and staff of an agency, and especially about the strong position of the head in relation to other managers at the agency who have, after all, been appointed by the head. It therefore recommended that the cabinet resume appointing managers below the agency head, so as to ensure that people in these positions would dare enter the fray with their agency heads. To date, the cabinet has taken no action on any of these suggestions. The principle that agency heads cannot be made accountable unless they are entitled to act as they see fit, including appointing their own agency managers, is likely to continue. However, there is growing awareness that some cohesion is needed and that central government should be regarded as a single, large concern. This warrants central monitoring of pay, working conditions, training and educational levels, a system for classifying positions, and a programme for managerial recruitment and training. Some greater centralisation is therefore likely to appear to constrain the exercise of the staffing and pay flexibilities which the agencies now have.

References

PARLIAMENTARY AUDITORS (1995). *Statlig personalpolitik* (*Central Government Staff Policy*). Report 1994–95.12. Stockholm: Fritzes.
PETERSSON, O. and SÖDERLIND, D. (1993). *Förvaltningspolitik* (*Administrative Policy*). Publica.
SCHAGER, N. and ANDERSSON, P. (1996). *Continuity and Reform in the Public Sector Pay Determination in the European Union: Analysis of the Centralised and Decentralised Response to Managing Labour Market Change, The Swedish Case* (draft). Swedish Agency for Government Employers. November.
SOU (1997a). *Arbetsgivarpolitik i staten, för kompetens och resultat* (*Employer Policy in the Central Government, for Skills and Performance*). 1997:48. Stockholm: Fritzes.
SOU (1997b). *I medborgarnas tjänst* (*In the Citizens' Service*). 1997:57. Stockholm: Fritzes.
STATISTICS SWEDEN (1998). The Government Agency for Statistics. Stockholm: Fritzes.
SWEDISH AGENCY FOR ADMINISTRATIVE DEVELOPMENT (1998a). *Produktivitetsutveckling i statsförvaltningen 1990–97* (*Productivity Trends in Central Government Administration, 1990–97*). Report 1998:23. Stockholm: Fritzes.
SWEDISH AGENCY FOR ADMINISTRATIVE DEVELOPMENT (1998b). *Staten i omvandling 1998* (*The Swedish Central Government in Transition, 1998*). Report 1998:15. Stockholm: Fritzes.
SWEDISH AGENCY FOR GOVERNMENT EMPLOYERS (AGV) (1997). *Studier av lönebildning på det statliga området* (*Studies of Pay Formation in the Central Government Sector*). March. Stockholm: Fritzes.

11 The Netherlands: Towards Personnel Flexibilities

Theo van der Krogt, Erik Beersen and Antoinette Kemper

Public administration in the Netherlands is highly complex and diverse. It has been changing continuously during the last decade but in the context of low 'central steering'. Therefore, it is difficult to provide an accurate picture of the present situation. This chapter does not offer a comprehensive account of human resources flexibilities in the Netherlands but focuses primarily on developments at two levels of government – central and local. It excludes the military, judiciary and police, as well as the vast not-for-profit sector which encompasses education, health and social welfare services. The reasons for these exclusions are explained below.

THE PUBLIC SECTOR IN THE NETHERLANDS

According to the constitution, the Netherlands has three autonomous levels of government: central government, 12 provinces and local government. However, at the lowest level there is another 'government': namely the water boards, a functional government organisation with water management tasks such as water control and waste water management. The autonomy of the provinces and especially local government is limited, because central and sometimes provincial government can overrule local government or give binding instructions. This is especially the case where local government tasks emanate from central government policy. There are also regions in the Netherlands but these have no constitutional status. They are voluntary associations of local authorities which collaborate on certain tasks, although the boundaries of the regions are determined by central government. There have been several attempts to give regions separate status and power but up to now these attempts have failed.

In the Netherlands major social services, such as education, health care, social work, care for the elderly and social housing are delivered to citizens by not-for-profit organisations, which are regulated and funded by central or local government. There are some public schools, such as local government primary schools, but they are becoming more and more rare. An exception in education is public universities which are still state organisations. There are also a few public hospitals 'owned' by local government but again they are exceptions along with academic hospitals. This situation is not a result of a vast programme of privatisation but has its roots in Dutch socio-cultural history. Since the mid-nineteenth century the Netherlands has been characterised as a 'pillared' society (Lijphart, 1975). This means government has stayed away from the delivery, although not the funding, of most social services in favour of delivery by 'societal actors'. Under this subsidiarity principle all social services were delivered in triplicate by Protestant, Catholic and labour/humanistic organisations. Since the 'depillarisation' of Dutch society in the 1960s, and growing concern for efficiency by central government, many of these organisations, particularly the Catholic and labour/humanistic ones, have merged into 'neutral' not-for-profit organisations. This history explains why the personnel policies of these organisations have been more or less different, at least between sectors, and developed more or less independently from personnel policy in government, with the exception of remuneration policy.

As in many other OECD countries, privatisation became popular in the Netherlands during the 1980s. Due to the existence of the large not-for-profit sector, the scope for privatisation was relatively small but some changes did occur. As stated above, government paid almost all the costs of not-for-profit organisations, via grants, and regulated their operations in more or less detail. From the 1980s the regulations were reduced and delivery-contracts took the place of grants. One of the outcomes was that personnel regulations were relaxed. One peculiarity had always been that personnel working in education, including those working in not-for-profit schools, had personnel regulations, including payment and pensions, that were almost the same as those of public employees. Other services differed although they also 'followed' the public sector to a large degree. An example of 'difference' is that these other sectors have their own pension funds.

There have been some 'real' privatisations in the Netherlands. The national coal, chemical and steel industries were privatised in large part in the 1960s and their stock sold. Although electricity and public transport remain as public enterprises, Dutch PTT has been sold off and the Dutch railways are almost privatised and have had to accept competitors on their network since 1997. In a few regions there are also experiments with tendering for bus routes. All these organisations have adopted market-oriented personnel policies, although some-times with bridging regulations for 'old' employees. Most of the time the 'old employment rights' are 'bought' out by the offer of new con-tracts with slightly improved new salaries and regulations, although employees may keep their rights. Another phenomenon of New Public Management (NPM) is putting public organisations 'at arm's-length'. This has become very popular in the Netherlands although putting organisations at arm's-length does not usually result in per-sonnel policy becoming very divergent from that in other government organisations.

RECENT DEVELOPMENTS IN CENTRAL GOVERNMENT

At the end of 1997 there were 111,800 public employees working in central government, excluding the armed forces and judiciary (Tweede Kamer, 1998: 86). Nearly 30 per cent were women and the average age of all personnel was 41.1 years, 1.1 years more than in 1994. The distribution of staff over the function levels was very uneven. There are 19 levels in all. In 1997, 14.4 per cent of staff were part-timers, of which around 75 per cent were women. The personnel costs for 1997 were 3.95 billion guilders (Min BZK, 1998: 48, 51, 54, 55 and 93). Table 11.1 outlines the size and relative distribution of staff employed in the public sector.

The Home Office is the 'employer' for the central government sector. It is the policy of central government that responsibility for personnel management lies at the lowest possible level of the organi-sation, corresponding to levels of responsibility and competency for the organisation's output (Min BZK, 1995, part 1: 18). Within the Home Office the Directorate of Personnel Management in Central Government (*DPMR: Directie Personeelsmanagement Rijksdienst*) is responsible for co-ordinating personnel management across min-istries. A council of Secretaries-General of the ministries is an impor-tant co-ordinating committee. DPMR develops the conditions within which the individual ministries carry out personnel management

Table 11.1   Staff (fte) employed in the public
sector in the Netherlands, 1997

Central government	103,500	14.0%
Local government	151,800	22.2%
Provinces	11,450	1.7%
Armed forces	76,400	11.2%
Police	43,700	6.4%
Water boards	8,250	1.2%
Judiciary	2,200	0.3%
Education	271,200	39.7%

Source: Tweede Kamer, 1998.

and attempts to co-ordinate to ensure cohesion, efficiency and effectiveness (Min BZK, 1996a: 9). In 1993, a report: *Towards Nuclear Ministries; Choosing for a High-grade and Flexible Central Government*, was published (Min BZK, 1993). This report recommended a smaller central government that would have capacity to adapt to changing circumstances and demands in a *flexible* way. Flexibility is described as the extent to which the organisation is capable of adapting the deployment of human resources and other means to the ever-changing demands from the environment and work processes (Min BZK, 1995: 53). Government has responded to the report in a number of ways.

Flexibility in labour relations

Government organisations have responded to the report which reflects the contingencies of the Dutch system of public administration. Most public employees have tenure and the opportunities for temporary appointments are limited. The circumstances under which this can be done are listed in the law governing the status of civil servants. Seasonal peaks in the workload are one of the circumstances. Government and unions are investigating whether this regulation of temporary jobs is geared to the need for increasing flexibility of working and opening hours. It is the experience of employers that, in some situations, it is easier to hire someone via a temporary employment agency, than to get permission for a temporary job, although it is expensive and leads to higher costs than are strictly necessary (Min BZK, 1995: 53–7).

The hiring of external personnel (i.e. personnel not on the payroll of the organisation) has increased enormously in the last decade in the Netherlands, not least in government. The hiring of external personnel and contracting out must be distinguished. In statistical and financial reports this distinction is not normally made, so the magnitude is not easy to determine. Contracting out to non-government organisations diminishes flexibility problems for government. Especially for non-core tasks, contracting out is a politically attractive alternative, although financially it can be more expensive. Hiring of external personnel can be caused by peak workloads, need for expert work or work where independent judgement is necessary. The formal policy is that when choosing between the hiring of external personnel and use of internal personnel, necessity and costs have to be taken into account. Internal staff have to be used, especially when there is redundant personnel elsewhere in the organisation. Also use of interim jobs (see below) is encouraged. Deliberation of these options is the responsibility of line management who can choose within the limits of their budget (Min BZK, 1997a).

The most used form of external flexibility in central government is hiring extra personnel, through temporary employment agencies. Their importance in the labour market is still growing, as is the diversity of contracts with workers. The traditional contract is one in which workers are paid when there is work for them to do. Nowadays, however, workers in high demand areas are 'guaranteed' work and get a kind of permanent contract. There is a collective agreement for this branch of work and the latest one foresees a form of tenure for personnel who work for the agency for a long time, including secondary conditions of employment like pensions and training.

In an attempt to cope with changing workloads, some larger government departments have resorted to use of internal temporary employment pools. In 1996 temporary employment pools were researched (Min BZK, 1996b) and three categories were distinguished: 'flexibility' pools, 'influx' pools and 'outflow' pools. Flexibility pools are primarily intended to cope with changes in workloads, but they also increase the employability of staff, especially those in higher functions. Besides the cost effectiveness of internal pools, another advantage is the organisational experience of their members. If the pool is unable to 'deliver' appropriate staff, management may turn to either other government pools or for-profit temporary employment pools. Sometimes the management of internal pools is contracted out to a for-profit temporary employment agency. Influx pools also aim to improve the labour market position of certain categories of job seekers including school-leavers, emigrants and the long-term unemployed and subsidies are paid on each of these. Finally, outflow pools are used in the framework of outplacement where redundant personnel fulfil temporary jobs in the hope of finding another permanent job.

Most internal temporary employment pools are oriented to lower administrative functions. However, one ministry, Agriculture, Nature and Fishery (LNV), has an internal pool of policy functionaries (Min LNV, 1993: 18). The idea is that these functionaries work on policy issues on a project base and are sometimes also used for interim management. After two years in this pool, workers get a 'normal' line function. Another ministry, Traffic and Water Works (V&W), uses 'expert clusters' (one for legal advice in complaint and appeal cases and one for job description and assessment) for tasks in units which lack such expertise. Similar pools exist in the Home Office for project management, Ministry of Public Housing, Land Use and Environment (VROM) for interim management and in Education, Culture and Science (OC&W) for all kinds of 'difficult jobs'. There is one interdepartmental pool for EDP-audits, which is a collaboration of the accountant units of all (but five) ministries. There is another interdepartmental pool, flexpool, which is an informal collaboration between five ministries, and aims at enlarging possibilities for mobility.

Employees on tenure have the possibility to fulfil another function, inside or outside their own organisation, on a temporary basis (six months to two years) with the right to come back, a kind of secondment. The 'sending' unit continues to pay the salary but the 'receiving' unit pays compensation to the former. A contract is made to regulate the secondment. Formally, secondments aim at broadening the horizon of employees, but they can be used as an outplacement instrument, to help cope with workload problems in the receiving unit. Table 11.2 indicates the scale of this practice in selected ministries. Collegial lending has the same aims as interim function fulfilment; the difference being that there is no formal contract between units. This mechanism is used for shorter periods, less than six months, because of the uncertain status.

Working hours have been a 'hot issue' ever since unions were established. A distinction can be made between working hours, number of hours per week an employee works and is paid for, and business hours, the number of hours per day/week the organisation is functioning. In all organisations this distinction is now being made,

Table 11.2   Number of vacancies and interim function contracts in selected Dutch ministries, selected years

Ministry	Employees	Period	Registration	Vacancies	Number of IF-contracts
Traffic and Waterworks (V&W)	4,500	1994–96	220	285	156
Agriculture, Nature Conservation and Fishery (LNV)	4,000	1994–95	266	Unknown	166
Public Health, Welfare and Sport (VWS)	2,000	1994–95	180	46	65
Education, Culture and Science (OCW)	2,400	1991–94	230	375	257
Public Housing, Planning and Environment (VROM)	4,088	1994–96	256	244	105

Source: Min EZ, 1997.

due to the reduction of working hours to 36 hours, on the one hand, and extension of business hours on the other. For example, since 1996 shops are allowed to be open till 9 p.m. and also during some Sundays. Until recently, working before 8 a.m. or after 6 p.m. or at weekends resulted in extra compensation, above the normal hourly rate. In more and more collective agreements, changes in this system have been made, including the most recent collective agreement for central government. The 'arithmetic average 36 hours working week', which is now law, aims at a reconciliation between the days and hours employees work and the needs of management. At the level of individual organisations and internal units, management has to negotiate with their personnel on this issue, resulting in custom-made timetables that can vary from day to day, week to week or period to period, depending on the specific characteristics of the work. Also what is chosen for fixed working hours can vary: four days of nine hours, four days of eight hours and one day of four hours, one week of 5×8 hours followed by one week of 4×8 hours. Reduction in working hours has been negotiated by the unions primarily to enlarge the number of jobs. This is very difficult, especially in the higher levels and for specialist functions. The outcome appears to be that the same is done but in less time.

Mobility and employability of personnel

Mobility is seen as an important target in personnel policy. First, this is because of the pressure government is under to reduce its costs and therefore size. Due to conditions of employment which make it almost impossible to lay off public servants, and even where possible, because of high unemployment payments, it is in the interest of the employer to help employees to find other jobs. Second, additional reasons for promoting mobility especially for higher level employees and management (levels 10 and higher) include the capability of the organisation to adapt to changing circumstances and the capability of management to be effective in different settings. Knowledge and skills have to be developed constantly and experiences in different functions are necessary, including training on the job. Employees are expected to be active in seeking education and new challenges through new jobs (Min BZK, 1997a).

Since 1993 personnel in the categories V and VI are appointed in 'general service', which means that they can be asked to take positions in other departments without resigning their old position. All departments of central government are considered as one organisation in this respect. In practice inter-departmental mobility is relatively low with only 548 persons transferring in 1997, while the influx from outside was 8,697 persons (Min BZK, 1998: Table 1.11). By stimulating outflow and functional circulation, an attempt is made to enlarge the number of vacancies. Three instruments are used in central government to stimulate interdepartmental mobility. First, there is the mobility bank which is the central point where all vacancies are collected and made available to all employees, not just those who are redundant. Second, under the Collective Labour Agreement (CAO) 1997–99 management has to discuss education with each employee and at organisational level education has to be part of personnel policy, after deliberation with the works council. Extra money for the education of older employees will be available through the A + O-

Fund. The A + O-Fund (Labour and Education Fund) is an autonomous foundation, which finances projects aimed at stimulating education in government. It gets its money from central government. The CAO 1997–99 creates the possibility of extra money when an employee is willing to move to another region. Also management can waive the pay back of the costs of education or parental leave in the case of mobility.

Third, in September 1995, the Higher Civil Service (*ABD:Algemene Bestuursdienst*) became operational after many years of discussion. It consists of the top 300 (levels 17, 18 and 19) employees in central government. There are plans to broaden the target group for the ABD to include level 16, an extra 1,000 staff. The aims for the ABD are to develop skills, especially management skills, promote mobility, internationalise experience and develop an *esprit de corps*. ABD personnel are to circulate every five years and preferably not stay in one job for longer than seven years. An elaborate system of training and assessment is being developed and co-ordinated by a special ABD bureau within the Home Office All vacancies at level 17 and above go through the ABD-bureau which facilitates and directs recruitment and selection. Besides this orientation to the whole of central government, the ABD aims at a seamless connection with departmental management development and career policy for levels below 16. One of the projects here is redesign of the Central Government Management Course (Min BZK, 1996a: 47).

The exchange programme of the ministries of LNV, VROM and V&W for level 10 to 14 employees in management and policy advice functions deserves separate mention. Within this programme temporary placements (for at least six months) in the same kind of job in another ministry are arranged, aimed at improving relations, information exchange and learning from each other. The exchange involves no cost but there are clear benefits in raising the employability of staff.

There are no figures for intra-departmental mobility but it is seen as being equally important as inter-departmental mobility. Management is seen as responsible for ensuring the performance of all staff. Education combined with job mobility, to obtain work experience, are seen as keys to good performance. It has been recognised that it is not always in the interest of managers to stimulate mobility and lose their best staff. Two ministries have experimented with the assessment of the efforts of their managers in stimulating mobility (Min BZK, 1997a). In particular they are assessed in terms of their willingness to use the instruments outlined above, including mobility banks and collaboration with other organisations.

DEVELOPMENTS IN PAY DETERMINATION AND CONDITIONS OF SERVICE

Formally all public employees have a special status and are 'designated in public service'. This is based on a legal act which denies them the right to strike. The Home Office decrees their conditions of employment although *de facto* this is determined by collective bargaining. There have been important changes in conditions of employment since the 1970s. Up to that time changes in the salaries of public employees were 'coupled' to the movement of salaries in the profit sector, the so-called 'trend policy'. The same held for the employees of not-for-profit organisations in the social, health and welfare sector, the so-called 'premium and subsidy sector'. On a voluntary basis the latter followed developments in the public sector and were called 'trend-followers'. Although there is not so much to negotiate, their conditions of employment are regulated formally in around 60 collective agreements (Albeda and Dercksen, 1993: 99–102).

In 1976, government decided upon a one per cent cut in the salary increase in order to dam the increase in public spending. This continued for several years, along with other measures including the lowering of starting salaries and freezing of number of public employees. After a pause in 1981, cuts continued throughout the decade with a growing gap between pay in the profit and non-profit sectors. Gross salaries in the profit sector had risen by 19 per cent between 1980 and 1988, whilst those in the public sector had fallen by more than one per cent (Albeda and Dercksen, 1993: 116–17). However, between 1981 and 1994 the profit sector and public sector had salary rises of 35 and 18 per cent respectively (Min BZK, 1994a, part 1: 45).

In 1979 the not-for-profit sector was forced by cabinet decree to follow developments in the public sector and cut salaries. From 1980, this measure had a temporary legal basis as 'unwanted' elements in collective agreements could be overruled by central government. However, this was a law that was against the European Social Charter, so in 1986 a new law (Law on the Developments of the Conditions of Employment in the Premium and Subsidy Sector – *WAGGS: Wet Arbeidsvoorwaardenontwikkeling Gepremieerde en Gesubsidieerde Sector*) was passed to regulate negotiations in the not-for-profit sector.

This law permits negotiations between employers and employees but government decides on the scope for development.

Up to 1967, trade unions were 'heard' by the Home Secretary before he decided upon changes in conditions of employment. Since 1967 the law (General Regulation Civil Servants Status – *ARAR: Algemene Regeling Ambtenaren Rechtspositie*) prescribes 'consultation' with the unions organised in the CCGOA (Central Commission of Organised Deliberation on Civil Service Issues – *Centrale Commissie voor Georganiseerd Overleg in Ambtenarenzaken*). Although this consultation is formally restricted to conditions of employment of public employees working in central government, the outcome more or less determines terms and conditions for public employees working in the educational sector, provinces and local government and for those working in the not-for-profit sector, because all these organisations are completely dependent upon central government for their budgets. These budgets were compensated for rises in salaries in central government.

The above developments in the determination of the salaries in the public sector, which resulted in industrial action and limited recognition by judges of the right to strike for public employees, led to renewed discussions about the position of public employees. Prohibition of the right of public employees to strike was withdrawn in 1980, although government wanted to exempt the right to strike from the European Social Charter (Albeda and Dercksen, 1993: 193). More and more is spoken about 'normalisation' of conditions of employment, which means moving in the direction of conditions in the private sector. Politicians emphasise the overprotection of the public employee, whilst unions stress the importance of normal negotiations over the terms of employment. Because of differences between the several layers of government, both sides agree on the desirability of more decentralisation so that local government bodies can negotiate for themselves. In 1984, the first step in the normalisation process took place with the creation of the Advice and Arbitrage Commission (*AAC: Advies en Arbitrage Commissie*) which can be asked for advice by any of the parties or for arbitration when both parties agree on that.

In 1989, the unions and government agreed on an experiment aimed at a more decentralised system within the existing rules of consultation (Protocol for the Experimentation Consultation Conditions of Employment 1989: *Protocol voor de proefnemening arbeidsvoorwaardenoverleg 1989*; Albeda and Dercksen, 1993: 118–21). What was new in this experiment was the requirement that changes in conditions of employment had to be agreed with a majority of the unions. 'Majority' here means a majority of represented employees. There are four groups of labour unions: ACOP (General Centre of Public Employees) unions who belong to the FNV (Federation of Dutch Unions; CCOOP (Christian Centre of Public and Teaching Employees) unions belonging to the CNV (Christian National Union); unions of the AC (Public Employees Centre; independent); and the unions of the CMHF (Centre for Middle and Higher Functionaries) which belong to the MHP (Unions Centre of Middle and Higher Employees). If there is no accord among the four then conditions stay the same. Also new was the preliminary consultation of all public employers, and the division between those subjects to be discussed at central level (salaries, pensions, social security benefits, employment measures) and those to be decentralised, i.e. all other elements of the conditions of employment, unless the decentralised bodies want central agreements. Government decides on a set of measurements and an accompanying budget as an input to the central negotiations. After agreement at central level, room for decentralised negotiations becomes clear.

Since 1993, negotiations about conditions of employment take place at three levels: national, sectoral and individual organisations. The public sector has been divided into eight sectors: central government, education and science, police, judiciary, local government, provinces, water boards and the armed forces. In those sectors where there is more than one autonomous organisation (education, local government, provinces, water boards) employers' organisations have been founded. All employers organisations together form the Association of Public Employers (*Verbond van Overheidswerkgevers*), the 'counterpart' of the Centres of Public Employees (*Centrales voor Overheidspersoneel*), where the unions work together. The employers and employees discuss common matters in the Council for Public Personnel Policy (*Raad voor het Overheidspersoneelsbeleid*). However, negotiations at national level are between the Home Office and Centres of Public Employees in what is called the Central Organised Consultation with respect to Public Employees' Affairs (*Centraal Georganiseerd Overleg inzake Ambtenarenzaken*). At this level only pensions and the legal framework for the public employees' social security are negotiated.

The most important negotiations nowadays are at sectoral level, where general terms of employment, working hours, social security over and above legal levels, salaries, early retirement, sickness benefit and holidays are negotiated. Central government, however, still has an important influence on these sectoral level negotiations, because all sectors depend on central government for their budgets. For example, local government can decide to give a bigger pay rise to their employees than central government but they have to find the money from within their budgets. Practice indicates that the unions 'co-ordinate' their strategies in the different sectors (employers try to do the same) and sometimes use a 'rich' sector (e.g. the water boards) as a lever in negotiations in other sectors. Of course, negotiations in the larger sectors, local government and education are influential.

All other conditions of employment such as job evaluation systems, rules for performance pay, holiday scheduling, working times and so on are negotiated at the level of individual organisations but as a sector they can decide to negotiate on these points at sectoral level. Also they can individually decide to use 'formats' designed, for example, by the Association of Dutch Local Governments (*Vereniging van Nederlandse Gemeenten*).

RECENT DEVELOPMENTS IN LOCAL GOVERNMENT

Because of the complexity and diversity of local government in the Netherlands, there is no overview at present of policies on flexibility. However, we undertook a limited investigation with some larger cities. The following observations are based on interviews with personnel officers of the following cities: Arnhem, Leeuwarden, Zwolle, Rotterdam, Den Haag, Tilburg, Enschede, Almelo, Utrecht, and Eindhoven. Further information was obtained from the Association of Dutch Local Governments (VNG). In local government, as in central government, the most important motive for flexibility and mobility has been reduction of costs. Policies were aimed at averting tenure whilst mobility was sought to get rid of redundant personnel. The number of employees in local government fell by 17 per cent in the period 1986–96 (Weggemans and Dawson, 1997: 12–13).

Types of contracts and working hours

Most local government employees are on permanent, unlimited contracts .The grounds for a temporary appointment are restricted, as in central government, to temporary tasks; pending a reorganisation;

replacement for a temporarily absent employee and for a trial period. Once the reason for the temporary appointment has lapsed, dismissal or tenure follows. Local authorities try to avoid this situation by 'hiring' employees from a temporary employment agency for a couple of months, renewing the temporary appointment again afterwards (revolving door policy). This policy is illegal, however. A temporary appointment for an indeterminate time is possible but when this appointment ends, local authorities are obliged to offer tenure unless 'other grounds resist against this'. Fluctuations in work and number of personnel are common in local government but the position of both employers and employee unions is that tenured staff should normally deal with these fluctuations. More flexible forms of employment can be used only when this is not possible. Then 'call-in employees' are preferred above other forms such as posted and temporary personnel (College voor Arbeidszaken, 1995: 14). However, use of flexible contracts is rising. In 1995, 5.5 per cent of all local government employees had some kind of flexible contract, rising to 7.2 per cent in 1997. Another two per cent worked in jobs for special categories of the unemployed (Weggemans and Dawson, 1997: 15). In 1997 3.8 per cent of employees worked via a temporary employment agency (Weggemans and Dawson, 1997: 15). In some local authorities these employees are not hired from commercial agencies but from a 'foundation' established for this purpose. This arrangement saves VAT and no formal labour contract arises. Most of the time, management of these 'foundations' is contracted out to commercial agencies.

Part-time employment is normal in local government where 27 per-cent of all employees have part-time jobs (Weggemans and Dawson, 1997: 16). Since April 1996, employees in local government have the right to work part-time, unless the interests of the organisation conflict with this (College voor Arbeidszaken, 1996: 55). One way of increasing flexibility is to increase temporarily the number of part-time positions. However, in some situations, employees are entitled to unemployment pay, if the appointment reverts to a full-time post again. Hiring employees on a 'call-in' basis is also possible under the UWO-local government agreement (UWO = *Uitwerkingsovereenkomst* (Consequences Agreement). This agreement, negotiated between local authorities and the unions at sectoral level, relates to 'local' labour conditions and states that at least 15 hours a month will be paid to all 'call-in' staff and that the minimum of a call-in will be two hours. When the level of call-in hours is higher then 15, then full-time hours have to be guaranteed. This is done to achieve a balance of interests between both parties (College voor Arbeidszaken, 1995: 41).

In the Collective Labour Agreement 1995–97 an 'average working week' of 36 hours starting in January 1997 was agreed. At the same time, agreements were made to realise more flexibility in deploying the workforce. The maximum working hours per day is nine, while during one day a week it can be 10 hours. The actual number of working hours varies between 30 and 42. The annual hours to be worked are set at a maximum of 1836 hours. Although employees can deviate from this in any one year, over a longer period the total must equal out. Overtime is generally compensated in free hours and results in extra payment only when more than two hours per week, or when it is on Saturday or Sunday (College voor Arbeidszaken, 1996: 10 ff). The above means a big change in labour conditions. It provides more room for flexibility but the wishes of employees must be taken into account and details must be worked out in negotiations with local union representatives, and with the labour council. The aim of the unions in reducing the working week to 36 hours is to enlarge the number of jobs. However it is expected that only around 50 per cent of 'released hours' will be re-occupied (Weggemans and Dawson, 1997: 17).

Mobility and employability

The necessity for greater mobility and employability is widely recognised throughout local government but lies far below the average of all other organisations in the Netherlands. In 1996 there were 2.5 internal job changes per 100 employees, while there were 5.4 new employees per 100, and 4.8 departures. The respective figures for all other organisations were 6.4; 7.9 and 8.8. The average age in local government is 41.4 years (39.1 in other organisations) and average years with the organisations is 12.9 years (11.3 in all other organisations) (Zonneveld *et al.*, 1998: 9–10). The employers' organisation of local government wants a large-scale mobility policy, especially for higher functions (College voor Arbeidszaken, 1997: 22). However, the results to date are minimal and a report to VNG states that local authorities lack strategic personnel policies. The instruments are there but they are not used jointly to realise flexibility (cited in College voor Arbeidszaken, 1998: 15). In a recent brochure of the Board of Labour Issues (*College voor Arbeidszaken*, the formal employers association for the local government sector) the following personnel instruments are seen as crucial for greater flexibility and mobility: recruiting and selection, remuneration, career development, age-conscious personnel policy, and especially education and training. All these instruments need to be used within the context of strategic human resources planning and development (College voor Arbeidszaken, 1998).

In the Collective Agreement on Labour Conditions in local government 1997–99, it was agreed that every local government should have an education plan and further education and training needs should be discussed annually with every employee. An employee is entitled to training where this is necessary for effective job performance. A new study-facility agreement can be developed, with more costs of training being compensated through subsidies of the A + O-fund (Labour and Education fund). This is a fund to which both the employers' association and unions contribute. In particular, it prioritises training programmes for older employees (Letter to local governments from the College voor Arbeidszaken on the results of the negotiations, September 12, 1997).

In the city of Tilburg there is an explicit policy that 50 per cent of all vacancies must be filled from internal candidates. In Utrecht, there is a special committee, which discusses all vacancies at level 13 and above and offers them also to internal candidates. Employees are not forced to accept a new function but need strong arguments to resist. An interesting instrument is used in The Hague, where trainees are appointed who follow a couple of 'internships' before they get a 'normal' function.

As stated above, for many years the biggest problem for local authorities was reduction in staff numbers. In the 1980s, the first mobility bureaux were established. Because they mainly dealt with compulsory mobility, they were seen as dealing with the worst personnel (in Dutch these are called '*kneuzen*': bruised ones) (College voor Arbeidszaken, 1998: 40). But this is now changing. Some local authorities have established their own mobility bureaux, others, especially smaller ones, act collectively. Most bureaux are a subsidiary or a joint venture of a commercial temporary employment agency. Many local authorities also work together with other public and not-for profit organisations in mobility projects. Data are available from four of the largest joint mobility bureau: Northern Netherlands, Randstad Holding (the largest temporary employment agency in the Netherlands), Mobility Bureau KAN-local governments, and Start Mobility Bureau. Together these served 390 local authorities in 1997.

Between four and nine per cent of employees in these local authorities is registered with these bureau, of whom between nine and 22 per cent have found another, sometimes temporary, job. Although mobility bureaus have become more important, most vacancies are filled with candidates from other sources (Weggemans and Dawson, 1997: 38–9).

Some local authorities have sought to change their reward systems to attract and keep employees and encourage good performance. These experiments, however, have met with limited success. In Rotterdam they are committed to using the value an employee has for the organisation to be one ground for extra reward. Taking courses can also be a ground for extra rewards. However, as less than two per cent of the total of personnel costs can be distributed on a reward basis this has had little effect (College voor Arbeidszaken, 1998: 57). In several local government organisations employees are compensated, for a certain period, when they accept another job, within or outside local government, that pays less. The Hague has recently had to abandon an existing compensation for voluntary horizontal mobility for cutback reasons.

More and more local authorities are using the appointment 'in general service' to create conditions for greater flexibility. Such an appointment is sometimes combined with agreements about the period for which a function is to be taken. This makes employability or mobility more clear-cut but the disadvantage is that a new function must be available as the old one expires (College voor Arbeidszaken, 1998: 48). In some local authorities a first step is being made to broaden function/job descriptions in order to have some flexibility when necessary. Instead of detailed job descriptions, a responsibility level is established and yearly output or production agreements made.

CONCLUSION

Flexibility and mobility are 'hot issues' in the Netherlands, in both central and local government, where policy is to increase both. The stimuli for action have come from the need to reduce costs and solve the problem of redeploying personnel with tenure but also to achieve wider experience for personnel and injections of new blood into government from the private sector. The main mechanism for achieving the latter has been to use mobility bureaux. Although the problem is that these still have the image of working primarily for redundant personnel. Flexibility in the use of existing personnel has been greatly assisted with the introduction of the 36-hours working week in local government and accompanying collective agreements on working time. Education and training is also seen as one of the most important instruments to help people to become more flexible and mobile. More and more organisations are developing strategic education and training plans, although there is evidence that training is still oriented to dealing with immediate skills gaps.

References

ALBEDA, W. and DERCKSEN, W. (1993). *Arbeidsverhoudingen in Nederland* (4th edn). Alphen a/d Rijn: Samsom.
COLLEGE VOOR ARBEIDSZAKEN (1995). *Flexibele arbeidsrelaties.* The Hague: VNG-uitgeverij.
COLLEGE VOOR ARBEIDSZAKEN (1996). *Arbeidsduurverkorting en flexibilisering.* The Hague: VNG-uitgeverij.
COLLEGE VOOR ARBEIDSZAKEN (1997). *Beleidsplan College voor Arbeidszaken 1998–2000.* The Hague.
COLLEGE VOOR ARBEIDSZAKEN (1998). *Employability en mobiliteit.* The Hague: VNG-uitgeverij.
LIJPHART, A. (1975). *The Politics of Accommodation; pluralism and democracy in the Netherlands* (2nd edn). Berkeley: University of California Press.
MIN BZK (Ministerie van Binnenlandse Zaken en Koninkrijksrelaties). The Hague:
(1993) *Naar kerndepartementen; kiezen voor een hoogwaardige en flexibele Rijksdienst.*
(1994a). *Mensen en management in de Rijksdienst.*
(1994b). *Inschakeling van intern en extern personeel.*
(1995). *Mensen en management in de Rijksdienst 1995.*
(1996a). *Mensen en management in de Rijksdienst 1996.*
(1996b). *Uitzendpools bij de Rijksdienst.*
(1997a). *Mensen en management in de Rijksdienst 1997.*
(1997b). *Kerngegevens Overheidspersoneel 1996.*
(1998). *Mensen en management in de Rijksdienst 1998.*
MIN EZ (Ministerie van Economische Zaken) (1997). *Jaarrapportage Interim Functievervulling.* The Hague.
MIN LNV (Ministerie van Landbouw, Natuurbehoud en Visserij) (1993). *LNV op weg naar 2000.* The Hague.
TWEEDE KAMER (1998). *Trendnota arbeidszaken overheid 1999,* Tweede Kamerstukken 1998–1999, nr. 26207. The Hague.
WEGGEMANS, J.H. and DAWSON, W. (1997). *Arbeidsmarkt Binnenlands Bestuur Trendrapport 1997.* Alphen a/d Rijn: Samsom.

WEGGEMANS, J.H. and DAWSON, W. (1998). *Arbeidsmarkt Binnenlands Bestuur Trendrapport 1998.* Alphen a/d Rijn: Samsom.
ZONNEVELD, J., HOFMAN, K. and KOUWENHOVEN, C. (1998). *Een mobiliteitsproject als vliegwiel voor de beweging van personeel; een praktische handreiking voor gemeenten.* The Hague: A + O-funds.

12 Human Resources Flexibilities in UK Public Services

Sylvia Horton

This chapter examines changes in public sector personnel policies in Britain in the last two decades and evaluates the extent to which they have led to more flexible human resources systems. After describing the policies and practices associated with the traditional bureaucratic model of people management it explores three key aspects of personnel – modes of employment, functional flexibility or mixed skilling and pay and rewards. Looking at both national and local levels of government it points to evidence of greater flexibilisation across the state system. It also evaluates the extent to which these changes have transformed traditional bureaucratic personnel systems to a new paradigmatic model of people management and achieves the objectives claimed for flexible human resource systems.

THE TRADITIONAL BUREAUCRATIC MODEL OF PEOPLE MANAGEMENT

Since the 1970s the scope, organisation and management of the public services in Britain have changed radically. The changes were largely externally and politically driven by Conservative administrations with a new right ideology and a belief in the superiority of markets over politics and private management over public administration. Arguing that the private sector is the wealth creating sector and the public sector a drain on national resources, successive Conservative governments throughout the 1980s and 1990s sought to reduce and transform the 'overloaded, inefficient and unresponsive bureaucratic state' into a 'lean, enabling, customer oriented and value for money organisation'. Governments abandoned the view that only the state could provide public and merit goods in favour of a mixed economy of welfare. Many public services were transferred to the private sector, whilst others were contracted out. Further, private sector manage- ment practices were introduced into the remaining public organisa- tions in the belief that this would lead to better management, greater efficiency, value for money and responsiveness to consumers and users of public services.

The search for greater flexibility, interpreted as greater responsive- ness to the external environment, occurred at both the macro and micro level of government policies. At macro level governments sought to remove rigidities in the labour market and allow the forces of supply and demand to operate in an unfettered way, assuming that this would push down the general price of labour and resolve the problems of obtaining and retaining labour in areas of short supply. Changes in the law regulating trade unions weakened their powers to resist managerial changes. Employment protection was also reduced through the abolition of wages councils, which set minimum wages in low pay sectors, and the increase from six months to two years before employees had protection against unfair dismissal (Farnham and Pimlott, 1995). 'In particular the government was keen to make the labour market more flexible by restoring incentives and changing workers attitudes towards pay and jobs' (Spencer, 1997: 73). This was done by reducing direct taxation and encouraging the use of perfor- mance and profit related pay.

At micro or organisational level, government sought greater flexi- bility in organisational structures and in working practices. This was achieved in the public sector through the creation of agencies in the civil service, trusts in the National Health Service (NHS) and encour- agement of purchaser/provider splits in local government. The aim was to create more organic and less mechanistic structures and delayer and decentralise management responsibility. At operational level, managers were expected to search for numerical, functional and pay flexibility to ensure tighter control over costs, get pay back for the reduction in the standard working week, meet equal opportunities pressures and be more responsive to consumer demands. The intro- duction of new technology provided both the opportunity and means to transform work processes. It both undermined previous job and skill boundaries and necessitated the reshaping of jobs to match the different skills and competencies needed to operate new equipment. New technology also gave an impetus to management preferences for operating with a flexible workforce unconstrained by multiple job grades, skill demarcation lines, payment systems and work patterns.

Public managers have been encouraged to look to flexible working patterns to act as a buffer against demand fluctuations and seasonal variations although this is not new in local government and the NHS, as we see later in the chapter. What is new, in the more market oriented public sector, is the need in many agencies to guard against the effects of loss of service contracts by moving towards more fixed-term employment contracts and temporary modes of employment. Flexibility, in its many manifestations has been widely accepted as a good thing both within the private and public sectors. There is evidence, however, of both advantages and disadvantages of flexible organisations depending from whose perspective – employer, employee or citizen, it is viewed.

The changes identified above had implications for personnel policies throughout the public services. These include the civil service, which covers central government departments and agencies and some non-departmental bodies; the National Health Service: and the local government service, which includes the education service and the police service. There are also a small number of nationalised industries and public companies and a larger number of non-departmental public bodies of which there were some 2,000 in 1998 (Cabinet Office, 1998a). None of these are staffed by civil servants. Within each major service there are a number of 'employers' including some 40 government departments and over 130 agencies in the civil service; 500 trusts, 200 health authorities and some 11,000 general practices in the NHS; in local government there are over 400 local authorities in England and Wales, 32 in Scotland and 26 single tier authorities in Northern Ireland (Carmichael and Knox, 1999). The systems in Scotland and Northern Ireland vary in some respects from England and Wales although not significantly. The number of public offices, rights of public employees and their remuneration are not rooted in public or constitutional law, unlike in many continental European countries. Public employees are employed under civil contracts of employment and have no different status under the law than employees in the private sector with some minor exceptions in the civil service, the Armed Forces and the protective services. This means that it is easy to change public employment relationships in the UK, by unilateral decisions of employers, collective bargaining or by ordinary statute (employment) law initiated by government or the European Union (EU).

Traditional public personnel administration in the UK had several distinctive characteristics. First, government determined strategic personnel frameworks with operational policies determined by senior managers within each service. Second, public services generally operated in a dual external labour market, a national labour market in recruiting senior and middle managerial and professional staff but local markets for more junior staff and manual workers. Third, public services traditionally had internal labour markets providing career structures and promotion opportunities especially for professional, technical and managerial staffs. Finally, public organisations tended to operate in excess of national minimum standards seeking to act as model employers in order to attract and retain staff and set an example of good employee relations. Farnham and Horton (1996a) identify five further characteristics of traditional people management (TPM) in the public services which are highly centralised personnel systems, standardised employment practices, paternalistic styles of management and collectivist patterns of industrial relations. There was little delegation of policy discretion to senior or operational managers and policies on pay, grading, pensions, recruitment, promotion and union recognition were centrally established and largely uncontroversial throughout the period from 1945 to the 1970s. High employment security and promotion rooted in seniority bred both an institutional conservatism and a collegial and supportive mentality, associated with the public services ethic. Senior officials were generally supportive of subordinates and their employment interests. Staff were not driven through patronage or fear of losing their jobs but rather by loyalty or the realisation that by conforming they would eventually be rewarded by promotion. Personnel policies were uniformly applied and regulated by rules and procedures set down in voluminous codes relating to each public service.

Collectivist patterns of industrial relations characterised all public services with trade union membership ranging from 65 to 98 per cent. All but the uniformed services, top civil servants and doctors and dentists had their pay and conditions determined by collective bargaining and the scope of collective bargaining was very wide. Over the years, public services were generally in the forefront of enlightened and progressive personnel policies and practices and came to offer secure employment, training and career development, equal opportunities and good pensions though there were pockets of low pay and less secure employment especially in local government and the NHS.

This normal pattern of traditional people management (TPM) reflected public employers' need to harmonise people management practices if they were to provide uniform public services across the country. It was also necessary for governments to impose some uniformity of personnel policy upon the growing public services, as they became more costly to support and public expenditure had to be controlled.

NEW PEOPLE MANAGEMENT

Throughout the 1980s and 1990s the organisational paradigm outlined above was challenged as new organisational structures, processes, roles and cultures emerged (Farnham and Horton, 1996b; Horton and Farnham, 1999). A new paradigm of public management began to replace both the traditional bureaucratic models of public administration and TPM. The key characteristics of this paradigm when contrasted with the traditional model are

- decentralisation is preferred to centralisation
- diversity to uniformity
- performance management to routinised administration
- entrepreneurship to consistency in practice.

There is no longer a commitment to a broadly uniform system of people management across the public services although the reality may still be more uniformity than is expected. There is evidence that the broadly universalistic and homogeneous set of policies described as TPM are being replaced by greater diversity and heterogeneity and a new people management (NPM) model (Farnham and Horton, 1996a).

Managing human resources is now acknowledged to be *the* major function of management in the public services where staff accounts for 70 per cent of total costs. There is an enhanced status for the personnel function headed often by human resource directors who are members of top management boards and involved in integrative and pro-active planning of corporate objectives. Personnel strategy is now central to the business planning cycle and is continually reviewed and updated. With this new strategic role for the personnel function, most tasks have been devolved to line managers including recruitment and selection, performance management, staff appraisal, rewards and training and a central feature of emerging employment practices amongst public employers is their focus on flexibility. In contrast to job stability, planned career pathways and employment security of the past the public sector is now resorting to more open recruitment, and diverse modes of employment and working patterns (Fowler, 1993), adopting many of the practices associated with the 'flexible firm' (Atkinson and Meagher, 1986). There is also greater flexibility in pay and benefits and pay is increasingly related to performance. A third area of greater flexibility is in the opening of the public services to outside recruits. Applicants from the private sector are actively encouraged at every level including the top posts of chief executive. Finally, there is more flexibility in jobs as demarcation boundaries are removed and multi-skilling is introduced.

A new industrial relations is also evident. National collective bargaining is still the norm for non-managerial staff but key groups of public employees, including all medical and nursing staff in the NHS, teachers in schools and top civil servants, have their pay determined by pay review bodies which recommend pay increases to the government which it normally accepts, although it can deviate if it so wishes. Senior management are also outside collective bargaining as they are on individual contracts and receive PRP. This dualist system is now the norm. Employers are still using collective bargaining channels but at the same time are encouraging joint problem solving and non-adversarial approaches, including non-union representation of employees. Single table bargaining, harmonisation of working conditions, the use of quality circles and team briefings are signs of new managerial practices. There is also evidence of a 'New Pay' approach, which White (1998) describes as essentially a person-related, rather than a job-related approach to pay structures. It is also organisationally specific and rooted in the idea of the market worth of an individual employee.

Finally, there is a move away from the traditional model employer role towards a new model based more upon the private sector employer. Driven by the need to reduce staff numbers, increase productivity and constantly deliver efficiency savings, public employment no longer offers security or the attractions of progression and 'fair' wages. Forced competition between public and private bodies, management by contract and the dis-aggregation of public organisations into purchasers and providers have led to internal markets and competition between separate public businesses aimed primarily at satisfying client needs in the market place but under conditions of resource restraint. The employment function of the state is being subordinated to its business function and the state is treating its employees as 'human resources', which need to be used efficiently and effectively rather than as public servants serving the state and public interest. The new mode employer encompasses legacies of the past but the evidence is that the search for flexibility and the ability of the state to respond to the changes in its environment are clearly having significant impacts on people management although they vary between parts of the public sector and within sectors. Drawing upon research into changes in people management the next section highlights some of the key findings. *Some of the key*

THE CIVIL SERVICE

Faced with cuts in expenditure, enforced staff ceilings and demands for increased efficiency, senior civil servants were forced, throughout the 1980s, to look for ways of restructuring the service's activities, reducing staff and increasing workforce flexibility.

Numerical and working time flexibilities

The civil service workforce fell from 732,000 staff in 1979 to fewer than 480,000 in 1998. This was achieved through a combination of transfer of functions and staff to the private sector and contraction of staff using non-replacement, early retirement or redundancy. Downsizing is a continuous process. Each year departments and agencies are set efficiency targets, which imply staff reductions. Accompanying contraction, there has been a growth of both part-time and temporary jobs. Women, who make up 52 per cent of the service account for 47,000 of the 50,000 part-time posts and a majority of the 15,000 temporary ones. Most women are concentrated in lower grades but there has been a significant increase in part-time work in the higher civil service.

Flexible working was first introduced in the 1970s to offset the then-anticipated 'demographic time-bomb' and to meet a commitment to equal opportunities. During the 1980s, however, the focus turned to devising ways of retaining highly qualified and trained staff and achieving greater numerical flexibility. The Mueller Report (1987) recommended a wide range of alternative working patterns including flexible hours, job-sharing, term-time working, recurring temporary appointments, on-call arrangements, home working and career breaks.

These diverse modes of employment are all used enabling the civil service to reach new labour markets and respond to the personal needs of staff, particularly women.)

Contractual and distancing flexibilities

Although full-time contracts are still the norm, fixed-term and temporary contracts are being introduced, especially in the new Senior Civil Service (SCS) which covers 3,000 posts. Each member of the SCS has a personal contract and posts, which include chief executives of Next Steps Agencies (see below), are normally recruited through open competition. This offers flexibility to attract people from the private sector and other public bodies who have specific skills and competencies and to bring in 'new blood'. Personal contracts also offer scope for getting rid of managers failing to perform to a satisfactory standard and so dispel the perception that civil servants have 'jobs for life'.

Since 1988, government has pursued a policy of agencifying and distancing in the civil service. This has resulted in the creation of some 150 agencies, each carrying out an executive function and headed by a chief executive. Agencies are still accountable to ministers and Parliament and staffed by civil servants but each agency is organised and managed in ways appropriate to its mission. Framework documents set down the powers and responsibilities of the agencies, whilst their objectives and targets are negotiated annually with their parent departments. Agencies have clear quasi-contractual relationships with departments. They must submit efficiency plans showing how they intend to meet their objectives within running cost limits and demonstrate how they will promote competition and encourage private-sector involvement to improve value for money. They are expected to market test their activities, which has led to further sub-contracting. There are wide variations in the extent of out-sourcing and in-house provision of services. Some agencies have sub-contracted their non-core activities such as security, cleaning, reprographics, IT services, personnel and payroll services (Medicines Control Agency, 1995). Others have retained their support services in-house but with staff reductions and new terms and conditions of employment (Public Record Office, 1995). In the second half of the 1990s, internal markets were introduced within larger agencies so that all relationships are now regulated through service agreements or contracts between purchasers and providers, whether in-house or external. Agencies are currently identifying their core and non-core functions and, in many cases, abandoning out-sourcing or privatising non-core functions. Efficiency is also being achieved through benchmarking and the incorporation of the Business Excellence Model into the work of agencies and departments (Samuels, 1998).

Task and functional flexibilities

Functional flexibility is a popular term in the civil service and training and development focuses on competencies and encourages versatility and continuous development on the part of staff. A new framework for action, introduced in July 1996, reiterates the need for broadening and deepening the skills of civil servants, so that they can meet the challenge of continuous improvement in an increasingly fast changing world (Cabinet Office, 1996). Each department and agency has produced its own action plan for implementing the programme, which has three key elements:

- a commitment to Investors in People; by 2,000 all civil servants will be employed in IiP organisations
- a new drive to raise skills and awareness of staff at all levels, linked to a flexible approach to recruitment and secondment
- encouraging people to be responsible for their own development and careers.

Larger agencies and departments are now adopting Human Resource Development (HRD) approaches within performance management systems. HRD strategies are aimed at improving the skill base and expertise of staff, improving performance, and achieving cultural and behavioural change, staff commitment and staff motivation. Another aim is to ensure that training is well targeted, cost effective, offers value for money and is flexible. The civil service is fast becoming a competence-based organisation, which identifies core skills needed at each level and within each branch of the service. Competencies are the basis for recruitment, development, performance appraisal and review. First developed by the Civil Service College to aid the training of the SCS, it is being cascaded down to cover all staff at every level. Competency frameworks are used at lower levels to encourage development of National Vocational Qualifications (NVQs) and clarify the step changes involved in moving into different types of jobs and levels.

Pay and personnel flexibilities

Only the appointment, promotion, pay and conditions of the SCS are still centrally determined. In 1990, personnel responsibilities were devolved to agencies and departments and in 1996 agencies were given complete pay and grading flexibilities for staff below grade 5. This means that departments and agencies now have full powers to recruit all staff below the SCS, decide on promotion, training and development, determine an appropriate pay and grading structure, exit staff and deal with grievance and discipline. They can also design their own management structures and staff communication systems. Only larger agencies are exercising all these powers whilst small agencies more generally adopt the policies of their parent department.

Agencies are not completely autonomous, however, as all flexibilities have to be operated within the constraints of agreed running costs and other financial requirements and the civil service management code. The latter imposes rules on merit-based recruitment and equal opportunities. Agencies operating as trading funds, however, have more leeway than directly funded units, as they can finance from their own receipts. Research indicates that most agencies prefer trading fund status and are working towards obtaining it (Massey, 1995).

It is in pay flexibility that many changes are currently occurring. Traditional, centrally determined pay structures relating to separate occupational groupings and grades are now being replaced. The move is towards harmonisation of terms and conditions, paying a rate for the job rather than grade and having a single pay spine for all staff. In the new SCS, the old grading structure has been replaced with nine overlapping pay bands topped by pay ranges for permanent secretaries. The new system is intended to strike a balance between cohesion and flexibility. Each pay band relates to a number of jobs, which are assigned to a pay band using a job evaluation system known as JESP (Job Evaluation for Senior Posts). Adjacent bands overlap in terms of JESP scores and salary, so departments can decide which pay band is appropriate for each individual by taking account of performance record, skills and marketability (Review Body on Senior Salaries, 1996). It is also up to departments to determine how staff progress through pay bands, move to a higher band, whether pay increases are consolidated or not, and the resources available each year to fund salary increases. PRP was first introduced into the civil service in 1986 and covered the whole service by 1990. It is currently under review and agencies may decide to retain individual PRP, move to group PRP or abandon it. Evidence shows that PRP is heavily criticised, although most civil servants support the principle (Review Body on Senior Salaries, 1996; Pilbeam, 1995, 1998).

When the government announced the end of national collective bargaining in 1994 they sought to force departments and agencies to act in more market oriented ways and to introduce contingent pay systems. By 1998 most agencies and departments had introduced their own pay and grading structures although their freedom is subject to strict Treasury control (Talbot, 1997). Pay is now more contingent on local circumstances and there is more variable pay because of IPRP. Other variations to the former standardised and uniform pay system (White, 1998) include changed entitlement to paid sick leave (Benefits Agency), single spine grading structure for all staff (Inland Revenue) whilst significant incentives, amounting to up to 25 per cent above normal pay scales, have been paid to attract Next Steps chief executives in a number of agencies (Horton, 1996). With greater pressure to recruit from the private sector, this practice of negotiated reward packages is likely to continue. It is clear that discounted salaries of senior civil servants, because of their security and pension benefits, are no longer easy to defend and, as a result, gaps between public and private sector salaries are closing. The principle that is emerging is 'what the market will bear'.

THE NATIONAL HEALTH SERVICE

Flexibility trends in the NHS are similar to those identified in the civil service, although there is greater variation and change is taking place more slowly. Agencification and introduction of an internal market has resulted in the NHS being fragmented into 500 trusts which are 'provider' units and some 200 'purchasers' which are Health Commissions. In addition general practitioners act as both providers and purchasers where they are directly funded. NHS Trusts have considerable devolved powers, like Next Steps Agencies, but are required to compete for contracts in the health market and derive their revenues from successful bidding. This structure is in the process of being reorganised again (Department of Health, 1997) to eliminate the problems associated with internal markets, to further reduce costs and to improve services.

Numerical and working hours flexibilities

Flexible modes of employment have always existed in the NHS, which has large numbers of part-time and shift workers amongst its one million employees. In 1994, 41 per cent of employees were part-time and of these 88 per cent were women (Hughes, 1995). Although the size of the workforce has not changed significantly over the last decade, its composition has. There has been a large increase in managerial and administrative staff (some 40 per cent between 1986 and 1996) at the expense of nurses and other medical groups (13 per cent fall) and ancillary workers (49 per cent FTEs reduction). At the same time, there have been increases in part-time and sub-contract workers. Pressure on resources and problems of high turnover and absence rates have also led to increased use of temporary contract workers and employment of agency and bank staff to work as required. The problem of obtaining and retaining staff is widespread (White, 1996) but is most acute in London where turnover is between 30 and 40 per cent per annum. According to the Royal College of Nursing there were 8,000 nursing vacancies in 1998 (Peston, 1998). Throughout the NHS, the nursing workforce, and to a lesser extent medical staff, provide clear examples of increased numerical flexibility. Income Data Services (1997) confirmed a significant increase in both temporary and short-term contracts (7 per cent of the NHS in 1997). The main reason for this was uncertainty in funding due to the short-term nature of the contracting process. This may be relieved by New Labour's policy to extend the duration of contracts to inject more stability in trust incomes. In addition to temporary staff, there has been a significant increase in casual staff. Internal 'banks' of staff willing to work additional hours plus external agency staff are important sources of mainly nursing casuals but in recent years also doctors and para-medicals. The causes of the large peripheral workforce are partly cost, to keep labour costs down, but also labour market factors – the difficulty of recruiting and retaining nursing staff. The leakage of trained staff, especially nurses and midwives, is very high.

Contractual flexibilities and distancing

Fixed term contracts were first introduced in the mid-1980s for the new general managers. Some trusts are now extending fixed term contracts to nurse managers and other posts at middle management levels. Once staff sign new contracts, they are no longer covered by collective agreements and so some trusts are willing to offer generous incentives to gain more managerial control. Fixed-term contracts are also attractive because they remove the need for redundancy if a trust contract is lost.

Both before and since the introduction of the internal market in 1990, hospitals have market tested their domestic and blue-collar support services. Most tenders have been won in-house but this has generally resulted in reductions in jobs or hours, as well as changes in terms and conditions of employment. Where contracts went to the private sector in the 1980s, there were often redundancies or staff transferred to the new employer often on lower wages and inferior conditions. Since the rights of public employees under the Transfer of Undertakings Protection of Employment Regulations 1981 (TUPE) have been confirmed, private companies have had to take on the *status quo* wages and conditions of transferred staff. This may explain, in part, the high proportion of successful in-house bids in the NHS.

With the advent of the internal market, all activities are now open to market testing and this has injected a degree of uncertainty for all employees. Although in most areas, the first years of trust status were accompanied by a continuation of existing provision of services, that steady state has since been adjusted. Trusts are now competing for business amongst themselves and with a growing private sector. There has been a significant increase in cross-boundary contracts, especially in the speciality areas of acute medicine and with private hospitals. Purchasers of services are keenly aware of both cost and quality criteria and seek to obtain best value for money by shopping around.

Trusts have to meet financial criteria set down by the Department of Health and need to maximise their revenue; failure to do so risks possible bankruptcy and liquidation. Although there are no examples to date of trusts being wound up, many hospitals and other health facilities have been closed and there are an increasing number of mergers and amalgamations. There have been many redundancies and reductions in staffing since 1996, as trusts were directed to de-layer their management structures. This resulted in fewer clinical directorates, extensive delegation of financial, personnel and clinical responsibilities and smaller strategic management cores. Many central support services are currently being market-tested, as in the civil service, and some are being subcontracted to the private sector or other public-sector organisations. Personnel, training and IT are particularly vulnerable to this type of out-sourcing. There is likely to be more rationalisation and restructuring of provider units over the next few years as the New Labour reforms of the NHS are implemented and they anticipate opportunities for further economies alongside increases in performance and quality.

Task and functional flexibilities

Functional flexibility is being achieved in the NHS through strategies of mixed skilling. This practice is found across the medical, paramedical and nursing fields as nurses perform minor day surgery operations and carry out tasks traditionally performed by doctors; imaging technicians carry out routine tasks, whilst radiographers concentrate on more advanced work; and health care assistants (a new and cheaper grade introduced in 1990) feed, bath and care for patients nominally under the supervision of qualified nurses who are either managing or attending to the clinical needs of patients. Multi-skilling is also found in non-professional areas where ancillary staff are performing a range of tasks across catering, portering and cleaning. The issue of multi-skilling is hotly debated as it is seen as a way of reducing costs and in conflict with the quality standards set by the professions. It is also thought to be having an effect on career structures and thus the attractiveness of the professions and contributing therefore to the shortfall of nursing staff generally.

Pay and personnel flexibilities

The NHS has traditionally been one of the most highly unionised parts of the public sector, with a complex system of national collective bargaining and Pay Review Bodies covering over 40 different occupational groups. Since 1979 the national system of collective bargaining has been slowly dismantled and greater pay flexibility has been introduced. In 1983, nurses, midwives and paramedics were taken out of collective bargaining, although their pay was still determined nationally by Pay Review Bodies (PRBs). From the early 1990s, government put pressure on trusts to develop their own pay structures and to move towards performance reward strategies, requiring them to have local pay machinery in place by 1995. Each trust now has its own pay and grading system, although most trusts are reluctant to move too far away from nationally recommended terms and conditions and more than half of NHS staff are still covered by PRBs. In those trusts where there are local pay systems they tend to be following a similar pattern to that identified in the civil service – namely a single spine with jobs located on the spine according to a job evaluation exercise. The movement to local pay bargaining was given a spur by the government's refusal during 1995 and 1996 to fund the whole of the Pay Review Bodies recommendations and some variations in pay began to appear. Since 1997, however, government has encouraged PRB recommendations to be adopted by all trusts and have provided funding for it but there is little evidence of PRP except for management staff and merit pay for doctors.

The traditions of Whitleyism, high trade union membership and pluralistic industrial relations are still an important part of NHS culture and few trusts appear to be derecognising unions or seeking to end joint regulation of the employment relationship (Corby, 1999). There has, however, been a shift towards prime union systems and single table bargaining where not all unions are represented although they are still recognised. Whilst joint regulation remains a key feature of the new industrial relations in the NHS, new and direct forms of employee involvement are also being widely used. Unions have to compete with new managerial practices associated with performance management and HRM. Systems of performance review and staff appraisal are establishing a basis for more performance based reward systems, as in the civil service. Similarly, there is now great emphasis placed on TQM and IIP, as the vogue of new management ideas spreads throughout the public services.

LOCAL GOVERNMENT

Local government has also undergone considerable change since 1979. There is more extensive use of flexible working patterns, although, as in the NHS, they are not new to this part of the public sector. Employment in local government has fallen by almost a third in the last two decades and the structure of the workforce has changed as more use has been made of Compulsory Competitive Tendering (CCT) for both manual and professional staff and the core role of local government has moved from service provision to community leadership.

Numerical and working time flexibilities

There are currently around 2.1 million people employed in local government in England and Wales, a fall from three million in 1979. Much of this contraction is due to the transfer of services out of local government such as higher and further education in 1988 and 1992 respectively. But there has also been a sharp fall in the numbers and proportion of manual workers due mainly to CCT and new technology. Other changes are a rise in the proportion of non-manuals, a reduction in the number of full-time posts and a significant increase in part-time employment. In June 1998, there were 970,000 part-time and 1.1 million full-time employees or 1.47 million full-time equivalents (FTE). Nearly 48 per cent of employees were in part-time posts and 52 per cent were full time. Seventy per cent of all employees were women but they account for almost 90 per cent of part-timers. Most women are employed in lower manual, clerical and professional grades, whilst men make up 95 per cent of chief executives and 91 per cent of chief officers and deputies. This gender segregation persists in local government, despite equal opportunities policies and positive action programmes.

Local government has always operated a flexible workforce, because so many of the services it provides require 24-hour coverage or the work is seasonal or irregular. Shift work, un-social hours and irregular work patterns are therefore widespread. The large numbers of both men and women in part time jobs (16 per cent of men and 60 per cent of women) are well above the national averages of eight and 46 per cent respectively. Most jobs, however, are permanent, with only nine per cent of men and 11 per cent of women on temporary contracts.

The incidence of part-time work has increased in local government along with the national trend with the highest increases in those areas 'with the least previous experience of employing part-timers. In services other than education and social services, the proportion of part-timers increased from 15 per cent to 24 per cent between 1994 and 1996' (LGMB, 1997a). Thirteen per cent of managers now work part-time, which is twice the national proportion. Many of these work in the 24-hour services and other 'out of hours' services such as leisure centres, residential homes and libraries. Part-time staffs, especially in services such as education and social services, carry out much of local authorities' 'core business'. Thus the core-peripheral model which suggests that part-time workers are part of the peripheral work of an organisation (see chapter 1) is not descriptive of local authority employment strategies. However, as discussed below part-time workers are three times more likely to be on temporary contracts than their full-time equivalents.

One type of part-time work is short-hours, that is working fewer than 10 hours per week. About 10 per cent of the total local government workforce and 25 per cent of part-timers fall into this category. Short hours contracts tend to be found mainly amongst manual employees, although more than 25 per cent of part-time teachers fall into this group. The number of employees working fewer than 10 hours per week in their main job has been increasing in local government, rising by 10 per cent between 1994 and 1996. The reasons for this increase are not clear but as employees in this group tend to be in younger and older age groups some of the reasons may be combining work with study or taking short hours to supplement pensions after early retirement or redundancy. Clearly from the employers perspective there are both service and financial factors at work. Some services such as 'school dinners' require a very limited number of hours. However, in other cases it is clear that employing people on low pay for limited hours avoids employers paying National Insurance contributions.

In 1997 nearly 20 per cent of the local authority workforce worked a flexitime pattern, nearly twice the national average (LGMB, 1997a). If teachers and social services staffs are excluded, this rises to over one third. It is also more common amongst full-time staff than part-timers. Flexitime has been operated within local authorities to enable employees to adjust their working time to the fluctuating demands of the job and their own personal requirements. There is some evidence, however, that it has become inflexible in practice and that it is in need of reform (LGMB, 1998). In addition to flexitime, two per cent of men and 25 per cent of women work term-time only. These are found mainly in education. Fewer than 10 per cent of staff have annualised hours, which cover five per cent of men and eight per cent of women. Only two per cent of local authority employees work on job-share schemes although this again is double the national figure. Job-share was introduced in the 1980s to promote part-time working in areas that had traditionally been seen as full-time. It is found mainly in non-manual posts and almost entirely benefits women.

Local government has a lower record of working long hours than the economy in general although in 1997, excluding teachers, some 10 per cent of local government managers worked more than 48 hours in a normal week. This compares with an average of 64.5 per cent of chief officers nationally. The recently implemented EU Working Time Directive is likely to see some change in the long hours culture, which characterises both the private and public sectors in the UK, and may have some knock-on effect on staffing levels.

Contractual flexibilities and distancing

In local government there is a high proportion of employees on temporary contracts, nearly twice the national figure. Nearly one-in-eight local government employees are temporary. Temporary contracts are particularly common in the education sector and other personal and protective services and lowest in managerial and administrative staff. Although some use is made of agency temping and casual workers, fixed-term contracts are more common. There is a definite trend towards employing more temporary staff in local government and their numbers increased from 11 to 13 per cent between 1992 and 1996. The use of fixed-term contracts is not new, as they have been traditionally used to cover maternity leave and long-term sickness. They are also used to employ staff on time-limited projects or to buy in expertise for specific tasks. There is evidence that now, however, short-term contracts are being used as a device for dealing with annual budgetary uncertainties. As the LGMB (1997b: 18) states 'Implicitly this new trend suggests that authorities may be endeavouring to become flexible organisations through making a high proportion of newly recruited staff dispensable'. The reasons why people take temporary contracts are mixed. Some take them because there is no permanent work available. However, there is some anecdotal evidence that temporary forms of working appeal to those individuals wishing to develop 'portfolio careers' and to move between jobs to gain experience and advancement.

Outsourcing is not new to local government, which has always employed private companies to undertake major capital programmes. Since 1980, however, contracting out has increased because of the enforced policy of CCT. At first it applied only to building and maintenance but was extended to refuse collection, cleaning, catering, ground maintenance and vehicle repair and maintenance in 1988, street lighting and sport and leisure facilities in 1989 and professional and technical services including personnel, training, IT, legal, financial and engineering services in 1992. Most contracts put out to tender under CCT have actually been won in-house (Shaw, Fenwick and Foreman, 1995) but many local authorities have used the threat of contracting out to restructure their operations and make their workforces more cost effective and competitive. According to White and Hutchinson, CCT has impacted particularly upon manual workers (1996: 204–5):

> CCT has led not only to major reductions in employment but also to less favourable working conditions and a major intensification of work . . . there have been reductions in bonuses and holiday entitlements and increases in working hours. Some authorities now have annualised hours to allow for peaks and troughs in demand and seasonal variations in daylight hours. Overtime has also been significantly reduced.

Dickens (1998) has also shown that distancing has not been gender neutral with women suffering disproportionately in terms of job loss, job insecurity and deterioration in terms and conditions of employment.

Task and functional flexibilities

The pressure on local government to cut costs and, at the same time, increase productivity and quality, has led it to introduce new systems of performance management, like those found in other public services. Staff appraisal and performance reviews have given management opportunities to control the work process more closely, although not all local authorities have yet implemented organisation-wide appraisal systems. Increasingly, however, with the focus on controlling the outputs of the organisation rather than inputs, staff now expect to be assessed on their performance. Effort is also being made to extend the skills of staff and break down functional barriers by redesigning or upgrading jobs. In order to raise performance, local authorities are placing emphasis on HRD and skills inventories; with training needs analyses identifying skill deficiencies. Internal training is now focused less on professional qualifications and more on developing transferable management skills and competencies, preparing the organisation for change and supporting organisational learning. There is emphasis on Investors in People, National Vocational Qualifications, Total Quality Management and obtaining quality marks and British Standards Awards, as in other public services.

Whilst large local authorities have their own training departments and training specialists, smaller local authorities rely more on external training consultants, local colleges and universities. The Local

Government National Training Organisation set up in 1997 is designed to help meet the business needs of local government and to monitor and guide standards throughout the service. The new single status agreement in local government (see below) is expected to stimulate a great deal of training and HRD, since Part 3 of the agreement sets out a framework and structure for training and development at local authority level. Providing flexible services, maintaining security of employment and achieving equality of opportunity are, it is argued, all dependent on excellence in training and HRD (Farnham, 1998).

Pay flexibilities

Although each of the 400 local authorities in England and Wales are independent employers, their pay and grading structures have traditionally been determined nationally through collective bargaining although agreements have always allowed for local interpretation. Since the 1980s, there has been a slow drift towards greater decentralisation driven by labour market factors, financial and political pressures and CCT. Difficulties in recruiting and retaining key groups of workers such as teachers, accountants, IT staff, architects and chief executives led to the use of pay supplements, supplementary benefits or advanced entry on basic scales. Pressure to reduce costs led to attempts to negotiate a new national floor of minimum rates but when this failed in 1989, 40 local authorities removed themselves from the national system and were operating their own local systems of pay determination by 1994 (Joyce and McNulty, 1994). Today fewer than 10 per cent of local authorities are opted out and none have done so in the last five years. The major impetus to local bargaining for manual workers was CCT with most local authorities reducing non-pay terms and conditions more in line with private employers but retaining basic national pay rates.

In 1997 a new single status deal was agreed between local government employers and the unions. This has a unified spine but without any specified rates of pay for particular jobs. Such flexibility enables employers to respond to local labour market conditions and to reward performance and thus results in local variations. Implementation of single status will not be easy for local authorities, as it involves placing both white and blue-collar workers on a single pay scale, as well as offering identical conditions of employment. This can only be done at a local level and therefore will increase the amount of decentralised local bargaining. Few jobs now have nationally prescribed pay rates and every local authority will decide where each job is placed on the single pay spine. Local government is always constrained, however, in what it can pay its employees because central government imposes ceilings on overall expenditure.

PRP has not made much impact in local government although 40 per cent of local authorities, mainly in Southeast England, have PRP for at least some staff (LGMB, 1994). It is largely confined to managerial staff although some direct service organisations link pay to income from contracts and efficiency gains whilst others pay bonuses for achievement of targets. There is some evidence that PRP is being abandoned by some local authorities whilst others are looking to group schemes. The other changes at local level have been the move towards single table bargaining, no strike clauses, pendulum arbitration and, in a small number of cases, some derecognition of trade unions. What is more general amongst the 400 local authorities is the growth of new types of employee communication systems, which are individualised and side step collective channels of union representation. Similar moves have been noted in both the NHS and civil service. What is most noticeable in local government, however, is the limited extent of the move towards decentralisation and the continuation of nationally determined structures and pay systems. Although there is a loosening up of the system and more flexibility is evident, local government employers appear to be committed to national collective bargaining and recognise its advantages in making the planning of pay management easier and avoiding pay competition.

DISCUSSION

It is evident that flexible working practices are widespread throughout British public services. More people are on fixed term, temporary and part-time contracts than in the past and they are more likely to be job-sharing, on annualised hours or working from home (Hegewisch, 1998). The latest workplace survey (Cully and Woodland, 1998) confirms that access to flexible and family friendly arrangements are significantly higher in the public sector than in the private sector (see Table 12.1). It is also clear that functional flexibility is increasing although this varies widely from the general redesign of work in the civil service, the enlarged managerial role of professionals in the health service and education, to the introduction of team-

Table 12.1   Access to flexible working arrangements in the
public sector by sex

	Men %	Women %	All employment (public and private) %
Flexitime	37	39	32
Job sharing	23	24	16
Parental leave	35	33	28
Working from home	13	9	9
Child care support (creches/subsidy)	6	9	4
None of these	40	34	36

Source: Adapted from Cully and Woodland, 1998.

based working in community care and job intensification in all the public services. Finally pay flexibility is also increasing although there has been some effective resistance to change in this area.

The major forces driving these changes have been political and financial, though the impact of modern management and organisational ideas should not be underestimated (Pollitt, 1993; Kirkpatrick and Martinez Lucio, 1996). Successive governments since the late 1970s have sought to roll back the state, reduce the claim of the public sector on the economy's limited resources and get more for less from what remains. Their policies of deregulation, privatisation, restructuring, contractorisation, and decentralisation have resulted in increased numerical, contractual, functional and pay flexibilities. Social push factors have also been driving forces behind increased flexibilisation as employers have responded to the needs of employees, especially women, for more flexible working patterns and the public for more user friendly and accessible services. Equal opportunities legislation and EU directives and court decisions have reinforced these on the one hand whilst Citizen's Charters, user satisfaction surveys and the introduction of a service oriented culture have put pressure on the other. This has meant reviewing access to services, extending opening hours, setting up one-stop services and moving towards 24-hour electronic government (Bellamy, 1999; Cabinet Office, 1999). New technology opens up opportunities for teleworking, 24-hour services, virtual organisations and many other flexibilities but all these changes need more flexible staff with appropriate skills and competencies.

Responses to these forces have not been uniform throughout the public services, although some generalisations are possible. First, the former unified public services have been fragmented and decentralised. Second, collectivist traditions in public services are giving way to particularism, individualism and competition between rival 'businesses'. Hospitals are competing for contracts, universities for students and all public bodies with the private sector because of CCT and market testing. Other forms of collectivism, including trade unionism and professionalism, are also in decline. Both cut across the boundaries of the new units and appear less relevant to individual employees. As individual contracts and performance management take hold, individuals become more organisationally oriented rather than committed to the service or their profession.

Third, the changes are affecting behaviour. For many employees a major contraction in the numbers employed in the public services has meant redundancy, early retirement, relocation or transfer of employment to the private sector. The job-for-life expectation is no longer part of the psychological contract. Operating within markets and CCT, or carrying out restructuring and market testing, is also changing the way people behave, even though they may not entirely support what they have been asked to do. Public officials are now cost-conscious and driven increasingly by financial objectives rather than by professional or bureaucratic ones. They accept greater uncertainty in their jobs and career structures and have learned to cope with constant change, although not without high levels of stress.

Fourth, there is a uniform movement towards HRM and performance management systems and public organisations now have strategic personnel or human resources units, which develop plans and policies that are integrated into the organisation's business and corporate plans. HRM is enabling management to control the labour process more effectively and use flexibilities to control costs and to encourage conformist behaviour. The movement towards individual contracts, PRP, and locally determined pay structures is giving management more freedom to take decisions in the interest of the 'business' as well as reflecting the particular local conditions in which the business operates. Some public organisations, however, have sought to pursue high commitment and high performance strategies by involving staff in a variety of ways (Cully and Woodland, 1998).

There is no doubt that there have been many positive outcomes of decentralisation and flexibilisation strategies in the public services. There is evidence of greater efficiency as over-staffing has been eliminated, restrictive practices have been removed and costs are closely controlled. Functional flexibility and job enlargement are producing more interesting work and post-bureaucratic organisations offer more opportunities to people to influence their working lives. Women, in particular, have benefited from more flexible working patterns and men are increasingly taking advantage of them too. Services are more responsive to customer needs and there is more variation and innovation as employees are encouraged to be entrepreneurial.

These benefits should not be exaggerated, however, and must be balanced by some of the negative effects of the changes (Hoggett, 1996; Ferlie *et al.*, 1997; Painter, 1999). In many ways, new structures, procedures and flexibilities have strengthened hierarchies and reduced the autonomy that many professionals previously had. There has been an increase in managerial control of the labour process, in the guise of decentralisation and flexibilisation. And in some instances bureaucratic characteristics are more pronounced. This is manifested in both the powerful centralising tendencies to ensure continuing control over the exercise of devolved powers but also in the new layers of internal bureaucracy engaged in contract specification, quality control, audit and inspection. Decentralisation has also resulted in fragmentation, which has created a co-ordination deficit.

Tensions have also been present in the management reforms, as they have sought to move to a new system of people management (Farnham and Horton, 1996a). On the one hand management is seeking to motivate and gain commitment of staff to change through sophisticated HRM and HRD strategies and on the other resorting to job contraction, CCT and job intensification to achieve reduction of costs. There is evidence of high levels of dissatisfaction and stress, whilst low morale appears to be at an all-time high in some public services, especially the NHS and education (Bogg and Cooper, 1992; Caplan, 1994; Cooper and Kelly, 1993). A study of PRP by the Institute of Personnel and Development in 1998 (unpublished) found that more than 50 per cent of public sector respondents believed that IPRP had a negative effect on staff morale as compared to only 34 per cent in the private sector. Although the public services still have a good record on equal opportunities there is also evidence that many of the changes in organisational structure, pressure on costs and contracting out are threatening progress and generally tend to disadvantage women disproportionate to men (Corby, 1998). Change towards individual contracts is also increasing labour mobility, especially among the higher skilled, and as mobility between public and private sectors increases this is undermining public service as a career for life. This can be seen most clearly in the civil service where the career SCS is under threat as government is imposing open recruitment and inter-changeability between top officials and their private counterparts (Cabinet Office, 1994, 1996). A career SCS is giving way to open access and top government jobs based on prescribed qualifications and managerial competencies, rather than traditional generalist skills, knowledge of the machinery of government and long service. This is likely to have constitutional as well as political consequences.

Although there has never been uniformity across public services, there has been a distinct public-service culture. In some public services, such as education and health, this has been rooted in professional codes of practice, as well as a public-service orientation. With the transition to managerialism, these professional cultures are being at best adapted and, in many cases, subverted by economistic values. Whilst the official claim is that all public services are now more consumer-oriented and committed to quality, limited resources and constant pressure to look for greater efficiency and economy undermines those aims. Many professionals now find contradictions between their own standards of quality and the performance indicators by which their work is judged. Professionalism and managerialism coexist, at best, within a context of creative tensions. In other public services business and economic priorities such as business need, cost minimisation, innovation and flexibility for managers to deploy resources, are also imposing new values which conflict with the public service ethos based on values of standardisation, probity, risk aversion, equity, fairness and detailed procedural rules.

The New Labour government is committed to modernising government and has set out a package of reforms which are clearly designed to respond in part to the negative effects of previous changes (Cabinet Office, 1998b, 1999). In particular it aims to substitute partnership, co-operation and collaboration for autonomy, competition and fragmentation and to promote both vertical and horizontal integration between government, private and voluntary organisations by means of 'joined-up government'. Reforms of local government, the NHS and civil service will all focus on making each more responsive to public needs and expectations and more able to be pro-active in meeting and managing change. There is a strong commitment to public service which the government states 'has for too long been neglected, undervalued and denigrated' It asserts it is committed to the 'public service values of impartiality, objectivity and integrity. But we need greater creativity, radical thinking and collaborative working . . . and must move away from the risk-averse culture inherent in government. We need to reward results and to encourage the necessary skills . . . we must be more flexible in bringing people in and . . . get more movement within the public service. We must get more flexibility within the public service so that it can meet the varying needs within our diverse society . . . The public service must become a learning organisation (Cabinet Office, 1999: 55–6). The government's programme includes reform of public sector pay systems, increasing diversity by addressing under-representation of women, ethnic minorities and the disabled at senior levels, extending family friendly policies and ensuring public officials have up-to-date skills and competencies through continuous development. There is no indication that the 'flexibility assault' is ended as the government expects constantly rising productivity and cost control of public services. And it is also fully committed to integrating the private sector still more into the public services through the Private Finance Initiative. In spite of the rhetoric there are still likely to be winners and losers in 'the flexibility game'.

References

ATKINSON, J. and MEAGHER, N. (1986). *Changing Patterns of Work: How Companies Achieve Flexibilities*. London: NEDO.
BELLAMY, C. (1999). 'Exploiting Information and Communication Technologies', in Horton, S. and Farnham, D., *Managing Public Services in Britain*, London: Macmillan, pp 107–27.
BOGG, J. and COOPER, C. (1992). 'Job Satisfaction, Mental Health and Occupational Stress among Senior Civil Servants'. *Human Relations*. 48 (3), pp 327–41.
CABINET OFFICE (1994). *The Civil Service: Continuity and Change*. (Cm 2627.) London: HMSO.
CABINET OFFICE (1996). *Development and Training for Civil Servants: a Framework for Action*. (Cm 3321.) London: HMSO.
CABINET OFFICE (1998a). *Public Bodies 1997*. London: The Stationery Office.
CABINET OFFICE (1998b). *Modern Public Services: Results of the Government's Comprehensive Review*. London: The Stationery Office.
CABINET OFFICE (1999). *Modernising Britain*. London: The Stationery Office.

CAPLAN, R. (1994). 'Stress, Anxiety and Depression in Hospital Consultants, General Practitioners and Senior Health Service Managers'. *British Medical Journal.* 309, pp 1261–3.

CARMICHAEL, P. and KNOX, C. (1999). 'Towards "a new era"? Some developments in governance in Northern Ireland'. *International Review of Administrative Sciences.* 65.1, pp 103–16.

COOPER, C. and KELLY, M. (1993). 'Occupational Stress in Head Teachers: A National UK Study'. *British Journal of Educational Psychology.* 63, pp 130–43.

CORBY, S. (1998). 'Equal Opportunities: Fair Shares for All', in Corby, S. and White, G., *Employee Relations in the Public Services*, London: Routledge, pp 95–113.

CORBY, S. (1999). 'The National Health Service', in Horton, S. and Farnham, D., *Public Management in Britain*, London: Macmillan, pp 180–93.

CORBY, S. and MATHIESON, H. (1997). 'The NHS and the Limits to Flexibility'. *Public Policy and Administration.* Winter, pp 60–72.

CULLY, M. and WOODLAND, S. (1998). *The 1998 Workplace Relations Survey* First Findings London: DTI.

DEPARTMENT OF HEALTH (1997). *The New NHS Modern – Dependable.* (Cm 3807.) London: The Stationery Office.

DICKENS, L. (1998). 'What HRM Means for Gender Equality'. *Human Resource Management Journal.* 8 (1), pp 23–40.

FARNHAM, D. (1998). 'Human Resources Management in British Local Government', paper presented at an international workshop on New Public Management, Humboldt University, Berlin, and Anglo German Foundation for the Study of Industrial Society. December.

FARNHAM, D. and HORTON, S. (1996a). *Managing People in the Public Services.* London: Macmillan.

FARNHAM, D. and HORTON, S. (eds) (1996b). *Managing the New Public Services.* 2nd edn. London: Macmillan.

FARNHAM, D. and PIMLOTT, J. (1995). *Understanding Industrial Relations.* London: Cassell.

FERLIE, E., ASHBURNER, L., FITZGERALD, L. and PETTIGREW, A. (eds) (1997). *The New Public Management in Action.* Oxford: Oxford University Press.

FOWLER, A. (1993). *Taking Charge.* London: IPM.

HEGEWISCH, A. (1998). 'Employment Flexibility', in Corby, S. and White, G., *Employee Relations in the Public Services Themes and Issues.* London: Routledge, pp 114–35.

HOGGETT, P. (1996). 'New Modes of Control in Public Service'. *Public Administration.* 74, pp 9–32.

HORTON, S. (1996). 'The Civil Service', in Farnham, D. and Horton, S., *Managing People in the Public Services.* London: Macmillan, pp 93–148.

HORTON, S. and FARNHAM, D. (1999). *Public Management in Britain.* London: Macmillan.

HUGHES, A. (1995). 'Employment in the public and private sectors'. *Economic Trends.* No. 495, pp 14–22.

INCOME DATA SERVICES (1997). *Pay in the Public Services: Review of 1996, Prospects for 1997.* London: IDS.

JOYCE, P. and MCNULTY, T. (1994). 'Local pay bargaining: a public sector response to the development of the contract state', paper presented at the Employment Research Unit Annual Conference, Cardiff. October.

KIRKPATRICK, I. and MARTINEZ LUCIO, M. (1996). 'Introduction: the contract state and the future of public management'. *Public Administration.* 74 (1), pp 1–8.

LOCAL GOVERNMENT MANAGEMENT BOARD (1994). *The Changing Role of the Human Resource Function.* Luton: LGMB.

LOCAL GOVERNMENT MANAGEMENT BOARD (1997a). *Local Government Workforce Statistics.* Luton: LGMB.

LOCAL GOVERNMENT MANAGEMENT BOARD (1997b). *Flexible Working Key Issues.* Luton: LGMB.

LOCAL GOVERNMENT MANAGEMENT BOARD (1998). *Flexible Working Patterns in Local Authorities and the Wider Economy.* Luton: LGMB.

MASSEY, A. (1995). *After Next Steps: Report to the Office of Public Service and Science.* London: Cabinet Office.

MEDICINES CONTROL AGENCY (1995). *Annual Report.* London: Medical Control Agency.

MUELLER REPORT (1987). *Working Patterns.* London: HMSO.

OECD (1996).

PAINTER, C. (1999). 'From Thatcher to Blair: Public Service Reform-A Third Way'. *Parliamentary Affairs.* 2 (1), pp 94–112.

PESTON, R. (1998). 'Nurses on lower pay in line for 5% increase'. *Financial Times.* 14/15 November.

PILBEAM, S. (1995). 'Current Trends, Issues and Dilemmas in Performance Related Pay', unpublished MSc dissertation, University of Portsmouth.

PILBEAM, S. (1998). 'Individual Performance-Related Pay (IPRP) Believers and Sceptics'. *Croners Employee Relations Review.* Issue No. 5, June, pp 9–16.

POLLITT, C. (1993). *Managerialism and the Public Services: the Anglo-American experience.* Oxford: Blackwell.

PUBLIC RECORD OFFICE (1995). *Annual Report.* London: Public Record Office.

REVIEW BODY ON SENIOR SALARIES (1996). *Eighteenth Report on Senior Salaries.* Report No. 37. (Cm 3094.) London: HMSO.

SAMUELS, M. (1998). *Towards Best Practice: An Evaluation of the First Two Years of the Public Sector Benchmarking Project 1996–98.* London: Cabinet Office.

SHAW, K., FENWICK, J. and FOREMAN, A. (1995). 'Competitive Tendering for Local Government Services in the United Kingdom'. *Public Policy and Administration.* 10 (1), pp 63–75.

STOREY, J. (1992). *Developments in the Managing of Human Resources.* Oxford: Blackwell.

SPENCER, P. (1997). 'Reaction to a flexible labour market', in Jowell, R. *et al,* British Social Attitudes: *The End of Conservative Values?,* 14th Report, Aldershot: Ashgate, pp 73–91.

TALBOT, C. (1997). 'UK Civil Service Personnel Reforms: Devolution,

Decentralization and Delusion'. *Public Policy and Administration.* 12 (4), pp 14–34.

WHITE, G. (1996). 'Public sector pay bargaining: comparability, decentralization and control'. *Public Administration.* 74 (1), pp 89–112.

WHITE, G. (1998). 'The Remuneration of Public Servants: Fair Pay or New Pay?', in Corby, S. and White, G. (eds), *Employee Relations in the Public Services*, London: Routledge, pp 73–94.

WHITE, G. and HUTCHINSON, B. (1996). 'Local Government', in Farnham, D. and Horton, S., *Managing People in the Public Services*, London: Macmillan, pp 185–224.

13 Human Resources Flexibilities in the United States

James Thompson and Raymond Cachares

In the United States, as in many other countries, there has been much tinkering and experimentation in recent years with the devices of governance. The public service generally, and civil service systems more specifically, have served as foci of investigation and change. This chapter provides an overview of some of the changes occurring within the American public service at federal, state and local levels. Particular emphasis is placed on developments in the federal government which tend to be of broader interest and where the data tends to be more accessible.

According to the Bureau of the Census, there were approximately 18.4 million public employees in the United States in 1990. Of that total, approximately 3.1 million (including the Postal Service) were employed by the federal government, 4.5 million by state governments and 10.8 million by local governments. The largest contingent works in the educational sector (eight million) followed by health (two million) and national defence (one million) (US Bureau of the Census, 1992). Federal government employees are generally categorised in three groups; the competitive service, the excepted service and the Senior Executive Service (SES). The competitive service, with approximately 52 per cent of all federal employees, includes all those whose terms of employment are governed by Title 5 of the US Code (US General Accounting Office, 1997a). When generic reference is made to 'the civil service', it is directed to this group of employees and this section of the law. However, a substantial number of federal employees are members of the excepted service and fall outside the provisions of Title 5. The excepted service includes multiple, separate personnel systems that have been created over the years to accommodate the particular needs of individual agencies. Included in the excepted service are diplomats within the Foreign Service, doctors and nurses in the Veterans Health Administration, and employees of government corporations such as the Postal Service. This diversity of personnel systems itself represents an important source of flexibility within the federal system. The SES includes the highest ranking members of the career service. With approximately 7,000 members, the SES is minuscule in comparison with the other two groups.

There is wide variability in human resource management structures, procedures and practices among the 50 federal states. Most state systems operate on the basis of merit principles although, as discussed below, one state, Georgia, has substantially revoked the requirement that merit serve as the primary basis of employment. Large urbanised states such as New York and California tend to have complex systems characterised by a high degree of regulation; smaller rural states operate less formally and with limited reliance on centrally created rules and procedures. Analysis of state personnel practices is complicated by the lack of any single, consolidated source of data on state personnel systems. The discussion below places particular reliance on a series of surveys conducted under the auspices of the Council of State Governments.

Gauging trends in personnel practices at the local level is particularly difficult. The estimated 80,000 plus units of local government in the US fall into a variety of different categories; counties, cities, towns, villages, school districts, and other types of special districts. Personnel practices vary not only between states but also between categories within states. Without data on general trends in personnel practices at the local level, the emphasis here is placed on identification of 'best practices' and reputational leaders among municipalities that may be suggestive of future trends.

HUMAN RESOURCE FLEXIBILITIES IN FEDERAL GOVERNMENT

To the extent that there have been identifiable trends in human resource management (HRM) practices in the American public services during the 1990s, those trends are highly congruent with the reform 'principles' identified by Osborne and Gaebler in their book *Reinventing Government* (1992). On the one hand, the principles themselves were derived inductively through the observation of 'best practices' among governmental units around the country; on the other hand, because of the book, many officials have made those principles a basis for their own changes. The book, and the principles identified therein, therefore, serve as a useful frame in which to understand much of the change that is underway. This is particularly true of federal government. President Clinton's management reform initiative, the National Performance Review (NPR), was substantially guided by the ideas set forth by Osborne and Gaebler. With regard to personnel practices, particular emphasis in the *Report of the National Performance Review* (1993a) is placed on the necessity of deregulating the processes of hiring, classifying, compensating, promoting and firing federal employees. According to the report, over-regulation of the federal personnel practices is epitomised by, '850 pages of federal personnel law – augmented by 1,300 pages of Office of Personnel Management (OPM) regulations on how to implement those laws and another 10,000 pages of guidelines from the Federal Personnel Manual' (*ibid.*: 19). The report was further critical of the cost to taxpayers of the 54,000 personnel staff responsible for promulgating and enforcing these rules and regulations. Worst of all, the rules and regulations impede the flexibility that is requisite for good management. To solve these problems, the report included a number of specific reform recommendations guided by the following principles: a lessening of the extent to which line managers are subject to centrally devised rules and regulations in personnel matters, an accompanying shift in the role of the central personnel office from one of 'policeman' to one of 'consultant' and 'partner'; the granting to individual agencies of the authority to shape personnel practices to specific needs and objectives, and increased attention to quality of work life issues.

Vice President Gore and his staff employed a multi-pronged strategy to shift authority and discretion in matters of hiring, firing, promotion and compensation from professional 'personnelists' to line managers. First, legislation incorporating a series of changes to the civil service system as a whole was developed. Second, the President used his authority as head of the executive branch of government to direct certain changes. Third, there has been *de facto* deregulation driven by across-the-board reductions in human resources staff. And, fourth, individual agencies have sought and received exemptions from government-wide personnel rules.

Civil service reform

The NPR report and the accompanying report entitled, *Reinventing Human Resource Management* (1993b) made a number of specific recommendations for reforming the federal civil service:

- eliminate the Federal Personnel Manual, emblematic of what reformers perceived as a central problem with the federal personnel system; excessive central regulation
- decentralise responsibility for recruitment and examination to departments, consistent with the emphasis on allowing agencies to customise their personnel practices
- simplify classification systems in order to give managers more discretion in assigning duties
- allow agencies to design their own performance management and reward systems consistent with the objective of decentralisation
- make it easier to fire poor performers
- encourage development of broad-banding systems in federal agencies, whereby employees are assigned to pay bands rather than salary grades and managers are given more discretion in setting an employee's pay.

While some of these items could be implemented unilaterally by the President, others, particularly items 3–6, required Congressional approval. Soon after release of the NPR report, the administration entered into discussions with members of Congress and representatives of the large federal employee unions over civil service reform.

Draft legislation that surfaced in 1995 included a number of provisions consistent with the NPR report:

- permitting agencies to put broad-banding practices into place
- removing from statute the criteria according to which jobs are assigned to specific pay grades, thereby allowing job classification standards to be determined administratively
- removing 'time-in-grade' requirements whereby employees progress through a salary grade according to a specific schedule, thus giving managers more flexibility in the pay-setting process
- making it easier to remove poor performers.

Several provisions designed to offset the opposition of the federal employee unions to those provisions granting managers more discretion were also included in the proposed legislation. One was to expand the number of workplace issues subject to collective bargaining and another would have required binding arbitration in areas where management had traditionally exercised exclusive control. The draft bill would also have given unions more say in the numbers, types and grades of employees in federal agencies and in the methods and means of performing work (Barr, 1995).

Ultimately, however, the effort to gain a compromise with the unions on comprehensive reform legislation fell foul of opposition by Congressional Republicans, who took the majority in both the House and Senate in 1994, to any provisions which would have expanded union authority and power in the workplace. Subsequent to the failure of the initial reform thrust, the Clinton administration has made several attempts at more incremental change to the federal civil service. The key substantive element in a bill which surfaced during the 104th (1995–96) Congress would have expanded the Office of Personnel Management's (OPM) authority to commission 'demonstration' projects as a means of testing innovative personnel practices. Even this version of reform failed to gain much support however, and failed at enactment. One personnel-related recommendation of the NPR that did get enacted separately was to allow expiration of the Personal Management and Recognition System (PMRS), a government-wide pay-for-performance system for top managers. In its place, agencies were authorised to develop their own performance management systems.

Reform by disaggregation

Although attempts at systemic reform have, to date, failed, the Clinton administration has achieved some success with a fall-back strategy of allowing/encouraging individual agencies to work with their respective Congressional oversight committees to establish certain agency-specific exemptions from provisions of Civil Service law. Two notable recent examples of this phenomenon, the Federal Aviation Administration (FAA) and the Internal Revenue Service (IRS), have been granted various personnel flexibilities, but only after each had failed in an attempt at data systems modernisation. The FAA, with 65,000 employees, is responsible for regulating the nation's airways and airports. In 1981, the FAA initiated a project to modernise the nation's air traffic control system with the purchase of new computer technology. In 1994, the modernisation programme had to be restructured after cost estimates for a key component tripled and system capabilities were downgraded (US General Accounting Office, 1997b). In response to agency complaints that restrictive personnel and procurement practices had contributed to modernisation woes, Congress authorised the FAA to establish its own personnel system 'to provide greater flexibility in the hiring, training, compensation, and location of personnel' (Public Law 104–50).

The changes in personnel practices that have been introduced at the FAA are quite innovative in the context of the federal government's notoriously hide-bound system. For example, FAA managers can now pay interview expenses for job applicants, place newspaper advertisements, or start an employee above the base pay rate without the approval of the personnel office. Selection processes, which in many cases could take up to four to six months to complete, now require only a few weeks.[1]

The FAA is in the early stages of introducing a market-based compensation system which incorporates broad-banding principles to replace the 'general' pay schedule which covers most federal employees. The general schedule includes 15 separate pay grades with 10 steps in each grade. An employee starts at step one and progresses, within the grade according to longevity criteria until reaching the top. In the FAA compensation schedule, there will be fewer grades and each grade will cover a broader salary range. There are no steps and thus no pre-established progression through a pay grade. The manager can decide where, within the grade, an employee's starting salary should be set and what the progression, if any should be. The intention is that pay increases be granted on the basis of performance rather than seniority. Funds allocated for government's annual inflationary increase and for within-grade step increases will be divided among employees on the basis of two new performance-based measures. An 'organisational success' increase will be granted to all employees, provided FAA meets its performance goals, whilst the 'superior contribution' increase is an additional increase provided only to employees ranked in the top 15 per cent of their organisation based on performance and contributions (US Federal Aviation Administration, 1998).

In general, the pay practices being put into place at the FAA, particularly the emphasis on linking pay to performance and on basing compensation decisions on external market factors rather than internal equity considerations, are emulative of private sector pay practices. The FAA plan will undoubtedly gain a lot of attention within federal government as these practices are put into effect and evaluated. To the extent that they are perceived as successful, it is likely that other agencies will seek the authority to make similar changes.

Another agency which has been granted certain human resource flexibilities is the IRS, the government's tax collection unit. With over 100,000 employees, the IRS is one of the larger agencies in federal government. In circumstances similar to those of the FAA, the IRS was given personnel flexibilities by Congress subsequent to a high-profile failure of an attempt to modernise its computer systems. Largely in response to that failure, Congress passed the Internal Revenue Service Restructuring and Reform Act 1998 in which the IRS Commissioner was given the authority to hire up to 40 individuals for 'critical technical and professional positions' at a pay rate not to exceed the Vice President's salary of 160,329 Euro (US$175,400), substantially above the rate at which career officials in other agencies can be paid. The commissioner was also given authority to provide performance bonus awards to IRS senior executives up to one-third of each individual's annual compensation. The law waives the 'rule of three', a provision of Title 5 which restricts managers to choosing one of the top three ranked candidates for a position. Instead, candidates will be assigned a category based on an assessment of merit and the manager will be able to select any applicant assigned to the highest category (US House of Representatives, 1998a).

It is too early to tell how far this trend toward 'disaggregation' of the civil service system as embodied in Title 5 of the US Code will go. That two large and high-profile agencies such as the IRS and FAA have been allowed additional flexibility in terms of personnel practices is important. Whether or not the experience of these two agencies represents a 'trend' remains uncertain. However a recent proposal that all 800,000 civilian employees in the Department of Defense (DoD), the government's largest employer, be placed in a separate personnel system suggests that pressure on Congress and the President to allow the customisation of human resource practices by agency will continue.

Performance-based organisations

While the actions taken to provide both the FAA and IRS with additional discretion in personnel matters were not part of any grand strategy, the Clinton administration has been supportive of the trend toward disaggregation. This is apparent with regard to Vice President Gore's proposal to create 'performance-based organisations' (PBO) modelled loosely on the 'Next Steps' programme in the UK. Gore's proposal was that six, carefully selected, moderate- to small-sized agencies be designed PBOs. A chief executive officer would be hired for each on a short-term contract with pay and tenure contingent on success in meeting annual performance targets. The intention was to provide the head of each PBO with flexibility not available to most agency heads in matters of personnel, procurement and budgeting. Congress has not approved PBO status for any of the six agencies initially recommended by Vice President Gore in 1996, however, in 1998, Congress did grant PBO status to the Student Finance Agency in the Department of Education. Accompanying that designation are personnel flexibilities including the authority to grant the Chief Operating Officer (COO) a bonus of up to 50 per cent of salary contingent on performance and to allow the COO in turn to pay other senior managers a bonus of up to 25 per cent of salary, also contingent on performance. Under the law, the COO is given the authority to hire 25 'technical and professional employees' outside the provisions of Title 5; appointments which will not have to comply with the normal requirements regarding competitive appointment and pay (US House of Representatives, 1998b).

Demonstration projects

The emergent 'reform by disaggregation' strategy being employed by the Clinton administration as a means of introducing human resource flexibilities into the federal government has been facilitated by use of demonstration project authority granted the OPM under the Civil Service Reform Act of 1978 (CSRA). Utilising this authority, OPM is permitted to waive certain provisions of federal personnel law for the purpose of testing the feasibility of innovative personnel practices. There are various restrictions on the use of this authority. Departments have to apply to OPM to sponsor demonstration projects and OPM is not authorised to waive laws and regulations covering political activities, equal employment opportunity, leave and other employment benefit programs. The law also provides that no more than 10 demonstration projects could be undertaken at any one time and that each project could involve a maximum of only 5,000 employees and could last for only five years. Congress has, however, waived its own restrictions on size and duration in several cases and has undercut OPM's gate-keeping role in authorising some demonstration projects in law.

The first, best-known, and perhaps most successful demonstration project took place at the Naval Weapons Center in China Lake, California. Initiated in 1981, the project has been extended several times by Congress. The major innovation introduced at that facility was use of broad-banding to simplify the classification process and provide managers with more control over the pay of their subordinates and hence the ability to reward outstanding performance. An evaluation of the demonstration project conducted under the auspices of OPM found a high degree of satisfaction with the new system among both employees and managers and showed that this approach to compensation had effectively rewarded outstanding performers and facilitated both retention of high-performers and departure of low-performers. The evaluation also found, however, that salary costs have risen as a consequence of the changes.

The general success of the China Lake experiment caused Congress to authorise similar changes at 12 Department of Defense Science and Technology Laboratories, employing approximately 40,000 people in 1995. In 1996 Congress authorised yet another demonstration project with similar interventions for 50,000 employees in DoD's acquisition work force (Friel, 1997).

Although none of the other OPM demonstration projects has had as much notoriety as China Lake, each represents a continuing process of probing and testing of alternatives to existing rules and procedures. The National Institute of Standards and Technology in the Department of Commerce sponsored a project that tested interventions intended to facilitate the hiring and retention of scientists. Included was a broad-banding provision, a performance appraisal system that ties rewards more closely to performance, delegated examination authority and an expanded direct hire authority. The most notable features of the 'Pacer/Share' project in the Defense Logistics Agency were close co-operation between labour and management and a gain-sharing feature whereby employees shared in the savings from productivity improvements.

'De facto' reform

The administration has sought to ensure that deregulation occurs in fact as well as in theory by making OPM itself a target for cuts. Between 1993 and 1998, OPM experienced the largest proportionate reduction in personnel of any federal agency, going from approximately 6,900 employees to 3,600 employees, a reduction of 48 per cent (US Office of Personnel Management, 1998). The effect was to substantially weaken OPM's capacity to perform its traditional oversight and regulatory functions. As a result of cuts in appropriations, OPM is placing increased reliance on fee-for-service contracts for recruitment and examination services with operating agencies as a source of revenue. The cuts at OPM have been paralleled by cuts to human resources units within other federal agencies. As part of NPR's down-sizing initiative, total civilian employment within the executive branch was to be cut by 13 per cent between 1994 and 1999. 'Control' positions, such as 'personnelists', were to be a prime target for the cuts. The NPR recommended a 50 per cent cut in the number of these jobs. Although data collected by the General Accounting Office (US General Accounting Office, 1996) suggest that many agencies have not achieved cuts of this magnitude, most personnel staffs have, nevertheless, suffered serious reductions as a consequence of downsizing.

Quality of working life for federal employees

The NPR (1993a) addressed issues relating to the quality of work life of federal employees as well as changes to personnel processes and structures. One element of this was the emphasis placed upon empowering front-line employees and moving to team-based approaches to processing work. The Clinton administration encouraged movement in this direction with a directive that agencies reduce the ratio of supervisors to employees by half, from 1 : 7 to 1 : 15. A number of agencies decided to move at least a portion of their work force to team-based structures substantially as a consequence of that directive. Often accompanying the shift to teams has been delegation to employees of certain authorities including increased control over work flow and ability to set leave schedules. The extent to which restructuring of this type has occurred varies by agency. The Veterans Benefits Administration, with approximately 15,000 employees, has committed to organising its front-line workers into self-directed teams. At the Social Security Administration, with about 65,000 employees, teaming has taken hold in some organisational components but employee unions have opposed implementing the concept in the extensive network of field offices where a large proportion of the employee population works.

The administration has also worked to introduce 'family friendly' practices such as 'flexi-place' (flexible workplace) and 'flexi-time' (flexible work schedule) in federal workplaces. Under flexi-place arrangements, employees are authorised to perform their work responsibilities, either at home or at designated tele-centres as well as at their normal place of employment. In June 1996, President Clinton issued a memorandum directing executive departments and agencies to 'review, develop, utilise, and expand opportunities for 'tele-commuting' and setting an objective of 60,000 federal tele-commuters by 1998. The OPM has issued guidelines to agencies on the implementation of flexi-place procedures and the General Services Administration has promoted flexi-place practices through the establishment of tele-centres equipped with telephones, computers, modems and facsimile machines which can be shared by employees of multiple agencies.

HUMAN RESOURCE FLEXIBILITIES IN STATES AND LOCALITIES

Themes similar to those which emerge from the federal reform experience are apparent at state level as well. Concurrent with the Report of the National Performance Review, an 'agenda for state and local reform' was issued by the National Commission on the State and Local Public Service, also known as the Winter Commission after it's chair, former governor of Mississippi, William Winter. The report recommended a number of changes in state and local personnel practices, some of which closely parallel those of the NPR report: increasing managerial discretion over selection processes and decentralising authority over personnel decisions to line mangers. Evidence of the implementation of these ideas is apparent from a broad overview of state activities provided by the results of a series of surveys undertaken by the Council of State Governments.

In the 1996–97 *Book of the States* (Council of State Governments), 25 states cite reform activity in six or more of the 10 personnel functions listed; merit testing, classification, compensation, recruitment, selection, performance evaluation, training, employee relations, benefits and lay-offs, with many of these reforms providing enhanced flexibility in the application of civil service rules and procedures. For example, 27 states have initiatives in progress to reduce the number of job classifications. Classification systems were created as means of rationally sorting and categorising positions according to pay level. Reformers argue that excessively detailed classifications limit the discretion of managers to transfer and redeploy workers between functions and hence to make use of modern management techniques such as multi-skilling and teaming. The California civil service system includes 4,500 job classifications of which 1,600 contain five or fewer employees. Between 1986 and 1996, approximately half the states reduced the number of job classifications (Chi, 1998).

A few states have coupled a reduction in the number of separate job classifications with the application of broad-banding practices. In Washington State, a personnel system put in place for mid-level managers consolidates 750 job classifications into four broad pay bands. A minimum and maximum salary is set for each band and where each individual is placed within the band is at the discretion of the supervisor (Chi, 1998). The city of Charlotte, North Carolina also put a broad-band salary structure in place with separate bands for the following groups; support staff, technical and administrative staff, professional/supervisory staff, senior professional/management staff, middle management, and top management (Risher, 1997).

A number of states have extended the principle of enhanced managerial flexibility to selection procedures as well. The traditional 'rule of three', limiting the selection of job candidates to the three individuals receiving the highest examination scores has been replaced in a number of states with much looser criteria. For example, Minnesota uses a rule of 10 for internal hires and a rule of 20 for external hires. California has moved to the use of zone scoring whereby managers can hire any job applicant whose test score falls within the top range, typically 90 per cent and above. In Menlo Park, California, the shift to zone scoring allowed anyone passing the test for fire fighter to be appointed. This change, accompanied by an aggressive recruitment strategy, resulted in increased representation of minority groups. Public employee unions have opposed such changes in some states, such as in New York, but have remained neutral in others such as California and Minnesota (Ban and Riccucci, 1993).

Changes in performance evaluation practices in state governments are marked by a clear trend toward more widespread use of pay-for-performance practices traditionally associated with the private sector. According to the Council of State Governments, 12 states have state-wide performance-based pay systems and 17 allow agencies to design their own performance management and reward systems (Jackson, 1994). In 1996, the State of Michigan put a pay-for-performance plan in place for all division and deputy division directors. Under this programme, managers who meet expectations are eligible for merit increases or lump-sum bonuses of up to eight per cent; managers with poor evaluations can have their pay cut by up to the same amount. Georgia's pay for performance programme gives agencies the ability to set differential pay increases (0, 4, 5.5, and 7 per cent) based on evaluation of performance (Gossett, 1997). In a 1986 survey, 76 per cent of local officials, responding to a International

City Management Association survey, stated that performance appraisals in their jurisdiction were linked with wage increases (Ban and Riccucci, 1993).

While virtually every state is engaged in some degree of reform, only a few states have pursued radical reform of personnel policies and practices with the State of Georgia the most notable recent example. Under that state's Merit System Reform Act, all individuals hired after 1 July 1996 are assigned 'unclassified' status thereby depriving them of the normal protection accorded members of the civil service such as security of tenure, although employees who held 'classified' status on 1 July retain that status. Tests to evaluate job candidates are retained but there is no longer any 'appointable range' and agencies are free to hire anyone who takes the test. Accompanying the change was a decentralisation of authority over personnel functions from the central personnel office to individual agencies. Although the central personnel office continues to develop position descriptions for jobs common to more than one department, departments can identify any position as unique and assume classification responsibility for it.

In conjunction with the structural adjustments, many states have introduced innovative working arrangements for staff. Forty-four states allow use of flexi-time, allowing greater management flexibility in scheduling of employee work. Seven-day-a-week operational coverage can be accommodated with flexi-time scheduling for agencies that need to have employees working at week-ends. In addition, employees can benefit from flexi-time schedules with slightly longer work days yielding more full days off work per week or earlier/later start and finish times in their work day (National Association of State Budget Directors, 1995).

Thirty-three states now allow sharing of earned leave time with other employees who are in need. Under this system, earned vacation, sick, and/or personal leave time can be shared with fellow employees, particularly when faced with an unanticipated catastrophic illness or other personal emergency circumstance. This innovation fosters a sense of community among co-workers within the context of a movement toward fostering a 'team working' environment. The sharing of earned leave time typically incurs no additional expense to the agency (National Association of State Budget Directors, 1995).

Widespread use and availability of computers and other electronic communication technology has fostered the use of tele-commuting from home in over half the states. Employees benefit in terms of saved commuting time and expense make telecommuting an attractive work arrangement. It also benefits agencies serving widespread geographic areas where commuting to and from the central agency office may not be practical. Under tele-commuting arrangements employees are required to spend a portion of their time in the central office for major staff meetings as well as supervisory work reviews.

Nearly half the states offer credits or incentives for not using accumulated sick leave. Some agencies allow employees to trade in sick leave time for additional vacation leave, apply accumulated sick leave towards accelerated retirement, or earn additional personal leave time for not using earned sick leave in any given year. In most states, where these incentives and/or credits are offered, there is a noticeable decline in average sick leave use and a corresponding increase in on the job productivity (National Association of State Budget Directors, 1995).

Over two-thirds of states allow job sharing between individuals. Under this arrangement, two or more individuals divide the responsibilities of one full-time position into different working hours. This allows government to attract talented people into the work force who might otherwise be precluded from working on a full-time basis. It also affords flexibility in scheduling to accommodate individual needs. Job benefit packages vary under such an arrangement (National Association of State Budget Directors, 1995).

CONCLUSION

There is a great deal of reform activity in the American public service. Activity at federal level has been particularly intense, largely because of the NPR and the interest and attention being given to management reform by Vice President Gore. A substantial amount of reform activity is under way at state level as well. In general, that reform is incremental in nature although at least one state, Georgia, has implemented radical change. Deregulatory and decentralising trends are fairly pronounced and, should they continue, could lend a substantially different countenance to the public service over the next few years. However, it is difficult in many cases to evaluate the extent to which reforms are having their intended effect. One state that relied heavily on reinvention principles, Florida, substantially failed to achieve its reform objectives (Wechsler, 1994) and there is insufficient information available on which to evaluate most others. Should the change process falter, should incidents of abuse of the newly developed flexibilities emerge on a broad scale, then current trends could be slowed or even reversed.

Note

1. Personal Interview with Christopher Early, Supervisory Personnel Management Specialist, Federal Aviation Administration, 18 July 1998.

References

BAN, C. and RICCUCCI, N. (1993). 'Personnel Systems and Labor Relations: Steps Toward a Quiet Revitalization', in Thompson, F. (ed.), *Revitalizing State and Local Service: Strengthening Performance, Accountability, and Citizen Confidence.* San Francisco: Jossey-Bass.

BARR, S. (1995). 'Civil Service Reform Plan in Jeopardy'. *Washington Post.* June 19.

CHI, KEON, S. (1998). 'State Civil Service Systems', in Condrey, S. (ed.), *Handbook of Human Resource Management in Government.* San Francisco: Jossey-Bass.

COUNCIL OF STATE GOVERNMENTS (1997). *Book of the States 1996–97.* LexingTon, KY: council of State Governments.

FRIEL, B. (1997). 'Rethinking Pay, Appraisal'. *Government Executive*, cited in The Daily Fed, June 13, 1998.

GOSSETT, C.W. (1997). 'Civil Service Reform: The Case of Georgia'. Unpublished manuscript.

JACKSON, O. (1994). 'The [Oklahoma] Personnel Reform Act of 1994', paper presented at the annual meeting of the National Association of State Personnel Executives.

NATIONAL ASSOCIATION OF STATE BUDGET DIRECTORS (1995). *Workforce Policies: State Activity and Innovations.* Washington, DC: National Association of State Budget Directors.

OSBORNE, D. and GAEBLER, T. (1992). *Reinventing Government: How the Entrepreneurial Spirit is Transforming the Public Sector.* Reading, MA: Addison-Wesley.

RISHER, H. (1997). 'Emerging Model for Salary Management'. *Public Management.* April.

US BUREAU OF THE CENSUS (1992). *Statistical Abstract of the United States.* Washington, DC: Government Printing Office.

US FEDERAL AVIATION ADMINISTRATION (1998). *FAA's New Personnel Management System: Compensation, A Key Component of FAA's New Personnel Management System.* Washington, DC: Federal Aviation Administration.

US GENERAL ACCOUNTING OFFICE (1996). *Federal Downsizing: Better Workforce and Strategic Planning Could Have Made Buyouts More Effective.* (GGD-96-62.) Washington, DC: Government Printing Office.

US GENERAL ACCOUNTING OFFICE (1997a). *The Excepted Service: A Research Profile.* (GGD-97-72.) Washington, DC: Government Printing Office.

US GENERAL ACCOUNTING OFFICE (1997b). *Air Traffic Control: Improved Cost Information Needed to Make Billion Dollar Modernization Investment Decisions.* (AIMD-97-20.) Washington, DC: Government Printing Office.

US HOUSE OF REPRESENTATIVES (1998a). *Internal Revenue Service Restructuring and Reform Act of 1998.* Conference Report to Accompany H.R. 2676. (Report 105-599). Washington, DC: Government Printing Office.

US HOUSE OF REPRESENTATIVES (1998b). *Higher Education Act Amendments of 1998. Conference Report to Accompany H.R. 6* (Report 105-750.) Washington, DC: Government Printing Office.

US NATIONAL PERFORMANCE REVIEW (1993a). *Creating a Government that Works Better and Costs Less: The Report of the National Performance Review.* New York: Plume.

US NATIONAL PERFORMANCE REVIEW (1993b). *Reinventing Human Resource Management.* New York: Plume.

US OFFICE OF PERSONNEL MANAGEMENT (1998). 'Fact Sheet: Total Federal Civilian Employment'. Available on the internet at *http://www.opm.gov*.

WECHSLER, B. (1994). 'Reinventing Florida's Civil Service System'. *Review of Public Personnel Administration*. Spring.

Part III

International Themes and Comparisons

14 Pay Flexibility in European Public Services: A Comparative Analysis

Geoff White

Increasing pay flexibility has been identified as one of the key features of the modernisation of the public sector in the post-industrial societies of western Europe and North America. The term 'pay flexibility' is defined differently in different countries but the OECD (1993i) has identified four main ways in which pay systems can be made more flexible: (i) decentralisation of the determination of pay; (ii) variations in pay systems between different organisations and/or groups of employees; (iii) variations in rates of pay adjustment between different locations, different categories of staff, or different sub-sectors (e.g. health and education); and (iv) individual or group-based variations in pay for a given job or position on the basis of factors such as skills, responsibilities or performance. The OECD does not include within this list changes in method of pay determination (e.g. either moves towards or away from collective bargaining) but such changes are important elements in the way in which pay flexibility is managed.

Public sector pay determination has traditionally been conducted at central levels, even if the actual mechanisms have varied according to the political structures in each country. This prevalence of centralised pay determination in the public sector is largely explained by the 'important underlying theme of budget controls, if not reductions, and the fact that labour costs in the public sector easily constitute the highest budget item' (Hegewisch and Larsen, 1994: 6). Governments remain keen to ensure that they retain control over the size of overall public expenditure on remuneration, so that in the past this has meant a preference for strongly centralised national pay determination systems and structures. Even in the USA (at Federal level) and in

255

Japan, which have little tradition of centralised or industry-wide collective pay bargaining in the private sector, pay determination for civil servants, if not for other public servants, has remained centralised.

Despite this strong tradition of centralised pay determination for public servants, in the last two decades a number of countries have made attempts to reform their public sector pay systems (Treu, 1987; OECD, 1993i; Ferner, 1994; Hegewisch and Larsen, 1994), although there remain considerable differences in the degree and scope of pay flexibility among the different countries. Some countries have seen decentralisation as the key to reform whereas others have approached changes in pay systems from within existing centralised systems. It might be further argued that 'centralisation and decentralisation are not mutually exclusive' (Fowler, 1988: 29) and that, even where pay bargaining has been decentralised, control of the pay bill remains highly controlled by central government.

Moves towards pay flexibility have presented major challenges to the parties involved in pay determination. This chapter takes a thematic approach in analysing international trends and begins with a review of the issues driving changes in remuneration systems. It then considers general trends in public sector pay, including the relationship to private sector pay movements. The evidence for pay flexibility in the European context is then investigated by comparing and contrasting current systems of pay determination and pay structures and recent changes. This evidence is grouped under the following headings:

- **Changes to the methods and locus of pay determination.** Is pay determined through collective bargaining, by independent review, by Government regulation or through market forces? To what extent are there pay comparability mechanisms to keep public sector pay in line with the private sector? At what level is pay determined (e.g. national, sectoral or departmental/agency level)? What role do trade unions play?
- **Changes to grading and job classification.** What criteria are pay and grading levels and promotion related to (e.g. seniority, qualifications, skills, responsibility or performance)? How flexible are these pay structures?
- **Changes to pay progression systems.** On what criteria is pay progression based (e.g. service, performance or skills acquisition)? What is the balance between fixed and variable pay? To what degree has the pay of public servants been individualised?

Finally, the chapter draws out the key points from the comparisons and provides conclusions on the current international trends.

THE SEARCH FOR PAY FLEXIBILITY

The current search for pay flexibility in industrialised countries followed a period in which there had been increasing regulation of remuneration, either through growth in institutionalised pay setting via collective bargaining or through increasing state regulation of remuneration. This post-war period of growing pay regulation began to wane in the late 1970s. Guy Standing (1997) of the International Labour Organisation points out that the current vogue for 'wage flexibility' is an integral part of the prevailing emphasis on supply side economics, as opposed to the demand side economics which predominated in the immediate post-war period. The supply side economists' argument is that wage rigidity is an obstacle to 'market clearing' and, more specifically, is responsible for high and persistent unemployment in the industrialised nations. This new emphasis on pay flexibility has been fuelled by the process of economic globalisation which has placed increasing pressure on private sector wage levels in the industrialised nations, which must now compete with developing economies with much lower labour costs (including substantially lower or non-existent levels of social benefits). Wage flexibility has, says Standing (1997: 18), 'amounted in practice to a reduction of the fixed wage as a share of total remuneration, a cutback on direct benefits and conversion of more of the remuneration into monetised form, coupled with an erosion of minimum wage protection and constraints on union bargaining powers'. In industrialised countries this has led to an increase in income insecurity and a growth in wage differentials and pay dispersion. At the same time, argues Standing, wage flexibility has been easier to achieve in the advanced industrialised nations than elsewhere, because of the underpinning social wage components provided by the welfare state which give some security of income not dependent on the employer.

The public sector has not been immune to these general pressures on traditional remuneration systems. According to the OECD, pressure for reform of public sector pay systems has resulted from three main sources (OECD, 1993) – (i) labour market problems in recruiting and retaining public employees (i.e. in competition with the private sector); (ii) the requirement to improve managerial effectiveness to ensure that better quality, cost effective services are delivered to users; and (iii) the need to hold down public sector pay costs as part of macro-economic policy. Flynn and Strehl (1996) argue that pursuit of pay flexibility in the public sector has been driven by two beliefs: that performance-based pay systems lead to greater employee motivation and output and that flexible pay systems are likely to be less costly than fixed systems based on traditional seniority and equity principles. Recent OECD research has indicated that countries which have reformed their public sector pay systems – i.e. decentralised their systems – have been better able to control public sector pay growth than those which have less flexible systems (for example in Australia, Finland, the Netherlands and the UK (OECD, 1997)). As we discuss later, however, there are counter arguments which indicate that centralised pay systems, or at least co-ordinated pay systems, can be more effective in controlling inflation at the macro-economic level (Marsden in OECD, 1994i). There may, moreover, be strong contrary effects from pay flexibility on employee motivation and commitment (Marsden, 1997; Marsden and French, 1998).

Two 'idealised' approaches to public sector employment systems have been identified (OECD, 1994ii; Flynn and Strehl, 1996):

- Career-based or 'closed structure' systems in which public servants have life-time employment and security of pay progression, often underpinned by law, based on seniority and acquisition of skills, responsibility and experience.
- Flexible contract or 'open structure' systems, under which employees are recruited on short-term contracts, are paid largely according to their performance and output and who may switch back and forth between public and private sector employment during their working lives.

In reality neither of these idealised types exists in practice in Europe. Instead, there are degrees and variations in the extent to which the models have been adopted. In some countries, mainly in the UK and the Scandinavian countries, the career-based public service model has been weakened because such systems have been seen by governments and public sector managers as inimical to the promotion of a performance-oriented work culture. In contrast, in other European countries, such as France, Germany and Spain, there is still a strong attachment to employment systems which provide security and predictability for public servants in which increased employee commitment and productivity are being sought through other means, for example through functional flexibility in Germany (White and Löffler, 1997). The OECD (1994ii), however, argues that:

> In fact, the traditional dichotomy between these two types . . . no longer seems to be at the heart of the debate. The issue is rather the convergence of the private and public sector labour markets due to the increasing use of private sector human resource management techniques within the public sector, including wage bargaining procedures which were traditionally only found in the private sector.

Previous studies of developments in European public sector personnel practices have identified a number of changes in reward systems. Ferner (1994) indicates that European governments have sought to constrain public sector pay by imposing pay limits and ending established forms of pay comparability (such as indexation and special treatment of public servants' pay), leading in some cases to outbreaks of industrial militancy among public servants (e.g. public sector strikes in Germany in 1992 and in France in 1995). There have also been proposals to reduce public servants' pension rights (for example in France, Italy and Germany). A second development has been the 'use of pay as a tool of managerial flexibility, in line with the emerging emphasis on market-driven service provision' (Ferner, 1994: 59). This development is partly an employer reaction to perceived rigidities of existing pay systems, with their emphasis on inflexible job categorisation and seniority-based pay progression. Attempts have also been made in some countries to make pay more reflective of local labour market conditions and individual employee performance.

Nevertheless, as Ferner (1994) suggests, there have been conflicting processes in the reform of public sector pay determination systems. While in some countries there has been a substantial shift away from centralised pay determination systems and traditional payment structures (notably in Sweden, Finland, the UK, and the Netherlands), and in some cases a weakening role for trade unions in pay fixing (e.g. the UK), in other countries there has been a movement towards more institutionalised pay arrangements and a growth in trade union involvement, notably in those countries which have moved from dictatorships to democratic government since the 1970s (e.g. Greece and Spain). For example, in Greece an employee right and employer obligation to bargain was introduced only in 1990 and in Spain, too, pay increases have been subject to negotiation only since 1990. In other countries, for example Germany, there has been pressure to move away from unilateralist systems of pay determination towards greater use of collective bargaining (White and Löffler, 1997), although so far with limited success. In the Netherlands fully fledged collective bargaining in the public sector was introduced only in 1989.

Two main approaches to the reform of public sector pay systems have been identified (OECD, 1994i):

- maintenance of relatively centralised systems and the development of flexibility in ways other than pay flexibility – for example in France, Spain and Germany; or
- organisational restructuring of the public services and the decentralisation of pay determination to lower levels, allowing more management decision making at sectoral or local level – for example in the UK, Sweden and Finland.

The first of these approaches places emphasis on central budgetary controls while the latter emphasises decentralisation of budgets away from central government and towards local managers, allowing more local decisions on pay (albeit often within central budgetary frameworks). In general, unilateralist systems of pay determination – those where pay is determined by management alone – tend to lead to more predictable outcomes than those where collective bargaining or some independent assessment of pay is involved. As the OECD states: 'If collective bargaining is to be in good faith, then there is necessarily some unpredictability in the final budgetary consequences' (OECD, 1994i: 17). The OECD observes that unilateralist systems, therefore, have the advantage of greater control over pay costs. In contrast, while budgetary outcomes may be less certain under collective bargaining, 'the potential gain to the employer side is that employee involvement will bring greater consent to the final outcome, and thus a more co-operative working environment' (OECD, 1994i: 17).

Despite some generalised trends towards public sector pay reform, the OECD (1994i) reports that there is little sign of any convergence towards a particular model. In the industrialised countries of the world there remains a great diversity in public sector pay systems, due to institutional/constitutional forces which reflect strong historical traditions in both industrial relations and public administration practice.

The major influences upon public sector pay systems have been identified as the prevailing industrial relations traditions of each country and the legal status of public servants (Marsden, 1997). For example, countries with strong traditions of centralised pay bargaining in the private sector have tended to have similar patterns in the public sector, for example (at least until recently) Sweden and the Netherlands. Similarly, where pay bargaining at the level of the enterprise was relatively undeveloped in the private sector, it also tended to be similarly underdeveloped in the public sector, for example in France and Spain.

There are, however, exceptions to this generalisation. For example, in Germany the prevailing system of pay bargaining in the private sector is at the level of the individual German state (the *Land*) but in the public sector pay bargaining has been centralised at Federal level since a period of strong labour market competition between the different *Länder* in the 1960s. This led to considerable geographical variations in pay levels between employees of different *Länder* and resulted in an amendment to the Federal Pay Act to ensure that pay scales applied nationally. Similarly, in the USA pay determination for the Federal civil service takes place at Federal level for the whole country, despite the fact that centralised or industry-wide pay bargaining is almost non-existent in the rest of the US economy.

There is also a difference between those countries where public servants are governed by separate employment legislation than private employees. This legislation may include special status in return for legal restrictions and responsibilities, such as absence of a right to strike (e.g. *Beamte* civil servants in Germany). In some cases, there have been moves to end such special status. For example, in Italy the decree law passed in 1992 ended separate legal status of some 3.6 million public servants and brought them under private sector employment law (although the armed forces, the police, executive grade State civil servants, diplomatic staff, university teachers and magistrates retain their public labour contract status). Clearly where pay determination systems are enshrined in public sector law, such as France, Germany and Spain, it is much more difficult for employers to make changes, especially where those legislating may themselves be public servants and hence have a self-interest in the *status quo*. On the other hand, withdrawal of special status may require new protective measures for employees, such as the rights to collective bargaining and to strike.

Table 14.1 Pay costs and pay bill as a share of general government final consumption expenditure

	Compensation costs		Pay Bill	
	as a share of final consumption			
	1990	*1995*	*1990*	*1995*
Australia	53.8	47.9	53.8	47.9
Austria	60.6	59.1	44.5	44.8
Canada	54.5	55.5	54.5	55.5
Denmark	73.7	70.3	73.2	69.9
Finland	77.1	71.4	54.1	51.3
France	61.9	58.0	49.1	46.0
Germany	53.2	52.1	42.2	41.3
Ireland	80.7	78.7	–	–
Italy	71.7	56.7	52.0	46.9
Netherlands	59.2	58.3	52.0	49.9
New Zealand	65.8	65.3	59.9	60.5
Portugal	74.1	78.7	68.9	59.3
Spain	71.7	70.2	57.6	–
Sweden	76.7	62.3	54.3	45.6
Switzerland	73.1	77.7	59.8	64.6
UK	59.6	53.2	–	–
USA	46.2	50.1	46.2	50.1

Source: *Public Sector Pay and Employment Data Update*. PUMA. OECD. June 1998.

TRENDS IN PUBLIC SECTOR PAY

Growth in public sector pay costs has slowed across most of the OECD countries and these costs account for a diminishing share of government consumption expenditure and of GDP (OECD, 1997). Table 14.1 shows the changes in pay costs and pay bill as a share of general government final consumption expenditure for a range of OECD countries. This fall in the relative share of public sector pay may result from structural changes in employment, with the transfer of public activities to the private sector (e.g. Finland, France and Sweden). It may also reflect reforms in public service management and efficiency (Australia, New Zealand and the UK), which may also be associated with structural changes. The policies of wage restraint which have applied in the 1990s has also had an effect – public sector average pay movements have only just exceeded inflation in most countries. It should be noted here that in some European countries there have continued to be national pay moderation policies at various times, which have limited pay growth for both private and public sectors (e.g. Belgium, Ireland, the Netherlands and Spain). For example, in Belgium both public and private sector pay is automatically linked to inflation. In Italy an agreement between the social partners in both the private and public sectors covering 1994–97 placed limits on labour costs growth although indexation was abandoned in 1993.

In terms of pay dispersion, changes have been most marked in those countries which have altered their pay determination systems. Pay dispersion widened in Australia, Finland and Sweden in the early 1990s, although in the UK pay dispersion in the public sector narrowed between 1992 and 1995 (OECD, 1997). This counter trend in the UK is partly explained by the fact that this period was before the full decentralisation of pay determination in the UK civil service in 1996, which should lead to greater pay dispersion in future, and also reflects the continuing effects of centralised pay systems in the NHS, education and local government. In France pay dispersion slightly decreased between 1990 and 1995.

In terms of pay comparisons between the public and private sectors, research by the European Institute for Public Administration (EIPA, 1997) on public/private sector pay growth over the period 1990 to 1995 indicates that there have been different outcomes in different European countries. Four distinct groups of countries are distinguished:

- countries where public sector pay has grown considerably faster than the private sector – for example, France, Luxembourg and Sweden
- countries where public sector pay has grown more or less at the same rate as the private sector – for example, Ireland, Finland, Germany and the UK
- countries where public sector pay has grown slower than the private sector – for example Belgium, Denmark, Italy, the Netherlands, Austria and Portugal
- countries where public sector pay has lagged considerably behind the private sector – for example Greece and Spain.

In terms of real wage levels (taking into account the effect of inflation upon wage levels), the EIPA research indicates that there is no clear relationship between the relative pay increases between the public and private sectors and growth of real wage levels in the public sector. Thus real wages declined between 1990 and 1995 in Belgium, Spain, Italy, Luxembourg, the Netherlands, Finland, Sweden and the UK. On the other hand, Austria and Denmark show positive gains in real wages and even higher increases have been achieved in Portugal and France.

Pay comparability between public servants and the private sector has been an important strand in remuneration systems in the public sector in many countries. These comparability mechanisms have included indexation to earnings and/or price movements; consideration of comparative pay information by independent pay review committees or special inquiries; or a shadowing of private sector pay settlements. In recent years, however, there has been some weakening of such systems. For example, in Finland the 'guaranteed earnings development clause', which linked civil servants' pay increases directly to pay movements in the private sector, was abolished with the introduction of performance-related pay. In the UK the civil service pay comparability system was similarly dismantled with the introduction of delegated pay bargaining.

The countries which have continued to stress comparability systems most include Denmark, Ireland and Sweden. For example, in Denmark, there is a compensation mechanism in the event that pay increases in the private sector exceed those in public administration. In Sweden, local budget allocations can be increased on the basis of an index measuring private sector wage increases. Countries where pay comparability is just one of a number of factors taken into account include Belgium (where budgetary limits and collective bargaining play a role alongside indexation); Germany (where *Beamte* pay increases tend to shadow the collectively agreed increases for non-*Beamte* public servants); and Italy (where there is now a distinction between those public servants on public employment contracts and others who are not). In France, pay comparisons are taken into account in the discussions between the social partners and in the UK pay comparability still plays some part in the determination of remuneration of those public servants covered by the independent pay review body process. In Greece, Spain and Austria pay increases are primarily determined by fiscal objectives.

CHANGES IN THE METHOD AND LOCUS AND PAY DETERMINATION

As mentioned above, public sector pay determination systems in Europe and the USA have followed a diverse pattern. According to a study by the OECD, pay systems can be viewed along two axes (see Figure 14.1) – one in which there is some form of joint regulation or independent involvement in pay fixing and one in which pay is simply a matter for government or the employer to determine (OECD, 1994i). On the first axis, the form of pay determination ranges from fully-fledged collective bargaining at one end (e.g. the Netherlands, most UK civil servants) to some form of independent pay review at the other (e.g. Japan, Canada, pay review bodies in the UK), whilst on the other axis it ranges from complete management discretion (e.g. Greece and *Beamte* civil servants in Germany) to systems of 'fixed rule employer regulation', where rules have been established for the automatic linkage of pay increases to one or more criteria – for example, indexation in some form or another (e.g. US Federal Civil Service). Of course, many countries fall between these two axes and are hybrids.

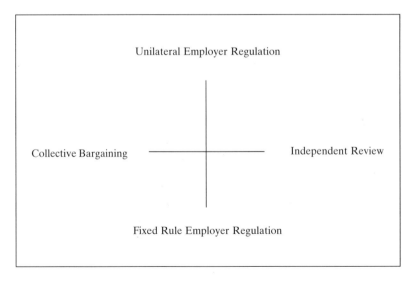

Unilateral Employer Regulation

Collective Bargaining — Independent Review

Fixed Rule Employer Regulation

Figure 14.1   Forms of public service pay determination
Source: OECD (1994i).

The complexity of pay determination systems between and within countries makes generalisations difficult. In some countries civil servants' – or at least senior civil servants' – pay will be determined unilaterally while other public servants may have collective bargaining (e.g Germany and the USA). Few countries allow completely unfettered collective bargaining – in most countries negotiating parameters will be set by government (for example in France, Belgium and Canada the outcomes of the collective bargaining are subject to Government ratification). On the other hand, unilateralist systems may either follow bargaining trends in other parts of the economy or allow trade unions to submit evidence or lobby (for example in the US Federal civil service or in the case of *Beamte* in Germany). Collective bargaining is the major method of pay determination in the Scandinavian countries, the UK (for non-Review Body groups), Germany (for non-*Beamte*), Australia, Canada, Ireland, Italy and the Netherlands. It is less important in Spain and France, where public sector salaries are set by law, although some bargaining does take place.

It has been argued that centralised pay determination can have advantages, although these differ between collective bargaining and unilaterist pay determination systems. As mentioned above, unilateralist systems may be quite inflexible whereas those involving joint decisions may be more open to change. Centralised collective bargaining can lead to resolution of problems arising from competitive pay bargaining between different employee groups (as was the aim in Germany when public sector pay determination was centralised in the 1970s) and there is also evidence that those countries with nationally co-ordinated pay bargaining are more likely to be able to control inflationary pressures (Marsden in OECD, 1994i). Other advantages for centralised pay determination are that it provides transparency, and hence the confidence of employees, and also facilitates job mobility between different parts of the public sector or within particular public services.

On the other hand, centralised pay systems have been criticised for failing to address significant differences in labour markets between locations and inhibiting development of pay innovation. Most importantly, pay is the largest single item of expenditure for most public services but, if budgetary control is decentralised without devolution of pay determination, local managers will have their options severely limited. Research by the OECD suggests that countries with decentralised pay determination systems (such as Sweden, Finland, the

Collective level

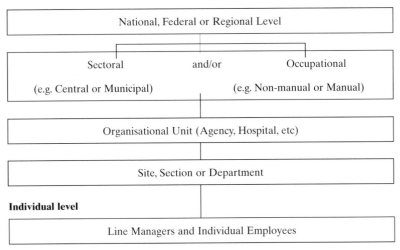

Figure 14.2   Level of devolution of payment systems in the public sector

Netherlands, Australia and Canada) have experienced lower pay bill growth than those with more centralised systems (OECD, 1997).

Collective bargaining can exist at several levels – national, service or industry-wide, regional, departmental or sectoral, and site or workplace level. Figure 14.2, shows the dimensions of bargaining from centralised at national level to local and individual level. It is important to state here, though, that bargaining may take place at more than one level – for example, in Sweden there is a framework agreement at national level and then further negotiations take place at the level of the individual agency. Table 14.2 provides details of the arrangements in 12 countries.

Within Europe, the countries with the most decentralised public sector pay determination systems include the UK, Sweden and Finland, where pay management has been decentralised to the level of individual government agencies within the civil service (OECD, 1997). The least decentralised countries are Germany, France and Spain (although there are differences between these three countries). In between come countries such as Italy and the Netherlands where there has been partial decentralisation from national level. In the USA attempts to decentralise Federal pay arrangements have been

Table 14.2   Pay flexibilities in the public services

Country	Changes to pay determination system?	Changes to grading?	Individual performance-based pay?
Belgium	Yes. Centralisation of pay determination from local level. New fixed-salary scales for all public servants.	Yes. 'Financial careers' (a form of broad banding) allow progression without grade change.	Yes. Performance premiums for managers. Also progression through the 'financial career' partly based on performance
Denmark	Yes. New pay system from 1998 but flexibility within a national structure.	No. National grading system for all public servants but in the process of change.	Yes. Not yet widely used but new pay system from 1998 allows more individualised pay.
Finland	New pay system in 1992 based on agency level agreements. But national negotiations set pay policy guidelines.	Yes. Old single national pay scale abandoned. Each agency can now establish own job classification system.	New system sets 3 main criteria for individual remuneration: nature of post; individual performance; and group performance.
France	No. Some experiments in delegation of pay budgets. But collective bargaining at national level for all public servants. Government agreement required.	No. National grading systems for each 'corps'.	No. Basic pay constitutes 80% pf total pay. Local allowances add further 20%. A few experiments with group and individual incentives.
Germany	No. Pay still determined at Federal level for Beamte (civil servants) and Angestellte (public servants) but some recent freedom to allow limited local variations.	No. National grading systems.	Yes. Limited freedom from 1997 to introduce performance incentives at local level.

Table 14.2 Continued

Country	Changes to pay determination system?	Changes to grading?	Individual performance-based pay?
Ireland	No. National negotiations for seven sectoral agreements since 1987.	No. National grading systems for each sector. Service based progression.	No. Basic salary usually 100% of total pay. Some local allowances. Civil service heads eligible for performance pay.
Italy	Yes. Protocol of 1993 created new system of bargaining with eight sectoral agreements. A central negotiating body for employers created – ARAN. Increasing decentralisation of bargaining in local government and health.	Yes. New grading systems in local government, health, public agencies and civil service. New four grade 'broad banded' system used in all sectors.	Yes. Progression through the grade now wholly dependent on performance.
Netherlands	Yes. In 1993 national system decentralised to eight sub-sectors. Some issues still negotiated at central level.	Yes. Each sub-sector now has own salary scales and job classification system.	No. Basic salary makes up 93–100% of total. Progression based on seniority but individual merit bonuses under consideration.
Spain	No. Centralised determination remains but autonomous bodies (which will have two thirds of public servants in future) free to determine own pay.	No. National grading structure for those with civil servant status. Five major but overlapping pay bands. Local agreements for other public servants.	Yes. Productivity bonuses can be paid on an individual basis at departmental level (4.3% of pay bill in 1995).
Sweden	Yes. Two-tier bargaining. Central framework agreement sets minimum levels	Yes. National level grading system abolished in 1989. Grading and pay structures now	Yes. Salary scales no longer used (except for 20,000 central level employees).

Table 14.2   Continued

Country	Changes to pay determination system?	Changes to grading?	Individual performance-based pay?
	and agency pay budgets, followed by agency level agreements covering individual pay increases, conditions and hours of work.	decided at agency level, using job classification scheme based on job families and five levels.	Individual increases decided at agency level through local negotiations.
UK	Yes. Decentralised bargaining in civil service. Health, local government and education generally retain national systems.	Yes. New grading systems, often based on broad bands, at departmental and agency level in civil service. Health and education retain national grading systems in the main. Local government has new single status agreement, allowing more local flexibility, from 1997.	Yes. Individual performance pay for all civil servants and for senior managers in health, education and some local government.
USA	No. Centralised for Federal civil servants. No collective bargaining for civil servants (except postal service). State and municipal governments each have own arrangements.	For Federal civil service 50 different grading systems but four major groups. In 1995 presidential draft law to reform civil service pay system but defeated in Congress. Some agencies have established new broad banded systems.	Yes. Progression based on seniority and performance for most civil servants. National performance pay system for top managers abolished. Some agencies allowed to develop own performance pay systems.

Note: This chart summarises often complex differences in terminology between different countries and also often complicated differences in the composition and structure of the public sector. In general, this chart deals only with public services. The chart should therefore be understood as an indication of trends in different countries.

limited but some agencies now have their own terms and conditions (see Chapter 13).

In the UK, Sweden and Finland, there has been organisational restructuring of the public services into autonomous agencies, trusts and departments but there are marked differences. In Sweden, civil service pay is determined at two levels – centralised negotiations take place between the Swedish Agency for Government Employers (AgV), which represents more than 200 central government agencies, and the trade unions representing public employees and then further negotiations take place at agency level (OECD, 1997). Framework agreements are centrally negotiated and deal with working conditions and salaries. Negotiations at agency level deal with individual salaries but increasingly involve working conditions and hours of work. In Finland, a pay system, launched in 1992, establishes pay determination at the level of the agency or department. The UK systems vary across the three major sectors (civil service, local government and health). In the civil service, from 1996 all national level negotiations between government and trade unions have ended and all agreements are now reached at departmental and agency level. In the National Health Service (NHS) local bargaining arrangements were planned for 1995 but national pay structures continue for most NHS grades because of the prevailing influence of independent pay review bodies. The number of local level NHS agreements is increasing but slowly (IDS, 1998) and national systems still predominate. In local government the pattern is similar to Sweden – a national framework agreement for the majority of staff with local negotiations on the detail. Decentralised bargaining in Sweden, Finland and the UK has developed hand in hand with individual performance related pay systems.

At the other extreme, Germany operates at national level for most public servants, although there are three separate types of public sector worker, each with their own arrangements (i.e. *Beamten, Angestellten* and *Arbeiter*). These three groups exists in federal, state and municipal government and in the social security department (see White and Löffler, 1998). While the pay and conditions of *Beamten* (established civil servants) are subject to unilateral government control, collective bargaining (with legally binding outcomes) at national level exists for the other public servants.

France and Spain are also very centralised. In France (see Chapter 6), collective bargaining at national level covers five million state employees in central and local government and in general hospitals.

The outcome of this bargaining, however, is simply a recommendation to government which the government is not obliged to accept. In the absence of a collective agreement (which is then enacted as a decree), the government is free to set pay unilaterally. In Spain (see Chapter 9) national collective bargaining, which is a relatively recent phenomenon, covers civil servants' pay and the outcomes of bargaining are legally binding. Autonomous communities and local authorities tend to follow suit, although they are in theory free to determine the pay of their workforces within the limits of the framework law.

In between these extremes come Italy and the Netherlands, where national systems have been subjected to decentralisation to sectoral level. In Italy (see Chapter 8), central bargaining now takes place between the Public Administration Negotiating Agency (ARAN) and employee organisations within eight separate sectors – ministries (except education and health); autonomous public administrations; non-economic public bodies; search bodies; national health service; schools; universities and regional and local administrations (OECD, 1997: 63). In the Netherlands (see Chapter 11), bargaining has also been decentralised away from national level to eight sectoral levels – ministries, education, police, defence, judiciary, provinces, municipalities and Polder (water) Boards. The first five in this list – central government departments – are given a budget within which they have to decide their own pay priorities. The three non-central government bodies have their own budget setting powers and thus more freedom to decide about pay priorities. In some respects this is similar to the difference between central and local government in the UK.

Collective bargaining remains the major method of pay determination within European public services, even where pay determination has been decentralised. In the UK some key groups are excluded from bargaining and have independent pay review bodies instead (doctors and dentists, nurses and paramedics, school teachers, senior civil servants, armed forces officers and judiciary). In Germany *Beamte* civil servants are also excluded from collective bargaining and in the USA federal civil servants are barred from bargaining.

CHANGES TO GRADING SYSTEM

In the public sector the traditional system of grading or job classification for pay purposes has been based on the principles of bureaucratic and hierarchical organisational structures – fixed salary scales with pay progression dependent on seniority, qualifications, level of responsibility and experience. In many countries, this remains the norm with national pay scales laid down for all employees, irrespective of their location or sector. For example, in France (see Chapter 6) careers are structured by grade or *corps* and employees are defined by their grade, not what they do. Each *corps* is divided into grades and each grade into points (*echelons*) which correspond to salary points or increments. Promotion of echelon (a pay increment) is based on years of service while promotion to a higher grade is based on merit (the *corps* decides this, not the line manager). The allocation of grade in a *corps* gives tenure, determines salary level and other remuneration, and belongs to the official, whatever the post held. On the surface this appears very simple but in reality there are all kinds of exceptions to the rules, adjustments and supplementary provisions. Pay scales rarely allow for extra pay to cope with labour market variations. Under the law, pay includes basic salary, residence allowance, family allowances and other work-related allowances.

The German, Italian and Spanish grading systems are similarly centralised, although there has been some flexibility introduced into the national structures in Germany and Spain in terms of pay progression and/or local merit bonuses. In the USA there are four main 'national' grading structures for federal civil servants, the largest of which – the General Schedule – covers 1.4 million white-collar civil servants. Presidential attempts to reform this system have so far been thwarted by Congress (see Chapter 13).

There is evidence of more radical change in grading systems, however. In Italy, new grading systems have been introduced into the civil service, local government, health and public agencies, with a new four grade 'broad banded' system now in operation. In Belgium new 'financial careers' (see Chapter 4) – a form of broad banding – allow more pay progression within the grade, rather than through promotion. In Finland and Sweden national grading systems have been abolished and each agency is now free to establish its own structure. In the Netherlands each sector now has its own salary scales and job classification system. In the UK the delegation of civil service pay bargaining to departmental and agency level has led to separate grading systems at that level. Also in the UK a Government consultation paper published in February 1999 proposes a new simplified system of three separate grading systems for the NHS which will allow much more local flexibility (DoH, 1999). A new 'single status' agreement covering local government in Britain, agreed in 1997, has also introduced a more flexible pay structure, allowing more local flexibility (see White, 1999).

CHANGES TO PAY PROGRESSION SYSTEMS

The third way in which public sector pay systems are being made more flexible is through changes in the criteria on which individual pay progression is determined. The main change here has been the introduction of individual performance related pay progression in some countries (notably the UK, Finland and Sweden). In general, however, variable pay forms a small proportion of most European public servants' remuneration. The spread of individual performance-related pay on the scale of the UK (or indeed other English speaking countries such as Australia and the USA) remains limited – not just in the public sector but also the private sector in much of Europe. In the USA the national performance pay system for senior federal civil servants has been abolished but pay progression remains based on a mix of seniority and individual performance assessment for those civil servants on the General Schedule (see Chapter 13).

In Germany, under the reform law of 24 February 1997, locally determined performance-related payments have been introduced into the structure but these are strictly controlled (White and Löffler, 1998). To date there is little evidence of employers utilising this new freedom (see Chapter 6). In Spain, too, a productivity bonus can now be paid on an individual basis by each department, although within a budget and rules set by the Finance Ministry (OECD, 1993ii; OECD, 1997). This is the only local element allowed in the national pay structure. In Italy, abandonment of automatic pay indexation in 1993 has led to more flexible structures which allow for some linkage of pay to productivity. The new pay and grading systems introduced in 1998 are based on four pay bands, each of which has four to six steps. Progression through the band is now wholly dependent on performance appraisal against defined objectives (see Chapter 7).

In the cases of Sweden, Finland, the UK and the Netherlands grading and progression have become much more flexible. In Sweden (Chapter 10), salary scales are no longer used in the main and jobs are now rated according to a number of criteria, allowing individualised and differentiated pay (OECD, 1997). There are 81 job families, each with five levels of difficulty (or competency). Agencies are free to determine their own pay system, allowing for elements including experience, skills, performance and market value to be taken into account. Annual pay increases are usually divided between a general pay increase at agency level and individual negotiations at local level. Agencies can introduce a bonus system if they choose. In Finland pay increments are decided at agency level and pay progression is now based on a combination of seniority, qualifications, and personal and work group performance. In the Netherlands, a performance-related pay system covers all civil servants although progression remains nationally determined. Performance is rewarded through bonuses, temporary allowances and accelerated incremental progression. Individual performance-related progression has probably gone furthest in the UK civil service, where all progression is now related to individual performance in most agencies, with no basic cost-of-living increase. Grading structures often consist of a few wide salary bands, with no guaranteed increments, and grade allocation may be based on assessment of each individual's personal competencies (PTC, 1996; IDS, 1998). Unions negotiate the size of the pay budget but not its individual allocation. Performance-related pay is also present in the UK for managerial grades in the NHS and in some parts of local government. The British government launched new proposals for individual performance related pay for school teachers in December 1998 (DfEE, 1998).

As mentioned above, in many European countries basic salaries are supplemented by a variety of fixed allowances and supplements. In many cases these are laid down in elaborate regulations at national level. These can relate to a number of factors – function or department; marital status and family size; risk or abnormal working conditions; overtime working; special duties or responsibilities; location supplements for working in areas of high living costs; and performance bonuses. In France such allowances can add up to 20 per cent to gross salary. There are also holiday and end-of-year allowances which are common in both private and public sectors in some European countries. In some countries, the only local management discretion allowed in the pay system is the allocation of these allowances and pay supplements. These payments are sometimes equated with 'variable' pay but in reality they are usually based on fixed criteria and are quite different to Anglo-American concepts of 'at risk' pay.

In the UK, after a growth of such pay supplements in the 1980s to combat skill shortages, there has recently been a movement within the public services to consolidate such payments into basic salaries (for example, regional allowances). In civil service agencies, location allowances and the many special allowances previously paid for particular aspects of the job (e.g. language allowances, typing proficiency allowances, etc) have been incorporated into individual salaries and the emphasis is now very much on individual merit and worth, rather than a rate for the job. In the European context there is less evidence of this trend and in some cases, new supplements and allowances are being introduced as part of the shift to more flexible payment systems and away from fixed salaries. Indeed, a first step towards performance-related pay may be the introduction of one-off merit pay supplements.

CONCLUSION

In reviewing the changes which have taken place across the various European countries, the variety and complexity of remuneration practices suggests that no clear model is emerging and that there remain large differences among countries and even between sectors within countries. This chapter has considered the changes in pay systems under three main headings – the decentralisation of pay determination; changes to grading systems; and changes to pay progression criteria and systems. Clearly these developments are often linked and the three categories are not mutually exclusive. Nevertheless, while decentralised management control of pay can provide the basis for increased pay flexibility, it is clear that flexibility can still be achieved within national frameworks.

While some element of decentralisation can be detected in many countries, degrees of change vary. At one extreme, highly centralised national systems are being loosened to allow some local variations and management discretion over pay. But this is within a grading and progression framework which remains national in scope, often supported by law, for example in Germany and Spain. At the other extreme one finds the wholesale fragmentation of pay determination to departmental or agency level, with local managers given new powers to appoint staff at their 'market value' and to determine individuals' pay progression by management discretion alone, for example in Sweden, Finland and the UK.

Increased pay flexibility is therefore occurring at different levels and to different degrees but it is also happening with different ideological objectives. This may reflect the politics of the government in power, but there are also quite clear differences between political parties of similar persuasion (compare the approaches of the social democratic governments in power in France, Sweden, the UK and Germany). Individualisation of reward and diminution of trade union influence over pay appears to be more common in northern than in southern Europe, although Germany presents a very large exception to this trend. In part these differences reflect both different industrial relations traditions in the UK and Scandinavia (where voluntary systems have been more common than legally regulated systems of employment regulation) and partly different traditions of public administration. Germany and Belgium share with the southern European countries a tradition of both constitutionally defined employment rights and separate public administration law. It is also probably the case that the UK, Netherlands and Scandinavian countries are more influenced by US views on remuneration practices than their European partners.

In conclusion, it is not entirely clear where greater pay flexibility is leading. As Marsden has argued: 'To be successful in the longer run, this depends upon building a consensus among public sector employees, and therefore upon convincing them that the procedures adopted give them a fair chance of obtaining the kind of outcomes they feel are acceptable and fair' (Marsden, 1997: 82). Consensus is needed, says Marsden, at two levels – at the individual and collective level. Traditional systems may have restricted management power, but their objectives were employment security rather than the potential for high incomes. If new systems are to work, this need for employee income security must be built in if pay flexibility is not to be undermined by reduced employee commitment. A recent survey of performance related pay in the UK found that public sector managers were, compared with those in the private sector, 'much less likely to feel that their schemes are generating beneficial outcomes for their organisation on virtually every indicator' (IPD, 1998: 6). There is currently discussion about the future of performance-related pay in the UK civil service and a Cabinet Office review of delegated pay and grading, including the link between pay and performance, is expected sometime in 1999.

This chapter has not addressed important issues raised by the impact of national and regional cultures upon pay systems. National and regional cultures might, however, be expected to have an important influence over pay systems, with more collectivist cultures favouring more long term approaches to pay design and determination (which might mitigate against more performance based systems) and more individualistic cultures favouring more personal variations in pay (see for example Hofstede, 1980; Gomez-Mejia and Welbourne, 1991). The objection to individual performance related pay in Germany has been linked to a general national characteristic of egalitarianism (see Chapter 7). This might suggest that there is no single, 'best practice' approach to public sector pay systems design. It is also important to place recent developments within an historical context. In Germany and the UK for example, centralisation of public sector pay determination followed earlier decentralised systems. Centralisation followed increasing conflict and competition between different public authorities and was partly the result of pressure from trade unions for greater equity between different public sector employers. Taking a longer term perspective, there may have been more divergence of public sector pay systems in recent years than convergence, particularly at the extreme ends of the spectrum.

References

BLENK, W. (1987). 'Labour Relations in the Public Service of the Federal Republic of Germany', in Treu, T. *Public Service Labour Relations. Recent Trends and Future Prospects. A comparative survey of seven industrialised market economy countries.* Geneva: International Labour Office.

DFEE (1998). *Teachers: Meeting the challenge of change.* Cm 4164. December. London: Department for Education and Employment.

DOH (1999). 'A Modern Pay System for a Modern Health Service. Fairer pay structure with local flexibility'. Press Release. Monday, 15 February. London, Department of Health.

EIPA (1997). 'Remuneration policy in public administration compared to the market sector'. Report compiled by the European Institute of Public Administration, Maastricht.

FERNER, A. (1994). 'The State as Employer', in Hyman, R. and Ferner, A. (eds), *New Frontiers in European Industrial Relations.* Oxford. Blackwell.

FLYNN, N. and STREHL, F. (1996). *Public Sector Management in Europe.* London: Prentice Hall.

FOWLER, A. (1988). *Human Resource Management in Local Government.* London. Pearson.

GOMEZ-MEJIA, L. and WELBOURNE, T. (1991). 'Compensation Strategies in a Global Context'. *Human Resource Planning*, 14 (1), pp 29–42.

HEGEWISCH, A. and LARSEN, H. (1994). *European Developments in Public Sector Human Resource Management.* Cranfield School of Management Working Papers, Cranfield University.

HOFSTEDE, G. (1980). *Culture's Consequences: International differences in work related values.* Beverly Hills, CA: Sage.

IDS (1998). *Pay in the Public Service. Review of 1997/Prospects for 1998.* February. London: Incomes Data Services.

IPD (1998). *IPD 1998 Performance Pay Survey.* Executive Summary. London: Institute of Personnel and Development.

MARSDEN, D. (1997). 'Public service pay reforms in European countries.' *European Review of Labour and Research.* 3 (1), May, pp 62–85.

MARSDEN, D. and FRENCH, S. (1998). *What a Performance. Performance related pay in the Public Services.* Centre for Economic Performance. July. London: CEP.

OECD (1993i). *Pay Flexibility in the Public Sector.* Public Management Studies. Paris: OECD.

OECD (1993ii). *Private Pay for Public Work. Performance-related Pay for Public Sector Managers.* Public Management Studies. Paris: OECD.

OECD (1994i). *Public Service Pay Determination and Pay Systems in OECD Countries.* Public Management Occasional Papers. 1994 Series No. 2. Paris: OECD.

OECD (1994ii). *Trends in Public Sector Pay: A study of nine OECD countries (1985–1990).* Public Management Occasional Papers. 1994 Series No. 1. Paris: OECD.

OECD (1997). *Trends in Public Sector Pay in OECD Countries.* 1997 edn. PUMA. Paris: OECD.

OECD (1998). *Public Sector Pay and Employment Data Update.* Activity Meeting on Human Resources Management. 25–26 June. Paris: OECD.

PTC (1996). *Whatever Happened to a National Civil Service?*, Research Brief No1. London: Public Services Tax and Commerce Union (PTC).

STANDING, G. (1997). 'Globalization, Labour Flexibility and Insecurity: The Era of Market Regulation', *European Journal of Industrial Relations*, 3 (1), pp 7–37.

TREU, T. (1987). *Public Service Labour Relations: Recent Trends and Future Prospects. A Comparative Survey of Seven Industrialised Market Economy Countries.* Geneva: International Labour Office.

WHITE, G. (1999). 'The Remuneration of Public Servants: Fair Pay or New Pay?' in Corby, S. and White, G. *Employee Relations in the Public Services: Themes and Issues.* London: Routledge.

WHITE, G. and LÖFFLER, E. (1998). 'Pay flexibility in the German and British civil services', *Croner's Employee Relations Review*, 4, March 1998.

15 Flexible Working Patterns in European Public Administration

Koen Nomden

Public services are becoming increasingly characterised by the importance of flexible working patterns. These flexible working patterns allow public services to manage their staff in line with the needs of the organisation and to offer public servants flexibility when it comes to adapting working patterns to individual preferences. Flexible working patterns are one of the elements which Farnham and Horton refer to as the 'New People Management' (Farnham and Horton, 1997b). This contrasts with 'Traditional People Management', which is generally characterised by standardised, largely inflexible employment practices. The aim of this chapter is to give some insight into the importance of flexible working patterns in European public services.

FLEXIBLE WORKING PATTERNS

Hondeghem, Farnham and Horton define flexibility as the departure from standardised modes of employment, which enables employers to adjust the size and mix of labour in their organisations (Hondeghem, Farnham and Horton, 1997: 127). When discussing the flexibility debate in the United Kingdom during the 1980s, Farnham and Horton (1997a: 162) distinguish two broad categories of flexibility, namely labour market flexibility and flexible working practices. Labour market flexibility as a public policy is directed at maximising employment and labour productivity by the efficient matching of labour supply and labour demand in the market place and seeks to make the economy more dynamic and reduce unemployment by making the labour market more flexible (e.g. easier dismissals, more enterprise-based agreements, greater possibilities for temporary employment).

Flexible working practices are sets of organisational and personnel policies of employers designed 'to adjust the size and mix of labour in their organisations, in response to changes in demand for their goods or services so that they do not carry excess labour or have rising unit labour costs' (*ibid*: 62).

Labour market flexibilities and flexible working practices are inter-linked with each other. Farnham and Horton (1997a: 164f) make clear that both stem from similar factors – uncertainty and volatility in product markets, increased international competition and acceler-ating technological change in the workplace, particularly in terms of information and communication technology. The link between both forms of flexibility becomes clear when considering part-time employ-ment. Part-time employment is both a flexible working practice and an instrument used by several governments to combat unemployment and increase the labour force participation rate of women.

In this chapter, the term 'flexible working patterns' is used instead of 'flexible working practices'. The concept of flexible working pat-terns was developed by Atkinson (1985) and Atkinson and Meagher (1986) in their theory of the flexible firm where they distinguish four types of flexibility: numerical, functional, distancing and pay. A study by the European Association of Personnel Management subsequently identified six categories of flexibility, which are: flexibilities in working hours; flexibilities in length of working life; contractual flexibilities; flexibility in the location of work; task flexibilities; and pay flexibili-ties. This chapter explores the range of working patterns found in selected European public services and is based on available compar-ative information. It does not deal with all the above categories but focuses particularly on flexibilities in working hours and length of working life. Contractual flexibilities and pay flexibilities are explored in Chapters 2 and 14 respectively and other forms of flexibility are discussed in the country studies.

FLEXIBILITY OF WORKING HOURS

Flexibility of working hours includes a range of different working hour patterns. For the sake of clarity the following distinctions are made. The most common form of flexible working hours – part-time employment – is discussed first, together with job-sharing. Subse-quently there is examination of flexi-time and flexible daily, weekly and annualised hours.

Part-time work and job-sharing

There are different definitions of part-time employment including self-definitions, company, statistical and legal definitions (Wedderburn, 1995). At international level, both the International Labour Convention No. 175 on part-time work and the European Framework Agreement on part-time work contain definitions of a part-time worker as an employed person whose normal hours of work are less than those of comparable full-time workers calculated weekly or on average over a given period of employment. The term comparable full-time worker refers to a full-time worker who (i) has the same type of employment relationship; (ii) is engaged in the same or a similar type of work or occupation; (iii) is employed in the same establishment or, when there is no comparable full-time worker in that establishment, in the same enterprise or, when there is no comparable full-time worker in that enterprise, in the same branch of activity as the part-time worker concerned; and (iv) due regard is given to other considerations which may include seniority and qualification/skills. The importance of the International Labour Convention (ILC) as well as the European Framework Agreement (EFA) on part-time work is that these are also binding on employees working for public services. Job-sharing can be defined as a full-time job that is shared by usually two persons and is therefore a particular form of part-time work.

Both the ILC and the EFA focus on the issue of proportional treatment of part-time workers in comparison with full-time workers. Clause 4 of the EFA contains the principle of non-discrimination. This means that 'part-time workers shall not be treated in a less favourable manner than comparable full-time workers solely because they work part-time unless different treatment is justified on objective grounds. Where appropriate, the principle of *pro rata temporis* shall apply'. The agreement allows for some conditions to be fulfilled like periods of service, time worked or an earnings qualification, which are justified objectively. More generally, the EFA tries to remove all obstacles to part-time work.

The ILC is more specific in mentioning areas where no discrimination is allowed. Article 4 of the Convention states that measures shall be taken to ensure that part-time workers receive the same protection as that accorded to comparable full-time workers in respect of (i) the right to organise, to bargain collectively and to act as workers' representatives; (ii) occupational safety and health; and (iii) discrimination in employment and occupation. The Convention focuses on equal pay for part-time workers, proportional to the number of hours worked. It seeks measures to ensure that part-time workers receive conditions equivalent to those of comparable full-time workers in the fields of (i) maternity protection; (ii) termination of employment; (iii) paid annual leave and public holidays; and (iv) sick leave. Certain groups of part-time workers, whose hours of work or earnings are below specified thresholds, can be excluded from the scope of certain statutory social security schemes, but not employment injury benefits or maternity protection. However, the thresholds are sufficiently low as not to exclude an unduly large percentage of part-time workers. The Convention focuses on the fact that transfers from full-time to part-time work or *vice versa* should be voluntary.

Undoubtedly, the legal force of the ILC is less in practice than that of the EFA. The part-time work Convention is only binding on those members of the ILO which have ratified it. So far there have been three (Cyprus, Guyana and Mauritius), enough for the Convention to have come into force. The EFA was negotiated by the European social partners (UNICE and CEEP acting for the employers together with the European Trade Union Confederation) in the framework of the European Social Dialogue. It was adopted as a Council directive (97/81/EC) which must be transposed into the national law of all EU Member States by 20 January 2000.

Part-time employment can be seen from different perspectives and touches upon topics like the organisation of work, employment, quality of life, social protection (Wedderburn, 1995), as well as access to the labour market of women (Walter, 1997). Whether aspects of part-time employment are seen as advantages or disadvantages depends very much on the position from which part-time employment is looked at. From an employer's perspective, part-time employment can make the organisation more flexible. It can permit greater flexibility in responding to market requirements eg by increasing capacity utilisation or extending opening hours (Bollé, 1997). Part-time employment also has advantages when looking at productivity. A study by the McKinsey consultancy company in the United States estimated the productivity of a half-time employee at 64 per cent that of a full-time worker. The figures for those working 60 and 70 per cent of full-time work are 77 and 87 per cent respectively (quoted in Walter, 1997).

The disadvantages of part-time employment from an employer's perspective include the higher costs of employing part-time workers.

Part-time workers need training, office space or equipment and may only be used at partial capacity, and part-time work does not necessarily require a smaller amount of administrative input than full-time work. There is a need for more co-ordination between workers and scheduling working hours becomes more complicated. In this respect, improved time resource management is required (see Dinkgreve, Zwolsman and Jansen, 1997). The Joint Committee on the Public Services of the ILO (1994) further argues that management of personnel moving from full-time to part-time work, recruitment of temporary or permanent part-time workers to handle the resulting workload, and redistribution of work amongst existing staff, consumes valuable management time.

From an employee's perspective, part-time employment allows for a better adaptation of working time to family responsibilities, training, leisure or civic activities. It makes it easier for workers progressively to enter the labour market or to retire from employment. But there are often several drawbacks to part-time employment such as low pay, limited career opportunities and lack of social protection. Part-time workers tend to be employed in low-grade, poorly paid jobs. Sometimes they are even paid lower hourly rates than full-time workers for equivalent work within the same establishment (ILO, 1993). Part-timers are more likely to be excluded from supplementary payments such as bonuses, holiday and sickness pay, training allowances, seniority payments and so on. Premium payments for overtime are often not made until a part-time employee has worked the equivalent of full-time hours (ILO, 1993). There are few career opportunities for part-time workers and they tend to be excluded from supervisory posts. As regards social protection, in many countries thresholds exist relating to a minimum number of hours worked or minimum earnings in order to be eligible for certain social benefits like an employer's pension contribution. Certain part-time workers work 'on call', without any guaranteed minimum weekly or monthly number of hours, and are often excluded from certain employment rights and benefits. It is significant that women are over-represented in part-time jobs.

From governments' perspective, part-time employment can be seen as an instrument for reducing unemployment and increasing labour market participation by women, handicapped people and older workers. More critically one could add that it can lower politically sensitive unemployment rates without requiring an increase in the total number of hours worked (Bollé, 1997). It is not surprising that many governments have made part-time employment attractive in order to reduce unemployment or improve the female labour participation rate. Part-time employment could also become a too easy option for employers if, through fiscal measures, it were to become financially more attractive to hire part-time workers than full-time staff.

The Joint Committee on the Public Services (1994) reported that a number of unions had expressed concern that increased use of part-time personnel could weaken the position of trade unions and public service employee associations because part-time workers were much more difficult to organise. Similarly the OECD has also argued (1991) that part-time employment may be an obstacle to unionisation, stating that the evidence indicates that part-time workers are less likely to be unionised than full-time workers.

One can conclude from the above, on the one hand, that part-time employment increases the quality of working life by reconciling working time and family responsibilities. In this case part-time employment corresponds to the wishes of employees. On the other hand, it is evident that part-time working can be precarious employment and insufficient to provide a reasonable income for individuals or their families. It may be a negative choice because of the difficulty of finding full-time jobs or because of lack of child care facilities.

When considering the advantages and disadvantages of part-time work, an essential point is whether part-time employment is freely chosen, and therefore voluntary, or whether it is involuntary, because a full-time job was not available. Involuntary part-time workers can be individuals who are working fewer hours than normal, compared with full-time jobs or normal part-time hours, because of insufficient demand. Others might work part-time because full-time work could not be found (OECD, 1995). Involuntary part-time work refers directly to the concept of 'underemployment'. Bollé (1997: 578) remarks that 'policies designed to promote part-time work by lowering its cost below that of full-time employment are likely to have the perverse effect of increasing the proportion of involuntary part-time workers, i.e. underemployment, with adverse consequences both social . . . and economic, depressing demand, growth and employment'.

Statistical evidence on the incidence of part-time work

Labour statistics show that there are wide variations in levels of part-time employment throughout the European Union and the US.

The general trend, however, is that it has become an increasingly important pattern of employment. The European Commission (1997) concluded that continued growth of part-time work is a structural rather than cyclical phenomenon. Moreover, net growth of employment is caused by an increase in part-time work. Part-time employment is especially high among women. In 1997, female part-time employment only fell below 10 per cent in Greece. More than 35 per cent of women work part-time in Germany and Sweden and 46 per cent in the UK. The highest proportion of part-time employment among women is in the Netherlands, which reached 67.6 per cent in 1997. Part-time employment rates for men are considerably lower. It was below five per cent in Germany, Greece, Spain, Italy, Luxembourg and Austria in 1997 and only in Denmark and the Netherlands was it over 10 per cent. Table 15.1 shows the percentages of part-time employment in the member states of the EU for 1989, 1996 and 1997. The figures in the table are based on self-assessment.

Between 1989 and 1997 part-time employment increased in all

Table 15.1   Part-time employment in Europe as a percentage of total employment

Country	Part-timers as % of male employment			Part-timers as % of female employment			Part-timers as % of total employment		
	1987	*1996*	*1997*	*1987*	*1996*	*1997*	*1987*	*1996*	*1997*
Belgium	1.9	3.2	3.3	24.2	34.0	31.4	11.7	15.9	14.7
Denmark	9.3	11.4	12.1	42.2	35.1	34.4	24.5	22.4	22.2
Germany	2.0	3.3	4.2	29.5	33.6	35.1	13.0	16.7	17.5
Greece	2.7	2.6	2.6	10.8	5.7	8.1	3.7	3.7	4.6
Spain	2.4	2.6	3.2	13.9	16.5	17.4	4.1	7.6	8.2
France	3.5	5.3	5.5	23.1	30.0	30.9	12.2	16.7	16.8
Ireland	3.1	5.7	5.4	15.8	22.2	23.2	8.0	12.9	12.3
Italy	3.2	2.8	3.3	10.4	12.4	13.7	5.2	6.5	7.1
Luxembourg	1.7	1.3	1.1	17.4	18.1	20.2	6.9	7.6	8.2
Netherlands	13.8	16.7	17.0	57.5	68.7	67.6	30.9	38.5	37.9
Austria	n/d	3.0	4.0	n/d	28.7	29.0	n/d	14.2	14.9
Portugal	3.5	1.6	5.7	10.4	8.3	15.0	3.7	4.7	9.9
Finland	n/d	6.5	7.6	n/d	15.2	15.6	n/d	10.9	11.4
Sweden	n/d	8.3	9.2	n/d	42.6	39.9	n/d	25.6	23.9
UK	5.3	7.5	8.7	44.7	44.2	44.8	22.6	25.0	24.9

Source: Eurostat, *Labour Force Survey*.

member states except Denmark. No comparisons are possible with the three new member states which joined the EU in 1995. Although the trend was generally upwards in all countries, there was a slight fall between 1996 and 1997 in five member states – Belgium, Denmark, Ireland, the Netherlands and Sweden. One explanation for this could be the increased strain on the labour market. When comparing 1996 and 1997, we see that the decrease in the percentage of female part-time employment is largely responsible for the general decrease in part-time employment in the five above-mentioned countries. The percentage of men in part-time employment is decreasing in two countries, namely Ireland and Luxembourg.

Part-time employment in public administration is generally higher than in industry, but lower than in other services. Table 15.2 shows the relative importance of part-time employment in public administration compared to agriculture, industry and other services. It is striking that in certain countries part-time employment in public administration is particularly low. This is the case in the Mediterranean member states of the EU – Greece, Spain, Italy and Portugal – where less than five per cent of staff in public administration work part-time. In Belgium, France and Luxembourg in contrast, part-time employment in public administration is higher than the national average. The highest figure for part-time employment in public administration is found in the Netherlands (23.6 per cent).

Part-time work and job-sharing in public administration in EU member states

There are no comprehensive studies available on the relative importance of part-time work in public administration. Available informa-

Table 15.2 Share of part-time employment in Europe, by sector of activity, 1997

Data 1997	B	DK	D	EL	E	F	IRL	I	L	NL	A	P	FIN	S	UK
Agriculture	7.0	12.4	16.3	9.6	7.6	15.7	6.9	12.8	2.7	31.2	16.4	31.3	18.1	21.8	18.8
Industry	4.5	9.4	8.0	2.3	2.6	5.8	4.2	4.1	2.0	16.4	6.4	3.9	3.6	9.0	8.1
Public Administration	15.9	14.9	13.1	0.9	2.6	18.9	5.9	4.3	10.1	23.6	10.8	1.3	5.3	12.5	14.5
Other services	19.5	28.7	24.4	4.2	12.0	21.5	18.2	8.5	10.4	44.0	19.7	9.1	14.7	30.7	33.0
Total	14.7	22.2	17.5	4.6	8.2	16.8	12.3	7.1	8.2	37.9	14.9	9.9	11.4	23.9	24.9

Source: Eurostat, *Labour Force Survey*.

tion in Polet and Nomden (1996) suggests that in the core administration of central government (central government departments and
agencies) figures for part-time working are clearly lower than in
local government. Part of the explanation of the high part-time employment figure in French local government stems from the
fact that half of employees in municipalities of less than 1,000 inhab-
itants work part-time. Another trend is that non-established staff
in public administration are more often in part-time jobs than 'established civil servants'.

From the legislative point of view, public services have undergone
tremendous changes which have made part-time employment a more
normal working pattern. In 1970 the Joint Committee on the Public
Services of the ILO still found that 'as a rule, civil service statutes do
not make provision for adjustments in working hours to allow for
part-time work for civil servants' although there was a trend towards
recognition of part-time work for some categories of workers such as
mothers, students, workers wishing to continue their training or
studies, and retired persons (quoted in ILO, 1994). This situation
completely changed during the 1970s and 1980s and the 1988 report
noted that part-time work was being actively encouraged in public
services in Canada, France, Germany, New Zealand, Norway, UK and
the US (quoted in ILO, 1994).

Both the right to work part-time and the social rights of part-time
workers in public services vary considerably within the general trend
of increased possibilities and increased incentives to work part-time.
In Portugal and Spain, the possibility for civil servants to work part-
time is quite restricted. In Portugal, applications for part-time work
must be sent to the competent minister and are subject to a ministerial decision entering into force at the time of publication in the
Portuguese Official Journal. They have to be accompanied by due jus-
tification, which must first have been submitted to the Director-
General. Only public servants or employees with at least three years'
effective service can ask to work part-time. Senior public servants are
excluded from the scheme. In Spain there are no specific regulations
concerning part-time work for staff with public servant status. It is
possible to opt for a shorter working day but this does not apply to
the administration as a whole (one notable exception being so-called
special activity areas). Contractual staff, however, may use a variety
of part-time working schemes.

In most countries rules have been adopted for part-time work. In
Belgium, it is possible to opt for the 'voluntary four-day week' and

10.5 per cent of the workforce had done so in 1996. In Luxembourg, only 25 per cent of part-time schemes concern persons with civil servant status, 75 per cent of these concern other categories of employees. A striking aspect in France is that 95 per cent of staff with public servant status working part-time are women. The most popular part-time scheme is one in which the employees work 80 per cent of a full working week (54 per cent of cases). In France the proportion of part-time work is much higher among non-established (*non-titulaire*) staff than among established (*titulaire*) staff (35 per cent against eight per cent) (see Chapter 6).

Several member states of the EU offer an extensive range of options for part-time work. In France, for example, it is possible to opt for part-time work as a proportion of 50, 60, 70, 80 or 90 per cent of full-time employment. In Belgium, it is possible to opt for schemes in which employees can work $\frac{1}{2}$, $\frac{2}{3}$, $\frac{3}{4}$, or $\frac{4}{5}$, of standard working hours. In Germany, part-time work is granted without any specific conditions but it must not amount to less than 50 per cent of a full-time working week. In Austria, part-time work options range between a third and 100 per cent. Some countries, such as Portugal, Luxembourg and Ireland, have as yet only set up one part-time option (half normal working hours) for public servants.

In certain countries, including Belgium and France, part-time employment has been actively promoted by making it financially attractive through a higher than proportional payment of salary in comparison to the number of hours worked. For example in France, remuneration for an 80 per cent working week amounts to 85.7 per cent of a full-time salary and 91.4 per cent for a 90 per cent working week. Therefore, it is no surprise that 54 per cent of all part-time workers in the French public service work 80 per cent of normal working hours. In Belgium part-time staff receive the salary payable for their reduced working hours, plus a gross salary bonus of 80 Euros per month. Also in Spain the salary payment is higher than proportional. For five hours worked per day, 75 per cent of salary is received.

There are also a number of possibilities for organising part-time work over the week. In Finland, the 20-hour week is the most common type of part-time work. Generally speaking, Ireland operates a job-sharing scheme on a week on/week off or mornings/afternoons only basis but the Irish government is currently looking into the possibility of new schemes (e.g. a four-day week or a three-week month) with a view to introducing part-time options other than half the standard working hours. France traditionally organises part-time work on a weekly or monthly basis but the French administration is also experimenting with yearly part-time schemes.

In several countries, public bodies openly use part-time work with a view to 'job sharing' and combating unemployment. Thus, in Belgium contract staff are supposed to be taken on to compensate for employees who opt for the 'voluntary four-day week'. In Ireland, the creation of part-time jobs in the public service comes under the job-sharing scheme introduced in 1984. Creation of two part-time jobs out of one full-time job thus assumes that two people will be recruited on a part-time basis and that they have reached an agreement as to the manner in which they will alternate their working hours (mornings/afternoons, week on/week off). Likewise in Finland, government's desire to use part-time work as a means of combating unemployment has led to a grant being given for converting a full-time post into two part-time posts. This applies to employers in both the public and private sectors (Employment Decree 51/94).

Interesting subjects for research are: to what extent possibilities for part-time work have increased personnel satisfaction, to what extent part-time work has led to increased productivity and improved quality of public service delivery and, last but not least, whether measures to stimulate part-time work have had an effect on the overall unemployment rate? As regards the public sector, there is a lack of international comparative research with regard to the issues of personnel satisfaction, productivity and quality of public service delivery. As regards unemployment and part-time work, research is widely available but is not conclusive as to the positive or negative effects that part-time work has on unemployment. Roche, Fynes and Morissey (1996) conclude, however, that the effects on employment may be positive when they concern government-initiated schemes in the public sector.

Flexitime, flexible daily, weekly and annual working hours

As regards the organisation of working time over a working day, most member states of the EU have introduced systems offering flexibility of working days on the basis of different time bands. Certain time bands are regarded as fixed or compulsory, in the sense that all employees must be at work during these periods. The total duration of these fixed bands generally varies between four hours per day (Portugal, Ireland), four and a half hours (Luxembourg), five hours

(Belgium) and five and a half hours (Spain, Germany), or even six hours in some departments (Germany). These fixed bands may be grouped together over a continuous period as for example between 9 a.m. and 2.30 p.m. in Spain, or split between the morning and the afternoon as for example, in Ireland, where the so-called 'core bands' are split between 10.00 a.m. and 12.30 p.m. and 2.30 p.m. and 4.00 p.m. Alongside these fixed bands, there are also so-called mobile, variable or flexible bands. These include between 7.30 a.m. and 9.00 a.m. or between 2.30 p.m. and 7.00 p.m. in Spain, between 8.30 a.m. and 10.00 a.m. and between 4.00 p.m. and 6.30 p.m. in Ireland, between 6.30 a.m. and 9 a.m. and between 3.15 p.m. and 7.00 p.m. in Finland.

This organisation of daily working hours has, in all cases, come about as a result of consultation between interested parties and the administration to which they belong. In addition, in most countries these arrangements are subject to the rule that total monthly or weekly working hours, spread over fixed and variable bands, must comply with statutory working time. In Luxembourg, for example, the positive balance for the month may not exceed 10 working hours and the negative balance may not exceed six hours. In Belgium, the number of extra hours worked may only exceed 12 hours, compared with the normal monthly regime, in a particular department if the manager in charge is able to specifically justify this on the basis that it is required by the department. Further, extra hours worked must be compensated for during the following month in the form of time off in lieu (a maximum of one and a half days) or by making up a number of time bands. By the same token, the work deficit may not exceed eight hours per month and the missing hours must also be made up the following month. This method of organising working hours on a day-to-day basis is practised on a large scale in some countries. In Austria, for example, half of all personnel make use of flexitime on a day-to-day basis and in Finland, 60 per cent of staff in government agencies use this type of flexible system.

Some countries have developed schemes allowing considerable flexibility in organising the working week. In Finland there are two alternative ways of organising the 38.25-hour week: either by using a five-day week, with five days of equal length (seven hours 40 minutes), or by having a week with one day of six hours and a quarter and four days of eight hours. In 1996, 26 per cent of all personnel made use of this system. A very flexible organisation of the working week also exists in the Dutch civil service where there has been a development towards an *à la carte* weekly system. This is the consequence of the adoption in central government of the 36-hour week. There are several ways to fill this working week, for example, by working four days of nine hours per week, five days of eight-hours days per week, with a free choice as to when to take the additional four hours as time off in lieu. This alternative includes the option of taking a longer period of leave if one works 40 hours per week for several months or years up to a maximum of seven years. Yet another alternative is to have a 40-hour week over five days followed by a 32-hour week over four days.

The Finnish public service is developing a system of compensating for overtime in an original scheme known as the 'working hours bank' or 'compensatory free time system'. In this system, it is possible to accumulate overtime up to a limit of 78 hours over a period of 26 weeks. This overtime is then credited to the employee and may be compensated for by granting leave for a period of time corresponding to the accumulated total of overtime. This system is laid down in collective agreements. It enables employers to introduce flexibility in the long-term management of working hours, whilst avoiding the additional expense associated with payment of overtime. In 1996 this system was used by six per cent of the workforce.

FLEXIBILITIES IN LENGTH OF WORKING LIFE

Here a distinction should be made between career breaks and early retirement schemes. Career breaks concern temporary absence from work. Early retirement refers to retirement at an age below the statutory retirement age. Several countries have introduced the possibility of taking special personal leave, for a sabbatical or career break, for periods that usually range between several months and one year. Of these countries, some have developed schemes for replacing people who are on leave, the aim of these schemes being to reconcile career breaks by employees in post and providing a training opportunity for job-seekers. Two examples of career breaks are found in Belgium and Finland. In Belgium, an employee can take career breaks in periods of a minimum of six months and a maximum of 12 months, with the total of these career breaks not exceeding 72 months during an entire career. In the case of special personal leave, pay for the leave period is not based on the employee's full-time salary. Nevertheless, the employee does receive a 'monthly career-break allowance', which varies from 258 Euros to 307 Euros. The originality of this flexible scheme lies in its link with employment problems, since the absent employee must be replaced by an unemployed person.

Finland is experimenting with a similar scheme known as 'job alternation leave'. This experiment was conducted within the Finnish administration between 1996 and 1998. An agreement between the employer and employee means that it is possible to replace employees for the duration of their leave, which is between 90 and 359 days. Replacements receive a salary from the employer but employees who are on leave do not. However, the latter can receive compensation equivalent to 60 per cent of the daily unemployment benefit that persons receive if they are unemployed, subject to a maximum limit of 760 Euros per month.

Early retirement schemes in public services have existed for several years in most countries. Early retirement implies retirement earlier than is normally required. In most countries there is a general retirement age but, especially in public services, some occupational groups have their own retirement age. Early retirement in these cases means early retirement compared to the specific retirement age for the occupational group within the public service to which somebody belongs. In Germany, for example, public servants who have reached the age of 55 may take advantage of unpaid leave during the period leading up to their due retirement date, on condition that this does not run counter to the interests of the department. In France, the so-called end-of-career leave (*congé de fin d'activité, CFA*) is available to public servants aged 58 or older who have completed 37.5 years of contributions or 40 years of public service. It allows such employees to retire up to two years before the normal retirement age of 60. In 1997, CFA affected 10,000 people in the state public service alone. In the United Kingdom civil servants may retire from the age of 50 and receive immediate payment of a reduced pension called 'actuarially-reduced retirement', based on the 'Principal Civil Service Pension Scheme'. In the Netherlands a new system for early retirement came into force on 1 April 1997. It grants the option of early retirement for public servants between the ages of 55 and 65, provided there is a continuous period of service of at least 10 years. An employee who takes early retirement is entitled to a pension before the age of 65 of in total 210 per cent of his/her annual income, paid out over the whole period of early retirement, based on 40 years of pensionable service. This means for someone who retires early, at age 62, the annual flexible pension that is enjoyed can be 70 per cent of his/her last income.

It is evident that early retirement has been used by governments in recent years to achieve reductions in the size of public organisations. But what is the future of early retirement schemes? One of the fundamental problems with early retirement schemes is that pensions are not only paid out for extra years but also that necessary pension capital accrues for fewer years (Anderson, 1997). It is therefore no wonder that some member states, including Germany and Austria, want to make it more difficult to seek early retirement and that other countries including Italy, the Netherlands and the UK are introducing measures to promote early retirement do so with reductions in pension payments (EIPA, 1998). Moreover, retirement age is generally increasing rather than decreasing because of the financial pressure on pension schemes due to demographic change. Ageing populations throughout Europe and the OECD countries have dramatically changed the balance between pensioners on the one hand and pension-premium payers on the other. Estimates indicate that the effect of supporting the elderly in Europe, expressed as the number of old age pensioners in relation to the working population, is expected to double from just over 20 per cent in 1990 to over 40 per cent in 2040. As a consequence financial demands on the pension systems will increase accordingly (Ekebrand, 1997).

Several countries have recently introduced the possibility of part-time work schemes at the end of a career. In Portugal, a retirement transition scheme for public servants based on a part-time working arrangement is under consideration. In Denmark, there are specific possibilities for organising working time at the end of a career, with particular emphasis on part-time working options. These arrangements apply both to public servants and salaried employees in the private sector. In Austria, the possibility of giving certain categories of public servants, namely teachers, the opportunity to opt for part-time work after the age of 55 is being considered. In Spain, public servants who have less than five years to work before they reach retirement age can have their working day reduced by up to half on request, provided that this does not contravene their conditions of service. Finland has also made it possible for employees at the end of their career to work part-time, either by reducing their workload, or by transferring to a part-time post in a different job. In France, there is a so called gradual suspension of professional activities (*cessation progressive d'activité, CPA*) which has been in operation since 1982. Under this scheme, employees who can demonstrate 25 years of public service are able to transfer to part-time work on reaching the age of

55. French ministerial departments have a general policy of compensating for the hours released by part-time work by recruiting permanent public servants.

From the point of view of wages policy, there is a big incentive to switch to part-time work if this policy proposes additional pay for the candidates in addition to the paid salary corresponding to reduced working hours. The Netherlands has recently introduced innovative legislation in this area. The scheme known as Partial Employment of Older Employees (*partiële arbeidsparticipatie senioren, PAS*) allows public servants who have reached the age of 57 and have been in continuous service for the last five years, to reduce their working hours to an average of 30.32 hours per week, ie a 15.8 per cent reduction in working hours, in return for a reduction in gross salary of only five per cent. Then, after the age of 61, it is possible to reduce working hours even further to an average of 22.76 hours per week, ie a 36.8 per cent reduction, in return for a reduction in gross salary of only 10 per cent. Compensation may be claimed for additional hours if the total number of hours worked in practice proves to be higher. Finally, public servants who join the PAS scheme are still eligible for existing schemes with respect to early retirement. Beneficiaries see their leave entitlement reduced. The additional annual days' holiday that are acquired at the ages of 55 (21.6 hrs) and 60 (28.8 hrs) are repealed and basic days' holiday is reduced in proportion to the actual reduction in working hours. Additional earned income is deducted from the salary obtained under the PAS scheme so that public servants at the end of their career are not encouraged to seek to reduce their working hours purely for financial gain.

CONCLUSION

This chapter has sought to show the diversity of flexible working patterns that have developed in the public services of member states of the EU. After defining the concept of flexibility and making a distinction between different flexible working patterns, flexibilities in working hours and flexibility in the length of working life have been subject to further analysis. As regards flexibilities in working hours, one can conclude that in almost all member states rules and regulations exist allowing public servants to work part-time. This is true for both established and for non-established staff. Some countries even provide financial incentives to work part-time by providing remuneration which is higher than proportional in view of the number of hours worked. As regards length of working life, in many civil services there are possibilities to retire earlier than at official retirement age, with the agreement of the employee. Some governments have restrictive policies on these schemes which are relatively expensive, whilst in others flexibility is created by offering more choice to the employee regarding age of retirement but with consequences for the pension received. Research is still needed before we can gain a more profound insight into the relative importance and effects of different patterns of flexible employment in the public service. One of the questions to be addressed is the extent to which flexible employment patterns as distinguished here are really flexible in practice – whether employees really have more choice as regards their employment and whether managers in the public service have more freedom in managing their staff.

References

ANDERSON, D. (1997). 'The True Cost of Early Retirement Schemes', in *Civil Service Pension Schemes, SIGMA-Papers No. 10*. Paris: OECD.

ATKINSON, J. (1984). *The Flexible Firm*. Brighton: Institute of Manpower Studies.

ATKINSON, J. and MEAGHER, N. (1986). *Changing Patterns of Work: How Companies Achieve Flexibilities*. London: NEDO.

BOLLÉ, P. (1997). 'Part-time work: Solution or trap?', in *International Labour Review*, 136 (4) (Winter), pp 557–79.

DENKGREVE, R., ZWOLSMAN, J. and JANSEN, B. (1997). *Arbeidstijd-management in perspectief, op weg naar 2007*. Deventer: Kluwer.

EKEBRAND, S. (1997). 'Pension Systems for Civil Servants', in *Civil Service Pension Schemes, SIGMA-Papers No. 10*. Paris: OECD.

EUROPEAN COMMISSION (1997). *Employment in Europe 1997*. Brussels.

EUROPEAN INSTITUTE OF PUBLIC ADMINISTRATION (1998). *Reform of the Pension Systems for Civil Servants in the Member States of the European Union*. Maastricht: EIPA.

FARNHAM, D. and HORTON, S. (1997a). *Flexibility and the Public Services in Britain: Some Conceptual Issues and Empirical Evidence*. Budapest: EGPA/Centre for Public Affairs Studies.

FARNHAM, D. and HORTON, S. (1997b). 'Employment Flexibilities and the New People Management in the Public Services: the Case of the UK', paper presented at the Annual Conference of the EGPA.

HONDEGHEM A., FARNHAM, D. and HORTON, S. (1997). *Working Report*. Budapest: EGPA/Centre for Public Affairs Studies.

HORTON, S. (1997). 'Editorial, Employment Flexibilities in the Public Services: Concepts, Contexts and Practices', in *Public Policy and Administration*, 12 (4) (Winter), pp 1–13.

INTERNATIONAL LABOUR ORGANISATION (1993). *Part-time work*. Report V (1), International Labour Conference, 80th Session. Geneva: ILO.

JOINT COMMITTEE ON THE PUBLIC SERVICES (1994). *Terms and Conditions of employment of part-time and temporary workers in the public service*. Fifth Session, Report II. Geneva: ILO.

OECD (1991). *Employment Outlook*. Paris: OECD.

OECD (1995). *Employment Outlook*. Paris: OECD.

OECD (1998). *Employment Outlook*. Paris: OECD.

POLET, R. and NOMDEN, K. (1996). *Employment in the Public Administrations of the EU Member States*. Maastricht: EIPA.

ROCHE, W.K., FYNES, B. and MORISSEY, T. (1996). 'Working time and employment: A review of international evidence', in *International Labour Review*, 135 (2), pp 129–57.

WALTER, J.-K. (1997). *Le travail à temps partiel*. Rapport présenté au nom du Conseil économique et social. Paris: CES.

WEDDERBURN, A. (ed.) (1995). 'Part-Time Work', in *BEST*, No. 8. Dublin: European Foundation for the Improvement of Work and Living Conditions.

16 Flexibility in Personnel Policies in International Organisations

Charles Montin

Though international public service organisations cannot compare in size with their national counterparts, except with those of the smallest countries, and though they are not fully homogeneous, the international civil service (ICS) provides an additional example of a type of public administration constantly adapting (or failing to adapt) to new environments or new objectives set for it. Recent changes may be construed as signs of the introduction of some flexibility in internal processes. But because of the specific nature of international organisations, the meaning and purpose of flexibility may be expected to differ from its national equivalents and the measurement of its success or failure may also be at variance. The degree of flexibility required may be quite different from what is useful in either the private or public sectors of member states. This chapter describes not only indicators of flexibility but also limits of this concept in the international environment. It also examines the status of the flexibility issue and how it may come into conflict with some of the basic prevailing principles of the ICS, which derive directly from the values and concepts of European civil services.

AN INDEPENDENT OR SUBORDINATE MODEL?

Before examining flexibility within the ICS, it is necessary to give a brief description of the type of system under review. Although close by its origins and its continuing links with national administrations, the ICS, which employs some 120,000 permanent staff, has developed over the years, in its own environment, to meet the requirements set for it by member states. It is now a fairly homogeneous model which can be viewed as a separate system, undergoing, sometimes with delays, the same trends as appear in the national contexts. Though shielded in many respects by statutes from some of the harshest realities of present-day economies, some international organisations (UNESCO, UNIDO) have been faced with the choice between changing their ways or disappearing. The pressures for change, however, have not always been managerial. As most IOs are composed of people originating from the nations surveyed in the country studies, and others throughout the world, lessons may be learnt from analysing what may appear as a possible synthesis of national solutions. However, political influence may be wielded by some national organisations and changes introduced into management practices are not viewed as neutral. Reforms may be interpreted as vindicating some national experiments and may be supported or opposed on those grounds, not on the intrinsic effects on the organisation concerned.

Although there is great diversity of missions, structures and operating modes within international organisations, there is an underlying unity in the ICS. Around 200 organisations are operating on the international scene and this figure includes only inter-governmental agencies, not non-governmental bodies which are even more numerous. Each agency has been created by official representatives of member state governments and the resulting organisation can be viewed as inheriting some of the traits of the countries most dominant in its inception. In the majority of cases they will have established an early influence and then striven to retain it whatever the fortunes of the agency may be. The diversity of locations of world agencies (UN in New York, ILO and WHO in Geneva, UNESCO in Paris, IMO in London) is a sign of unity, indicating that the main contributors attempt to distribute the influence and the returns to be derived by hosting international organisations. Participating nations have also sought to structure these bodies to preserve the effectiveness of their control. The United Nations (UN) status of specialised agencies has provided a framework for operating the 16 technical bodies which all report, sometimes indirectly, to the UN General Assembly. In spite of the diversity of their geographic membership, the co-ordinated organisations have a strict set of common rules concerning conditions of service, which is designed to prevent competition between agencies hiring the same specialists. The unity of the ICS is further enhanced by frequent meetings between officials and mobility, at senior levels, of staff who develop an expertise in the management of such organisations. This enhances mobility of ideas, especially in management values and practices. The same type of co-ordination exists in two other groups of organisations, though it seems to be limited to statutory matters:

- European Union agencies, where a civil service-type status protects all the '*fonctionnaires*', except a number of temporary staff categories
- western co-ordinated organisations system of NATO and OECD, which brings together six agencies operating with a membership wider than Europe to encompass other industrialised countries. In this system, only pay and pension rules have been harmonised and do not prevent a diversity of personnel policies being implemented.

It has been indicated that member states can be seen as competing to exert their influence within international organisations, either to further their direct interests in the handling of the core business of the agencies or to promote their national reputation and secure long-term advantages. One of the signs of this struggle for influence is competition to secure the higher positions in agencies for their nationals, as this is a means of obtaining access into decision-making processes. Though officials often come, after a few years, to identify with the multicultural outlook of their employer, and do not necessarily promote the ideas of their country of origin, they are inevitably marked by their original outlook and tend to try to convince colleagues that their outlook is more efficient or more acceptable than others. This situation is interesting from an academic perspective, as international organisations can provide a test-bed for current management theories emanating from different countries, where ideas are actually competing for recognition by practitioners, as well as trying to prevail over existing theories and practices.

SPECIFIC TRAITS OF THE ICS

The ICS has been the subject of a number of very thorough investigations (Amerasinghe, 1994; De Cooker, 1990; Plantey, 1977), although the approach has been mainly political, systemic or legal (Riss, 1993). Very few have studied the management problems faced by these organisations, as underlined by Jéquier (1985: 201). The 'elasticity' or possible impact of flexibility policies are largely determined by these traits.

Autonomy

The basic principles underlying the ICS are close to the classic rules of the public service in European countries. One of the first documents on the subject (Balfour Declaration, 1920), in the early days of the League of Nations, transposed values from the British civil service such as its independence and its moral qualities. The Noblemaire Report (1921), which is still a charter for many aspects of the UN service, confirmed that recruitment and career should be based on merit rather than on national protection. After the Second World War, the organisations became more numerous and more efficient and their independence more clearly defined. Direct involvement of member states became less frequent, as the ICS became increasingly aware that loyalty to the mission entrusted by a group of states had to take precedence over national allegiance. Such principles were incorporated into staff rules and regulations, and confirmed in litigation brought before newly established administrative courts. In summary, the specific medium in which international organisations have to operate, dominated by member states pursuing their own objectives, requires that independence *vis-à-vis* national interference be guaranteed in statutes, in the same way as some institutions are protected inside national systems. Examples include the judiciary, which must be shielded against excessive influence by the executive branch of government, or the central bank, which is now only just being freed from government influence. The consequence of this independence is precisely a loss of control by governments, with the corresponding risk that guidelines, for greater efficiency, may not be followed. As autonomy is considered as an objective in its own right, it is not surprising that a fair share of studies on the ICS concentrate on the issue of the preservation of this independence, and the threats it faces, rather than increased efficiency (IIED, 1984: 270; Beigbeder, 1988: 170).

One of the most effective guarantees of autonomy has been provided by the emergence of an 'independent' ICS, structured by regulations and subject to arbitration for resolution of disputes. This may be seen, as within national administrations, as a possible obstacle to more results-oriented management styles. One consequence of the principle of autonomy is that management of international organisations must integrate the political dimension at international level. It is not insignificant that the external partners of the international manager are representatives of sovereign states, not other ministries of similar rank in the same government. In some cases, the number of such constituents can be high, as in the case of UN agencies, and their influence is to be felt not only directly, but indirectly by way of coalitions between which the agency must mediate, furthering the collective interest. As one of the stakes can be the internal structure, goals and means of the organisation itself, management combines the tasks of the executive as well as the legislative arm of government. In such a context, criteria of success are not the same as in national administrations and the emergence of bureaucratic methods of work is difficult to contain (see Jéquier, 1985: 219, for a theory of the three bureaucracies at play, and Bertrand (in De Cooker, 1990) for the 'superposition of bureaucracies'concept).

Member state distribution

Within the management of international organisations, diversity of origin of staff, which is both an objective and a constraint, affects the ways they are managed. Member states, which are their funding authorities, naturally insist on some type of 'return-on-investment', in the guise of policies safeguarding their interests, or expenditure incurred in their currency. These spin-offs are often difficult to ensure, or to measure, and attention then focuses on the distribution of posts in the complement of staff. Accordingly, managers within the IOs must take this into account in the recruitment process and are often faced with 'political' appointments as a result. These are cases where, in the presence of several 'equally qualified' candidates, preference is given to the applicant whose country is less represented on the international staff. The difficulty arises chiefly from the ambiguity of the notion of equally qualified in a multicultural context. As described by Bertrand (in De Cooker, 1990: p.II.2/3–8), control of recruitment leads to 'fierce battles' between member-states and a 'sort of osmosis' between national diplomatic services and the UN Secretariat.

Co-ordination

International organisations are created as the need to formalise inter-state co-operation in a particular field occurs or as the result of a new international situation. Considering the variety of areas of co-operation covered, with differing memberships, and the correspondingly large number of bodies, delegates from member states do not have an overview of the situation and agencies are set up in a rather disorderly manner, with varying statutes and modes of operation.

Thus, there is a need for co-ordination in order to improve effectiveness of management control, avoid costly duplication of efforts and limit competition for the same skills. Where there is confrontation of national interests affecting management choices, decisions tend to shift from within the organisations to co-ordination level. This process entails, in some cases, lack of consistency between the positions of member states expressed at co-ordination level and agency level. There is also, in some cases, a more technical and at times more financial approach to the issues, once they are further removed from the immediate pressure of operations. One needs to ascertain to what extent co-ordination, which concerns nearly all international organisations, increases or decreases the flexibility of internal management policies. One of the consequences is that the remuneration structure bears little relation to the recruitment and retention difficulties in a particular organisation or agency or with the problems of an individual occupational group such as lack of flexibility.

AN OVERVIEW OF MANAGEMENT STYLE IN THE ISC

In spite of a variety of organisations, the specific traits of the ICS, described above, are sufficiently numerous and distinctive to allow some generalisations about the style of management to be made. There is in fact less difference between the way the UN and the EU operate than between the American and German administrations. This stems from the necessary blend of national civil service traditions and newer requirements of increased accountability. In this management context, flexibility does not appear to be the main objective of the system. Those aspects inherited from national public services include:

* public law: though staff are either in a regulatory position (EU) or in a contractual situation (elsewhere), there is always a statutory text defining rights and duties of personnel in relation to their employer (Amerasinghe, 1983). The fundamental obligation of loyalty, discretion and independence *vis-à-vis* member states is universal and is compensated by varying degrees of security of tenure. Labour law of the country of residence does not apply, except to certain categories of temporary staff, who are not part of the ICS. Social protection itself is often organised on an independent, private basis to ensure consistency with international standards

- arbitration: litigation related to employment in the ICS is not referred to national courts but to 'administrative tribunals' such as those set up by the UN, the International Labour Organisation or 'appeals boards' like in NATO. These bodies generally apply the same principles as those enforced in national administrative courts such as limits to the discretionary power of the chief executive of the organisation, requirement for motivated decisions and respect for due process (Pellet, 1982)
- representation of staff and consultation on regulatory changes: an array of joint bodies are generally consulted before any change of regulations can be submitted for approval to the legislative body which is often the Council of member states. In some rare cases, such as the EU, staff representatives are also associated with decisions concerning promotions and appointments.

Those aspects deriving from managerial constraints include the:

- primacy of availability of funds: when an international organisation can no longer secure its contributions, it must take measures to adjust to the limited resources, as remaining members are reluctant to bear the original charges
- progressive use of fixed term contracts as the legal basis of employment, for large numbers of the staff, with the duration of the post connected to funding. This is a trend observed in nearly all bodies and life-long employment has virtually disappeared
- introduction of new approaches to human resources management (HRM), performance assessment and pay, though this trend is more widely discussed than implemented. Many nations are still repelled by such talk, as appeared recently during the UN Fifth Committee's consideration of the issue. 'The founding fathers of the Organisation had no intention of establishing an institution which functions on the basis of "value for money". It is of extreme importance that the new direction towards the so-called "corporate" mentality does not destroy the fabric of the international civil service' (Amb. Incera, on behalf of the group of 77 and China, 25 October 1996).

On the whole, the legal set-up of the ICS still gives precedence to binding rules, enforced under the control of an independent arbitral system upholding traditional civil service values. This system tends to favour stability of staff rules, placing the burden of proving good faith and true external constraints on agencies wishing to modify conditions of service. This structural resistance to change is best expressed by the notion of 'acquired rights' (Appril, 1983) which is frequently put forward by staff battling reductions in benefits or new requirements and viewed by many managers as the main obstacle to internal adaptations.

In conclusion, the meaning of flexibility must be qualified when examining the capacity of the ICS to adapt to a more cost-conscious, client-oriented mode of operation. Except in specific cases, where a new management style has been imposed through the choice of a particularly proactive leadership, traditional administrative values, such as security of due process and hierarchical reporting, are still very much predominant. In most cases this is based on consensus amongst members of the organisation itself more than resistance to change within its structures. Now that this framework has been established, to serve as the background against which the success or not of flexibility policies can be measured, it is time to examine, at a more practical level, the nature of efforts towards flexibility in personnel policies and the obstacles they may have had to face. Two specially significant areas are examined: staffing, and remuneration. These two areas have been selected because they have tended to focus the attention of member state delegations, intent on streamlining or downsizing agencies while trying to preserve their influence through maintaining their quota of national posts.

STAFFING FLEXIBILITIES

One of the criticisms often made about public bodies is that they outlive the purpose for which they were created. Once recruited, staff expect to stay in office till they retire. In a world where no position can be considered a life-long privilege, and contributions to international organisations must be justified in terms of return on investment, this attitude is no longer acceptable. The question is: do IOs adjust to the evolution of their mission by terminating staff as easily as they hire extra personnel when additional activities are required by their member states? As the increase of staff does not usually pose a difficulty, once the appropriate funds have been made available, attention centres on reductions. An answer can be sought by examining the legal questions involved in changing or terminating employment, on the one hand, and management of staff complements on the other.

Except in the EU, where most employees hold permanent tenure, employment may be terminated for reasons linked to the future of the organisation, if a decision to do so is taken at the appropriate level. This results from the employment regime of the ICS, where personnel are employed under contract, even if the contract is of indefinite duration. All statutes allow termination of contract in the event of changes affecting the number or nature of posts approved in the budget and generally provide for compensation. NATO regulations, for instance, mention the suppression of the budget post, changes in duties of the budget post, general staff cuts including those due to a reduction in or termination of the activities of the organisation, the withdrawal of the member country of which the incumbent is a national, transfer of headquarters or any of its units to another country and several other cases including an all encompassing 'specific staff policy as agreed by the Council'. In other statutes, there is not such a detailed list of cases, but a general formula such as 'if the necessities of the service require abolition of the post or reduction of the staff'. From these examples, it appears that chief executives have wide powers to adjust levels of staff to their needs. This power, however, remains rather theoretical, except in special circumstances. The statutes generally provide for compensation for loss of job, at a level which makes it difficult to contemplate massive reductions of their complement. Other problems include loss of morale amongst remaining staff and national pressures in the selection of areas for cuts.

In this situation, where flexibility of staffing is theoretically allowed by statute, but made difficult by shortage of funds and political interference, how can managers adjust the complement if required? Most bodies have recently experienced one or more 'social plans' aimed at reducing, or 'rejuvenating' staff complements. The purpose of these plans is generally to secure funds to initiate terminations, by offering those willing to leave a financially attractive package. The main argument for deciding such a package is often the 'economic' advantage to members: the separation indemnities are lower than the future salaries which would be paid until the retirement of the staff concerned. In CERN, there were three such schemes in the 1980s and early 1990s and a scheme is currently being discussed at the European Space Agency. Contrary to what usually happens in the private sector, schemes rest on the willingness of staff to take the package on offer. If the incentive is too generous, there will be a deluge of applicants. Not all will be accepted, which will create disappointment and leave staff de-motivated and inflame member states which are funding the exercise. If conditions are too ungenerous, generally for budget reasons, there will be insufficient interest in the scheme and it will be considered a failure. In extreme cases, national representatives call for terminations without appropriate compensation but they have not generally succeeded. In summary, social plans purporting to buy out staff members are expensive because job security comes at a premium. They are also inefficient as the leavers are generally the most efficient staff, not those the organisation prefers to shed. All-in-all, social plans, which are compatible with existing regulations, are only used in extreme circumstances when member states are intent on drastic downsizing and can face high costs. In other cases, a more gradual approach is adopted, drawing on progressive results through a less generous contract policy.

Though there is still a general feeling that access to the ICS should be the beginning of a long career of public service, there have been signs that staff can no longer expect life-long employment. Through budgetary control and political guidance, national representatives have managed to reduce the frequency of indefinite duration contracts, though this does not necessarily entail any precariousness in employment. Initially, it was felt by member states that excessive security of tenure not only impaired the possibility of adjusting staffing levels, but also could lead to lack of motivation and loss of productivity. On this assumption, either a ban was placed on indefinite contracts or they became *de facto* difficult to secure, through self-imposed discipline inside the organisations. In some cases, this led to some injustice because indefinite duration contracts were statutorily defined as a right, as well as a guarantee against arbitrary staff reductions, chiefly because of the higher level of compensation awarded in case of termination.

However, there are other limits to the flexibility that was supposed to result from the spread of definite duration contracts. The first is reluctance by managers to exercise their right to terminate contracts when the incumbent's performance becomes less than optimal. Though such a facility should directly result from the nature of the contractual link, the civil service tradition, supported by case-law of international arbitral courts, has led to the notion of 'legitimate expectancy' of renewal of contract which the management has to reverse to justify a non-renewal decision. The special, multi-cultural, atmosphere has not been sufficiently accustomed to performance evaluation to use its findings to legally justify a separation. In practice, apart from those occupying the most senior positions, which are under more direct political scrutiny, staff are generally allowed to stay until they can find employment elsewhere, whatever the precise wording of their contracts.

This lack of flexibility would not pose an insurmountable problem if staff could be retrained and re-deployed as the needs of organisations change. Here again, the civil service type of statutory constraints limit the flexibility allowed to managers. Chief executives generally experience difficulties in transferring staff from one service to another, although this applies mainly to the management of vacancies. Comfortably accustomed to their contractual duties, staff do not usually see the point of a lateral transfer without promotion. In some organisations, such transfers are in any case accessed through competition, which enhances its appeal as a reward for performance at the lower grade, more than a tool to bring about organisational change. In times of structural reorganisation, and provided the moves have been prepared and carefully discussed with the staff and groups concerned, transfers can usually be effected in a satisfactory manner. They entail, however, a lengthy process which must be professionally managed.

PAY FLEXIBILITIES

This is probably the area where the ICS displays least flexibility. Conditions of service, especially financial packages, tend to be agreed at the co-ordinated level (see above), irrespective of the importance or efficiency of the specific agencies belonging to the group, and rarely allow for personal adaptations to cater for special technical skills or performance. The issue of flexibility should therefore be examined at two levels: agency and individuals. The question of flexibility frequently arises when top management of a specific agency is experiencing difficulties in attracting appropriate staff. Rejection of job offers by applicants and last minute defections of high-level candidates can result in a shortfall as well as poor applicants in the competition for vacancies. Recruitment is sometimes entrusted to an external consultant such as Hay Management for the UN or Watson-Wyatt for co-ordinated competition. Though co-ordination systems have been set up to avoid agencies stealing each other's best staff, there is no global system and a UN executive may well be tempted by an EU job carrying a 30 per cent mark-up of remuneration. Far from being hypothetical, this type of situation was actually the source of bitter debate within the UN system in the early 1990s, when two

Geneva-based organisations decided to award additional bonuses (Beigbeder, 1990). The discussion was closed only after heated exchanges in the UN General Assembly and the two 'rogue' agencies were forced to withdraw their initiative. In spite of the general agreement that high technical activity can warrant extra compensation, there is a reluctance to depart from the grade system, which rests on established classifications. These determine, in a precise way, the position of each job in the salary scale, through an analysis of responsibility, scope of position, mental effort and several other factors. The introduction of 'occupational rates' would disrupt a balance between professions which has not shifted much in the last 30 years. In the UN, the problem is made more acute by the growing lack of competitiveness in salaries, as measured against those awarded by other organisations, and the private sector, and the corresponding shift in recruitment which is welcomed by many member states. Uniformity of grade-pay across the system can be viewed as a tool for eliminating candidates from more demanding backgrounds, i.e. countries where salary levels are higher, irrespective of the conditions of the employment market. In such a context, flexibility is presented as a self-serving mechanism invented to circumvent financial discipline.

Though it finds its origin in budgetary considerations, the debate on 'affordability' currently pursued in the co-ordinated system may lead to salary differentiation, at the initiative of the agencies concerned. The purpose of such a proposal is, however, not to reward performance of staff and managers, but to reduce the overall wage bill. The trend of recent discussion in the co-ordination system is to give governing bodies of each affiliated agency power to suspend cost-of-living adjustments on the basis of the budgetary constraints placed by member states. Strongly opposed by staff representatives, and criticised by agencies themselves, this method may see its legal standing challenged within the arbitration courts of each organisation. 'Agency rates' have never really stood a chance in the ICS, against the combined pressures of civil service tradition and strict budget control, but there is a chance that flexibility might be introduced at the level of the staff member.

Traditionally, the multicultural setting of international organisations encouraged the view amongst managers that difficulties of agreeing on what constitutes efficient performance precluded any serious moderation of pay according to results. This opinion is reinforced by those who hold that international civil servants must be protected against undue pressure from member states, a view sometimes relayed through their nationals on the international staff. This situation is slowly changing. Widespread criticism of international bureaucracy, accused of being insensitive to the needs of member states or the public, has led some chief executives of agencies to require increased efficiency from their staff, with a willingness to reward merit. In CERN, a merit-oriented advancement was introduced in 1992 to allow grade promotion without a change of job position and without re-classification. This system was devised to reward high performance with a swifter step increase and promotion to the next higher grade after a number of years of excellent service. But in general, though considerable attention has been given to monitoring and assessing performance, especially in the UN system, very little has been achieved in the way of practical measures.

This may, however, be changing. By resolution 51/216, the UN General Assembly has asked that proposals for the introduction of performance awards and bonuses be developed as a priority. Representatives of agencies' executive heads have been studying the issue since 1994, under the impetus of the Consultative Committee on Administrative Questions (CCAQ), largely at the initiative of Eccleston, Executive Secretary to the Committee. But it will be difficult to break away from grade-related pay. The CERN scheme does not introduce a new method for calculating pay but simply modifies the rhythm of advancement within grades and increases the possible span of careers. None of the main agencies have set up performance-linked bonuses such as the '*prime de rendement*' widely used in the French central administration and in several other systems.

In summary, the problem of measuring of efficiency in a multicultural context has been somewhat overcome by agreeing that some objectivity could be achieved by measuring performance against agreed work targets, explained to and understood by the staff member concerned and monitored over a sufficiently long period. In some cases, staff appraisal is being introduced and newly appointed supervisors have received training on assessment of staff.

CONCLUSION

This chapter has endeavoured to show the problem of flexibility is not posed in the same way in international organisations as in the national context. The 'political' drive for reform and greater personnel flexibility does not take the same form as it cannot be easily imposed from above. Most governing bodies tend to proceed by consensus rather than by majority rulings. Resistance to change cannot be dismissed as the mere expression of special interests or of antiquated management methods. The usual justifications for increased flexibility, cost-efficiency and adaptation to new missions, do not go unchallenged. Accusations of ideological bias are made, on the basis that such reforms show a productivist attitude and disregard the traditional values of the civil service (independence, objectivity), without compensating gains. In addition there is opposition because change would be accompanied by a corresponding loss of service for some of the constituents concerned. However, some elements of greater flexibility in human resource management are evident particularly in the areas of contracts and to a lesser extent in pay. Overall, however, this assessment of the recent evolution of flexibility in the international context shows that the traditional 'bureaucratic' approach to staff administration is still dominant and defended as meeting the perceived needs in some international public services. At the same time, this does not rule out the possibility of improved cost-awareness and adaptability but it ensures a slow incrementalist approach to change.

References

AMERASINGHE, CHITTHARANJAN F. (1983). *Staff Regulations and Staff Rules of Selected International Organizations,* Washington, DC: Office of Executure Secretary World Bank.
AMERASINGHE, CHITTHARANJAN F. (1994). *The Law of the International Civil Service.* Oxford: Clarendon Press.
APPRIL, Cl. (1983). 'La notion de droits acquis dans le droit de la fonction publique internationale', in *RGDIP*, 87 (2), pp 315–58.
BEIGHBEDER, Y. (1988). *Threats to the International Civil Service.* London, Pinter Publishers.
BEIGHBEDER, Y. (1990). *Le BIT contre le système commun.* Milan.
BETTATI, M. (1987). *Le droit des organisations internationales.* Paris: Presses universitaires de France.
CHARPENTIER, J. (1987). *Institutions internationales.* 8th edn. Paris: Dalloz.
DE COOKER, C. (ed.) (1990). *International Administration: Law and Management Practices in International Organisations.* Dordrecht, Boston, London: Martinus Nijhoff Publishers.
DORMOY, D. (1995). *Droit des organisations internationales.* Paris: Dalloz.
INSTITUT INTERNATIONAL D'ÉTUDES DIPLOMATIQUES (1984). *L'avenir des organisations internationales.* Paris: Economica.

JÉQUIER, N. (ed.) (1985). *Les organisations internationales entre l'innovation et la stagnation.* Lausanne: Presses polytechniques romandes.

LIPATTI, V. (1993). 'Les organisations internationales'. *Revue internationale des Sciences sociales*, France.

LIPATTI, V. (1995). 'Le financement des organisations internationales'. *Revue française de Finances* publiques.

MOUSSÉ, J. (1997). *Le contentieux des organisations internationales et de l'Union européenne.* Brussels: Bruyland.

PELLET, A. (1982). *Les voies de recours ouvertes aux fonctionnaires internationaux.* Paris: Editions A. Pédone.

PIQUEMAL, M. (1998). *Problèmes actuels de la fonction publique internationale.* Montreuil (France): Ed. du Papyrus.

PITT, D. and WEISS, T.G. (1986). *The Nature of United Nations Bureaucracies.* London & Sydney: Croom Helm.

PLANTEY, A. (1977). *Droit et pratique de la fonction publique internationale.* Paris: CNRS.

ROUSSEAU, C. (1987). *Droit international public.* Paris: Dalloz.

SCHWOB, J. (1987). *Les organes intégrés de caractère bureaucratique dans les organisations internationales.* Brussels: Bruylant.

RUZIÉ, D. (1996). *Rapport général présenté à la journée d'études de a SDFI sur le contentieux de la fonction publique internationale.* Paris: Pédone.

SICAULT, J.D. (1990). 'L'évolution récente de la jurisprudence des tribunaux administratifs des Nations-Unies et de l'OIT en matière de droits acquis', in *RGDIP*, tome 94/1990/1.

WOOD, D.M. and YESILADA, B.A. (1996). *The Emerging European Union.* Harlow: Longman Publishing Group.

17 Evaluating Human Resources Flexibilities: a Comparative Perspective

Sylvia Horton and David Farnham

In this concluding chapter, we offer some observations about the patterns of human resources flexibilities, which are evident from the country studies in this book, work carried out by the OECD and other researchers. Our purpose is to highlight the trends, similarities and differences among countries and to analyse what appear to be the factors influencing the ability of governments to introduce flexibilities and bring about organisational change in the public services. We also identify some of the effects of the movement towards human resources flexibilities upon government, managers, public workers and users of public services. Finally, we examine the relevance of theories of flexibility to the public sector.

DEVELOPMENT OF THE FLEXIBILITY MOVEMENT: THE THREE WAVES

Although the flexibility movement has been ongoing since the 1960s, it is possible to discern three waves in its emergence and growth. The first wave (1960s and 1970s) occurred during a period of full employment, an expanding workforce and a concern with shortening and improving the quality of working life. A combination of social pull and economic push factors led industry and governments to try to reduce working hours, provide for flexible working patterns to attract women into the labour market and ease older workers out of the labour market to make jobs for the younger generation. The underlying assumptions were that continuing economic growth and rising productivity would enable improved welfare services to be provided and support both the working population and the retired. Growing tax revenues funded expanded public services and increased public sector employment. But in several countries, governments resorted to prices and incomes policies, indexation of public sector pay and centralisation of public sector pay regulation, to keep some control over rising public expenditure and inflation. There was also a desire on the part of governments to provide equal opportunities for women and ethnic minorities in line with the extended concept of citizenship rights.

A second wave of pressures for flexibilities in the 1980s stemmed from the effects of increased economic competition, globalisation, structural changes in the economy and the impact of new technology on work. Although some social pull factors continued, in particular the need to accommodate the needs of the growing female labour force, the pressures were to find ways of reducing labour costs and restructuring the labour force in both the private and the public sectors. Managers sought more control over the labour process to raise efficiency and improve competitiveness. Studies of industrial responses to market instability and uncertainty suggested a distinction was being made within firms between core and peripheral workers and full-time permanent employees and an expendable range of short-term, temporary and part-time staff. This pointed to a strategy for increased flexibility, described as the 'flexible firm' (Atkinson and Meagher, 1986). This model was later transposed to the 'flexible state'.

The third wave, in the late 1990s, reflects the transformation taking place within the economies of western Europe and other OECD countries. In increasingly knowledge-based economies, there is a premium on a highly educated, skilled and flexible workforce, continually learning and continuously adaptable to change. Functional flexibility is the key requirement for core employees. The emphasis is on 'flexible people' rather than flexible systems or organisations. Social-pull factors in the workplace continue to be related to issues of equal opportunities with disabled people joining women and ethnic minorities as target groups. New social pressures have emerged, however, such as the rising expectations of employees to be trained and developed and be provided with opportunities for greater participation in the management process. There are also rising expectations of customers, consumers and service users for high quality, accessible, responsive and user-friendly services meeting *their* needs rather than those of producer interests. Economic pressures continue to drive flexibility but there is evidence of a change in the strategies being adopted by those leading private and public services in response to these new pressures. The model being adopted is the 'learning organisation' rather than the 'flexible firm'.

These macro-contexts provide common settings for developments in human resources flexibilities in both the private and the public sectors. It is evident from the studies carried out by the OECD (1990a, 1993, 1996b, 1997, 1998b, 1999) that similar responses can be observed in all advanced economies, although there are also significant differences. During the 1960s and 1970s, equal opportunities legislation and incentives for women to enter the labour market were slowly introduced throughout OECD countries. This was stimulated in Europe by commitment to equal opportunities and equal pay by the European Community. In part to improve quality of working life but also to harmonise European practice, shorter working hours, better health and safety, longer periods of paid holiday and opportunities for early retirement were also introduced. Trade unions were generally in a strong position to demand these improvements because of full employment. In all countries, the public sector tended to be the trend-setter by providing the standard of 'good' employment practices for private industry to follow.

The 1980s saw governments being confronted with demands for reduced public expenditure, lower taxation and deregulation of labour and product markets to enable the private sector to respond to changing global markets and increased market competition (Bacon and Eltis, 1976). In particular, the post-war welfare states and Keynesian demand management economic policies were challenged by New Right economic ideas and political ideologies (Farnham and Horton, 1996). In several OECD countries (UK, US, Canada, New Zealand and Australia), strong anti-statist and pro-market movements challenged the scope of government and demanded privatisation of state activities. Private sector management was held up as the model for the public sector to follow to reduce costs, increase efficiency, engender a competitive, entrepreneurial and risk-taking culture and become more responsive to service-users. The changes resulting from these pressures are collectively referred to as New Public Management (NPM) First introduced into the Anglo Saxon states of the OECD, it spread to continental European countries, although at differing rates and in differing forms (Flynn and Strahl, 1997; Farnham *et al.*, 1996; OECD, 1998c).

An important element of NPM was the search for cost reductions, workforce restructuring and 'downsizing' or 'rightsizing'. Throughout Europe and the US, governments sought to reduce public sector staffing through imposing staff ceilings and across the board targeted reductions, transferring activities to the private sector or restructuring public organisations to enable public managers to operate with greater flexibility. The new cadre of public managers was encouraged to look for ways of increasing organisational efficiency, reducing costs, delivering quality services and providing value for money to taxpayers and citizens. Performance management became the vogue and the range of contractual, numerical, pay and functional flexibilities identified in chapter 1 were gradually applied to public services.

PATTERNS OF HUMAN RESOURCES FLEXIBILITIES

As Table 17.1 indicates, all 10 countries in this study have adopted various forms of contractual, working time, pay, working life and task or functional flexibilities. The weightings attached to each of the categories reflect the assessment of the authors of each country study and the editors of the book. This delphi method has its limitations but the ratings do not contradict OECD surveys on pay and working time flexibilities.

All 10 countries use fixed and short-term contracts and temporary forms of employment but permanent unlimited contracts of employment or service are still the norm. Even in Sweden and the UK, where there is no legal security of tenure in public services, long service is still commonplace. All states have reduced the size of their public services since the 1980s, although there are wide variations in the extent of downsizing and in the strategies adopted to bring this about. Most countries have used a combination of non-replacement, natural attrition and privatisation to bring numbers employed in public services down and redundancy has not been widely practised, even where there are no legal restrictions on shedding labour. The policies of governments have varied, with the UK and US both imposing targets which public agencies have had to achieve or, as in Finland, using budgetary controls to force agencies to reduce their staffing but leaving them to decide by what means. Both these approaches have had consequences which are reviewed later in the chapter.

Scope for using more flexible forms of employment and contracts such as short term and limited hours contracts varies widely across OECD countries. Legal controls over the length and duration of atypical contracts in France, Spain and Belgium have undoubtedly limited this form of managerial flexibility, while greater freedom in

Table 17.1 Types of flexibility by country

	Contractual				Working time							Pay		Working life			Functional
	Fixed Term	Short Term	Sub- Contracting	Temporary	Part- Time	Job Share	Flexitime	Annual Hours	Shifts	Overtime	Flexi hours	Local CB	PRP	Earl Ret	Career Mobility	Special leave	Task
Belgium	XX	X	X	X	XXX	X	XXX		X	X	XX		XX	X	XX	XX	X
Finland	XXX	XX	XX	XX	XX	X	X			XXX	XXX	XX	XX	X	X	XX	XXX
France	XX	X	XX	X	XX		X	X			X	XX		XX	XX	X	X
Italy	XX	X	X	XX	X	X	X	X		XXX	X	XX	X		X		X
Germany	X	X	XX	X	XX	X	X	X	XX	XXX	XX	X	X	XX	X	X	XX
Spain	X		X	X	X		X				X	X	X	X	X		X
Sweden	XXX	XXX	XXX	XXX	XXX	XXX	XXX		XXX	XXX	XXX	XXX	X	XXX	XX	XXX	XX
Netherlands	XXX		XXX	XX	XXX	X	X		X	XX	XX	XX	XXX	XXX	XX	XX	XXX
UK	XX	XX	XXX	XX	XXX	X	X	X	X	XX	XXX	XX	XX	XX	XX	XX	XXX
USA	XXX	X	XX	X	XX	XX	X	X	X	X	XX	X	X	XX	XX	X	XX

Key
XXX important and extensive use of flexibility.
XX important but not extensive use of flexibility.
X limited use of flexibility.

Sweden, Finland and the UK to adopt temporary and short term contracts has enhanced it. In the US federal government managers have used contractors to create 'a contingent workforce' because they were constrained by staff ceilings in employing temporary staff (Ban, 1999: 49). Variations in the use of part-time contracts appear to be related closely to the feminisation of the labour force (Breugel and Hegewisch, 1996) as well as to historical, institutional and legal factors. There is very little part-time work in either Spain or Italy, where participation of women in the labour market is relatively low, although in both countries the public sector has more part-time workers than the private sector has. Female participation is also affected by institutional factors such as the availability of childcare facilities. The definition of part-time employment varies widely among the countries in this study, ranging from anything less than a standard working week, such as 'four day' contracts in Belgium, to nil hours contracts requiring workers to be 'on call' until the employer wants them, as in some social services in the UK. This makes comparisons difficult but there is a definite trend towards more part-time contracts.

This is pronounced in the UK, where, in addition to a general increase in the use of part-time workers in traditional areas such as local government and the NHS, there has been an increase in part-time senior managerial and professional positions. A similar trend is also found in Finland and to a lesser extent in the US. In many continental European countries, the increase in part-time work is linked to governments allowing workers to have more control over their working lives by choosing whether to work part or full time. In Sweden, parents with children under eight can opt to reduce their hours to 75 per cent of the norm and in the Netherlands, since 1996, public employees have the right to work part-time. Governments in Belgium have also favoured part-time work. In Germany, the Netherlands and since 1998 in France (Bodiguel, 1999) it is used to counter the problem of unemployment. All these countries have policies permitting early or partial retirement with enhanced payments for those who opt for shorter working hours. Combined with a reduction in the standard working week, this has been seen as a way of providing at least part-time employment for the unemployed. It has resulted in part-time jobs being created in traditionally male areas of employment, providing an increase in the number of men in part-time employment (Thurman and Trah, 1990).

Although job-sharing is on the increase throughout Europe, it is still less common than in the US, where there is job-sharing in two-thirds of American states. Similarly, use of tele-commuting is increasing quite rapidly in the US, more slowly in the UK, but is still not widely used in Europe. Flexitime is more widespread, with most countries adopting the principle of core and peripheral hours. There tends to be more rigidity in the traditional core civil administrators than amongst other groups of officials, however, who are in the front line and dealing with the public. Career mobility and use of special leave can be found in all the study countries. Mobility is especially high in those countries where there is a career structure and security of tenure; in the absence of redundancy provisions civil servants must be found alternative positions. Spain, France and Germany have all resorted to Employment Plans and internal mobility to deal with this problem, as has the Netherlands. Most European public services have traditionally provided scope for individual officials to leave the service, by secondment, to pursue political careers, retrain or develop, improve their professional profiles or take positions in private industry. Most countries place restrictions on the maximum length of time individuals can be absent from the service but this is now being extended. Secondment has recently been adopted as a strategic human resources development policy in the Senior Civil Service in the UK and is also practised widely in Scandinavian and Nordic countries. Many *Beamten* and *Fonctionnaires* in Germany and France take extended leave to serve in national, local or European assemblies as elected representatives.

Functional or task flexibilities, in the form of redesigning jobs, encouraging staff to become multi-skilled and promoting the development of autonomous, self-managed, multi-functional team-work is the most recent focus of flexibilisation (Vickery and Wurzburg, 1996). In Germany functional flexibility has been the preferred approach to improving performance rather than more traditional NPM methods (see Chapter 7). In the UK recruitment and training is now competency based for administrative, professional and technical employees and staff appraisal systems focus on meeting training needs and encouraging personal professional development as the basis for rewards. White shows in chapter 14 that there is evidence of changes in pay determination systems, grading systems and the movement towards performance related pay in some countries but only limited change in others. All countries have sought to constrain public sector pay, as it represents the major element in public expenditure. They have resorted to various tactics including imposing pay limits and abandoning comparability with private sector pay. However, there is no single pattern or trend that emerges, as countries have varied in their strategic approaches. In some, such as the UK and Sweden, there has been both increased centralisation and decentralisation. In the UK, teachers, health workers and top civil servants have their pay determined by national pay review bodies, which recommend pay levels to the government, which it usually accepts. On the other hand, there has been a move towards some decentralised collective bargaining in the UK for other public employees, as hundreds of agencies and health trusts have delegated powers to determine their own pay and conditions. In Sweden, where collective bargaining is the means of determining pay and conditions for all public employees, national bargaining sets down a framework within which hundreds of independent employers have flexibility in the interpretation and application of national agreements. A similar approach has been adopted in Finland.

In contrast to these are those countries within which highly centralised systems continue to operate including Germany, France, Belgium and Spain. Countries which come in between include Italy and the Netherlands, where there is partial decentralisation and the US, where although attempts to decentralise federal pay fell foul of Congress, some agencies have been given delegated powers to determine their own terms and conditions. Whilst it is impossible to generalise about trends in pay flexibility in the countries in this study, some forms and degrees of flexibility are occurring in all of them. There are, however, significant differences between northern European countries on the one hand, and central and southern European countries on the other. The former are tending towards more performance related systems and the latter are retaining their more collectivist, egalitarian and security focused reward strategies.

The countries displaying the most extensive range of human resources flexibilities are Sweden, Finland, the Netherlands, UK and the US. These have adopted most forms of human resources flexibility, identified in Chapter 1, although their extent varies across levels of government and administration, among public services and within public services. A second group of countries, consisting of Belgium and France, practise a lot of flexibilities, although not as widely or extensively as in group one. The third group, comprising Germany, Italy and Spain, appears to contain the most rigid systems, with less human resources flexibilities in each of the five categories. However, this is a relative positioning and in each country there are trends towards more part-time, temporary and fixed term posts especially in employee and contract status groups but also amongst established statut civil servants (Derlien, 1999; Parrado-Díez, 1997). In particular there is evidence of an increasing move towards more flexible practices at local level and in their decentralised, autonomous regions. Although there is a general trend towards greater flexibility in human resources policies and practices there are clearly major differences. How can these be explained?

FACTORS INFLUENCING FLEXIBILITIES

The countries examined in this study share many broad political and economic similarities. They are all liberal democracies and advanced industrial societies participating in the international economy, which has been the source of great instability and uncertainty since the late 1970s. They are, therefore, subject to a common unifying factor namely pressure to succeed economically in an increasingly competitive world market. With the exception of the US, they are also members of the European Union and thus operate within a framework of rules and regulations imposed by European institutions. Furthermore, only Sweden, UK and the US are not part of the new Euro-zone with its single currency – the Euro.

There have, however, been different responses to these external environmental pressures among the 10 states. In particular the reforms associated with New Public Management have varied. The UK has gone furthest and quickest in adopting the public management paradigm and has been a model for some of its European partners, in particular the Netherlands, the Scandinavian countries and to a lesser extent the US (OECD, 1998b), each of which has adapted UK practices to their own systems. In some countries, such as Germany, the UK model has been largely rejected in favour of their own strategy for re-engineering government. Even in Germany, however, some local governments have adopted NPM and HRM with greater enthusiasm (Röber, 1998) Other countries have developed their own policies and priorities which deviate quite significantly from the UK model. But there is very little evidence to-date that their good practice has been adopted or adapted by the UK.

One must be careful not to draw the wrong conclusions about the reasons for the similarities and differences in the 10 country studies in this book, as one is confronted with a vast array of factors influencing the way countries respond to pressures for change. Some of these were touched upon in Chapter 2. They include a country's:

- perception of the state
- constitution, political system and political culture
- administrative traditions and the role of administrative law
- public service structures
- system of industrial relations and the relative power of staff associations and public sector unions to impede or promote change
- political leadership, which is difficult to measure and provides a chance element, which renders prediction of the direction and speed of change very risky.

There is a clear difference between the Anglophone countries and the rest of Europe in their perception of the state. Britain does not recognise the state as an institution in law and civil servants are servants of the Crown, not of the state. The orders they enforce are made in the name of ministers and there is a great deal of discretion exercised by civil servants who act with the authority of ministers, not of the state. In contrast, elsewhere in Europe, public officials represent the state and exercise state authority. German civil servants are 'the bearers of state sovereignty'; while French civil servants perform 'acts of public authority'. This legal recognition of state officials is reflected in a special employment status given to them. It is a service relationship, not an employment relationship. Job security and permanency is provided in return for the state official's loyalty and services to the state. It protects and rewards their loyalty but also restricts and regulates their activities.

Second, there are differences stemming from the nature of the constitution and the political system in each case. Belgium, Germany and the US are federal states. Italy and Spain have devolved structures with strong provincial governments, while the remaining states of France, Finland, Sweden and the Netherlands are unitary states. The UK, formerly a centralised unitary state, has, since 1999, joined Italy and Spain with a devolved provincial structure, though it is too soon to know how powerful the governments of Scotland and Wales will become. All but the UK have written constitutions, which are normally the source of the basic law regulating civil servants. Special procedures are needed to change that law. The political structures of the state may also be a key factor in facilitating or impeding the ability of governments to change public service practices. Attempts by the Clinton Administration to introduce major changes in the Federal civil service, in the mid 1990s, failed because of the US's separation of powers, and the President's inability to carry Congress with him. Similarly attempts to change laws relating to *Beamten* in Germany have been frustrated by the fact that public officials populate the *Bundestag* (lower house) and the *Bundesrat* (upper house) and procedures for changing the basic law require weighted majorities. Weak political parties in the US and multi-party systems in Germany are also significant in explaining those outcomes.

Political culture is important in understanding responses to change too. In the Netherlands, for example, the role of the state is rooted in the Protestant principle of 'Sovereignty within its sphere'. This leaves a great deal of autonomy to functional private or semi-government bodies providing public services funded by the state. In Belgium and Germany underlying public sector culture is the Catholic principle of 'subsidiarity' and abstinence of government in the delivery of public services. In these countries privatisation has been less attractive to political authorities, as voluntary and private bodies already provide most social services. In the UK, in contrast, where monopoly of state provision was the norm, privatisation was a radical structural solution to the situation. There are clearly forms and nuances of flexibility reflecting particular public service cultures. For example in spite of criticisms and efforts to modify the structure and behaviour of public services in France, continuity in office and neutrality remain prominent values and the ideal of the career civil servant is a strong obstacle to temporary workers. In contrast in Anglo-Saxon countries (Pollitt, 1990) responsiveness to politicians and to citizens' demands seem to have gained importance.

As pointed out in *New Public Managers in Europe* (Barlow *et al.*, 1996) the tendency for Anglophone states to be more receptive to public management and human resources flexibilities can be explained by both cultural factors and language. The literature on flexibilities, HRM and NPM is almost entirely written in English and is more widely disseminated in countries in northern Europe than in the south. This may account for the greater influence of Anglo-American management ideas and British administrative practice in Scandinavia and the Netherlands. Common language also facilitates networks through which ideas and innovatory practices can be articulated. There is no doubt that public officials in northern Europe have been greatly influenced by American management ideas, which were in large part the underpinning for HRM and NPM (Casey *et al.*, 1997). International organisations, such as the OECD and World Bank, whose major language is English, have also been instrumental in supporting the principles of the 'free market', market deregulation and new managerialism for over a decade.

All but the UK have administrative law systems with codified laws which regulate the exercise of power by state officials and provide a legal framework defining the structure of the public service, the rights and responsibilities of public officials and procedures for regulating their behaviour. Legalism and traditions of legal control thus impose limits on managerialism and the powers of public managers. In France and Germany, in particular, HRM is constrained by special laws that regulate civil servants. More significantly, in these countries, the traditional theory of the state, translated into public laws, imposes limits on public managers, and places constraints on their personal discretion. Laws, for example, regulate recruitment, training, promotion and remuneration. All of these constrain the development of more flexible systems of management and HRM.

There has been a movement to a private law or civil law base for public servants in some countries, such as Spain, Italy and Sweden. In Italy, since 1993, only general rules on recruitment and specific services, such as the diplomatic *corps*, magistrates and armed forces, remain under administrative law. In Spain, while the civil service remains subject to administrative law, new agencies created since 1990 operate under private law. There is some evidence that this change is producing more flexibility in their systems and is resulting in some convergence between the private and public sectors in those countries. It is also contributing to a growing convergence in practices between administrative law and private law based countries.

The structure of the public service is another key variable. The OECD makes a distinction between 'career based ' (life long tenure) and 'job-based' (appointment to post) public services (OECD, 1998c). The majority of the countries in the OECD operate with career based systems, although most countries have a mixture of the two. One in four public servants are non-career based in France and around one-third in Finland. The career-based system is generally associated with an underpinning legal culture and job-based systems with a managerialist culture. In the latter, there is an assumption that contractual employees are hired to carry out particular functions, and if those functions end or change, there is no guarantee of continued employment, although the employees may have some protection through redundancy agreements or other policies such as redeployment. In contrast, the career-based rationale is that public service offers a job for life and if a job ceases to exist another will be found for the public official. It also assumes that if officials move out of the public service into the private sector, they retain the status of public officials with the right to return. This system of *pantouflage*, traditional in France, Germany and Spain, is becoming more widespread throughout the OECD in the guise of 'secondments'. While both career-based and job-based rationales can be found in individual countries, the tendency is for there to be a shift from career to job systems.

However, many categories of public workers, who are not 'permanent' officials, still have protection against redundancy or dismissal. In Germany, for example, both *Beamten* and *Angestellten*, as opposed to those contracted as workers, have full job security and this probably accounts for the small reduction in their civil service compared to the considerable reductions in the UK and Sweden. But even in job-based systems, public officials tend to have more protection than in the private sector. In Sweden, where there is no special law for the public sector and no such thing as a civil service, workers receive up to 12 months on full pay and assistance in finding another job either within or outside the public service. In Spain, Employment Plans ensure that redundant public officials are given priority in filling vacant internal posts and assistance in moving between agencies and areas.

Another important factor in the structure of public services is the presence of *corps* or specialised groups. The rigid structuring of the public services into *corps* and classes, in continental Europe, greatly reduces the scope for innovation and change. In contrast, the absence of a single structure in the UK and the US, leaving wide discretion to public organisations and managers to innovate, has allowed faster change to occur. Resistance to change is often strongest among vested interests in the public services themselves. This can come from staff organisations protecting the interests of their existing members, either against the usurpation of promotion prospects or against the flexibilisation of employment conditions For example, the French and Spanish *corps* protect their fiefs against 'outsiders', such as other *corps*, while public sector unions seek to protect existing employment rights against any relaxation of them. Rouban (1996, 1998) has shown how the *grands corps* have been most resistant to change in France, while the technical *corps* have embraced managerial reforms more readily and widely. Attempts to merge or remove *corps* have met with only limited success in both France and Spain, where their opposition to change has impeded the reform process.

A further key factor influencing the extent and form of flexibilisation in individual states are their systems of public sector industrial relations. Public service unions are relatively strong in most European countries because of their rights in law and the widespread tradition of concertation and social partnership with governments and employers. In Sweden, where almost all aspects of pay and terms of conditions of public employees are determined through collective bargaining, the unions have been positive, proactive and supported reform. In contrast, in France unions have tended to resist change and, along with the *corps*, have been a block on reconstruction and modernisation. Even in the UK, where governments have done most to weaken trade unions, collective bargaining is still a constraint on managerial power. In countries where public officials make up a large part of elected assemblies, as in Germany, France and Italy, such groups are able to block reforms and changes in the law or greatly modify them in their own interests.

Finally, in the public sector, it is the preferences of politicians that determine the policy frameworks within which public managers have to operate. Although all OECD governments appear to have adopted common perceptions of the problems facing them, and to have similar goals, they have evolved different policies to achieve them. This in part reflects the differing ideologies of the governmental parties in each country and the strength of their political leaderships. A combination of strong political leadership and a clear radical agenda, combined with a highly centralised and strong executive and a weak opposition, were key factors in explaining the transformation of the UK state between 1979 and 1997 (Barlow *et al.*, 1996). Other important factors, however, were the absence of a written constitution, no tradition of administrative law and public services that could be changed by managerial action, collective agreements or legislation. It is this contrast with the legalistic philosophy, administrative law tradition, weak coalition governments and strong public sector unions which lies at the source of the differences between most continental European countries and the UK.

SOME RESULTS OF HUMAN RESOURCES FLEXIBILITIES

Underlying human resources flexibilities are a number of assumptions about the effects they have for the parties introducing them or affected by them: governments, managers and public employers, public service workers and users of public services. There is little evidence of any systematic evaluation of their impact or their costs and benefits and so any evaluation here has to be based on limited and often anecdotal evidence.

Governments

From the evidence provided in this book, it appears that the search for human resources flexibilities in European and US public services, unlike in private services, has been driven primarily by governments seeking reductions in public expenditure and value for money in the ways in which public services are delivered to their citizens. Reduced public expenditure enables government to demand less from its taxpayers in funding the modern state and to reduce its own borrowing from the private sector. This effectively transfers resources from the public to the private sector and thus stimulates the market economy. Taxpayers and businesses benefit from this strategy as human resources flexibilities keep public spending down. Second, governments can use non-standard atypical patterns of employment to further employment policies. Where there are high levels of youth unemployment, the state can try to deploy the young unemployed into non-permanent job vacancies in the public services, especially if it costs less to employ them than it does older workers. Third, the state can promote equal opportunities policies in public organisations, for women, ethnic minorities and the disabled, as a means of implementing its social policies and improving its image as a 'good' employer and acting as a model of 'best' employment practices for other employers to follow. Fourth, government can encourage greater customer orientation in the provision of public services, through skilful utilisation and deployment of a flexible workforce. The OECD (1997) has shown however that there has been no reduction in levels of public expenditure as a proportion of GNP since the 1980s and in most countries the proportion has risen. There has, though, been a decline in the numbers of public employees. Levels of taxes have not changed significantly either, although in the UK there has been redistribution away from direct to indirect taxes. Governments have been successful in instilling the need for improved efficiency and a more performance management approach, particularly in the Anglo-American and northern European states. While the public management paradigm has taken root throughout OECD countries, some governments have been constrained by the factors identified above.

There have also been some unexpected consequences of the use of human resources flexibilities for governments, as well as some disadvantages. The disadvantages include the potential loss of control over semi-autonomous agencies and adverse effects on the standardisation and quality of service provision. In the UK the New Labour Government, elected in 1997, inherited a wide range of problems identified with the structural fragmentation and specialisation carried through by previous Conservative governments. Their response has been to reintroduce forms of central co-ordination, regulation and control and to require greater co-operation and partnership between units of government at both horizontal and vertical levels. The aim is to eliminate the co-ordination deficit that has been an unexpected outcome of greater flexibility (Cabinet Office, 1999).

Other social and economic objectives of governments, furthered by use of flexible working patterns, such as equal opportunities and job creation have had mixed results. There has been an increase in every country in the number of women employed in public services and an improvement in their advancement within public organisations. This is most pronounced in northern European countries and the US. The number of jobs created for the unemployed and young workers, by introducing early retirement and part-time employment options, has not been recorded but anecdotal evidence suggests the policy has not been as successful as governments had hoped as public organisations, committed to reducing expenditure, have not sought to take on new staff, even with the financial incentives offered.

Managers

For managers, as representatives of public employers, the main advantages of human resources flexibilities are, first, that they have greater freedom to determine their own human resources strategies, adapt the number and quality of personnel to changing circumstances and take advantage of a pool of often cheaper labour from which to recruit and select relevant staff. In some countries flexibilisation enables them to by-pass cumbersome procedural controls or to compensate for personnel cutbacks. Second, flexibilisation potentially provides opportunities, if they are effectively managed, of improved service provision for citizens or users of public services by meeting their specific needs.

This can be done by using flexible working patterns to resource late opening of offices or 24-hour telephone or email contact. Third, with functional and task flexibilities, there are possibilities for recruiting and managing a multi-skilled workforce, adaptable to change and the demands of post-bureaucratic public organisations. The EPOC survey, carried out in 10 countries in 1994 (Geary, 1994; Wickham, 1998), shows that managers practising forms of direct participation and consensus building techniques, linked to functional flexibility, believed it had positive effects on output costs, throughput, absenteeism, and sickness. In other words there had been positive effects of operating as 'learning organisations'. Fourth, external contracts ensure that staff are less disruptive to the organisation as they operate external to the normal administrative structure and managers sometimes use external contracts to union-bust (Kettl, 1997). Fifth, public managers can personally benefit from certain human resources flexibilities, such as pay flexibilities, through performance-related pay, share options and profit sharing in successful public enterprises. It is clear that many countries have PRP for managerial staff and that salaries of public managers have moved closer to their private counterparts.

The disadvantages to public managers of human resources flexibilities are, first, that they can result in poor employee commitment to the organisation and the public service ethic, as well as weakening employee performance, as shown in Chapter 3. In an international attitude survey on the rewards of work covering Italy, UK, Sweden and Germany (Russell, 1998), there was evidence that commitment is related to a sense of job security, good social welfare systems and level of qualifications and education of workers. Those workers who were in temporary and insecure jobs expressed lower levels of commitment than those in secure, permanent jobs, although 'somewhat surprisingly those on fixed term contracts of over one year do not differ significantly from those with permanent contracts' (*ibid.*: 83). This coincides with the findings of Virtanen in the Finland study (Chapter 3). Attitudes were also affected by level of social support available for those who became unemployed. In those countries with high levels of social support, such as Sweden and Germany, there were the highest levels of commitment to work, whereas the lowest levels were found in the UK, where levels of social support are also lowest. Russell states that 'fixed term contracts are found often to reduce work commitment and have an extremely damaging effect on organisational commitment. Employers it seems are sacrificing productivity and loyalty for short-term flexibility gains' (*ibid.*: 93). Other studies such as Burchell (1994) have also linked perceived insecurity with high levels of stress and absenteeism.

Second, there are high transaction costs in managing flexible organisations, associated with activities such as constantly replacing short-term contracts, contracting out services and inducting new staff. These costs are rarely computed. Third, with flexibilisation, there can be practical, logistical problems in effectively planning, managing and executing work, when relatively large numbers of non-permanent, insecure staff do it. Furthermore, use of outside contractors leads not only to a loss of direct control but also, over time, to loss of expertise and informed purchaser status. Fourth, because flexible staff are not always trained effectively, quality of service provision can suffer, resulting in dissatisfied customers and clients. Finally, downsizing can be very disruptive when tight ceilings are imposed on managers who have no choice over which staff will be replaced or which will be encouraged to go. This can result in the loss of key personnel.

Public service workers

One advantage of human resources flexibilities for public workers, both civil servants and employees, is that they have greater choice about life styles and how and when they should work. With contractual and working time flexibilities, they might also have more leisure time to spend with their families and dependants. Second, flexibilisation provides some workers with job opportunities that might not be available on a full-time, permanent basis. Third, with multi-skilled flexible working arrangements, public workers can have more interesting jobs and improved working conditions. The evidence suggests that women in particular benefit from a range of flexibilities, particularly part-time work, flexible hours and flexi-time. In the UK most women working part-time do not want to work full time (Social Trends, 1998). Young persons, especially students and older workers, wanting to supplement incomes or pensions with part-time jobs or to reduce their working hours are clear beneficiaries too.

There is, however, a darker side to flexibility as there is normally less job security for flexible staff and a two-tier employment structure of 'rich-work' and 'poor-work' emerges. Although there are exceptions among managerial and professional staff on temporary or part-time contracts, most workers on atypical contracts are in low paid, low status jobs. They also have fewer opportunities to get effective training and development from their employers. People in temporary jobs are also more likely to become unemployed. Evidence shows that women, in particular, are disadvantaged as they make up the majority of part-time workers in all countries. They also have less training, earn lower incomes and receive less promotion than their male counterparts. Temporary employment also usually disadvantages workers in terms of social security provision (Ban, 1999).

Public service users

The main advantages of flexibility to those using public services are better access to the services being provided, lower costs to users and improved quality. In most systems committed to improved quality of service, users are consulted and able to influence, albeit in minor ways, development of policy. Their most effective means of prompting change, however, is by using appeals and complaints procedures which tend to receive more attention than the feedback questionnaires. There is some evidence in the UK that standards of service have risen, users, consumers and clients of public services are more involved and services are more responsive to their demands (Cabinet Office, 1998). One disadvantage of flexibilities is that the services delivered by temporary staff might be at a lower quality standard than that provided by permanent staff. There may be variations in the services provided by agencies in different parts of the country and there may be an accountability gap where purchasers and providers of public services are different. At the present time there is little hard evidence to make any real comparisons.

DISCUSSION

There is clearly a trend in the 10 countries in this study and in international organisations (see Chapter 16) towards more flexible patterns of employment in public services, as responses to economic pull and social push factors. There are, however, wide variations in public policies on flexibility, which reflect the contingent factors identified above. In every country there are also areas of resistance and here too one finds significant similarities as well as differences. Resistance comes in some cases from politicians opposed to the deregulation of internal and external labour markets or loss of control over human and budgetary resources (Spain). Public officials seek to maintain their privileged and protected status, with its considerable financial benefits, and resist attempts at legal reform (Germany and France). Special interests challenge the impact of flexibilisation, especially devolved responsibilities for human resources management, because of its impact on equal opportunities (Corby, 1998). The key debate amongst students of public administration, however, is to what extent the increase in unorthodox employment patterns and the more general movement towards greater flexibility is 'a threat to the permanent civil service and its values of professional neutrality and consistency' (Gow and Simard, 1999: 5). Whilst some consider recent changes as a positive step to a more adaptive, competent, efficient, responsive and cheaper government, others defend permanent bureaucracy as a way to promote professionalism, consistency, neutrality and dedication in the exercise of public power. Open competition, appointment on merit, life-long careers and fair rewards are the hallmark of representative and responsible bureaucracy, an essential element in both liberal and social democracy. These characteristics of traditional public services are intended to avert the problems arising from open entry, nepotism and sectionalism on the morale, competency, honesty and integrity of public officials. Permanency, it is claimed, aids continuity and consistency and ensures dedication of public officials to the service. Although most public services have political appointments and the dividing line between the administrative and the political has always been a shifting one, the role of the permanent public service has been to exercise the authority of the state or, in the UK, the Crown in an impartial and politically neutral way. New public management and human resources flexibilities represent a challenge to this.

There has clearly been some cultural shift as new approaches to public management have introduced business-like conceptions of the administration of public affairs although again this varies between countries and within public services. Civil servants are increasingly perceived as 'resources' to be used and exploited and motivated by performance related pay or team performance. They are also required to be innovative and entrepreneurial in the 'business of government'. Traditional government professionalism is in decline as managerialism comes into conflict with professional values (Cabinet Office, 1999 (UK); De Closet Report, 1989 (France); Gore Report, 1993 (US); Sherwood, 1997). There is also a growing concern about ethical issues as the OECD Report on *Ethics in the Public Service* (1996) indicates. Public scandals have occurred in many countries revealing lapses in the behaviour of public officials as well as politicians. There are many officials who look back to a 'golden age' of public ethos and regret its passing. They argue that in adopting private sector techniques and practices and recruiting outsiders the public service ethos is being corrupted (Lawton, 1998). Others challenge that view pointing to the corruption found in the past and the need for a new public ethics to match the changing role of government and new public management (Hondeghem, 1998a). The theme of the EGPA Conference in Leuven 1997 was *Ethics and Accountability in a Context of Governance and New Public Management* (Hondeghem, 1998b).

Finally, there is an awareness of the ambivalent nature of flexibility which Dahrendorf points out can be the flip side of rigidity but also the opposite of stability and security which are the pre-conditions for the existence of civil society and political liberty (cited in Cella, 1999). There is now a growing recognition of the need to 'square the circle' (Wickham, 1998) and balance the need for workplace flexibility with social protection. The European Commission is currently seeking to promote flexibility as a means to achieve both through the model of the 'flexible firm'. This high trust, high skill, flexible model it claims can offer a win-win situation with managers and workers in partnership. The model, presented in the Commission's green paper on 'Partnership for New Organisation of Work', is rooted in the European social model of inclusion based on social partnership and an inclusionary social welfare system. It is central to the third phase of the ongoing flexibility debate.

References

ATKINSON, J. and MEAGHER, N. (1986). *New Forms of Work Organisation*. IMS Report 121. Brighton: Institute of Manpower Studies.
BACON, W. and ELTIS, W. (1976). *Britain's Economic Problem*. London: Macmillan.
BAN, C. (1999). 'The contingent workforce in the US federal government: a different approach'. *International Review of Administrative Science*. 65, pp 41–53.
BARLOW, J., FARNHAM, D., HORTON, S. and RIDLEY, F (1996). 'Comparing Public Managers', in Farnham, D. *et al.*, *New Public Managers in Europe*, London: Macmillan, pp 3–25.
BEECHY, V. and PERKINS, T. (1987). *A Matter of Hours: Women, Part Time Work and the Labour Market*. Cambridge: Polity.
BLANCHFLOWER, D. and CORRIE, B. (1987). 'Part-time Employment in Great Britain: an Analysis using Establishment Data: Research Report 57'. Department of Employment.

BREUGEL, I. and HEGEWISCH, A. (1996). 'Flexibilization and part-time work in Europe', in Brown, P. and Crompton, R., *A New Europe? Economic Restructuring and Social Exclusion.* London: UCL Press, pp 33–57.

BODIGUEL, J.-L. (1999). 'Non-Career Civil Servants in France'. *International Review of Administrative Sciences.* 65, pp 55–70.

BURCHELL, B. (1994). 'The Effects of Labour Market Position, Job Insecurity and Unemployment on Psychological Health', in Gallie, D. *et al.*, *Social Change and the Experience of Unemployment,* Oxford: Oxford University Press.

CABINET OFFICE (1998). *Next Steps Report 1997.* London: The Stationery Office.

CABINET OFFICE (1999). *Modernising Government.* (Cm 4310.) London: The Stationery Office.

CASEY, B., METCALF, H. and MILLWARD, N. (1997). *Employers Use of Flexible Labour.* London: Policy Studies Institute.

CELLA, G. (1996). 'Work and social protection: the transformation or decline of industrial citizenship'. *Transfer.* 4/96, pp 561–73.

CORBY, S. (1998). 'Equal Opportunities Fair Shares for all?', in Corby, S. and White, G., *Employee Relations in the Public Services,* London: Routledge, pp 95–113.

DE CLOSET REPORT (1989). *Le pari de la responsibilite: rapport de la Commission Efficacite de l'Etat.* Paris: La Documentation Française.

DERLIEN, H.-U. (1999). 'Unorthodox employment in the German public service'. *International Journal of Administrative Science.* 65, pp 13–23.

EUROPEAN COMMISSION (1997). Green Paper. *Partnership for a New Organisation of Work.* Brussels: European Commission.

FARNHAM, D. and HORTON, S. (1996). 'The Political Economy of Public Sector Change', in Farnham, D. and Horton, S., *Managing the New Public Services.* 2nd edn. London: Macmillan.

FARNHAM, D., HORTON, S., BARLOW, J. and HONDEGHEM, A. (eds) (1996). *New Public Managers in Europe: Public Servants in Transition.* London: Macmillan.

FLYNN, N. and STRAHL, F. (1997). *Public Sector Management in Europe.* London: Prentice Hall/ Harvester Wheatsheaf.

GEARY, J. (1994). *Conceptualising Direct Participation in Organisational Change: the EPOC Programme.* Luxembourg: Office for the Official Publications of the European Community.

GORE REPORT (1993). *Creating a Government that Works Better and Costs Less.* Report of the National Performance Review. Washington, DC: USGPO.

GOW, J. and SIMARD, F. (1999). Introduction, *International Review of Administrative Science.* 65, pp 5–12.

HONDEGHEM, A. (1998a). Introduction, *Ethics and Accountability in a Context of Governance and New Public Management.* Amsterdam: IOS Press.

HONDEGHEM, A. (ed) (1998b). *Ethics and Accountability in a Context of Governance and Accountability.* EGPA Year Book. Amsterdam: IOS Press.

HOOD, C. (1991). 'A Public Management for all Seasons'. *Public Administration.* 69.1.

HOOD, C. (1995). 'Contemporary Public Management: A New Global Paradigm'. *Public Policy and Administration*. 10, (2), pp 104–17.

KETTL, D. (1997). 'Privatization: Implications for the Public Workforce', in Ban, C. and Riccucci, M. (eds), *Public Personnel Management: Current Concerns: Future Challenges*, 2nd edn, New York: Longman, pp 295–309.

LAWTON, A. (1998). *Ethical Management for the Public Services.* Buckingham: Open University Press.

OECD (1990a). *Labour Market Policies for the 1990s.* Paris: OECD.

OECD (1990b). *Survey of Public Management Developments 1990.* Public Management Committee (PUMA). Paris: OECD.

OECD (1991). Public Management Developments 1991. PUMA. Paris: OECD.

OECD (1992). *Regulatory Management and Reform: Current Concerns in OECD Countries.* PUMA. Paris: OECD.

OECD (1993). *Public Management: OECD Country Profiles* Paris: OECD.

OECD (1994a). *Performance Management in Government.* Occasional Papers. Paris: OECD.

OECD (1994b). *Jobs Study: Facts, Analysis, Strategies.* Paris: OECD.

OECD (1995). *Governance in Transition: Public Management Reforms in OECD Countries.* Paris: OECD.

OECD (1996a). *Ethics in the Public Service: Current Issues and Practices.* Occasional Paper 14. Paris: OECD.

OECD (1996b). *Integrating People Management into Public Sector Reform.* Paris: OECD.

OECD (1997). *Issues and Developments in Public Management: Survey.* Paris: OECD.

OECD (1998a). *Public Sector Pay and Employment Data Update.* PUMA/HRM (98) 2. Paris: OECD.

OECD (1998b). *Public Sector Workforce Adjustments in OECD Countries: Interim Report.* Paris: OECD.

OECD (1998c). *Issues and Developments in Public Management: 1998 Country Reports.* Paris: OECD.

OECD (1999). *Structure of the Civil Service, Employment in 7 OECD countries* Paris: OECD.

PARRADO-DÍEZ, S. (1997). 'Staffing and Human Resources Flexibilities in the Spanish Public Services'. *Review of Public Personnel Administration.* xvii, 3, pp 46–56.

POLLITT, C. (1990). *Managerialism and the Public Services.* Oxford: Blackwell.

RÖBER, M. (1998). 'HRM in German Local Government', paper given at Anglo-German Foundation Workshop on Public Management Reform, Humboldt University, Berlin, December.

ROUBAN, L. (1996). France in Farnham, D. *et al., New Public Managers in Europe: Public Servants in Transition*, London: Macmillan, pp 151–68.

ROUBAN, L. (1998). *Le Fin Technocrates?* Paris: Presses de Sciences Po.

RUSSELL, H. (1998). 'The Rewards of Work', in Jowell, R. *et al., British and European Social Attitudes*. Aldershot: Ashgate Publishers.

SHERWOOD, F. (1997). 'Responding to the Decline in Public Service Professionalism', *Public Administration Review*, 57, (3), pp 211–17.

Social Trends (1998). No. 28. London: Office of National Statistics.
THURMAN, J. and TRAH, G. (1990). 'Part-time work in an international perspective'. *International Labour Review.* 129, pp 23–40.
VICKERY, G. and WURZBURG, G. (1996). 'Flexible Firms, Skills and Employment'. *The OECD Observer*, 202, 17–21.
WICKHAM, J. (1998). 'Squaring the circle? Participation, innovation and employment: some results from the EPOC survey'. *European Review of Labour and Research.* 4/2, pp 231–45.

Index